SILVER IN ENGLAND

ENGLISH DECORATIVE ARTS

SILVER IN ENGLAND
Philippa Glanville

ENGLISH GLASS
R. J. Charleston

JEWELLERY IN ENGLAND
Shirley Bury

ENGLISH DECORATIVE ARTS

SILVER IN ENGLAND

Philippa Glanville

Assistant Keeper
Department of Metalwork
Victoria & Albert Museum

Holmes & Meier
New York

UNWIN HYMAN
London   Sydney

First published in Great Britain by Unwin Hyman, an
imprint of Unwin Hyman Ltd, 1987

First published in the United States of America
by Holmes & Meier, 1987

UNWIN HYMAN LTD
Denmark House, 37–39 Queen Elizabeth Street,
London SE1 2QB
and
40 Museum Street, London WC1A 1LU

Allen & Unwin (Australia) Pty Ltd
8 Napier Street, North Sydney, NSW 2060, Australia

Allen & Unwin with the Port Nicholson Press
60 Cambridge Terrace, Wellington, New Zealand

Holmes & Meier Publishers, Inc.
30 Irving Place, New York, NY 10003

British Library Cataloguing in Publication Data

Glanville, Philippa
   Silver in England. – (English decorative arts)
1. Silverware – England – History
I. Title   II. Series
739.2′3742   NK7144
ISBN 0–04–748004–1

Library of Congress Cataloging-in-Publication Data

Glanville, Philippa.
   Silver in England.
   1. Silverware – England – History.   I. Title.
NK7143.G54   1987   739.2′3742   87–114
ISBN 0–8419–1139–8

Set in 11 on 13 point Bembo by Nene Phototypesetters, Northampton
and printed in Great Britain
by William Clowes Limited, Beccles and London

CONTENTS

LIST OF ILLUSTRATIONS

PHOTOGRAPHIC CREDITS

Crown Copyright; with permission of the Controller of Her Majesty's Stationery Office 20, 131; Mansion House, City of London 126; Town Hall, Stamford 128; Regalia Room, King's Lynn Plate 5; the Duke of Marlborough 28; Lady Victoria Leatham and the Burghley House Trust 27, 43, 76; the Prime Warden and Court of the Goldsmiths' Company 34, 57, 58, 61, 64, 66, 67, 117, 121; the Master and Court of the Mercers' and the Founders' Company 19, 110; the Governor and Court of the Cripplegate Foundation 123, 127; the Society of Antiquaries 108; the Governor and Court of the Bank of England 86; the Masters and Fellows of All Souls, Corpus Christi, New and Trinity Colleges, Oxford 3, 4, 12, 137; the Masters and Fellows of Christ's, Corpus Christi, Magdalene and Fitzwilliam Colleges, Cambridge, nos. 73 to 77, 104, 106.

Birmingham Assay Office 40, 41; Bristol Art Gallery 69; British Library (Manuscripts) 111; British Museum 1, 15, 37, 88; Castle Museum, Norwich 35, Plate 2; Grosvenor Museum, Chester 63; Guildhall Library 71, 72; Museum of London 23, 107, 113, 124, 136; National Maritime Museum (loan) 125; National Trust (Dunham Massey) 24, 33; Royal Albert Memorial Museum, Exeter (loan) 68; Temple Newsam, Leeds 36; Wellington Museum, Apsley House 101.

Art Institute, Chicago 26; Colonial Williamsburg 29, 65; Folger Shakespeare Library, Washington 11, 134; Bayerisches Nationalmuseum, Munich 109; Kunstindustrimuseet, Oslo 103; Metropolitan Museum of Art, New York, 21, 30, 98; Museum of Fine Art, Boston 8, 32, 84, 92; Richmond Museum of Art, Virginia 18.

Anonymous private collectors 50, 55, 59, 95; Christie's 39, 45, Plate 7; Timothy Coward 62; Kenneth Davis 42; Garrard's 100; F. R. Goodenough 78; Hancock's 56; John Harris 114; Cyril Humphris 16, 90; Mrs How 93; Jarrold's Plate 5; the late Hugh Jessop 80; Eric Shrubsole 46; Sotheby's Plates 6, 8; Spink's 31, 53.

Others not listed: Victoria & Albert Museum.

PREFACE

SILVER is unique among the decorative arts in that its raw material is both inherently valuable and infinitely reusable. Its ownership has been a social bench-mark and its form has exercised the skills of sculptors, designers, chasers and engravers, but ultimately it could be, and normally was, melted down and refashioned quite without sentiment. Because of this constant recycling, the survival of any individual object is quite random and unrelated to its uniqueness or otherwise in its period. Hitherto plate historians have focused on individual objects almost to the exclusion of the context – social or economic – from which they came but now that context is seen as crucial in understanding historic plate. So in the first section of this book each chapter considers contemporary attitudes and usage.

Departing from the pattern of Charles Oman's and Gerald Taylor's classic studies of English silver, this historical introduction is balanced by other approaches. In the past twenty-five years scholars have broadened their focus on material culture to consider design sources, working methods and goldsmithing in the less well-documented centres away from London. Under the spur of the social anthropologists, the sociological role of silver is another theme discussed here, with the significant shift from complete unsentimentality towards old plate to the prevailing collector's and curator's attitude of reverence.

This is not a book about bottle tickets, racing trophies, silver toys or caddy spoons; small silverware, which has attracted collectors for over a century, has its own rich literature to which the bibliography pays tribute. Nor does it discuss gold. Every grand household owned some gold vessels but their artistic significance, as tableware at least, is not great. Gold vessels were, by and large, grander, heavier, more expensive and more prestigious versions of silver, or rather silvergilt, ones. A very few gold objects survive to emphasise the point: a tumbler cup at the Cooks' Company, the Marlborough wine coolers at the British Museum, or Beckford's entirely conventional teapot in Birmingham.

Confusingly the term goldsmith customarily encompassed all those engaged in the craft, whether bankers, retailers, manufacturers, jewellers or plateworkers, although gold was so small a proportion of their raw material. The records of the Worshipful Company of Goldsmiths, which has governed the craft since the twelfth century, hold the clues to these relationships which are gradually being elucidated in successive volumes of their history.

Because many aspects of this enormous subject have already been amply covered, this book does not pretend to an equal treatment of all topics: the evolution of church plate, for example, is conveniently discussed in just two publications, Charles Oman's *English Church Plate* (1957) and the Victoria and Albert Museum exhibition catalogue *Victorian Church Art*

(1971). In other areas, such as the domestic use of silver before the Reformation, some care has been taken to adjust the common impression that silver was not widely used in England until the later sixteenth century. Another popular truism, 'that all the old silver was melted down in the Civil War', again appears less certain when set beside the reality, which shows that shifts of fashion and taste, especially the Stuart revolution in dining and drinking, were far more devastating. Because research on provincial goldsmiths is sometimes hard to find, I make no apology for summarising the recent work of G.N. Barrett, Tim Kent and Canon Ridgway.

The manuscript was completed in the autumn of 1984, although some additions have been made to the bibliography.

ACKNOWLEDGEMENTS

MERELY to give a list of names seems churlish to all those colleagues in museums here and overseas and friends in the trade and the Silver Society who have so generously shared their wisdom with me during the writing of this book; I hope that each will recognise his or her contribution and feel it is happily placed. For a constant flow of stimulating suggestions I must particularly thank Susan Hare; the Library at Goldsmiths Hall is the centrepoint from which all good studies of English silver are raised. For particular help I am very grateful to the following people: Judith Banister for her knowledge of the trade; Robert Barker, whose research on Jamaican goldsmiths brought him to the Department and whose enthusiasm is a delight; Elaine Barr whose unique familiarity with the Wickes ledgers she has allowed me to share; David Beasley; Shirley Bury and John Culme for details of nineteenth-century goldsmiths; David Dalladay for comments on assay office practice; Myrtle Ellis for the reference to a Van Vianen document at Hatfield; Mireille Galinou for the Mayday milkmaids; Mrs How; Tim Kent for sharing his research on West Country goldsmiths; Richard Parsons for a copy of the 1955 Tollemache sale catalogue; Kenneth Quickendon for sharing his research on the Rich epergne; Jean Schofield for hints and encouragement; Michael Snodin for advice on design sources; Gerald Taylor for his penetrating comments; and Clive Wainwright whose study of the antiquarian movement in England is a mine for all those concerned with material culture.

Others who have contributed in various ways, perhaps sometimes without realising it, include Claude Blair, John Davis, Robin Emerson, Godfrey Evans, Martin Gubbins, Brand Inglis, Titus Kendall, Jessie McNab, Jeremy Pearson, Anna Somers Cocks, Tim Schroder, Hugh Tait, Peter Waldron, Tim Wilson and my colleagues in the Department of Metalwork.

I was fortunate to have known and worked briefly with the late Charles Oman, who made a unique contribution to the study of English silver and had stimulating exchanges with John Hayward, Hugh Jessop and Tom Lumley whose recent deaths have so depleted the silver world.

I should like to thank Lyonel Tollemache both for his hospitality and for allowing me to quote from the Dysart and Tollemache family papers at Buckminster. For permission to quote from other manuscripts I am grateful to Westminster Abbey Muniments.

To Arthur Grimwade, who not only read the text and gave me the benefit of his criticism, but also remained willing, having done so, to write a foreword, I owe many thanks.

For their patience in turning manuscript into typescript I am very grateful to Victoria Keric, Louisa Lawson and Diana Rogers.

In gratitude for their tolerance and encouragement, I dedicate this book to Gordon, James and Matthew.

FOREWORD

IT is now over one hundred years since Wilfrid Cripps wrote the first comprehensive account of English silver following the first publication in 1863 by William Chaffers, the London dealer, of *Hallmarks on Gold and Silver Plate*. The ability to date and recognise the creators of the great heritage of English silver in communal and private hands must have sent a thrill of discovery through all interested in the crafts of the realm, and to every generation since then the interest and pleasure of recognition and artistic assessment remains viable.

The last thirty years or so have seen a remarkable acceleration in the study of the subject stimulated by a series of illuminating exhibitions at Goldsmiths' Hall and elsewhere and literary productions from 'Dial-a Mark' dictionaries to period studies and biographies of leading goldsmiths, who are now seen as prominent exponents of the decorative arts and major contributors to the taste and social manners of their day. In her present book, the author of *Silver in England* has shown herself a most receptive student of her predecessors' and contemporaries' mining in the gold-bearing veins of original sources and artistic influences that have raised our knowledge and appreciation of the subject to its present extent. There is little doubt that her work will speedily be recognised as a fascinating and valuable conspexus of what may fairly be styled 'The Present State of English Silver Knowledge'.

Arthur Grimwade

PART I

HISTORY

ONE

MEDIEVAL

E ARLY English silver is extraordinarily rare; fewer than 300 pieces made before the 1520s survive, a figure which is put into perspective when we consider that one London goldsmith, Robert Amadas who died in 1532, left more than 300 items in stock. For a more positive picture of the importance of silver from the early Middle Ages we must turn to contemporary documents, fleshing out their dry descriptions with examples drawn from the handful of surviving pieces.

Silver in the Early Middle Ages

First the Danes, and then their successors the Normans, virtually swept clear the monastic treasuries of Eastern and Southern England, with the result that curiously we are better informed about the goldsmithing of the pagan Saxons than their Christian successors, particularly through discoveries of burials at Sutton Hoo, Kingston and Taplow.

The custom of equipping dead kings and noblemen with rich grave-goods has, despite later grave-robbing, preserved goldmounted drinking horns and armour, jewellery, buckles and basins which together make up an overwhelming contribution to our picture of early Anglo-Saxon art. But this source died abruptly once the conversion to Christianity had taken hold, and there is pathetically little visual evidence to bring to life the glowing references to treasure of gold, silver and jewels, in Anglo-Saxon literature from the eighth century onwards, apart from chance survivals. A hoard found by tin workers at Trewhiddle near S. Austell, Cornwall in 1774 was deposited about AD 875. It contained a parcel-gilt chalice and paten; a silver hanging bowl found in the last century in the River Witham near Lincoln (and now slipped from sight again) enables us to say that niello, engraving, cloisons of enamel, filigree, parcel-gilding and cast figures were all techniques used by Anglo-Saxon goldsmiths in the eighth century, although it should be pointed out that a rather larger number of jewels, which are smaller and so more easily lost and found again, have been recovered to illustrate this aspect of the goldsmith's craft. The Alfred Jewel at the Ashmolean Museum, dated to between 871 and 899, is one; another (seventh century) found in Kingston-on-Thames is now in the Walker Art Gallery, Liverpool.[1]

From the earliest times horns were used as drinking vessels. They were particularly popular with the Anglo-Saxons since they lent themselves to competitive drinking; once filled, they could not be put down until emptied. A group of seventh-century graves found at Taplow in Berkshire in 1883 yielded six horns, one with silvergilt mounts and settings for gems, and seven were buried with the Sutton Hoo ship.[2]

Drinking vessels were inevitably the most personal and most adorned of a man's possessions and in later periods form the bulk of surviving objects. But more is known about Anglo-Saxon church art; chalices, statues, reliquaries and crosses of gold, studded with gems, and silver fronts to altars are all described in English wills and in lists of gifts to cathedrals. One masterpiece produced by a goldsmith working in the Anglo-Saxon tradition, if not actually an Englishman, belongs to Kremsmunster Abbey in Austria. This coppergilt chalice, made for Tassilo, Duke of Bavaria, between about 777 and 788, is engraved with Christ and the Evangelists in ovals, with chipcarved palmettes and interlace between. This scheme of decoration, carried out in silver and gilding, covers the entire surface area; its intricacy and the combination of techniques demonstrates why Anglo-Saxon goldsmiths' work was so highly regarded that the popes of the eleventh century delighted in its possession. This is clear from the lists of their holdings in the *Liber Pontificalis*, although none of their goldsmiths' work, as opposed to Anglo-Saxon needlework, can now be traced.[3]

Open-handedness was a prime Anglo-Saxon virtue and much of our information about their goldsmiths' work, as Professor Dodwell demonstrates, comes incidentally in accounts of gifts to religious houses. When King Cnut presented a group of relics to the New Minster in Winchester, they were encased in a gold cross; he is depicted with his wife in an Anglo-Saxon manuscript making the presentation. His other gifts included six-branched silver candlesticks and two large-scale effigies 'Finely adorned with gold and silver', as the chronicler William of Malmesbury described, so that 'the amount of precious metal fills visitors with awe and the splendour of the gems dazzle the eyes of the beholders'. The description is typically imprecise; nothing remotely like this has survived and the illustrations in Anglo-Saxon manuscripts are not much help, since they lack a sense of scale. However, one of Christ's Temptation by the Devil shows a drinking horn, a cup, a bowl, a silver-mounted sword and torcs for neck and arms, all examples of typical Anglo-Saxon work. The Norman William of Poitiers, writing shortly after the Norman invasion of 1066, described the native goldsmiths' work of England in hyperbolic terms, claiming that it would impress even the metal workers of Byzantium. More practically, he commented on their liking for drinking horns ornamented with silvergilt; Cnut is said to have used one of gold. The Atheling Athelstan left a silver-mounted trumpet to S. Swithin's shrine and gold-sheathed, or at least gilded, furniture is shown in several Anglo-Saxon manuscripts.[4]

In his stimulating study of Anglo-Saxon art, Dodwell has stressed both the enormous significance this society attached to precious metals and jewels, to the extent that they became a touchstone of beauty and were constantly used metaphorically by English writers, and the many factors which militated against Anglo-Saxon goldsmiths' work surviving. In 1066 the religious houses suffered a new rule and one that was disastrous for all works of art composed of precious metals, whether gold or silver vessels, embroidered textiles, chalices, reliquaries, or book bindings. Apart from the official depredations of William the Conqueror and William Rufus (to benefit their favourite home abbey of Caen) which stripped those abbeys which had stood out against the Normans, the incoming Norman abbots also removed treasures, sometimes to alleviate local disasters such as famine and fire, but more frequently to spend on their ambitious building programmes. Ely, for example, was despoiled in 1071 and again in 1076, losing among other treasures a life-sized statue of the Madonna and Christ child. Relics of England's Anglo-Saxon saints and kings were not spared; in a generation all the royal gifts of Cnut and Edgar to Winchester were destroyed.

Given the scale of this destruction or removal of Anglo-Saxon metalwork, it is hardly surprising that we have virtually nothing to show. The situation is little better after 1100, although we can at least consult the monk Theophilus (Roger of Helmarshausen) who wrote a handbook of techniques for goldsmiths, to see what goldsmiths working in England might be capable of. The exhibition on English Romanesque Art (1984) brought together from across the world an astonishing assemblage of items in both precious metals and base metal made between 1066 and 1200, bearing out the descriptions he gives of niello, lost wax-casting, inlay, gemsetting and enamel. A silver flask of about 1130–40, a unique secular survival, now in the treasury of the Abbey of S. Maurice d'Agaune, Switzerland, incorporates several of these; it is engraved with dragons with foliate tails found in English manuscripts of the twelfth century.[5]

Base metal objects (almost all made for liturgical purposes) can demonstrate the techniques and ornament found in the precious metals too. The inhabited scrolls and cast openwork of the coppergilt Gloucester candlestick (VAM), about 1104–13 and given to the abbey of Gloucester by Prior Peter, may be presumed to have had silvergilt precursors. A small group of coppergilt ciboria (standing bowls for the Host) of the late twelfth century, the Balfour and the Warwick in the Victoria and Albert Museum, the Malmesbury Abbey in the Pierpont Morgan Library, depict scenes from the Old and New Testaments while a unique silver ciborium (c.1200–10) also in the treasury of S. Maurice d'Agaune, Switzerland, has an unexpected mixture of classical and biblical imagery, with three Virtues in ovals on the foot and ten medallions with scenes from the Infancy of Christ on the bowl and cover; the finial is a three-dimensional group of Chiron and Achilles. The closest, indeed the only parallel for all these scenes are English manuscript paintings of about 1200 and it is clear that a model book was used common to several workshops.[6]

But the recent exhibition of Romanesque art emphasised the difficulty of ascribing nationality to metalwork, since both craftsmen and styles crossed the channel both ways. Two twelfth-century drinking cups found in a hoard on the island of Gotland, Sweden, are thought to be English work, one most unusually signed by a goldsmith called Simon working for a Slav patron called Zhalognev. Itinerant Limoges craftsmen visited England to make enamelled objects, like the Thomas à Becket *chasse* (box) on loan to the British Museum.[7]

Church Plate after the Norman Conquest

Virtually no secular silver and only a few liturgical pieces survive from before 1300. There is a gradual build-up of information from other sources – marginal drawings in manuscripts, for example – but only chalices and spoons provide more than a dozen examples before 1500. However, a fairly clear impression emerges of later medieval silver, that is after about 1400, even though it is impossible to be sure whether a given shape was new for its time, or already well established. Ironically, because of the depredations of Henry VIII and his son Edward, which required full inventories, more is known about ecclesiastical than about domestic silver; but even these descriptions can only push back the history of English plate half a century or so.

None of the early (pre-1400) chalices and cups now known survived the Reformation in church use; either they have been rediscovered in episcopal graves, or turned up as chance archaeological discoveries, or they were given later, perhaps preserved in a private family chapel. This position was reversed with domestic silver of the sixteenth and seventeenth centuries, which has been preserved from refashioning only because it was given for church use.[8]

Several extraordinarily elaborate and beautiful chalices survive in Ireland, such as the Ardagh (eighth century) and the recently discovered Derrynaflan (early ninth century, found with a metal detector in 1980), but the finest medieval example made by an English goldsmith is the Dolgellau chalice and paten of about 1250, found by a country road in 1890 and now exhibited at the National Museum of Wales. This superb piece is unusual not only in its ornament (it is both engraved and embossed) but because it is signed 'Nicol'us Me Fecit de Herfordie'; this is probably not the name of the goldsmith but of the dignitary, perhaps a bishop, who had the piece made. The largest group of medieval chalices to have been preserved are those found in bishops' and archbishops' graves, notably at York Minster, at S. David's, at Salisbury, Canterbury and Chichester.[9]

However, these are usually simple in form and either made specifically for the burial rite or chosen as the plainest in the cathedral treasury or the bishop's private chapel. They do not enable us to visualise the more elaborate chalices, monstrances, ewers and basins commonly used on the altars of the great cathedrals. The dry inventories of Henry VIII's commissioners can be supplemented, for Canterbury at least, by an account of a visit there by the humanist Erasmus.[10] He was particularly struck by the contents of the cathedral treasury, which were regularly shown both to pilgrims and to visitors with more secular interests; many of the items – relics and elaborate plate – he describes can be identified in inventories preceding his visit and at the time of dispersals a few years later. But most of the pre-Reformation church plate preserved is of no great artistic merit, standard items produced by goldsmiths to customary designs, as similarity between chalices from Coombe Keynes, Nettlecombe and the private chapel of the Bedingfield family, all of which date between the mid-fifteenth century and the 1530s, makes clear. Of rather higher quality is the late fifteenth-century cup from Lacock Abbey (on loan to the British Museum; Fig. 1), but this is secular in origin.

Common to these late medieval chalices are the bands of gilding to contrast with the burnished silver surface. It is clear from the Edward VI inventories that those who could afford it preferred gilt to white silver; a chalice gilt overall cost substantially more than one silver parcel (partly) gilt. Often additional ornament was added, such as an engraved panel on one cusp of the foot, normally showing a crucifixion. This cusped foot, on which there were six in-curving segments, lent itself to the use of cast applied terminals at the toes. These have rarely survived the attentions of later reformers and on the chalice from West Drayton, Middlesex (1507) the bowl was altered too, presumably to make it appear more like that of a 'decent communion cup'. These shaped feet on chalices were a new feature in the fourteenth century to assist in draining the tilted cup and prevent it from rolling. For 600 years at least,

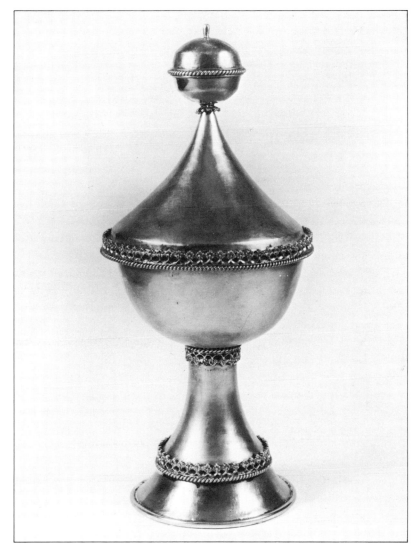

Fig. 1 **The Lacock cup**
Parcel-gilt *c.* 1450–80. The cresting, trumpet stem and high foot remained standard until the late 1520s.
British Museum

English chalices had customarily stood on circular feet, as can be seen in the earliest known, the ninth-century chalice from Trewhiddle in Cornwall and in the late twelfth-century chalice from Berwick S. James, Wiltshire (in the British Museum).[11]

A decorative element adopted by goldsmiths from contemporary architectural forms was the openwork gallery or arcade. One occurs on the stem and foot of the communion cup of S. Martin, Ludgate, originally made as part of a monstrance. Given by Stephen Peacock, citizen and once mayor of London, in 1530 it bears the hallmark for 1507 – it was clearly taken to the goldsmiths when the Bishop of London required the refashioning of mass chalices into communion cups, the offending top knocked off, and a decent Protestant trumpet-shaped communion bowl made and set on the stem to replace it. A collar of battlements and buttresses is found also on the 1527 chalice at Trinity College, Oxford, and another of two years earlier at Wylye in Wiltshire. The Oxford one was given by the college founder, Sir Thomas Pope. It is to be presumed that he, as one of Henry VIII's commissioners for the dissolution, had acquired it in the course of his official duties.[12]

Another Oxford college, Corpus Christi, retains the gold chalice given by Bishop Foxe, but, like the Lacock cup, this shows little artistic originality and is of interest primarily because of its associations and as the only English gold chalice known. These were not uncommon before the Reformation, both in private chapels and cathedrals; Salisbury (Old Sarum) had been given a gold chalice within a generation of the Conquest, plus seven silver gilt chalices, six candlesticks, crosses and reliquaries, all from its Norman bishop S. Osmund. By 1500 the new foundation owned far more, but still placed the reliquary containing the armbone of S. Aldhelm (Osmund's gift) on the high altar for services.[13]

A handful of outstanding survivals, such as the Dolgellau chalice and paten, may or may not represent the general quality of work for the court – we simply do not know. Given the competitive energy of donors it is likely that many were not content to follow standard designs, and descriptions of the altar plate given to chantry chapels in the larger and more popular churches are breathtaking. At S. Paul's Cathedral, for example, the chantry chapel established by Cardinal Beaufort in memory of John of Gaunt in 1446 was lavishly equipped. Figure sculpture was characteristic of altar crosses and candlesticks. Richard III gave York Minster a 'great cross standing on six bases, having six angels in the pinnacles of these bases and two angels on bases holding in their hands reliquaries'. A processional cross in the 1534 inventory of S. Mary's Guild, Boston, had two branches supporting gilt and enamelled images of Our Lady and S. John, 'with a sovereign of gold thereto nailed and offered by John Rede'; its carrying shaft of silver had a gilt roll and three gilt knots, 'everyone hath six roses enamelled with azure', in reference to the Virgin.[14]

Private chapels were often far more lavishly equipped than guild chapels or parish churches; Sir John Fastolf's contained over a thousand ounces of altar plate, plus some gold, in 1459.[15] Equipment for the Mass became more complex through the later Middle Ages; after Corpus Christi or the Feast of the Holy Sacrament was instituted in 1254, a monstrance to display the Host in procession became necessary. The crocketed monstrance containing S. George's heart which the Emperor Sigismund gave Richard Beauchamp, depicted in the Beauchamp Pageants about 1490, is convincingly similar to contemporary examples, although none of English make has survived. It seems that late medieval manuscript illustrations are relatively reliable as a source. Other Mass plate gradually appearing on the altar included candlesticks, a ciborium or covered vessel for wafers, cruets and the pax or tablet on which the priest passed the kiss of peace around the congregation. But poor churches might own merely a minimum of chalice, paten and pyx (for the Host) and that in copper gilt, not silver.

It is impossible to assess the value of the silver and to a lesser extent gold locked up in the holdings of churches, chantry chapels and monastic houses before the mid-sixteenth century.

No precise figure can be set on the Dissolution confiscations, although it has been estimated that bullion, plate and other treasures worth over a million pounds were sent to the Mint between 1536 and 1540. A further massive quantity was removed from the parish churches by Edward VI's commissioners in 1552 and more trickled quietly away, often taken surreptitiously by churchwardens, hoping for better times, in advance of the commissioners' visits.[16]

The wealth of plate owned by a prosperous town church such as S. Peter Mancroft, Norwich, before the Reformation can now only be reconstructed from inventories. This church, with its several side-chapels, owned several thousand ounces of silver and silvergilt; the largest and most elaborate piece was the processional cross which weighed 166 ounces; the arms were set with enamelled medallions, and figures of the saints and of the donor and his family stood around the base. Of the three pyxes (boxes to contain the Sacrament), one was made from an ostrich (or 'griffin's') egg, an exotic material more valuable even than the silvergilt in which it was mounted.[17]

When S. Mary's Guild at Boston in Lincolnshire made an inventory of its goods in 1534 shortly before it was dissolved, the jewels alone, that is all the altar plate, including six chalices, an engraved silvergilt cover for the Gospel book, an enamelled processional cross with images of Our Lady and S. John, and so on, came to 1,022 ounces of silvergilt. That was 100 ounces more than the corporation owned (and sold) 300 years later. In addition, there were reliquaries stored in the vestry and domestic silver (mostly gifts) in the chantry house. The guild had part of the finger of S. Anne 'closed in a hand of silver and gilt' and a point of another of her fingers 'with certain bones of the Innocents' plus a parcel gilt case containing three stones from the Mount of Calvary, the Sepulchre and the stone from which Christ ascended into Heaven. A silvergilt case with the image of Our Lady contained some drops of her milk.[18]

Church collections were not static and were treated, like private holdings, as potential liquid reserves. S. Christopher le Stocks in the City of London pledged a monstrance in 1530, as security for a loan. It was redeemed six years later, to be sold finally in 1538. Although the value of gifts to churches is inestimable, the bequests of George Talbot, fourth Earl of Salisbury, who died in 1538 may stand as an indication of their scale. This 70 year old courtier left sixpence each for a thousand priests to say masses, three priests for twenty years were to pray at his parish church in Sheffield and cloth-of-gold vestments were to be made for the Prior of Worksop and for his own church, with a long list of other gifts to churches and religious houses. John Lord Marney, the builder of Layer Marney, left £100 to buy three pairs of basins, cruets, sacring bells and candlesticks for his house chapel and his chantry chapel (which also had a chalice) with careful instructions as to their security, in 1525.[19]

However, after the Reformation for two generations there was no church building and all those resources were diverted to secular ends. The enormous and visible increase in expenditure on domestic comfort, particularly on plate, which was characteristic of the lesser gentry and bourgeoisie, was fuelled largely through this transfer.

What Men Owned: the Holland Inventory, 1447

Normally before the sixteenth century too few documents exist for us to be able to trace the history of a family or an institution's accumulated plate. Nor are medieval inventories usually more than brief lists recording weight and whether the object is silver, parcel-gilt or gilt, since these distinctions determined its bullion value. However, in the royal household or where a particularly important estate was concerned, such as that of John Holland, Duke of Exeter, the knowledgeable London goldsmiths were brought in as appraisers, they gave the inventory clerks rather fuller descriptions and also, from their specialised knowledge, quoted a range of resale values which hint at the degrees of elaboration of the various cups and salts listed.[20]

John Holland, Duke of Exeter and Earl of Huntingdon, died on 5 August 1447 after a life on active service in France. He had married three times and had several royal appointments commensurate with his status as one of England's premier nobleman, including serving as Lord High Admiral and Constable of the Tower. As a man of great personal wealth he had followed the normal custom and pledged some of his plate, to Richard Joynour, grocer of London, as surety for a loan to the king of £1,000. In addition he had large personal debts so when he died the king moved fast; all Holland's goods of any value, that is the finest of his plate, his clothing and his beds, were removed to S. Martin le Grand in the City so that once the sums were done his creditors could collect their due in kind, if not in cash. The resulting inventory, in the Westminster Abbey Muniments, was taken a month after his death and annotated with creditors' names and the goods they had taken. It lists a mouthwatering series of twenty-nine gold cups with a total value of over £900; in every case the bowls were of crystal, chalcedony or jasper, garnished with 'stone and pearl'.

It was customary to name distinctive and outstanding pieces of plate; one cup, called the Shepherd, made of gold and crystal and garnished with stones, weighing 40¾ ounces, was presumably a figural piece like the Huntsman salt in Oxford. Another was called the Swan, perhaps a heraldic device in reference to his first wife. Exeter's life story – marriage alliances, his reward of the French comte of Ivry and royal appointments – is reflected in his plate. One gold cup, ensuite with a ewer, was perhaps commissioned to mark his constableship; it was embattled with a castle in the top and weighed just over 43 ounces. One set of three cups had the arms of Huntingdon and of Stafford, the family of his first wife who had died fifteen years earlier. His second wife, Beatrice, was a natural daughter of King John of Portugal and widow of Thomas, Earl of Arundel but her arms – Portugal and Arundel – occurred only on silver gilt basins and a spice plate. The most highly valued pieces were set with jewels – 'stone and pearl'. Several were 'chased Wreathwise' and enamelled; values for the gold cups ranged from 28*s* to 22*s* the ounce, a clear indication that the valuers were considering resale rather than melt figures.

Very little white silver occurs in the Holland inventory but a great pan 'with the Arms of Exeter in the four quarters' was valued at only 2*s* the ounce, the lowest figure quoted. Armorial plate was clearly less desirable, although the device of removing an earlier owner's arms and substituting one's own was commonly adopted. Some plate handed over to the widow, or collected by the new duke from S. Martin's before the appraisal took place, gave the clerks problems of nomenclature, when presumably the goldsmith-appraisers were not on hand to advise. 'A great high charger with a basin thereto called a Chavying dish with My Lord's Arms' might be either a chafing dish or shaving dish, since both were normal equipment for a nobleman at the time.

The terms for drinking vessels also caused problems; the gold cups were, with the exception of one 'for the sacrament' with a 'cressent', all described merely as cups, although the decoration was specified, but distinguishing between the twenty-three silvergilt ones was clearly easier since they covered a wider variety of shapes. Most were covered and comprised 'bowl cups', cups with low feet 'enamelled in the bottom', plain without a knop and a standing cup 'with the pommell chased upright'. A set of five had no knops and one cover only, as ceremonial use required. One described as 'a low cup for sweet wine pounced' may have been for banqueting use and sounds like the font cups familiar fifty years later; others of white silver are described as of 'Rone' or Rouen fashion.

The Holland plate list was made with an eye to the most valuable and saleable items and so includes little in the way of cupboard plate, apart from three gold ewers *en suite* with cups and a ewer 'covered with a spout for a cupboard called a layer chased'. With the exception of spice plates, there is no serving or dining plate at all and there are no spoons. It may be contrasted with that made at the death of his near contemporary, Sir John Fastolf. Fastolf was a self-made man, profiting by his retainerships, and his plate clearly reflects this status; the arms of his royal and noble patrons occur on several pieces.[21]

The Fastolf Inventory, 1459

Although the original inventory made after the death of Sir John Fastolf in 1459 has disappeared, it was transcribed by the Norfolk antiquary Blomefield over 200 years ago and is one of the most complete and evocative descriptions of the household effects of a fifteenth-century adventurer. He left each of his houses lavishly equipped with plate and other rich furnishings. His newly built mansion at Caister, Norfolk, his principal residence, contained some gold plate and over 13,000 ounces of silver. At S. Benets Abbey, Holme, of which he was a patron, he had deposited a further 3,000 ounces for safekeeping in accordance with contemporary practice, and at his town house in Bermondsey there was another 2,500 ounces of silver.

One essential 'garnish' of Fastolf's serving plate, that is 12 dishes, platters, saucers and 3 chargers, alone came to more than 500 ounces. Virtually every piece, however otherwise decorated, bears a badge, device or coat of arms; many are those of Fastolf himself, like the 'six bowls, all gilt, with one cover, and a rose in the top, each enamelled in the bottom with my master's helmet'. Others indicated an earlier owner, like the basins and quart pots with gilt 'verges' or bands with the arms of Sir Robert Harling, Fastolf's companion-at-arms who was killed in the French Wars in 1435. Fastolf's long residence in France presumably accounts for his French-made silver and base metals. The finest were '6 Parys Cups of silver of the Months with no feet, the borders gilt'. Other pieces bore the badges of the Lancastrian kings and of Margaret of Anjou, whose columbine flower was enamelled on six gilt cups 'like fountains'. Fastolf's own arms and badges occur also on candlesticks, both coppergilt and silver.

In this great list there is little variety; the repetitive details of gallon and pottle pots, cups, flat pieces, basins and bowls is broken by one particularly handsome spice plate 'well gilt like a double rose, my master's helmet in the amell, with red roses of my master's arms' and a silver toasting iron. Two massive salts of architectural form remind us that this was a constant decorative element in fifteenth-century plate. One was shaped like a tower or 'bastel' and gilt, with roses, weighing seventy-seven ounces and the other, 'with many windows', weighed eighty-six ounces.

We simply do not know enough about medieval plate to be able to attribute Fastolf's silver to London rather than Paris. Undoubtedly, given English opportunities in the Hundred Years War, a proportion of the highly decorated plate owned by great English magnates emanated from France, as did the Royal Gold Cup (in the British Museum). Made in a Paris court workshop about 1380, perhaps as a gift for King Charles V, it came into the hands of John, Duke of Bedford who left it to King Henry VI in 1435. The Founder's cup, purchased by Oriel College, Oxford (with another) for £418s1d in December 1493, was almost certainly made in Paris in the previous century, although it has also been described as English too.[22]

A rare survivor of an aristocratic order for plate is a gilt covered cup presented to Christ's College, Cambridge by its founder, Lady Margaret Beaufort. Already 60 years old, it bears inside the bowl the arms of Humphrey Duke of Gloucester and his second wife. Although the Foundress's cup was presumably English-made, it is clearly in the mainstream of Northern European gothic design. Almost exactly similar covered cups are to be seen in manuscript paintings of feast scenes in the *Très Riches Heures* of the Duke de Berry. That there were recognisable differences we know since, to the clerks compiling fifteenth-century inventories, Rouen cups and Paris bowls were clearly distinguishable from English ones and it is unlikely that this was based merely on the ability to recognise marks. An inventory of Henry VIII's plate and jewels taken in 1521 lists plate of Flanders and the Rouen touch (hallmark), of Bruges-making, Paris plate, plus Almain-fashion (German) and Spanish-fashion. Although Almain-fashion, it has been suggested, referred only to a particular design known by that name, this is unlikely since the 'Spanish-fashion' pieces were gifts to Henry from the Spanish-born Queen Katherine of Aragon. The London touch was specified in only one of the 887 entries; either it was taken for granted or much of the plate was not fully marked. The date letter system and a general tightening of assay and marking procedure came in only a generation before this (1478).[23]

Lacking actual objects from which to make stylistic judgements, we are forced to depend on the accuracy of the inventory clerks. While some pieces in the Fastolf inventory are identified as being French – 'of the Parys touch' – the inventory clerk did not always try to pick out foreign-made plate. When Fastolf's bequests to his retainer William Paston were in dispute some years later, household servants deposed that a gridiron, a great charger and a pair of covered gilt basins 'pounced and embossed with roses and with great large amells in the bottom with certain beasts embossed standing within an hedge of silver and gilt upon the said amells' were all 'of the Parys touch'. None of these was so described in the earlier list.[24]

Only from the late fifteenth century can we identify with certainty the products of English workshops, with the additional, if ambiguous, support offered by hallmarks. Although many of the craftsmen were aliens, it is reasonable to call a piece English if it bears English hallmarks, since these indicate that it was made or offered for sale to an English customer.

There was effectively no legitimate export trade in wrought silver and licences were required even to take abroad the minimum personal allowance of plate and jewels, because of the constant fear of a negative bullion balance. English plate which travelled abroad, and inevitably a quantity did, went as diplomatic gifts or occasionally in payment of debts, not as trade goods; unfortunately the relative purity of our gold and silver coinage made both very desirable across the Channel.

Royal and some noble households are reasonably well documented but much less is known about the holdings of plate of the lesser nobility and gentry, men of the standing of, for example, Sir Richard (Dick) Whittington (d.1421). Collections of wills tell us what men valued and chose to give as specific bequests, but by definition these are treasured family pieces, not necessarily indicative of what was in everyday use; for example, the will of Sir Richard Weston of Sutton Place (1542) mentions only one bequest of silver, a 'Pownse Cup' but his inventory lists forty-eight cups of various types. Wills also rarely give any indication of weight or size and cannot be relied on to distinguish between an older item or a recent purchase, nor do they normally indicate where the plate was made. We cannot use them as evidence for when certain vessels first emerged, since we have neither dated examples nor adequate descriptions to rely on.

What is clear is the great wealth of ornament, lavished on relatively few forms, and the enormous quantities of plate required by magnates. But all, or virtually all, types except drinking vessels, salts and basins have vanished. Surviving objects are no true guide as to what was regularly in use before the seventeenth century and we are dependent on inventories to fill out the picture. To quote a slightly later instance, the plate inventory of Sir Richard Weston included that essential toilet article, a silver shaving basin, but the earliest identifiable such basin is over a century later.[25]

When the stewardship of Peterborough Abbey changed hands in 1460, the household goods of Abbot Richard Ashton were carefully listed. He had a good, but not lavish, stock of plate with no gold and no fashionable mounted crystal. The principal ornament was the arms of S. Peter, which appear on both cups and basins. Distinctions of rank were carefully maintained in the monastery as in lay households and expressed through both the placing and the dressing of tables. The prior and the abbot each had a set of six silver cups, presumably for those sitting at the second table in their respective chambers. The abbot had, as was customary, several sets of salt cellars, in pairs with one cover apiece, the largest of the sets for his own table in his chamber. Fourteen small salts, uncovered and weighing six ounces each, were presumably for the squires' table in his hall. It is not possible to be sure when the eight mazers were used, whether they were intended for casual or bedtime drinking outside formal mealtimes. One was inscribed 'Ave Maria', a standard motto found, for example, on the fifteenth-century mazer at the Ironmongers' Company and on a coconut cup at New College, Oxford.[26]

While a probate inventory does not necessarily survive for every will, there is a large group

13

from the Prerogative Court of Canterbury at the Public Records Office (about 800 before 1660) which inform us about those Englishmen and women who died owning property worth more than £5, in more than one diocese. This selection, while not statistically valid, does catch a cross-section of the non-noble but prosperous silver-owning classes. The inventory of John Alfegh esquire of Chiddingstone, Kent, taken in 1489, demonstrates that a man's silver could be his most valuable possession. Alfegh owned a newly-built house, well equipped with tapestries, bed hangings and furniture. Apart from his chalice and paten and his 'paxbrede graven with a crucifix, Mary and John', he possessed only a ewer and basin, 'a Paryse Boll (Paris bowl) with a cover chased codde round' and twenty-four spoons, but together these items were valued at £16, whereas his fifty-one cows in milk were worth only £15 6s. [27]

A list of plate pledged by William Paston on 24 October 1474, probably represents the holdings typical of a middling gentleman who had benefited through his service with a greater man, Sir John Fastolf. It consisted of standing cups, goblets, salts, a basin and ewer and spoons with 'oke knoles' (knops), all pledged against a loan of £40 which had to be repaid within two months. Many of the items had come from Fastolf's estate. [28]

Domestic plate below the artistocratic level was normally confined to vessels for drinking and washing, spoons and the cruets, pax bowls and chalice for the chapel. Another list of Paston plate of slightly later than 1479 includes, most unusually, a tiny egg spoon and six socket candlesticks with removable branches. [29]

Not much greater variety is to be seen in the plate holdings of Robert Amadas, citizen and goldsmith of London, who died in 1532. Although a man of exceptional wealth who lived in considerable style – he took on a family connection as supplier to the Jewel House and was by far the largest London contributor to the 1522 forced loan – his household plate is dominated by drinking vessels – thirty-three, all but four gilt. His chapel was richly equipped but his domestic gilt plate consisted only of spice plates, ewers, pots, candlesticks and salts. His white plate was severely practical – a porringer, a posnet, a chafing dish, a candlestick, saucers, platters and two flagons. He had only six silver spoons and none of the mounted glass or other composite pieces currently popular at court, except for some coconut cups (blacknuts). His household was large and it is possible that some of the many mazers (he had twenty-one of one sort and twelve of another) were for his household servants and not shop stock. The significance of this rather limited but massive collection of plate to his estate is apparent. He left movable goods worth £3,800; setting aside £2,000 owed to him, he had plate valued at almost £1,000 in stock in his counting house. His household plate, at just under £300, was therefore about a third of the total value of his goods. [30]

What Survives?

Of the medieval secular silver remaining today, by far the greater proportion is drinking vessels. Among these survivors, mounted pieces (horns, mazers and coconut cups) bulk large not because they were the most commonly used or most valued, but because the light weight and low value of their mounts has protected them from stripping and melting down. Most belong to institutions but this is misleading; there was no form of vessel peculiar to, say, colleges rather than private households before the seventeenth century. Most silver-owning households were both large and mainly masculine, and silver vessels for drinking, even before eating, were universally called for.

By contrast with the documentary evidence for plate holdings, a pathetic remnant of actual specimens survives. While many forms found later were already familiar – Count Amadeus of Savoy bought a silver urinal when staying in London in 1292, a coconut cup is first mentioned in a will of 1254, and salts, cups and spoons were in use from ancient times – we have virtually no idea of whether there was an English national style, even at court level. A continuity in both form and usage is evident until the mid-sixteenth century.

Drinking Vessels

The most spectacular piece of medieval secular plate is the so-called King John's cup, which was made about 1360 and already belonged to the town of King's Lynn in 1548. Its previous

Fig. 2 **The Studley Royal bowl**
Gilt *c*.1350–80. H.14 cm. Engraved with a black letter alphabet, divided by leafy branches. A drinking vessel, this formerly belonged to Studley Royal Church, Yorkshire.
VAM

15

history is not known, but there is no connection with King John. This brittle but elegant confection of translucent enamel and silver gilt has a bell-shaped bowl on a tall knopped stem, rising from a cinquefoil foot. The disc within the bowl depicts a woman with a hawk. Although the cup has been repaired and re-enamelled, most heavily on four occasions in the eighteenth century, and the present finial with its miniature steeple apes those on Jacobean standing cups, it is still a unique piece of secular goldsmiths' work. It has long been treasured as part of the 'regalia' of Lynn and appears in a trophy with the mace and the civic sword on a town map of 1725. Every surface, from the five flanges around the base, the knop and the sides to the cover is enamelled, a characteristic of medieval secular plate (Plate 5).[31]

A later fourteenth-century piece is a covered bowl, which belonged for many years to Studley Royal Church in Yorkshire until bought by the Victoria and Albert Museum (Fig. 2). It is engraved all over with a black-letter alphabet. Even the spaces between the letters are filled with floral sprays and the foot ring is pierced. Until the early sixteenth century, a print of clear enamel over an engraved silver disc or an enamelled boss was the typical central ornament for all cups, mazers and basins. Drinking vessels, whether mounted maplewood or totally of silver, were often also engraved with a possessory inscription or invocatory phrase, which led to their being referred to by name.[32]

Mounted Cups: Wood, Horn, Coconut

Mazers, turned maplewood bowls, followed standard forms; they were often made with tall stems which were sometimes detachable. One shown in the Beauchamp Pageants had been taken from its stand. Although mazers fell out of fashion in the sixteenth century, institutions with no pressing wish (or ability) to overhaul their plate collections retained them in regular use; several belonging to Harbledown Hospital can be seen in the Victoria and Albert Museum. Three of the mazers in the abbot's lodgings at Peterborough in 1460 had covers and gilt feet but the other five, described as 'wide', were flat-bottomed, four with silver rims and one without. The last may be compared with the late fourteenth-century Swan mazer at Corpus Christi College, Cambridge, which originally had a cover resting on three projecting strawberry leaves above the vertical lipband.[33]

Mazers conformed to standard sizes and their central prints or bosses also adopted certain popular subjects. They were usually enamelled over engraved or cast silver discs, with the Virgin and Child or S. George and the Dragon, or personal devices. The Saffron Walden mazer of 1507, from which Pepys drank, bore the Virgin and Child on its print; a Gloucester merchant in 1454 left his son one mazer with a dolphin in the bottom and another with 'John' on it.

Inscriptions were used on certain types of cups. They might be invocations with magical connotations, like the Jasper, Balthazar, Melchior on the Corpus mazer, or a grace; the plain silver cup at Peterborough in 1460 engraved with 'Blessed is he that cometh in the name of the Lord' was perhaps a grace cup. At Boston, one religious guild had a great mazer 'with an image of Almighty God sitting at the Judgement in the middest of four evangelists' plus seven others 'with various devices and legends and inscriptions' but only one large 'standing cup'; this was much heavier (46½ ounces) and so more costly to the donor.[34]

Fig. 3 **Covered mazer**
Maplewood and gilt *c.*1440. Given by Thomas Ballard Esq. whose arms are enamelled on the print.
Unusually this has retained its cover mounts, although the wood is a replacement.
All Souls College, Oxford (on loan to Ashmolean Museum)

The horn was a peculiarly Anglo-Saxon drinking vessel – the Bayeux Tapestry depicts Harold's men at Bosham drinking from horns while the Normans drink from bowls, and William of Poitiers found it another example of English barbarity. Drinking horns retained their popularity well into the sixteenth century and were often elaborately mounted, appropriately enough in view of their ceremonial function. Some were associated with feudal dues such as cornage; the best known of these is perhaps the Pusey horn (Victoria and Albert Museum) associated with Cnut's grant of land to the Pusey family of Berkshire in gratitude for services they rendered. Although the silvergilt mounts at present on the horn are no earlier than the mid-fifteenth century, the tradition might well be authentic; it was cited as such in 1684 when the Lord Chancellor gave judgement that the horn should pass with the land to the heir.[35]

Another horn, now in the British Museum, has been associated with the Stewardship of Savernake Forest at least since the late sixteenth century but was probably originally a cornage horn, from its decoration. It retains mounts of two different periods, the thirteenth and the fourteenth centuries. The earlier panels of French *basse taille* enamel depict hunting scenes with a king and a bishop, while the arms of the Earldom of Moray (extinct by 1347) appear enamelled on thirteen plates on the baldric. It was booty from Scotland, perhaps acquired by the Earl of Hertford after Henry VIII's campaign there in 1544.[36]

From the fourteenth century, several mounted horns are preserved; one at Cambridge was given to the brothers of the Guild of Corpus Christi before 1347 and passed to the college on its foundation in 1352. This, like the Pusey and the Eglesfield horns, is fitted with a silvergilt band and feet – although it has lost its cover. The mounts are battlemented and the horn is capped with a silvergilt turret. The improving hand of later stewards has added to both the Corpus Christi and Eglesfield horns (the latter is at Queen's, Oxford) but essentially these can stand as examples of a commonly-used ritual drinking vessel.

The large capacity of a horn made it peculiarly suited to communal drinking at festivals; in 1406 a Somerset man, William Carent of Montacute, left his son a horn with a cover of silvergilt 'In which I was accustomed to drink at the feast of the Nativity' and John Goldcorn gave the Corpus Christi horn with the stipulation that it be used 'fairly freely' on Corpus Christi day. As on so many medieval drinking vessels, phrases of good cheer are also incorporated; the mounts of the Eglesfield horn are inscribed WACCEYL in several places. The Guild of S. Mary at Boston, the premier fraternity of that prosperous town, had been given by 1534 both a hunting horn harnessed with silver, and a drinking horn 'ornate with silver and gilt, with 2 feet of silvergilt, set with a stone'.[37]

The Earls of Cawdor now own a horn which is said to have been presented by Henry VII to a Cardiganshire family in 1485. Its original appearance was recorded by an antiquarian visitor, Colonel Dineley, in 1684 when it was at Golden Grove, the home of the Vaughan family; it was then supported by the Tudor red dragon and the greyhound of York on an oval base chased with roses; the heraldic message confirms the likelihood that this was a royal gift from the newly installed king. But unfortunately the present horn bears little resemblance to the drawing of the late fifteenth-century original; presumably it was damaged, or otherwise disposed of, and a copy made some time between the 1680s and 1840 when the next illustration was published. The Tudor supporters and badges of a portcullis and a rose occur frequently on other pieces made at the order of the Jewel House as gifts, or for the royal household; a copy of the statutes for Henry VII's chapel, deposited with the dean and chapter of S. Paul's Cathedral in 1507, has both its silver seal boxes and its clasps so enamelled, and an elaborately decorated cabinet in Henry VIII's privy chamber was 'harnessed' with silvergilt and enamelled badges. The heraldic message is most clearly spelt out today in the metal grille in his father's chapel in Westminster Abbey.[38]

Another fifteenth-century horn has survived, although altered. The footed horn at Christ's Hospital was already at the school in 1567 and apparently had a new rim added at the expense of the hospital's benefactor Thomas Banckes in 1602. It is of no great artistic merit and probably typifies the standard of craftsmanship applied to the great majority of mounted horns by the late fifteenth century. A contemporary will shows that a canon of Wells Cathedral regarded his mounted horn as a fitting bequest for his servant in 1498.[39]

Although the earliest coconut cups we have, for example those belonging to New College,

Fig. 4 **Coconut cup**
Gilt *c*.1490. Probably given to the college by Robert Dalton, admitted 1472 and later Prebendary of
Chichester. Note the Lombardic D's. The nut is held by six oakbranches, growing from a paled
enclosure, probably for rabbits. One of seven coconut cups owned by the college in 1508.
New College, Oxford

Oxford and Gonville and Caius, Cambridge, are late fifteenth century, they were popular from early in the Middle Ages, combining the exotic and the practical, and continued so into the seventeenth century. When the stock of Robert Amadas, royal goldsmith to Henry VIII, was valued in 1532, he had mounted mazers, listed for their metal mounts at so much each, but his 'black nuts' were more highly valued, since the nuts themselves were worth as much as their weight in silvergilt. A little closet in his working shop contained 'old broken mazer trees small and great, old nuts, shells black and painted' stripped of mounts or ready for mounting. Nuts were often painted before mounting, although the only trace of this is a red internal coat on a nut in the Victoria and Albert Museum with marks of about 1625. Clearly there was the possibility of deception, of so thickly coating a nut before painting it as to increase the weight and the price paid.[40]

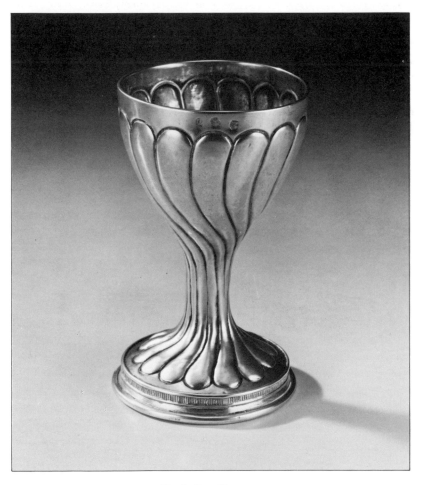

Fig. 5 **Standing cup**
Gilt 1493. Mark an escallop below a baton. H.14 cm. One of the earliest secular vessels with the London date letter, introduced in 1478. Formerly in use at S. Andrew's Church, Middleton, Yorkshire.
Goldsmiths' Company

Since the nuts were valuable in themselves, the mounts were sometimes carefully designed with imagery personal to the owner, as a coconut cup at New College demonstrates (Fig. 4). Clasped by six oak branches arising from a paled enclosure, the nut was probably the gift of Robert Dalton (known to have given a coconut cup), to whom the collar of Lombardic 'Ds' refers. The air of woodland fantasy of this piece is reinforced by small holes or burrows in the oakroots; cast rabbits, now lost, no doubt originally played about within the paling. This is a characteristic late medieval combination in both English and French silver; many pieces are described as having a field or bank of grass enamelled on the foot, with animals and birds or even human figures in a bower. But only the Huntsman salt at All Souls stands as a comparison today.[41]

The other New College coconut cup, also was about 1500, one of seven it owned in 1508; it is no less unusual in its mounts. Three demi-angels with scrolls, on turreted stands, form the feet; the stem of scales and feathers is like the near-contemporary flagon at Magdalen College. A black letter inscription 'ave maria gracia plena tecum benedicta' surrounds the rim, a standard late medieval drinking grace, and the cresting around the foot and at the base of the nut is crudely cast when compared with the crisp cast work on Warden Hill's salt, in the same collection, or Bishop Foxe's salt at Corpus Christi.[42]

Standing cups sometimes took fanciful forms. Albrecht Durer engraved a gourd-shaped cup on a twisted stem, which as a result is considered an early sixteenth-century German innovation; this design retained its popularity in England into the 1600s, but it had a longer ancestry. Cups 'like costards' (apples) occur in fifteenth-century inventories.[43]

There were in every large household sets of smaller (and cheaper) cups, often without covers and only a few inches high; these are either quite plain, like the Kimpton cup of about 1480 (VAM), or gadrooned, like one shaped like an eggcup at the Goldsmiths' Company (1493); (Fig. 5). These two little cups have survived the melt only because each belonged for many years to a church, whereas the handful of grander cups among the 'Founder's plate' owe their existence to their associations. Four sets of six cups at the Drapers' Company in 1489 had only one cover to each set; the individual cups weighed from only ten to twenty-two ounces.

Spoons

Spoons make up by far the largest category of surviving secular silver and cover the widest range of dates. Apart from those dated by context, examples with the leopard's head mark of the fourteenth century are known; marked spoons run more or less continuously well into the sixteenth century, when other types of silver exist for comparison. Although the artistic merit of spoons is small, they survive in sufficient numbers for us to know that they were produced to standard sizes and designs, by specialist spoonmakers, well before the end of the middle ages; they also provide a body of material from which to comment on decoration and craftsmanship. As a man's personal property, his spoon travelled with him and so was far more at risk of casual loss or theft than domestic or altar plate – which was carefully stored away when not in use – hence many of the chance discoveries. Those other spoons which were passed on as heirlooms, and survived into the eighteenth century, were by then probably protected from melting by their antiquarian interest.[44]

Although the fig-shaped bowl was more or less uniform in profile into the sixteenth century, there are tremendous variations in the shape of the knop. Several types are recognisable by 1500; already in the fifteenth century terminals are described as wrythen, acorn, slip, 'perle' and figurative, presumably referring to the owner's crest or other heraldic device. Apostle spoons appear by the mid-fifteenth century, with 'woodwoses' (wild men) a little later. About thirty years ago Commander and Mrs How attempted a complex dating classification by the shape of the leopard's head mark struck in the spoon bowl, which was to become in effect the London hallmark. But there are too few closely-dated specimens for this to be quite satisfactory and in any case by no means were all spoons so marked. This is one area in which new evidence does appear from time to time. A few years ago great publicity surrounded the sale of a diamond-point spoon, which had been found in the rafters of a Devon farmhouse. This fetched a record price for a single spoon. More recently, an unrecorded woodwose spoon – the wild man or green man of medieval literature – of the fifteenth century turned up in the United States, still owned by the family of Cornish extraction whose ancestress had taken it across the Atlantic in 1846. Mudlarks working on the Thames foreshore have also added to our stock of early spoons, although their discoveries are confined to spoons of the late fourteenth and fifteenth centuries.[45]

The most famous medieval English spoon, the anointing spoon still shown with the regalia at the Tower, apparently survived the Commonwealth. It was in 1660 repaired at a cost of £2. Although it has been argued that this spoon was entirely remade at some point, there seems no reason to doubt that much of it is twelfth century; the stem is decorated with interlace like that on contemporary Scottish spoons.[46]

Spoons were recognised as a means of marking entry to the senior membership of a society, whether a craft guild or a college, and some institutions were well stocked before 1500. Eton College owned a total of 200 spoons by 1456, although admittedly five dozen were from a single benefactor, and the Drapers' Company had eleven and a half dozen in 1489. So overstocked were the Drapers that by 1509, and probably long before, they had commuted the customary gift of a spoon to a payment called 'Sponesylver'. Set at 3s 4d, this reflected the price of a spoon half a century or more before; by 1509, 3s 4d would scarcely buy an ounce of silver and the spoons presented were normally well over an ounce in weight.[47]

Silver about the House

Turning to more utilitarian plate, a handful of basins, two at Corpus Christi, Oxford from Bishop Foxe's gift and one belonging to a London church, probably a post-Reformation gift – represent the simplest late medieval form of this useful vessel, with gadroons or 'bolyons' radiating from a central enamelled boss. But these date only from 1480 or later and more ornate versions no doubt existed before. The Foxe basins are interesting not for their ornament, which is confined to a central enamelled boss, but for the dog-faced spout which emerges below the rim of one. This basin, filled with scented water, was tilted above its pair to enable the user to wash his hands in the falling water. The gemellion, or twinned basin, is familiar in base metal and references occur in the fifteenth and early sixteenth centuries – there is one set in the 1521 royal inventory and another in a Pembroke plate inventory of 1561 – but

Fig. 6 **The Bermondsey dish (the reverse)**
Parcel-gilt *c*.1330–50. The central boss was originally coated with translucent enamel. The front of the
dish is illustrated on the cover.
S. Mary Magdalen, Bermondsey (on loan to VAM)

the method was superseded by the far more convenient ewer and basin even before 1500 and Foxe's pair, which were originally domestic plate, survived only because they were given for use in his college chapel.[48]

In church of course a basin could be used to collect alms even when its liturgical significance as a priest's ablution basin was dropped altogether. A 1524 basin now belonging to S. Magnus the Martyr, City of London, bears the later inscription 'for the ewse of the poorre 1564' and when the dean and chapter of S. Paul's Cathedral listed their minimum requirements for worship in the reforming days of 1547, their 'Certain thinges of necessary use' included two pairs of basins 'for to bring the Communion Bread and to receive the offerings for the poor'. The silver pair was for everyday use, the gilt for festivals.[49]

By far the earliest English basin, with no hallmark but an ownership mark, is parcel-gilt, again with a central boss once enamelled (about 1320–30; Fig. 6). Although it has belonged to Bermondsey parish church since the sixteenth century, it was made for domestic use and has a leopard's head engraved on the back, possibly indicating that it was once the property of the royal household, this being the 'King's mark'. All the royal plate stored at Caerphilly Castle in 1327, with the exception of the chapel plate, was similarly stamped and Hugh Kayle or Keal, a prominent court supplier in Queen Elizabeth I's reign, had a punch with which to mark all the royal plate he supplied.[50]

Examples of such punches to denote ownership are found extremely rarely but pewter issued to the Tudor battleship the Mary Rose, and so presumably all royal-issue pewter, was stamped; and the king's scullion at Caerphilly in 1327, John d'Podenhale, had to answer for three brass pots marked 'E', although this probably stood for the household department, the ewery, from which they were issued. Identification marks have a long ancestry; another sixteenth-century example is on the Leigh cup at the Mercers' Company which has a tiny maiden's head (the Company crest) punched inside the cover.[51]

Occasionally official marks can enable us to reconstruct with certainty the history of an object. William Bateman, Bishop of Norwich, the founder of Trinity Hall, Cambridge, died at Avignon in 1355. His silvergilt beaker, now at the college, has on the base the official punch used by those Avignon goldsmiths working for the papal court; this has been read as an indication that the beaker was taken into the papal treasury on Bateman's death, but it is now recognised as Avignon-made.[52]

Identification marks as a precaution against theft were common in all wealthy households. In the royal households each department responsible for plate had its own distinguishing letter, such as 'P' for Pitcherhouse, and the 1574 inventory lists several, although Collins points out that it is not always easy to distinguish between a reference to a date-letter and to a location mark.[53]

The chafing dish is another example of practical plate once in almost universal use but now vanished. Ceramic versions of this useful vessel are recorded from English archaeological sites of the mid-fourteenth century. Silver ones are listed in the Holland and Fastolf inventories – plus a 'chaufer to set upon a table for hotwater' – and John Howard, Duke of Norfolk, gave Lord Hastings 'a double dish for hot water' as a New Year's gift in 1481. Queen Elizabeth I inherited several chafing dishes, and one which from the 1574 description was also a food warmer. It was elaborate both in construction and decoration. Gilded and chased, it had two leopard's head handles surmounted by hollow scalloped shells to put hot water in 'to keep the meat hot without fire' and they were clearly commonplace in Tudor households. Yet the earliest silver chafing dishes date only from the later seventeenth century; Bishop Ken left one to Winchester College. Serving dishes, and 'saucers' to accompany them, normally came in sets or 'garnishes' of twelve but these do not survive; nor do the accompanying pair of chargers.[54]

The pierced perfume burner is another standard item of medieval household equipment, made for London housewives in greenglazed pottery, but a pierced silver version of 1628, now in the Los Angeles Museum of Fine Art, is a unique pre-Restoration survival.

Sconces, and candlesticks with detachable nozzles, were both familiar household objects in the fifteenth century, if not long before, but the earliest silver candlestick (which may in any case not be in original condition) is of *c*.1560–90; although illustrated in Jackson's *An Illustrated History of English Plate*, its present whereabouts is not known. The earliest sconce dates to just before the Civil War. It should be stressed that both forms of lighting can be found in base metal and in ceramic versions rather earlier, normally preserved in archaeological contexts (that is discarded in rubbish pits) a fate from which silver was normally preserved because of its high value.

Relatively few types of vessel were generally in use before 1600 and the difference between the very wealthy and the less wealthy silver-owning classes is one of bulk and ornament rather than function. There is of course no such thing as a typical list of plate but it is interesting to see what John Howard, first Duke of Norfolk, thought appropriate to take aboard his new 'Great Ship' in about 1481. This modest list may be taken to illustrate the minimum possible for a man of birth; apart from his chapel equipment of a chalice, he took four goblets in a case and a layer (jug) for his personal wine, a large salt and two small ones of crystal, a washing basin and two pots and a 'pyssying bassyn'. His immediate retinue presumably drank from the six white bowls 'Unkeuvring', that is without covers. The minimum holding, a personal cup and silver spoon, is represented by the establishment at a small chantry chapel with two resident priests at Bridport in Dorset. In its buttery in 1408, Munden's chantry had six silver spoons and three cups, but the priests' servant was expected to use latten.[55]

Notes

1   The Trewhiddle chalice is pl. 1 in Oman 1957.

2   Wilson 1962.

3   The Tassilo chalice is at Kremsmunster Abbey, Austria, Dodwell 1982, col. pl. 14.

4   Dodwell 1982.

5   Arts Council 1984, 'Metalwork' and refs cited there, 1984, 279. Oman 1932.

6   Oman 1958 and Arts Council 1984, 249 and col. pl. 73; 263–5; 288.

7   Arts Council 1984, 283–5; Oman 1932.

8   Hope and Fallow 1887. The Dolgellau chalice belonged for some years to Baron Schroder, Oman 1978, pl. 3 and 4, and Goldsmiths 1979.

9   Comparable with the Dolgellau chalice is the mid-twelfth century chalice and paten found in the tomb of Archbishop Hubert Walter at Canterbury in 1890; Arts Council 1984, 294–5 and Oman 1978, pl. 1 and 2. A plainer twelfth-century example came from a Chichester bishop's coffin. Oman 1957.

10   Legg and S. John Hope 1902.

11   Oman 1957, pl. 1; Arts Council, 1984, 293 and Jackson 1911, fig. 134; Campbell 1982.

12   Freshwater 1893. Oman 1957. For fifteenth-century secular cups too, Beauchamp Pageants 1908, pl. XX.

13   Campbell 1982. His gifts, made between 1078 and 1099, are in Nightingale, *Church Plate of Wiltshire* Appendix I. Appendix II gives the 1536 inventory.

14   National Portrait Gallery 1973; Thompson. 1856, 142. For enamels, Campbell 1983.

15   P. 11. A century later the Earl of Pembroke's chapel had over 1,600 ounces of plate; Pembroke inventory 1561, VAM.

16   For the value of confiscations between 1536 and 1553, see Challis 1978, 160–5. The canons of S. George's Chapel, Windsor sold altar plate worth more than £1,200 in 1548–9. Their gold chalice followed in 1552, for £260, Bond, 11–12.

17   A typical list; see *Norfolk Archaeology I*, 1847; 7, 1879.

18   Thompson 1856, 142.

19   Freshfield 'Will of George Talbot, fourth Earl of Shrewsbury 1468–1538', *Derbyshire Archaeological and Natural History Society Journal*, XXXI, 1909. Layer Marney (with other Essex bequests) Benton 1926, 318.

20 Westminster Abbey Muniments 6643.

21 *Archaeologia* 21, 1827. Serving plate, although normally undecorated, bulked large in inventories. At Caerphilly Castle there were 272 dishes and 279 'saucers'. On heraldry, see Ch. 10.

22 Lightbown 1977; Dalton 1924. Reddaway and Walker's biographies of London goldsmiths emphasise their potential wealth and standing, Appendix 2.

23 Inventory 1521. For marking, p. 145–7.

24 Paston 1971. Vol I.

25 Harrison 1893, Appendix IV inventory 1542.

26 Peterborough Cath. Lib. M52 'The Register of Abbot Richard Ashton' Myers 1969, Vol. IV, 1146–8. One cup in the Talbot will (cited note 19) was called 'my lady's nightcap'. The ritual attached to drinking is discussed in Eames 1971, 41–2. See p. 35.

27 See bibliography for inventions.

28 Paston 1971. Vol I, no. 95.

29 Ibid. Vol 2, no. 923.

30 Glanville *Proceedings of the Silver Society* forthcoming.

31 Norwich 1973, 27–8. See p. 197–8

32 Oman 1978, pl. 19. Five important standing salts in the early Tudor Jewel House had names: Collins 1955, 22.

33 Hope 1887. See also note 26. One at the Drapers' in 1489 with a silvergilt handle was called a 'bygget'. Fitzwilliam 1975, MTD2.

34 Between 1489 and 1518 the Drapers' were given twenty-five covered cups, plus four sets of six with a single cover; at least four, and one set, had invocatory drinking graces.

35 Jackson 1911; Stone 1961.

36 It is first mentioned in the 1607 edition of Camden's Britannia: *British Museum Yearbook II*, 1977, 201–11.

37 Somerset Wills 1901; Thompson 1856.

38 See note 35 and p. 200.

39 Penzer 1960; Somerset Wills 1901.

40 Oman 1979; Fitzwilliam 1975, MTD4 and refs cited there. PROB/2/486. One pledged (with a mazer) to the Drapers' about 1500 was valued at the white silver rate of 2s 6d per ounce.

41 Oman 1979, 296; Lightbown 1978.

42 Oman 1979, pl. 70. Campbell 1982, pl. 1–6.

43 Somerset Wills 1901.

44 How and How 1952; Culme 1985 and p. 276.

45 Sold at Phillips's 1982.

46 How and How 1952, 24, pl. I. For the Iona spoons, see Arts Council 1984, 280.

47 Oman 1971, 102. The Drapers' Company took seventeen payments in 1509–10 from apprentices completing their time.

48 Glanville *Pelican* 1984.

49 Freshfield 1893.

50 Oman 1952; Oman 1978, pl. 6. Inventory 1326. Collins 1955.

51 Inventory 1326. On security, p. 333.

52 Fitzwilliam 1975, 51; Lightbown 1978, 93, pl. LXXII.

53 Collins 1955, no. 1525, twelve gilt platters 'streken on their backsides with the lettre S' were almost certainly for the scullery.

54 Collins 1955, 502. Oman 1955. A Somerset knight, Sir Robert Hungerford of Heytesbury, left such a garnish to his wife in 1459, all with his arms.

55 Howard 1844, 275. Wood-Legh 1956.

TUDOR

> The most remarkable thing in London is the wonderful quantity of wrought silver. In one single street named Cheapside leading to S. Paul's, there are fifty-two goldsmiths' shops, so rich and full of silver vessels, great and small that in Milan, Rome, Venice and Florence I do not think there would be found so many.
>
> (*Italian Relation c.*1500)

FOREIGN visitors to England between the late fifteenth and late sixteenth centuries were struck by the amount of silver in regular use, although one over-enthusiastic Italian was misled by the high quality of our pewter into thinking that every tavern served its customers in silver mugs and cups. Certainly the sixteenth century saw a sudden rise in prosperity for a large section of the English population with, simultaneously, a new pattern of expenditure. Protestant Englishmen, no longer bound by custom and piety to dedicate resources to their spiritual protection after death, were able to invest in treasure on earth. As a crude but effective indicator the wills of London merchants, each with its litany of payments to chantry chapels, 'Singing Priests' and similar bequests before 1550, changed to lists of legacies, in money and material possessions, of which silver, with clothes and bedding, was by far the most important and valuable.[1] Inventories reinforce the picture of this enormous increase in the value and quantity of material goods which was, however, restricted to those prosperous enough to merit an inventory at all. When the Essex vicar William Harrison (1577) described the new domestic refinements in his rural community, comforts already commonplace among the London bourgeoisie rather earlier, he was clear about the timing of this new prosperity: 'In the past seventy years . . . the multitude of chimneys lately erected . . . amendment of lodging . . . the exchange of vessel, as of treen platters into pewter, and wooden spoons into silver or tin.'[2]

Of course this oversimplifies a far more gradual process in which not all social groups shared equally. Pewter, latten or pottery remained the normal materials for vessels in most homes.[3]

This enormous shift in expenditure directly benefited the goldsmiths, both through the programme of refashioning of Mass plate into decent Protestant communion cups and from the surge in spending on domestic plate by those profiting directly or indirectly from the redistribution of ecclesiastical property. Henry VIII's 'new men' not only had the wherewithal to spend on plate but were expected to do so to dress their handsome new houses, and their descendants built on their holdings. Conversely some livery companies, such as the Vintners and the Drapers, sold their plate in the 1540s to acquire property. It was a period of great fluidity in the land market.

While the spread of pewter through society in the late Middle Ages up to the late seventeenth century has recently been quantified, a similar exercise for silver has not yet been attempted.[4] However, by analysing the inventories of individuals from recognisable social groups, at least we can reconstruct what they were or were not using at any one time. In aristocratic or royal households, when there was a change of officers, or in all families when the owner died, careful inventories were made and as a result we know most about the top end of society.[5]

Royal and Aristocratic Silver

The Tudor and early Stuart royal collections are particularly well recorded in a series of documents from 1521 to the dispersals of 1649–50. From these lists one can see both the enormous variety of domestic vessels made in precious metal and the steady increase in their number. In Queen Elizabeth's privy kitchen, her cooks used massive 150-ounce boiling pots of silver, gridirons, chafing dishes, skillets, pie dishes, ladles and a cullender, all of silver. Her butler served her dessert of crystallised ginger or marchpane on gilt and mother-of-pearl plates and she ate the sticky sweetmeats with a silvergilt sucket fork. Another set of dessert plates inherited from her father had *verre églomisé* (painted glass) panels, a rare and costly technique of which the Vyvyan salt is an example (VAM, 1592). She cracked her nuts with a fifteen-ounce figure of a woman in silver gilt. Her toilet utensils, from her bedpan to her shampoo jug, were all of silver and most were personalised with her badge, initials or armorials. Shoehorns, setting sticks for ruffs, strainers, wine funnels, all were silver. Her looking-glass was of steel in a silvergilt frame with sockets for silver ear and toothpicks.[6] While some of the more elaborate items were gifts at New Year or on progress the household purchased more domestic pieces from the royal goldsmiths, in particular Hugh Keale or Kayle who several times supplied the queen with porringers and covers. Her expenditure on plate was perhaps rather less than that of her principal subjects since she inherited a collection of well over a thousand items (977 entries in the 1574 inventory; many of these being sets). These were by no means always newly made but were often old plate which in many cases had fallen to the Crown because of the impeachment or disgrace of their original owners. At least ninety items in the 1574 list can be identified as being from this source, either from the badges and arms described by the clerks or by a specific reference.[7]

After Cardinal Wolsey fell, his enormous collection of plate at York Place (now Whitehall), came into the Jewel House. Some of the gold plate bore both his device of a griffin holding a pillar (emblem of a cardinal) and, more provocatively, the friar's girdles of the French king Francis I who had presented them, with much other plate, in happier days when Wolsey was Henry's ambassador. These reminders of the past were removed by the royal goldsmiths Cornelius Hayes and John Freeman in 1532.[8] Some of his plate passed on to members of the court. Sir William Sydney had a gilt pot with a cover bearing his device in 1544 and several of his standing cups, pots and a casting bottle with a chain were wrought with the castle,

Fig. 7 **The Vyvyan salt**
Gilt and painted glass (verre eglomise) 1592. Mark WH and a flower. H. 40 cm. The architectural model
was popular for standing salts between about 1560 and 1620. Descended in the Vyvyan family of
Trelowarren, Cornwall.
VAM

pomegranate and sheaf of arrows indicating that they had been made for Katherine of Aragon.

Wolsey's income from his see and benefices was about six times as great as the wealthiest contemporary peer and he entertained lavishly on the king's behalf, a role in which his massive expenditure on silver and gold was shown to great effect, and might indeed be seen as an instrument of state policy. George Cavendish, his gentleman-usher, has left a vivid account of the display in the presence chamber at Hampton Court, put on for the benefit of a French embassy in 1527. A temporary cupboard running the full width of the room was dressed

> six deskes highe full of gilt plate very sumptious and of the most newest facion and uppon the nethermost deske garnyshed all with plate of clene gold and lit by two great silvergilt candlesticks. This cupboard was barred in round about that no man might come nigh it for there was none of the same plate occupied or stirred for there was sufficient besides.[9]

Much of the splendid effect of such buffets depended on the sheer mass of plate which would normally include, for the period of the meal only, all the chamber plate, that is ewers and basins for washing and livery pots and cups for the customary overnight provision of bread, wine and ale for each guest. However, such was Wolsey's stock that his display remained untouched and as Cavendish said:

> Every chamber had a basin and ewer of silver and some clene gilt and some parcell gilt and some two great pots of silver . . . and one pot at the least with wine and beer. A bowl or Cobbett and a silver pot to drink beer, a silver kandlesticke or two . . . thus was every chamber furnished throughout the house and yet the two cupboards in the two banqueting chambers not touched.

Aristocrats lived almost as lavishly. When the Duke of Northumberland was arrested in 1553, over 10,000 ounces of plate was removed from Durham Place, in London and Syon House. Forty-three pieces were retained for the royal collection. Edward Seymour, Duke of Somerset, beheaded a year earlier, was notorious for his expenditure on plate and had trouble persuading the Trappes family, leading London goldsmiths, to continue to supply him because of unpaid bills.[10] Even on his silvergilt cups, his enamelled and cast phoenix crest was in solid gold. Elizabeth inherited from his collection 'a great spice plate pounced wrought with Antiques with the Duke of Somerset's arms in the middle, gilt within, white without' weighing forty-nine ounces and two silvergilt spice boxes, one 'like a cofer with a lid, graven all over with Antiques and within the same a little gilt spoon, having a boy upon the top of the steel'. The other was much smaller and square, simply engraved with a phoenix within a garter.[11]

References to spice boxes, earlier called 'powder boxes', with accompanying spoons, occur with greater frequency into the seventeenth century. The familiar shell-shaped sugar box, very rarely found with a folding spoon, is the standard early Stuart form of this condiment container. A tiny square box with four compartments, the lid of each engraved with Tudor royal arms, unmarked but made about 1550 (VAM) may have been for spices but, given its small size, is more probably a forerunner of the familiar Jacobean pomander in the form of a segmented sphere.

Spice plates, spice boxes and gilt dessert cutlery were usually much more elaborately decorated than general dining plate. Kept by the confectionery staff, they were used at the small refined and private repasts of spiced bread, wine and candied fruit, which were occasions quite distinct from the main meal. Those attending the host were a select small group of friends – the banquet houses on the roof at Longleat hold six at the most – who were sharing delicacies, music and conversation. Sometimes the occasion was more solemn; after the funeral of John Islip, abbot of Westminster (1532), 'the mourners departed into a place over the chapel of the defunct where was prepared for them spiced bread, sucket, marmylate,

Fig. 8 **Hourglass and stand**
Parcel-gilt, English *c*.1530. A rare example of early Renaissance design applied to a practical object. The stamped floral panels are found on English terracotta work in the 1530s. For the dolphins on the frame, compare Fig. 13.
Boston, Museum of Fine Arts

31

Fig. 9 **Spice plate**
Gilt 1573. Mark RF monogram, for Roger Flynt. D.25.5 cm. From a set of six, all engraved with Old Testament subjects, here Abraham and Isaac. The engraver (unnamed) has drawn from three different sources; the rim is in the style of Vergil Solis.
VAM

spiced plate and divers sorts of wine a plenty'.[12] Similar repasts were held at the election of their masters by the livery companies; spice plates were central to these festive occasions. Several Elizabethan sets survive, distinguished by their superb engraving. Gilt, and bearing no knife scratches, they were clearly intended for the lightest and most elegant use. The accompanying cups, for sweet wine or hippocras, were often designated as such and were more ornately decorated in their bowls.

32

Mounted Exotica

The Renaissance taste for both natural and man-made wonders, expressed at its most sophisticated in the Medici collection of hardstone vessels, spread across the Channel and stimulated English goldsmiths into creating similar elaborate confections of exotic materials. A nautilus shell, an ostrich egg mounted as the body of a bird, turned serpentine, or panels of agate were mounted up into tankards, cups and salts.[13] The cheapest and most widely available was the coconut, which lent itself to carving and mounting.

Although the workmanship required for those mounted pieces preserved today is nothing exceptional, some high-quality court commissions offered more challenge. The mounted rock crystal bowl thought to have been designed by Holbein was a vehicle for both the crystal-cutter and the enameller.[14] The Stonyhurst salt (1577) in the British Museum is the result of a similar process. Here, to create an impressive standing salt, the goldsmith reassembled ten irregular lumps of rock crystal and fifty-two cabochon stones from earlier ecclesiastical settings of the fourteenth and fifteenth centuries. The resulting salt is intriguing rather than beautiful.[15]

Worked crystal became widely available in post-Dissolution London, and from being a rarity confined largely to church treasuries, it became almost commonplace and entirely in keeping with the general European taste for rare and prized natural materials. Two cups and a salt at the Goldsmiths' Company of 1545, 1554 and 1576 incorporate rock crystal cylinders; another Tudor cup (given to Yateley Church, Hampshire in 1675) has a crystal bowl and may be the work of a local Hampshire goldsmith. In the Cheapside hoard, the stock of a Jacobean goldsmith discovered under a cellar floor in 1912, there are several little crystal bottles awaiting mounting and a crystal salt and two tankards, perhaps old stock brought in to be stripped of their mounts.[16]

Natural curiosities were highly valued as gifts, if not for their bullion content. John Harrington gave Queen Elizabeth an agate salt with a steeple on the cover, another fashionable feature, in 1576 and a beer cup of serpentine with silvergilt cameos and agate heads, in the royal collection in 1550, may have been a New Year gift from Seymour, whose badge it bore. The cameos sound somewhat Parisian; there was of course no restraint on giving foreign plate, although it was strictly speaking illegal for a goldsmith to sell it unmarked after 1579.[17]

Doctor William Butler left to Clare, his Cambridge college, three imported curiosities in 1617 – a turned serpentine tankard, another of glass and filigree (both probably German made, about 1560) and a silver falcon standing on a box, made in Antwerp in 1561. These have survived later melting, presumably because of their relatively low bullion content. As Fuller commented, Butler 'was better pleased with presents than money, loved what was pretty rather than what was costly and preferred rarities before riches'.[18]

Of all the vessels in exotic materials, Chinese porcelain bowls were the most highly prized in Elizabethan England. Their aura of exotic mystery attracted legends to explain their presence here. A small porcelain bowl with a silvergilt foot, mounted for use as a standing cup (now in the Museum of London), is said to have belonged to Mary Queen of Scots.

Fig. 10   **The Glynne cup: a pelican in her piety**
Gilt 1579. Maker's mark a bird. H. 39 cm. Typical of the elaborate, often figurative, standing cups
popular in the sixteenth century. The body of the cup may originally have been a nautilus shell, replaced
by silvergilt.
Loan, VAM

34

In 1599 a bowl of blue and white Chinese porcelain was superbly mounted with double-tailed mermaid handles and caryatid straps by a goldsmith whose mark is IH (VAM). The property of a Dorset family, the bowl is said to have been a gift from Joanna and Archduke Philip of Austria who were wrecked on the Dorset coast in 1506. Their involuntary visit took place several years earlier than the date of manufacture of the porcelain but this bowl, and a companion piece, presumably attached themselves to this romantic episode of family history because their existence was otherwise inexplicable.[19] English-mounted porcelains have similar stories; one of the earliest is a celadon bowl presented by Archbishop Warham to New College, Oxford before 1530. Again he is said to have had it from Archduke Philip of Austria in 1506.[20]

Cups, Bowls and Drinking Pots

The first piece of silver people aspired to was a spoon, whether as a baptismal or a wedding gift, weighing 1½ or two ounces at most. This represented the minimum expenditure possible. The next step was to acquire a cup. A silver cup was a popular gift, regarded as appropriate to cement a relationship, mark a favour or as a bequest, as it had considerable ceremonial significance. When the Goldsmiths' Company set up their first permanent assay office in 1478, they decided to make two cups from the accumulated assay samples or diets.

The sixteenth century saw not only a greater spread of silver across society but a profusion of new forms such as tankards and casting bottles and, particularly for dessert, spice plates and boxes and sets of dessert spoons and forks. Cups formed a markedly smaller proportion of the plate holdings of wealthy families by 1600. Cups had almost always been supplied with covers, as were the new drinking vessels – tankards and pots – which emerged in the mid-sixteenth century. The reason was largely one of etiquette. The large household, characteristic way of life for many Englishmen before about 1600, had its own elaborate hierarchy and ritual of dining and drinking in which silver vessels were significant symbols of standing. Such a household might consist of two to three hundred people, all but a handful men, and plate holdings reflected this medieval tradition of hospitality with a strong emphasis on ceremonial drinking, hence the preponderance of gilt cups, goblets and bowls (with rather fewer salts and spoons) in late medieval inventories.[21]

To honour the lord of the household he, or the most senior person present, was always served with drink in the most handsome of the available covered cups. Other cups, uncovered, were then brought by the yeomen along the table to each guest in turn. When Tudor goldsmiths' bills itemise sets of cups or drinking bowls, normally one cover only is specified.[22] However, this customary ceremonial (a practice which survives in the baring of the head in the presence of superior authority or when going into church), which was strongly masculine in emphasis, lapsed in the seventeenth century as families retreated into private dining rooms and habits changed. A vestige of the ceremonial survives now only in societies where formal dining still occurs.

Very few of the surviving Tudor cups are still associated with their covers, even those given to such conservative institutions as livery companies. In those sets that survive together, the cover has rolled or been dropped often enough to require repairs which have

35

Fig. 11 **'A very rich Lotterie Generall without any Blanckes'**
Drawn on the steps of S. Paul's Cathedral, 1567. The prizes were partly money and partly plate:
candlesticks, salts, ewers and spoons but above all drinking vessels, covered bowls and beakers and
covered cups, some very elaborate, but no alepots.
Washington, Folger Shakespeare Library

36

Fig. 12 **The Campion cup**
Gilt 1500. Mark a covered cup. H.9.5 cm. Inscribed SOLI DEO HONOR ET GLORIA. A 'flat cup'
which may originally have had a cover, a type popular by 1450.
VAM

modified its original appearance. The Lambarde cup at the Drapers' Company, for instance, had its finial replaced twice and has now a version of 1912.[23]

The great variety of terms used in late medieval and Tudor inventories for drinking vessels – nests of chalice bowls, 'flat' cups, bowls, bowlets, 'cups bowl fashion or glass fashion', tun cups, beer cups with ears – cannot be tied up precisely with surviving examples. Cups, that is deep bowls on feet and with covers, were regarded as display and ceremonial plate and often elaborately decorated, whereas bowls were not always supplied with covers and were shallower, lower and more personal. There were also distinctive forms for beer and wine.[24]

The 'font-shaped' cup, so-called by historians of plate from its shape but probably called a flat cup or bowl 400 years ago, was popular from the mid-fifteenth century. Only three of the seventeen or so known font-shaped cups retain their original covers. The Cressner cup at the Goldsmiths' Company, made for John Cressner in 1503, bears on the cover a print enamelled with his arms under a disc of rock crystal. The earliest known, the Campion cup (VAM 1500, Fig. 12), has many of the characteristics of the group; the inscribed motto SOLI DEO HONOR ET GLORIA indicates that it was probably passed along the table after grace had been said. It has also a sturdy short stem and foot and shallow bowl. The ivory bowl in the Howard Grace cup

(VAM 1525) is as shallow as these others, without its misleadingly deep silvergilt lip-band; this also retains its elaborate cover, which the servant held while the lord of the feast drank.[25]

Later in the sixteenth century, this was superseded by a more elegant standing cup called by historians a 'tazza', that is a wide shallow bowl on a slimmer and taller stem. The function of these vessels, made also in glass and pottery, has been much debated, but it seems clear that they were regarded as drinking vessels at the time. Gilt standing bowls of this shape were offered as prizes, in company with a wide variety of other cups, in the 1567 London lottery. Their centres were always engraved or embossed, often with a head in a roundel, or, as on the S. Michael bowl set with a chased plaque, clearly designed to be glimpsed through the wine. One was given to Deane Church, Hampshire for use as a chalice in 1688, and another of 1586 to Cripplegate Ward to join the drinking vessels already available for the officers' comfort. The earliest is the Arlington bowl (1532) until recently in use as an alms dish in a Devon church, and several are depicted in the drawings of Tudor plate of the 1530s and 1540s, at the British Museum.[26]

For those not yet able to aspire to a silver cup, it was common practice to buy a relatively cheap but decorative German stoneware pot and mount it with silvergilt. The first purchases of John Bowyer, son of a yeoman who rose through the law to become a gentleman, in 1551 were two such pots, one 'with a flower on the side white' for 5*d* and the other 'a stone pot of dark colour' for 2*s*. 'Fashion', including silver lids engraved with Bowyer's cypher (he was not then entitled to bear arms) cost 4*s* and 5*s* apiece.[27] Bowyer's next purchase, a little gilt salt bought from Affabel Partridge at the Black Bull, Cheapside in 1554, cost well over a pound. When a shilling was a day labourer's wage, even these small silver items were luxury goods, inaccessible to all but a minority. These mounted stoneware pots are familiar collectors' pieces now, but were regarded as merely the first step in accumulating a plate cupboard. However, some became heirlooms because they epitomised how far the family had come up the social ladder.

At all levels of society the English had a strongly marked preference – apparently unique to this country and confined to the period from the 1530s to the 1560s – for squat bulbous alepots, which according to one's wealth might be made of silver, glass, maiolica, stoneware or coarse glazed earthenware. In 1558 a French visitor, Etienne Perlin, commented that the English drank their beer 'not out of glasses but from earthen pots with silver handles & covers & this even in houses of middling quality'.[28] At court in 1550, the king had several in coloured Venetian glass with silvergilt mounts of great elaboration; at the Inns of Court, hundreds were supplied regularly, in green-glazed Surrey pottery, for the law students. Typical is the mounted stoneware jug which David Gittings gave to the Vintners' Company in 1563 with a standard cast pomegranate and dolphin thumbpiece. It was personalised for Gittings with an engraved inscription around the lip and his merchant's mark enamelled on the boss.

Pot-shaped drinking vessels, like the Tyndale flagon at the Armourers' and Braziers' Company, were called 'Haunce' or 'hans' pots, possibly because of a perceived link with North Germany (derived from Hanse or Danzig). However, the term could derive from 'anse' or handle; a committee of goldsmiths setting prices in 1516 gave a list of components for plate which included 'bottoms of cups, haunsis of pots and coffins of salts'.[29]

Beer was also drunk from 'canns' – the term apparently indicates a straightsided vessel

Fig. 13 **Covered cup**
Gilt 1533. Mark indecipherable. H.21 cm. Given by Robert Morwent, President of the college 1537.
Corpus Christi, Oxford

Fig. 14 **Steeple cup**
Gilt 1599. Mark IE above three pellets. H. 50 cm. Given by Mrs Elizabeth Ludwell (with other plate) to
her parish church in 1765. The pinnacle cover was popular from about 1560 to 1640, for both cups and
salts.
SS. Peter and Paul, Charing, Kent

40

which increased in popularity from about 1550 and is paralleled in contemporary ceramics – the white Rhenish stoneware ones, known as canettes, were imported into England in large quantities. The origin of this shape is uncertain; it also may be Scandinavian or Baltic under Hanse influence. Sometimes Elizabethan tankards, such as the three presented to three Cambridge colleges by Archbishop Matthew Parker in 1571, have two horizontal ribs suggesting a wooden prototype and they are certainly very similar to the tapering wooden barrels, also called canns, in which drinking water was hawked about the streets of Elizabethan London. Inventories sometimes refer to 'barred' or 'barrelled' tankards so that clearly contemporaries saw a connection with a wooden prototype. Certain other materials were readily worked up into this shape and tankards of rock crystal, serpentine, glass and horn have survived; the British Museum has the Burghley tankard (c.1570).[30]

Steeple cups are a disproportionately large section of the existing late Tudor and early Stuart plate; over 150 are known today, of which 50 belong to churches. They were presentation and display pieces primarily and so have often been preserved by the corporations to which they were given; S. Albans and Barnstaple each own three. One at Lewes is well documented; Thomas Blunt, barber-surgeon and burgess, left 'a silver bowl double gilt of the value of 20 nobles' as a loving cup or 'poculum charitatis' to his fellow burgesses there in 1611.[31] These tall cups are often regarded as an early Stuart phenomenon, deriving the design of their characteristic pinnacle or pyramid-crowned cover from the Elizabethan device of the obelisk. This occurs on funerary monuments and buildings, for example on the Gate of Gonville and Caius College, Cambridge (c.1580). However, while the earliest now known are gilt cups of 1599, several salts and cups with steeples are listed in the Elizabethan royal plate inventory of 1574; one, a gold cup 'with a pyramid' Sir Nicholas Bacon gave Elizabeth on progress at Gorhambury in 1572 or 1573 and others are described in the 1561 Pembroke Inventory.

While the size of steeple cups varied with the generosity of the donor, their basic form became more or less standardised, with minor variations in the embossing on the bowl of stylised flowers (lilies of the valley, roses, daisies, acanthus), the bowl resting on three or four scroll brackets above a trumpet foot. Certain goldsmiths – AB conjoined (Antony Bennett?), CB monogram, TB, FT (Francis Terry) and TC seem to have specialised in producing or at least sponsoring these cups.

Sometimes steeples or obelisks surmount other forms of cup, such as the gourds or entwined stems popular in the sixteenth century. One in the Portsmouth civic plate was made in 1610. Another of 1608 at the Armourers' and Braziers' Company has a miniature out-of-scale woodman attempting to chop down the tree. This touch of fantasy is a feature more typical of German plate. A cup now at the Inner Temple was made in 1563 in the shape of a pomegranate bursting open to show the seeds within. A gold cup of about 1610, shaped like an acorn and also on a twisted trunk stem, was left to Stapleford Church in 1732 as a chalice. It is now in the British Museum.[32]

The steeple cup was designed entirely to enhance the splendour of the buffet display. One of the most stately, a cup presented to S. Ives, Cornwall in 1640, stands thirty-three inches high, by far the tallest of any cup, but the form was to fall rapidly out of favour as the buffet concept lapsed.

Salts

Until the mid-seventeenth century, the standing salt, that essential centrepiece of the dining table set always to the right of the host, was a symbol of luxury and status. A handful of important late medieval salts survive, notably in Oxford colleges, with a common characteristic of great elaboration of detail. Display pieces *par excellence*, they made use of exotic materials such as crystal or gems and incorporated painted glass panels, as on the Warden Hill salt (given by 1494). One described in a royal inventory, the Moryon salt, was in the form of a blackamoor holding up a gold covered bowl set with pearls, rubies and diamonds. It was returned to Henry VII by Richard Gardiner, alderman and mercer, to whom Richard III had pledged it for a hundred marks. This remained in heavy use (it was repaired twice in 1533) despite later Jewel House acquisitions with more fashionable 'antique' motifs. Its figure stem may be compared with the Huntsman salt at All Souls or the Monkey salt at New College, made about 1500 as a chimpanzee sitting on a cushion. On his head is a crystal disc supporting the salt bowl.[33]

Another popular late gothic form for the great salt was the hourglass. The salt given by Walter Hill to New College, Oxford, of which he was warden from 1475 to 1494, must stand for a whole vanished group; its pyramidal cover is set with panels of purple glass with a gilt diaper pattern and the cresting on the body set with pearls. A similar combination of colour, cast openwork and pearls makes up the Corpus Christi salt, given in 1517 to his college at Oxford by Bishop Foxe; this is even more elaborate in its construction. Rivetted to the body and cover is a series of openwork panels containing cast devices – the pelican badge of the founder, animals with foliage and scenes of the Virgin enthroned and an angel holding a scroll.[34] Where cast elements, modified by individual chasing, are used it is clear that the goldsmith anticipated a steady demand for such ornament, sufficient to justify the cost of the initial model and carving (probably in boxwood) and the making of the necessary moulds. Other labour-saving devices were in common use and account for the appearance of identical ornament on pieces by different makers. Bands of repeating strip ornament, used around feet, rims and covers, were produced by hammering thin silver sheet onto a bronze pattern supplied by a pattern-maker. Specialist die-cutters obviously supplied their wares in standard popular designs, although too few examples survive before about 1550 to demonstrate that goldsmiths used common dies.

Simpler small salts were certainly made in large numbers and the sumptuous survivals quoted should not be taken as typical. At the Ironmongers' Company are two hourglass salts of 1518 and 1522 which are parcel-gilt with the characteristic mid-Tudor ornament of alternatively plain and chased vertical panels. This was popular until the 1560s at least and may be seen on several two-handled covered cups, such as those given by Archbishop Parker to Corpus Christi, Cambridge in 1571.[35]

By far the most elaborate Tudor salt is one which encompasses all the most fashionable contemporary motifs – a hexagonal base with shell cameos of Roman emperors supports a crystal column which once contained a table clock. This piece, distinctly French in style, was made at the Paris court workshop. It was in the English royal collection by 1550, but whether it came there as a royal gift from Henry's rival Francis I, or less directly by confiscation, is not recorded.[36] The clock salt was bought in 1967 by the Goldsmiths' Company and is believed to be one of just three pieces preserved from the Tudor royal collection. In 1574 it was only one of eleven clock salts; there is no reason to assume that all the others were imports. We know from Holbein's two sketches for Sir Anthony Denny of a combined clock and hourglass (intended as a New Year's gift for Henry VIII) that there were London goldsmiths capable of such confections.[37] Since 1632 the Company has owned two other display salts, one made in 1576 and presented after a search for trade offences at S. Bartholomew's Fair. It is square with a central rock crystal cylinder enclosing a figure of Neptune. The four Ionic columns, each capped on the cover with a cupola, demonstrate the Elizabethan fascination with architectural motifs as decorative elements. Several pillared salts are known and a similar form was used for the Butleigh salt (1606), now at the Barber Institute of Art; the Vyvyan salt (VAM) also follows an architectural model. These were peculiarly English forms; the ceremonial standing salt has no exact parallel in French or German silver.

It should not be presumed that all diners were forced to dip their knives into the rather small and shallow bowls of such display salts. Smaller plain white 'low' salts were supplied in sets, sometimes ensuite with the largest, although very few Elizabethan examples have survived. In 1574 the royal household had a pair of square gold trenchers, each with its own salt and pepper box set in the surface; these were probably confined to royal use only, like the two 'trenchers of estate gilt with a spoon, toothpick and a little tun dish' at Hardwick in 1601.[38] The household book of George Rivers, Archbishop of York, describing the ceremonial preparations for his enthronement banquet in 1466, gives a vivid description of the precursor of the small individual silver salt, and incidentally explains why one of the shapes taken by silver salts was a flat triangle; the server is instructed to take a trencher (slice of bread) 'Then with your brode Knyfe take a little Salt and plane it on your trencher, tyll it be even. Then with your brode Knyfe cut your Salt quadrant' so each diner had a triangle.[39]

The 'honour' system about covering and uncovering applied also to display salts; only that set by the chief man present was permanently covered and, according to the Rivers ritual, two others were to be set at each end of the high table, surrounded by 'small saltes, which is made of bread properly triangled of halfe trenchers'.

A group of silver from Mostyn Hall bought by the Victoria and Albert Museum in 1886 includes one small salt of 1566. It consists of a simple embossed tube supporting a salt bowl with a cover, a shape found in Norwich and Exeter too. A salt of c.1580 by the Barnstaple goldsmith Thomas Mathew, is also in the national collection. Others, one of 1550 (Goldsmiths' Company) and another at Eton are hexagonal with alternate facets engraved, a shape called 'six-square' at the time. Although inventories distinguish between items by weight rather than by size, the repeated references to 'little' salts weighing five ounces or less indicate the general use of such small salts, despite the emphasis given by art historians to the more glamorous standing salts. Only one in two at most was supplied with a cover, for the reason described above. It is not possible to say whether any survivor would have had a cover, since these were interchangeable; Seymour had a set of five bell salts with one cover in 1546. 'Pantry' salts had no covers. They were made in sets and in standard designs; one in a private collection (1583) is by the same maker as, and virtually identical with, one in the Untermyer Collection at the Metropolitan Museum, New York.[40]

From the 1530s a popular shape for the salt was the so-called bell, which consisted of two tapering sections, each with a salt bowl, capped with a hollow cover which was pierced as a pepper-castor; this version of a double salt meant that the host still had his salt in a covered container, with his table companions presumably using the lower, uncovered section. Late Elizabethan examples are often flat-chased with strapwork and flowers and occasionally pounced with the arms or initials of the owner. So basic was the construction that it was a task left to the least skilled journeymen, as the preamble to a 1607 Goldsmiths' Company order on masterpieces makes clear: 'Many of the idler sort betake themselves to . . . one slight & easy part . . . nothing but bell salts.'[41]

Spoons and other Plate

As the use of silver spread outward to a broader society, a profusion of smaller lighter objects, such as beakers, salts and wine cups were made, and have survived, many of them with initials or devices rather than armorials; the classes who were beginning now to own silver were not necessarily armigerous. They were also perhaps more likely to be sentimental about their fairly small holdings of family silver, and more anxious to record its descent to later generations, than the wealthier aristocracy for whom silver was only so much tableware, to be refashioned as desired. A spoon from a set which belonged to the Postlethwaite family of Cumberland has the initials of seven generations on the bowl (VAM). A group of five apostle spoons handed down in the Plunkett family are unmarked but engraved with a love-knot, the initials IP and KL and the date 1538, apparently for John Plunkett and Catherine Luttrell who married in that year.[42]

Specialist London spoonmakers produced a range of standard designs, slip top, diamond top, seal top and from about 1450 the popular apostle spoons, to which pounced initials or arms could be added, often on the nimbus. Wealthier families had several sets of spoons, perhaps in different styles and occasionally personalised by a finial in the form of a crest, like the owl spoons presented by Bishop Oldham to Corpus Christi, Oxford in 1506 or a set with squirrel finials made for the Gilbert family in Devon at the end of the century.[43]

The initials on smaller pieces of plate are often arranged in a triangle with the surname above the husband's or wife's Christian names and sometimes with a date of marriage, although curiously with spoons the maiden name of the wife is sometimes indicated also. In the careful list of his family plate made by Edmund Bowyer, a rising Elizabethan lawyer who died in 1570, there are several references to the conjoined initials of himself and his wife and one to what sounds like a cipher of his surname.[44] His sons Benjamin, Matthew and John each received apostle spoons from godparents who shared their Christian names; presumably appropriate saints formed the terminals.

Practical plate, such as ewers and basins and livery pots, was not necessarily lavishly embellished and although gilded, perhaps bore only the arms of the owner and a minimum of engraved and enamelled ornament; normally the central bushel or 'amell' was engraved with the owner's arms or device and sometimes the rim also, as in the case of the 1518 basin from S. Magnus the Martyr Church in the City, which may be seen at S. Paul's treasury.[45]

All types discussed so far were parcel-gilt or double gilt, that is coated with a thicker deposit of gold to give a richer and more durable surface. It has been said that this was particularly appropriate for drinking vessels, since white silver imparts an unpleasant taint to wine, but at the time of the Goldsmith and the Grape Exhibition (1983) a committee of wine tasters could find no detectable difference between glass and silver. However, since the experiment was with modern wines of a rather different composition from the more acid earlier vintages, this is hardly conclusive, and it is more likely that the preference for gilt plate was one of pride.[16]

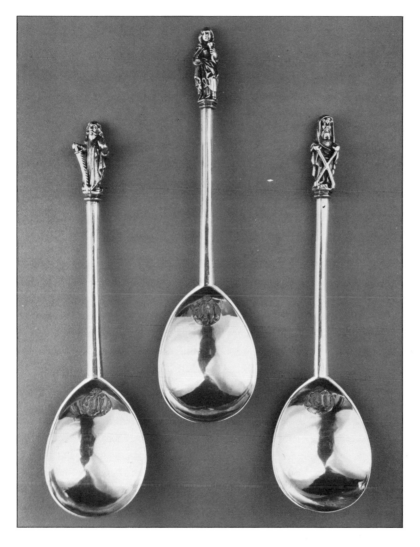

Fig. 15 **Virgin and two apostle spoons**
Parcel-gilt 1536. Mark a cornsheaf (?). From a set of thirteen; normally the Master, rather than the Virgin, makes up a set. Engraved with IHS and struck in the bowl with the leopard's head, customary location for this mark until the mid-seventeenth century.
British Museum

45

Gilding was reserved for chamber plate; items supplied for Henry Percy, Earl of Northumberland's personal use – fruit dishes, a posnet, sugar box and wax candlestick – were all gilded (probably by Francis Terry) in 1617.[47]

It is easy to plot the preference for gilt plate, since it is always listed and valued as such in inventories, with a separate category and price for parcel-gilt. Gilding made a difference of rather more than 10 per cent to the price per ounce of silver; when the plate of John Holland, Duke of Exeter, was appraised by goldsmiths in 1447 they valued the silvergilt items at 4s, parcel-gilt 3s and plain silver 2s8d. The price naturally crept up over the years; in 1532 Amadas's parcel-gilt was valued at 3s8d. A century later the Royal Mint at Oxford in 1642 paid compensation at 5s6d for gilt and 5s for white plate.[48]

Apothecaries stressed the advantage to health of preparing both food and herbal remedies in silver vessels and the silver posnet – a small three-footed saucepan with a cover, known in its larger form as a skillet – was widely used in the seventeenth century. Contemporary recipe books refer frequently to cooking in silver dishes and chamber-cooking, which in non-noble families was the responsibility of the lady of the house rather than a servant, also called for silver saucepans. The metal could be as easily cleaned as a glazed ceramic surface and was far more in keeping with contemporary ideas about status.

Plate made for the kitchen, in which food would be both cooked and served, was always white, although it was in use largely in aristocratic households only. Henry Percy, when stocking up in 1617, bought over 9,500 ounces of white plate made up of pie dishes, salad dishes and chargers, including twelve dozen trencher plates.[49] This enormous quantity may be compared with a typical gentry plate cupboard of less than a hundred ounces. Richard Smart, an Ipswich gentleman, left in 1608 plate valued at just over £20, a third of his movable property. He had '2 plain white silver canns', three little bowls (seven ounces each), two covered salts and a dozen spoons.[50]

Such small holdings allowed only a shadow of the ritual attached to dining plate, as the inventory of Ralph Creyke's plate, made in 1605, underlines. His 'Plate daily occupied in the house' consisted merely of an old salt, a dozen plain spoons and three bowls – that is wine cups. In the plate chest kept in his dining chamber was a larger selection for formal use: a basin and ewer, two livery pots, a double bell salt and a small trencher salt and a great bowl. He had two of the popular coconut cups with silvergilt covers and a 'mazer [wooden] sugar box wherein is the spoon and garnished with silver' but no plates or cooking implements, except a silver-trimmed toasting stick.[51] He, like most wealthy gentlemen, was still eating from pewter plates. To buy silver trencher plates, even for the senior members of the household alone, represented a very large investment, since an ounce of silver cost as much as half a pound of pewter. Given the high quality of English pewter, which was exported to Northern Europe and could be as readily personalised with engraved or enamelled armorials, it offered a perfectly adequate alternative.

Pots

The terminology for vessels to contain wine, beer and water is almost as obscure as that for cups. Pairs of large and heavy vessels, called pots, occur in most medieval and Tudor inventories. Relatively elaborately decorated, almost always with armorials or badges and also chased with scales or shells, they were both functional and display pieces. The finest and largest known, and virtually the only surviving examples clearly described in contemporary lists, are the two pairs of 'waterpots' sold from the Jewel House to John Acton in 1626 and bought by Tsar Mikhail.[52] Although references to silver spouted pots occur from at least the fifteenth century and the type is known in brass, no others have survived. The earliest English pot, although whether for water or wine is not clear, is that at Magdalen College, Oxford recently recognised by the late John Hayward. It is pear-shaped with a very narrow neck; by comparing its scale-chased decoration with that on hallmarked cups he dated it to the early sixteenth century. This was no doubt called a pot, sometimes qualified as a 'plain gallon pot'.[53] More elaborate was the ewer or laver, which could be both a large container for perfumed water and a small highly ornamented personal jug, often accompanying a cup. The French custom, when making diplomatic gifts, of presenting a cup with an accompanying ewer, seems to have lapsed in England by the mid-sixteenth century.[54]

Although the term flagon or 'stoup pot' occurs from the late fifteenth century, these seem then to have been bellied vessels. The tall tapering shape, lidded and with handle to serve wine or beer, emerges only towards the end of the sixteenth century. Confusingly the term flagon was also used simultaneously for another shape altogether. Until 1640 or so 'flagon-fashion' described a flattened oval flask with a chain handle (the shape we now call a pilgrim bottle), which was a popular shape for links in gold chains; cast miniature pilgrim bottles occur both as applied ornament and standing as feet on the Leigh cup at the Mercers' Company. Sir Richard Weston had in his plate store at Sutton Place in 1542 four silver flagons 'with their close staples and chains to them' and the casting or perfumed water bottles popular between about 1520 and 1560 were often described as 'flagon-fashion' implying a flattened pear-shape on a foot.

The change in their name came about during the next century.[55] The pilgrim bottles sent to Russia in 1604 and 1620 were called at the time 'great flagons'. This shape remained a standard element in ceremonial plate until the early eighteenth century but the set issued to Marlborough in 1701, when Ambassador Extraordinary to the States General, were by then called 'bottles'.[56]

This fluidity of nomenclature is a constant stumbling-block in the study of early silver; although the containers supplied for communion wine from the late sixteenth century were usually of the tall tapering shape, contemporaries had no one recognised term and in church records they are called variously pots, flagon pots, livery pots, or pots flagon-fashion.[57] When the Anglican Church was attempting to improve the quality of the eucharistic ritual in 1603, the order specified that wine for the communion should be brought 'in a clean and sweet standing pot or stoup of pewter, if not of purer metal'. Some churches have straightsided flagons, others bellied livery pots and others, like Tong in Staffordshire and Monken Hadley in Hertfordshire, have ewers with elegant curved spouts.[58]

At first no distinction was drawn between flagons for domestic and those for liturgical use. Both were originally made without spouts; until the late seventeenth century, spouts were confined to spout pots and ewers, the jugs supplied with basins for washing hands and face before and after meals. Only with the new hot beverages – tea, coffee and chocolate – did spouts became normal in tableware. The bellied jug-form then replaced the tall tapering flagon and few are found today outside churches, since once their domestic function had been superseded, they were refashioned.[59]

There is a broad continuity in English plate from the accession of Elizabeth until the Civil War. Traditional forms remained popular and ornament, whether embossed or engraved, suffered no radical innovations. The only exception, the arrival of the auricular style, was confined to a small circle at court, and was only to be more widely copied after 1660. Throughout the period, innovations in design can be attributed largely to alien influences; heraldry was still the most significant form of ornament to English customers, as discussed in Chapters 10 and 12.

Notes

1 London 1967. For Tudor silver: Brears, Bury, Suffolk inventories, Hernmarck 1977, Hayward 1976, Goldsmiths' 1951 and 1952, Christie's 1955.

2 Harrison 119; Emmison 1978, 1980, 1983. In 416 minor gentry and yeomen wills from the Waltham area, 1558–1603, sixteen specify at least one item of plate apart from spoons.

3 Pewter was, after silver, the most expensive material for tableware. Valued by weight, it was the largest item in fifteenth- to sixteenth-century rural probate inventories: Hatcher and Barker 1974, 54–5.

4 Hatcher and Barker 1974, 98–9, 106–7. An ounce of silver was valued at 5s, which bought six lbs of pewter; both could be refashioned. Silver pushed pewter down the social scale in the sixteenth century.

5 Inventory 1521; Collins 1955; Society of Antiquaries MS. 1891, 129; Hardwick 1601; VAM MS Pembroke inventory 1561 and bibliography.

6 Collins 1955, 574. The Earl of Pembroke had an equally elaborate toilet service with a shoehorn, pincers, eight tooth cleaners etc., all of engraved silvergilt.

7 Collins 1955, item 441, 554. On confiscations as a source of plate, see Collins, 118–30.

8 Collins 1955, 116–18.

9 Cavendish 1959, 69. Some had been issued by Amadas; BM. Add. Egerton 2603, f. 14–15.

10 In 1544: *Seymour MSS*, 94, 100.

11 Collins 1955, items 368, 478, 501, 502, 908. Plus other probables: no. 300, already in the collection by 1550, may have been a gift.

12 BM. Add. MS 5829, f. 61.

13 For example, a nautilus shell (1585) and ostrich egg (1610). Hayward 1976, pl. 661 and 662.

The Duke of Rutland has at Belvoir an ewer and basin of agate, London 1579. MacGregor 1983, 70–98.

14 Hayward 1968.

15 Tait 1964, 270.

16 Carrington and Hughes 1926; Christie's 1955, no. 66, given in 1675. A casting bottle (VAM, c.1540–50) incorporates a reused Islamic crystal of the tenth century.

17 Collins 1955, 101–8.

18 Fitzwilliam 1975; virtually every collection had exotica.

19 Glanville 1984.

20 But see Oman 1979: the mounts were almost certainly made for a hardstone bowl originally.

21 Eames 1971, 41–4; Glanville 1985 and Ch. 13.

22 The Drapers' Company owned six sets, each with one cover, in 1489.

23 Greenwood 1930; Cooper 1977 and 1979 reproduces the most important of the early Tudor drinking vessels.

24 Chased goblets, standing cup, standing and stone(ware) cruses and broad bowls, plus a pounced cup, were in the Weston inventory of 1542: Harrison 1893, Appendix IV. Glanville 1985.

25 Penzer 1958. One at Portsmouth (1525) was given to the town by Grace Bodkin, widow of a former mayor, in 1591. Oman 1965, pl. 5. For the Howard Grace cup, see Penzer 1946.

26 Hayward 1976, pl. 37, 40, 42. The Rochester bowls retain their covers, although not as originally matched. One of 1584 (Goldsmiths') has a towering cover; Hernmarck 1977, pl. 246.

27 Minet Library, Camberwell, MSVI/230; Glanville 1978. See Harrison, 89 and Ch. 14.

28   Glanville 1971, 1985; Oxford 1965, 192, 265.

29   Goldsmiths' Company MSS, minute book B and C: 4 November 1516, 'A book with rates for goldsmiths work both English and strangers'.

30   White stoneware canns were made in Cologne specifically for the English market; Hodges & Davey, 37–45.

31   Penzer 1959. Although Whitney, *A Choice of Emblems* (Leiden 1586) claimed the obelisk as an emblem of Queen Elizabeth 'A Mightie Spyre, whose toppe dothe pierce the skie . . . the Piller great our gracious Princes is', this had been popular already for twenty-five years. A standing cup in the Pembroke inventory had a spire; f. 10v.

32   Oman 1965b. One of 1608 in the Untermyer Collection is so like Nuremberg work that it is thought the steeple was added in London to an import; the silver content is markedly different. But two gourd cups given to the Earl of Pembroke at New Year 1562 were to this design: Pembroke inventory f. 10v. Other cups were specified as 'Almain facion', but not these two.

33   Oman 1979; Collins 1955, 290.

34   Campbell 1984.

35   And on a salt of 1550 (Goldsmiths' Company) and a cup at Corpus Christi, Oxford.

36   Toyeska 1969, 292–4: *Goldsmiths' Review*, 1972–3, 27–31.

37   Collins 1955, pl. II.

38   Hardwick inventory 1601. The Pembroke plate included one elaborate trencher of estate 'curiously wrought with the siege of S. Quentin' with a salt and a dragon on top and a case with cutlery, supported on four pillars with the Pembroke beasts, badges and arms: f. 15v.

39   Rivers Household Book, quoted by Oman, 'The Small Silver Salt', *Antique Collector*, May 1935, 113–16.

40   Indenture 1546: *Seymour MSS* 1581, Vol. IV, 122. The maker's mark is a bull's head, Goldsmiths' 1979.

41   Quoted in Hayward 1976.

42   Miles 1976, 15–19. Ch. 14.

43   Kent 1981; Wilson 1984. The Gilbert spoon was formerly on loan to the Exeter Museum: Royal Albert Memorial Museum, n.d.

44   Glanville 1978, 294 and 297.

45   Basins are very rare; one of 1569 and another of 1596 are at the Middle Temple, given by Viscount Rothermere: Clowes 1957, pl. 9 and 1.

46   Goldsmiths' 1983, preface. The S. George's, Windsor chapel plate, supplied by Christian Van Vianen in 1638, was described as 'triple gilt'.

47   Percy 1962, 109.

48   Holland and Amadas inventories. In August 1644 the Ironmongers' sold silver at slightly less, 5s 4d per ounce for gilt, 5s for parcel-gilt, 4s 11d for white: Nicholl 1866, 234.

49   Percy 1962, 108–9, 110. Only five saucers are mentioned, weighing a total of ten ounces; these were no longer purchased as part of a 'garnish'.

50   Suffolk 1981, 'Smart'. His silver was almost a third (£20) of the total personal property. A wealthy widow, Jane Ward, had much less: two mounted stoneware pots, twenty spoons and a small cup, salt and parcel-gilt pot; presumably the heir had taken the bulk.

51   VAM Archives (National Art Library): Inventory of Ralph Creyke 1605.

52   Oman 1961, pl. 39 (one of 1604 pair) and p. 60. These extraordinary pots were a large part of the 3,700 ounces sold to the tsar; they were probably always unusual.

53   Hayward 1983, pl. 6 and 7.

54   The Pembroke inventory refers to 'French leavers' or layers, as though they were distinctive. But the mayoral gold coronation cup was accompanied by a ewer before the sixteenth century: Blair 1979, pl. 54.

55   Collins 1955; Glanville 1978, 298. A stoup was an individual drinking pot, shaped like a tankard. One in the Guildford civic plate is helpfully engraved 'This stoup new made 1602'.

56   Oman 1961, pl. 11. But the 1663 embassy adopted the new term for large vessels. The pilgrim bottles were called 'bottle' (pl. 28) and the tapering straight-sided vessel was called a flagon (pl. 27) or livery pot: p. 39.

57   In 1630 and 1631 two donors termed their gifts as flagons and as livery pots, to describe identical bellied vessels. Christie's 1955, 56 and 61–2, pl. IX and X.

58   The earliest church flagons are at Cirencester (1577). Oman 1957.

59   One pair continuously in private ownership (the Paston and Bacon families, 1597) is in the Untermyer Collection.

S T U A R T

S TUART silver is rather more commonly found than Elizabethan. Historians often refer to the Civil War as a disaster for English silver but it brought only the best documented melt, a threat to which silver has always been subject. More significant for the study of seventeenth-century silver are the Restoration innovations in eating and drinking, particularly equipment for the new beverages of tea, coffee, chocolate and punch – and refinements in tableware. Therefore, 1660 rather than 1600 divides Elizabethan from early modern silver.

The silver taken by a Stuart emigrant to New England, Mrs Elizabeth Glover, tells us what was considered appropriate early in the century to 'a fair and full cupboard of plate . . . as might ordinarily be seen in most gentlemen's houses in England', as one of Mrs Glover's English-born servants described it.

The plate referred to, a collection reckoned to be worth more than £200, featured in several affidavits in a long court case over a disputed inheritance. It had been brought from England by Mrs Glover, who had sailed with her husband for Boston in 1638. She took with her 'a great silver trunk with four knobs to stand on the table and with sugar' (a sugar box) plus six trencher plates, a chafing dish or 'silver grate with a cover on it' and twenty-nine silver spoons, along with the usual cups, bowls, ewer and basin. The silver of the early settlers' families is well documented and two pieces of her collection can still be identified, her 'very fair salt with 3 full knops on the top of it' given to Harvard in 1644 (as her second husband, she married Henry Dunster, the first president) and one of her six porringers. The scroll salt still bear the initials of Elizabeth and her first husband, pounced in a triangle. [1]

This short list comprises almost all the recognisable Stuart vessels in common use. We can only occasionally reconstruct the holdings of individuals and must turn again to contemporary descriptions of the plate held by organised societies, with the bonus that many still retain some pre-Civil War silver. Colleges and livery companies, which were totally male and with a tradition of ritual gifts on admission to the senior ranks of membership, inevitably accumulated drinking vessels and these form a disproportionate part of their surviving silver.

The Civil War and after

A list of the plate sacrificed by Queens' College, Cambridge to the king on 3 August 1642, which is tactfully headed 'in these dreadful times of imminent danger for the security thereof deposited with the King', itemises seventy-two vessels, the majority of white silver, with their donors' names. Virtually all were for drinking – tankards between 13 and 19 ounces, beakers rather less, flagons of 37 and 41 ounces, bowls with covers 25 to 109 ounces (a wide class, meaning standing cups) and 'College pots' of 14 to 21 ounces. Three salts were the only exception[2]. Whether the Cornhill Ward covered mug was once a popular shape is not clear, but it survives as a reminder of the variety of forms taken by drinking vessels (Fig. 23). Most of the Queens' College drinking vessels had been given by fellow commoners in the preceding half-century and so were presumably the easiest to sacrifice, being neither of great age nor of great sentimental value. The rapid late Tudor expansion in university attendance had undoubtedly enhanced college plate cupboards and the Civil War forced loans did not necessarily extract their greatest historic treasures. At both New College and Magdalen College, Oxford, early plate was concealed and other pieces redeemed by members of the college and it is noteworthy that a few older items valued as 'Founders' plate' have often survived all the later pressures, both external and internal, to melt or sell. The growing cult of antiquarianism undoubtedly contributed to their preservation; see Chapter 13.[3]

Private families suffered differentially in the Civil War according to their accessibility. Richard Lybbe at Hardwick House in Oxfordshire contributed £40 in plate to Charles I's

Fig. 16 **Inkstand**
1639. Mark AJ, probably for Alexander Jackson. Although emphatically English in form the chasing and modelling of the putti candleholders are very close to Utrecht or Amsterdam silver.
Loan, VAM

Fig. 17 **Rosewater basin**
Gilt 1611. Mark SO for Simon Owen. Given in 1631 by Roger Snelson, a City dyer, to his church,
perhaps as a baptismal basin. Used later as an almsdish.
All Hallows the Great, City of London

forced loan in 1642; a year later he was raided again, by Parliamentary troops from Reading, and lost plate worth a further £182. This included three popular Stuart items – a chafing dish, a sugar dish and a mother-of-pearl bowl in gilt mounts as well as the usual salts, flagons, basins, bowls and spoons.[4] A greater variety of forms was generally in use in 1642 than a century earlier; a reflection of the increasing refinement of domestic comfort even before the Restoration, which is commonly seen as a watershed in English domestic life.

The history of domestic silver cannot be divorced from the evolution of the English country house plan. During the seventeenth century, both the number and social standing of residential servants declined. As casual visiting and open hospitality fell out of practice, the household shrank and formal dining in state became a rarity. The buffet display appropriate to a large communal dining chamber was inconvenient and unwieldy in the smaller ceiled room characteristic of the later seventeenth century.[5] Only in institutions such as colleges and corporations did the concept of formal dining, and thus the concept of the buffet laden with display plate, survived; hence their retention of such obsolete forms as the steeple cup and scroll salt (Fig. 20).

Meals were served to smaller numbers, with fewer dishes at each remove and the redundant buffet plate was often converted into more fashionable and appropriate forms, to be used only by the immediate family. Sets of livery pots, in which the nightly allowance of spiced wine or beer was provided for guests and principal servants, fell out of use and so were melted down and few survive today. The pair of 1594, now at the Goldsmiths' Company, were passed on to Westwell Church in 1630, an alternative solution to the problem of redundant plate.

In this process the Civil War confiscations were no more than a hiccup; when institutions and private individuals replaced their lost plate, they took the opportunity to revise it. The Drapers', one of the wealthiest City livery companies, sacrificed 2,500 ounces of their plate in 1642 and turned temporarily to the less valuable and expensive alternatives of Venice-made glasses and tin-glazed salts the following year. These large losses were not made up for fifteen years. When the Company received its first gift of silver trencher plates in 1671, it quickly added more and had six dozen by 1700, when all the existing plates were refashioned by John Leech. Each of these handsome broad-rimmed plates is engraved with the Company's arms and those of fourteen donors. However, each donor had originally given some other piece of plate altogether, forms no longer fashionable by the 1670s such as bowls, tankards, basins and ewers, salts, spout pots 'now of little or no use' and so refashioned into silver plates for the greater dignity of court dinners.[6]

General expenditure on plate rose markedly around the time of Charles II's return and continued to rise, with occasional troughs, as in plague years, until the end of the century. Figures for the plate taken for assay in 1660–1 show an increase, from 25,000 pounds weight to 37,000. Spreading from court circles, there was a growing demand, partly to replace that plate sacrificed in the 1640s but also in response to the taste for lavish interiors which characterised the Restoration court. Silver furniture – mirrors, tables, candlestands, fire implements – became briefly fashionable among the aristocracy, and for a rather longer period of about a century, women of standing expected to own complete toilet services of silver running to twenty-five or thirty items (Fig. 18).[7]

What was new was the scale of silver vessels. Silver wine cisterns, occasionally met with in the late sixteenth and early seventeenth century, became standard aristocratic dining room equipment, often supplied with an accompanying fountain for washing glasses (Fig. 33). From the 1670s, Ravenscroft's lead glass was popular both for serving and for drinking wine. Some dessert stands were made in glass too but tableware still occupied a large place in the plate room. Dinner plates of silver could be taken to indicate that a man had arrived both socially and financially; although his cups, candlesticks and tankards might be gifts, his plates represented a solid investment of capital. The attitude may be seen in Samuel Pepys's satisfied comment in his annual reckoning of 1666, when he was a rising civil servant of 33. 'I am come

Fig. 18 **Toilet service**
1679. Mark goose in a dotted circle. Engraved with the arms of Brownlow impaling Sherrard. The plaques set in the box sides are chased with lovers, contemporary (?French) dress, possibly taken from imported lead models.
Virginia, Museum of Fine Arts

to abound in good plate so as at all entertainments to be served wholly with silver plates.' He had thirty, enough for two or three removes.[8]

Pepys was characteristic of that class for whom many goldsmiths worked exclusively; his silver was in no way unusual or designed to his taste. When later in life he wanted to mark his long association with the Clothworkers' Company, he gave a ewer and basin of a familiar type, merely personalised by their beautiful engraved armorial panels.

Sets of Stuart plates are very rare; Jackson reproduced a travelling canteen of silver made for the Fortescue family in 1674–6 and there are twenty of various years from 1639 to 1644 in the Kremlin Armouries. Unlike much of the important English silver exhibited there, these did not form part of a royal gift; their very plainness and utility would disqualify them. They were presumably acquired from a returning Russian traveller.[9]

Dessert, the French term which replaced the void or 'banquet' of earlier times was by the end of the century generally served in the same room as the main meal; appropriate gilt plates and cutlery and salvers for glasses were set out on a side table, with a silver centrepiece dressed with fruit, flowers and sweetmeats. An early precursor of this centrepiece was the scroll salt, the last version of the large ceremonial standing salt from the 1620s until its general disappearance in the late seventeenth century. The scroll salt was apparently covered or 'dressed' with a small cloth, which might be extremely elaborate, with the dual purpose of hygiene and display.[10]

Salts

How the ceremonial salt evolved from its late Tudor form of a square or cylinder with a cover on brackets (for example, Fig. 8) to the massive but uncovered pulley salts of the 1630s is not clear. When the Earl of Arundel was carrying out his great-uncle's wishes (Henry Howard, Earl of Northampton, d.1614) and equipping the Trinity Hospital at Greenwich he ordered from the goldsmith Thomas Hawes for the master's table a tall and dignified heavy-gauge cylinder salt, quite plain except for an inscription, and a rather smaller cylinder for guests (both now at the Mercers' Company; one weighs twenty-four ounces, the other just over five). Neither was supplied with a cover, an early example of changing practice.[11]

Two years earlier, in 1617, the town of Coventry had been given an ornate cloth or 'cover-pane' for their salt, sewn with fifty-two gold buttons and pearls, indicating that it was dressed for formal use and probably had no metal cover. But it is not clear how generally this custom of using a cloth was followed here. Pepys, writing in 1662, evidently found it necessary to specify to himself that the four greyhounds and four eagles of the Seymour salt

Fig. 19 **Standing and trencher salts**
1618. Mark RW above a rose. H (of larger) 14.5 cm. Presented to Trinity Hospital by the Earl of Arundel, fulfilling the bequest of Henry Howard, Earl of Northampton (d. 1614). The earliest standing salt known without a cover.
Mercers' Company

(Goldsmiths' Company) were 'to bear up a dish', implying that this usage was not totally familiar to him.[12]

A simple drum-shaped salt belonging to Bridgwater Corporation and made fourteen years after the Trinity Hospital salts, in 1633, had the added feature of three 'arms' or 'scrolls in the new fashion'; they appear virtually simultaneously in both France and Holland, as we see in engravings of the 1630s by Abraham Bosse, although more examples survive in pewter and tin-glazed earthenware than in silver. The purpose of these scrolls has been argued back and forth. Certainly Dutch genre paintings show both napkin-draped scroll salts and others with dishes of fruit and nuts, handsome centrepieces for the dessert stage of the meal, but the visual evidence for the custom in England is lacking.

For thirty years from the 1630s, the waisted pulley salt with three or four arms was the shape preferred for 'master' salts, like the Dethick at the Mercers' (1638) and the Reeve at the Innholders'. Low trencher salts were round, oval or triangular and of course had no arms since they had not even a residual ceremonial function.

A set of four newly made Salts of State supplied by the Jewel House for the Coronation banquet of Charles II have drum-shaped bodies, elaborately embossed in the current Dutch manner with tulips and other flowers, and three arms terminating in serpents' heads but this form of ornament was not much imitated, most late Stuart salts relying for their effect on their simple strong lines (Fig. 19). The ceremonial or master salt was still distinctive and massive until the end of the seventeenth century. The latest of the type is the scroll salt by Augustine Courtauld (1730), now at the Mansion House, presented by Richard Dormer to the Sword Bearer's table eleven years after it was made.[13]

Perhaps under French influence, there were some experiments with the scroll salt after the Restoration; the Countess of Dysart was charged by the goldsmith Alderman Backwell for '2 Branches To Hold a Candle added to a Salt' at a cost of £3 16s 6d in April 1661, suggesting a recognisably French form of salt. She was well stocked with French plate, including a salt which she sold to Backwell at the same time but the branches were unsuccessful and these were credited to her account a couple of months later that year.[14]

The scroll salt was to remain popular until the 1690s but was then to disappear from view so totally that the Restoration Salts of State actually stood upside down at the Coronation of George IV, resting on their arms. At that time Rundell, Bridge & Rundell supplied four new silvergilt pans to fit inside the cavity thus exposed and to hold the salt, a misunderstanding of the original usage rectified only this century. Each of these Stuart salts, kept at the Jewel House with seven other Stuart Salts of State, is surmounted by a prancing horseman, presumably in reference to S. George on whose day the Coronations of both Charles II and James II were held.[15]

In the 1660s another variation emerged, still waisted like the pulley salt but octagonal or square with four scroll arms set at the angles. The Seymour salt, although its body is made of four slabs of crystal, is an octagon at foot and rim whereas the Moody salt of 1664 (VAM) attributed to Wolfgang Howzer, is square and chased with his favourite acanthus around the waist.

Fig. 20 **Salt of State**
Gilt 1660. Mark RL over a bird for Ralph Leake. H.25.5 cm. A grand example of the scroll salt.
HM Jewel House, Tower of London

Fig. 21 **Sweetmeat dish**
1627. Mark S over W. L.20 cm. The fluted body and upcurved shape are taken from a contemporary
Chinese hardstone brushholder: some Stuart silversmiths took Portuguese and Chinese forms as
models.
New York, Metropolitan Museum of Art

Plates and Dishes

New shapes emerged in response to the greater emphasis on privacy and so greater attention
to the details of dining plate. Because institutional, rather than private, collections have
tended to be preserved more or less intact, we are relatively ill-informed as to how some of
the domestic plate was used; family records are rarely as full and continuous as those kept by
the clerks of institutions.

The so-called sweetmeat or dessert dish is a decorated plate on a foot, called in inventories a
fruit or spice plate, weighing normally about fifteen to twenty ounces, with a shaped and
pierced rim, and often embossed overall, which appears in the decade before 1620.[16] The
descendant of the medieval and Tudor spice plate, it is very different in decoration from the
known Elizabethan spice plates, which in any case survive in engraved sets of six or twelve,
not supplied as individual items.

The embossed scalloped panels around the rims of early Stuart dessert plates are
reminiscent of the painted decoration on Chinese export porcelain, such as those blue and
white dishes recovered by Dutch marine archaeologists from the ship the White Lion (*Witte
Lieuw*), wrecked off Jakarta in 1613. Perhaps this decorated porcelain directly stimulated the
goldsmiths. However, a more immediate link is with the flimsy pierced and embossed dishes
made in Portugal at this time, which were apparently popular here. Portuguese plate had

certainly reached the royal household (Charles I sold nineteen Portuguese vessels when raising money in 1626) and several Portuguese dishes are now in English churches, given during the seventeenth century. Their intricate openwork designs were not originally part of the English goldsmiths' repertoire but clearly caught on here in the early seventeenth century. Small lightweight two-handled saucers or dramcups embossed with grapes, plums or simple bead ornament, now called 'wine-tasters', also follow Portuguese models (Fig. 21).[17]

It has been argued that these flimsy vessels, produced in large numbers between 1615 and about 1660, were a response to the worsening English economic situation but it is just as likely that they appealed on the grounds of their visual quality and novelty. As Oman pointed out, Portugal's goldsmiths certainly were short of bullion and suffered economic depression after the Spanish took over in 1580, but the English market was never under such strong financial constraints and these were probably intended for customers who a generation earlier had used pewter or stoneware. They were sold at regional fairs; provincial goldsmiths, such as James Plummer in York made them too.

Sugar Boxes, College Pots and Nests

Sugar boxes, for sweetening wine, were required in large numbers and made to a more or less standard weight of around twenty ounces. The Elizabethan scallop shell, with a section for a spoon, gave way to a coffer shape on four feet by the 1640s; an example at the Goldsmiths' Hall of 1651 is oval and completely plain with a flat lid. Post-Restoration sugar boxes are normally slightly domed, with a double coiled-serpent as handle. Some are chased with chinoiseries; more rarely they are found embossed with exotic flowers and long-tailed birds, like a box of 1683, perhaps by Philip Rollos (VAM Fig. 22).[18]

Although standard types can be recognised, ambiguity of nomenclature continues to cause problems. 'College pots' are thought to be the globular pots with two ring handles and without covers, now found only at the Mercers' Company, certain Oxford colleges and at Eton where two of 1698 were in everyday use to dispense a dole; these were also called 'strangers' cups' or 'Grace cups'. Queens' College, Cambridge sent ten college pots to the melt in 1642 but did not trouble to replace them after the Civil War.[19]

The earliest Stuart example of this distinctive shape, often described as an 'Ox-eye' cup, is that provided for Trinity Hospital in 1616. But when William Lambarde presented a covered cup to the Drapers' Company in 1578, he called it his 'college cup'. The name signified to him only the association of his gift with his newly built college or almshouse at Greenwich, of which the Company were to be governors. Clearly, at that time the term did not identify a particular shape. Lambarde's gift is a handsome but characteristic Elizabethan standing cup with a cover and without handles.[20]

Another term given too much precision by plate historians is 'nest', taken to mean a set of stacking bowls or beakers. In 1577 William Harrison, referring to the rising standard of living of Tudor yeomen, designated a typical plate collection as a salt, a dozen spoons and a bowl for wine, 'if not a whole nest'. No complete English nest of beakers has survived, although nine (from a set of ten) of 1615 are in the Kremlin Armouries, each only 4½ inches tall. But the term meant not necessarily such a stacking set, like the German *Statsbecher*, but merely several

Fig. 22 **Sugar box**
1683. Mark IS. L.21 cm. Flat-chased with ho-ho birds, palm (?) trees and a pagoda. Essential for sociable
wine-drinking, the sugar box was often highly decorated.
VAM

to the same design. When in 1630 John Banckes bequeathed some silver to the Mercers'
Company he listed 'A great nest of silver beakers . . . with the case'. His three massive
beakers survive, now gilt, but they could only with great difficulty (and instability) be
stacked one inside the other, since applied to each one are three cast maidenheads in high
relief, the badge of the Company. A 'nest' implied simply a matched set.[21]

The 'nesting' design was convenient for travelling and informal drinking and several sets of
tumblers are known from later in the seventeenth century, occasionally equipped with a
cover on three ball feet which could also be reversed to act as a stand, a vestige of formal
drinking practice. One set (Untermyer Collection, New York) is hallmarked 1688 and
retains its original case but references occur to sets of 'tumbling bowls' in the 1630s; in March
1661 the Countess of Dysart paid Alderman Backwell £26 13s 6d for seven tumblers weighing
just over ninety-three ounces. These were substantial heavy-gauge drinking cups, not to be
compared with the six to eight ounce specimens normally met with in the antique trade
today.[22]

While some drinking vessels described as beakers, such as the Banckes set, or Fig. 127,
apparently never had covers, the beaker shape retained its popularity throughout the
seventeenth century and some versions were covered. One termed a Mawdlin or Magdalen

Fig. 23 **Lidded alepot or 'stoup'**

1646. Mark double-struck and indecipherable. Presented in 1646 to Cornhill Ward. A unique Stuart
survivor of a drinking vessel popular since the late fifteenth century, preserved because it belonged to an
institution which gently decayed later and so had no impetus to refashion its silver: compare Fig. 127.
Museum of London

cup in inventories was so-called because of its similarity to the alabaster ointment jar with which Mary Magdalen is depicted in late medieval religious art; essential features were horizontal ribs on the flared body and the turned finial to the conical cover. Very few survive; one such covered beaker, at Manchester Art Gallery, is elaborately engraved. Another given as a chalice to Honnington Church in Lincolnshire, was made in 1577 (in Lincoln Cathedral treasury). The type continued popular well into the seventeenth century. In 1617 Henry Percy bought 'a Maudlin cup' plus a porringer, weighing thirty-eight ounces together, as part of his chamber or personal plate, as distinct from his dining plate.[23]

Two-handled Cups

Porringers, caudle cups and posset pots are terms often used interchangeably now (and perhaps also in the seventeenth century), and to avoid confusion Stuart vessels with handles, often with covers, are most safely referred to simply as two-handled cups. The porringer with its own stand has a long ancestry. Queen Elizabeth had several; one given in 1578 was 'standing upon an oaken leaf with a snail in the top' and the normal seventeenth-century form with two handles or 'ears' and a cover was familiar a century earlier. It was a personal eating vessel for chamber use, although it acquired an extra status as a formal gift, particularly from king to royal official.[24]

Where a covered cup survives still associated with its salver, as in the case of the Lowther set of 1660 (VAM, Fig. 133), it may be a presentation set; then it was described by contemporaries as a porringer and salver or state cup and dish. Whatever the term applied, these vessels contained sometimes alcoholic mixtures, more wet than dry to be drunk, and sometimes, conversely, gruel and other farinaceous mixtures to be eaten with a spoon. Pots with spouts for curdled mixtures or possets, occur in the 1635 Goldsmiths' Company searches; a rare Norwich one of 1642 is in VAM.

From inventory descriptions, 'posset pots' were often much heavier and so presumably larger than 'porringers', at least in the first half of the century. Two-handled cups were also used to take communion, occasionally by Anglicans and more frequently by nonconformists. When Lady Gooch in 1775 gave 'My gilt sacrament cup' to the chapel at William and Mary College, Williamsburg, she ensured the preservation of a typical handsome Stuart covered cup, with two cast handles and elaborate cutcard work.[25] Colerne Church, Wiltshire, has another handsome two-handled cup with its salver, each with silver openwork applied over a gilt body (c.1670).[26] Several less glamorous versions of late Stuart two-handled cups were used by dissenting communities such as four of 1694 belonging to the Scots Church, London Wall (S. Paul's treasury) and a pair, made specifically for communion use at the But-Lane Chapel and given by the two Swallow sisters in 1708 (VAM). Secular plate was still just acceptable for church use and vice versa.

The term porringer was ambiguous even in the seventeenth century. A covered cup given to Queen's College, Oxford by Sir Joseph Williamson in 1670 is called 'the Provost's porringer' but the term porringer was also applied to small bowls with one flat handle or 'ear', which collectors today sometimes call bleeding bowls.

Porringers, or two-handled cups, are found with the marks of many Stuart goldsmiths and

Fig. 24 **Pair of tankards**
1671. Mark TI, two mullets between, for Thomas Jenkins. H.25 cm. Engraved with the arms of Sir
Thomas Langham, father of the first Countess of Warrington. These gristly handles are found on much
silver of *c*.1660–70, particularly by the Limburg-born Jacob Bodendick.
National Trust, Dunham Massey

in standard sizes and designs with cast caryatid handles, often of extreme coarseness but recognisably from a common original model. In the 1640s, porringers were decorated with a repeating floral or geometric pattern, chasing and punching around the body, but embossing with flowers and animals in the Dutch manner rapidly became popular. Oman reproduces sixteen versions of the porringer in his *Caroline Silver,* all between six and eight inches tall and with handles, some facetted, others with cage-work bodies and cover. The accompanying salvers, standing on trumpet-feet (like cakestands) were decorated to match, often with armorials engraved both on the central field and on the porringer cover.

As their original function was forgotten, the porringer and salver were often split up. Salvers retained their usefulness as trays, plates or even patens. One by Benjamin Pyne engraved with wriggle-work, a technique peculiar to contemporary pewter, of 1691 was given to Durrington Church in Wiltshire a decade later.[27]

Salvers

Although Blount's *Glosso-graphia* (second edition 1661) is often quoted as evidence that the footed salver was an innovation at the Restoration, 'a new fashioned piece of wrought plate broad and flat with a foot underneath and is used in giving Beer or other liquid things', both footed vessels for dessert, and standing patens for church use, were familiar at least from the 1620s. In the 1620s and 1630s flagons or 'pots' for the altar were often supplied with under-plates of silver: neither as a stand for a drinking vessel nor as a footed plate was the salver-form new in the 1650s.[28]

By 1700 the general utility of the salver had become recognised and it had evolved into 'a silver plate to hold glasses or sweetmeats' as Cocker's *English Dictionary* described it (1704). At Gray's Inn in 1706 'two convenient silver salvas for collecting the Sacrament money' were purchased; weighing less than eleven ounces each, they were used later as patens.

The convenience of a 'salver' to catch drips was quickly extended to the service of wine and other beverages; illustrations of early eighteenth-century dinners, such as two paintings by Marcellus Laroon at Kensington Palace, depict servants bringing small flat-bottomed servers, each holding one or two glasses of wine. Wine was still distributed from a side table and the glasses only brought to table on this small silver dish when gentlemen 'took wine with one another'. From about 1720 salvers are frequently met with in sets of varying sizes which could be adopted for wine or teatable use, since neither cup nor glass would be passed by hand but always offered on a salver, waiter or 'presenter'.[29]

In the brief list of plate held by the Duchess of Lauderdale in 1690 were four gilt salvers. This list is indicative of what an elderly lady of quality but extreme indebtedness regarded as the irreducible minimum; she had mortgaged 5,000 ounces of her plate five years earlier to Anthony Ficketts of London, her goldsmith, and his executor lent her back a few items 'which I doe hereby promise to re-deliver and return on demand'. She had a warming pan, knife hafts (the goldsmith was of course concerned only with the silver, not with the steel blades) table and dessert spoons, four small salts, a gilt teapot, two pairs of candlesticks with a snuffer and pan and a caudle cup, in addition to the salvers. At just under 400 ounces altogether, this was a tiny quantity for a woman who had lived in the greatest ostentation at Ham House and in her other houses, where even the hearth furniture was of silver.[30]

By 1700, the salver had in addition acquired a ceremonial status. It was *par excellence* the means of advertising a court office; a great officer of state seeking an appropriate form for that perquisite, his silver seal of office, had it fashioned into a salver. These were sometimes round, like the one (now in the Burrell Museum in Glasgow) engraved by Simon Gribelin for Charles Montagu from the Exchequer seal of William and Mary, or more unusually square, like a salver made by De Lamerie for Sir Robert Walpole in 1727 and most beautifully engraved with representations of both parts of the Exchequer seal and a view of London; this has been convincingly attributed to William Hogarth, painter and engraver (Fig. 82). Other seal-salvers made between 1700 and 1800 show that these pieces, like the standing cups also sometimes engraved with seals, were primarily regarded as display items and so have often survived in perfect condition. Their associations with family or national history saved them from being melted as unfashionable and they have now acquired a considerable value as antiques, with the additional historical interest of the seal engraving: see Chapters 11 and 14.[31]

Changes in Tableware

The lavish Stuart attitude to silver was of course particularly expressed in silver for eating and drinking. Sadly Pepys's diary ends too early in the century for him to comment on the spread of the innovations in dining habits, which started with the aristocracy and were adopted only gradually by the professional classes. Food was presented with greater refinement and more elaborate equipment, but with less ceremony in 1700 than in 1600. The new elements – sets of cutlery, the tiered centrepiece, sets of cruets and casters, tureens, sauceboats, rings 'to support a dish and make a more handsome show' – imitated French practice and inevitably spread only gradually beyond fashionable aristocratic circles. Forks were slow to come in; one of 1632 is in the VAM but they were still unusual in the 1660s as a disgusted French visitor (De Monconys) noted. But by 1720 the new dining customs were sufficiently well established for standard designs to be produced by London goldsmiths for their gentry customers.

The first impulse came from aristocrats who had lived in France, like the Countess of Dysart who not only brought back Paris-made silver but expected her London goldsmiths to imitate these items. She bought 'a thing to hold sugar and gilt' in 1662, clearly a vessel unfamiliar to the goldsmith writing the bill; it might well have been a sugar caster, since sets of casters were coming in at this time.[32]

New forms for silver came both from France and from Holland; from the Restoration, a quantity of French plate flowed on to the London market. In 1659, the Countess of Dysart purchased from Alderman Backwell various pieces of French silver and she later paid £6 14s for '2 stands for dishes of the French fasion' which by their weight were predecessors of the familiar eighteenth-century dish ring.

From the mid-seventeenth century, stands on trumpet-shaped feet were commonly being used to support either a single dish, or a mass of small plates and cups, to 'make the feast look full and noble'; as Randle Holme explained. This straightforward approach to table layout was particularly suited to long tables and can be seen in engravings of formal banquets such as those of the Coronation and of the ceremonies of the Order of the Garter published by Elias Ashmole. However, the move to smaller, often round or oval, tables, encouraged a new approach to table layout and the simple stand was to be superseded by the rather more complex 'machine', *epergne* or *surtout de table* after 1700.[33]

The structure of dining altered from a large number of dishes served at one remove towards the modern idea of a menu constructed from several courses offered in sequence, a gradual process not fully accepted, even by the end of the eighteenth century. In the 1780s Parson Woodforde still offered his guests meals constructed in the traditional manner, mixing sweet with savoury dishes, although with relatively few dishes to each course, but in discussing innovations in table silver we are inevitably describing objects made for the leaders of fashion and particularly the aristocracy.

References to mustard pots or 'cups' occur from the 1660s; although a recognisably English pot is not known before about 1720, they were familiar items in Holland and France by the mid-seventeenth century and several New England merchants whose inventories were taken in the 1670s owned one.[34] Although the caster for 'powder' or spice originated much earlier – the Tudor pepper shaker set in a bell salt is a forerunner – the concept of a set of three, a pair for cayenne and black pepper (or dry mustard) and a single larger one for sugar was generally accepted, probably in response to French practice, from the 1670s.[35]

Those casters fitted with a blind sleeve inside the piercing are described as mustard casters or boxes and were supplied with a spoon, although the sleeve has often been removed later. A single caster with the arms of Oliver Cromwell (1658) recently passed through the London market; sets survive from the 1670s. Cruets for oil and vinegar were standard equipment, emphasising the importance of salad in the meal.

Although silver cruets by George Garthorne are known, sets of cutglass bottles fitted with silver caps and spouts, with scroll handles, rapidly replaced them in popularity after 1690. These bottles were then set in rings on a shaped frame. Some also have a set of three casters in a cinquefoil frame; good later examples can be seen at the Ashmolean Museum (De Lamerie, 1727) and at Woburn. There are often smaller rings to hold the bottle caps: this form, called by collectors the Warwick cruet because two sets of 1715 (formerly at Warwick Castle) were publicised in the late nineteenth century, was certainly being made by 1710.

By 1700 the list of utilitarian plate was lengthening: chamber pots, colanders, ladles, skillets, toasters, saucepans, and even warming pans all occur, although rarely survive. Noble households even baked their sweet tarts and puddings in silver. In 1723 Sarah Duchess of Marlborough bought a set of 'Ten scallop'd patty pans' secondhand; still engraved with the cipher of their original purchaser, the Earl of Radnor (d. 1723) they measure 4¾ inches across. When James II died in exile in 1703, he had all these domestic items, down to his apothecary's silver pestle and mortar, although this was to be sacrificed for his son's great seal. Despite financial pressure, James II was still equipped with a personal set of gold cutlery and two caddinets, the silvergilt stands for cutlery, napkins, salt and pepper which originated at the French court and whose use in England was peculiar to the Stuart royal family. His tableware, which included a mustard pot and spoon, was all gilt.[36]

Tea, Coffee and Chocolate Pots

From about 1600 English merchants and travellers were briefly in contact with the Japanese and almost continuously with the Chinese, and publicised their custom of drinking tea. At Fukien in 1637 'the people there gave us a certain Drinke called Chaa which is only water with a kind of herb boyled in it' as the Cornish traveller Peter Mundy described it. While the Japanese normally prepared tea by pouring hot water over the leaves in a bowl or cup, whisking it and allowing it to infuse, the Chinese used red stoneware pots, many of which reached Europe; these, and other porcelain vessels such as wine jars, were to be the most pervasive influence on European silversmiths in designing tewares.[37]

Although the earliest surviving English silver teapot, made in 1670 (VAM) is often described as experimental, since its tall tapering body and conical cover are very different from the later familiar pear-shape, it is clear that this shape was already in use for serving tea, at least to a large number of drinkers. Trade tokens issued by London purveyors of tea, coffee and sherbet in the 1660s depict such pots whose capacity was quite appropriate for serving a group drinking tea in a coffee house, as Samuel Pepys did for the first time in 1660. The 1670 teapot was presented, as its inscription records, by George Lord Berkeley to the East India Company, which initially monopolised the import trade in tea and with which he had close family and business ties. It, therefore, presumably follows the generally accepted form for institutional as against domestic teapots at the time; its construction is simple, a seamed tube with a straight spout.[38]

Fig. 25 **Teapot**
1670. Mark TL. H.33 cm. Engraved with the arms of the East India Company and of George, Lord Bakeley, who presented 'This Silver tea-pott' to the committee of the Company in 1670. Close to the shape adopted for coffee pots, perhaps from Middle Eastern brassware.
VAM

Although spouted posset pots were in use early in the seventeenth century, there was of course no precedent in English silver for a vessel to brew and to dispense a hot liquid to several people at a time, and several forms were tried before the pear-shaped teapot emerged about 1700. Small upright melon-shaped teapots with curving spouts, based on a Chinese hot water jar, are in the VAM and Ashmolean Museum (c.1685); their elegant silver handles are impossible to hold if the pot is full of boiled water. Another gilt pot, now in the Museum of Fine Arts of Boston, which is engraved overall, stands on three feet and has the curiously wrought handle of a Bodendick tankard. It is a forerunner of a shape briefly popular again in the 1730s.[39]

For tea equipment, gilding seems to have been customary, at least before 1700; the Duchess of Lauderdale had acquired two gilt teapots before 1684. An unmarked pot made by the Huguenot, David Willaume about 1700 (BM) is sometimes called a cordial pot because it has no internal strainer, but this rounded pot with its duckbill spout is equally suited to tea and is very similar to a slightly larger pot, also by Willaume and marked for 1706 (Assheton Bennett Collection, Manchester). The strainer's function could have been carried out instead by pouring through a strainer spoon, an item which early became a standard element in the tea service along with tongs and teaspoons.

Despite the cost of tea, the taste for drinking it spread quickly; le Pautre published elaborate teapot designs in Paris in the 1660s, the earliest English pot of any artistic significance (at Burghley) was made twenty years later, by Harache. In the 1670s, the potter John Dwight at Fulham turned out red stoneware pots to supplement wares imported from China; these were oval with facets and were to be the model for one shape adopted by goldsmiths after 1700.[40]

The pear-shaped teapot was established in England by about 1700 and remained popular, sometimes facetted, or with the addition of cutcard ornament and generally supplied with a lamp and stand, until the 1720s when it was supplemented by a rounded or bullet-shaped form. As tea became cheaper (it dropped from 50s a pound in 1660 to 8s or so for Bohea (black tea) in 1750), so the custom spread through society; stock shapes in silver are recognisable from about 1710.[41]

The problem of what to drink tea from arose very early in the English experience of the new beverage. A visitor in 1615 to the East India Company's toehold in Japan, its factory at Furando, described the local cups of tin or porcelain which were covered with silver saucers to keep in the steam while the tea infused. He preferred to use a familiar silver porringer 'to drink Chaw in'. Bowls or cups of silver were not satisfactory, since the hot liquid made them unbearable to hold but a few have survived; notable are a pair of gilt-handled bowls with saucers of 1688, as ornately engraved as the Boston teapot. Other simpler handled cups are at the Ashmolean and in the Burrell Collection. Cups without handles were made in white silver between 1700 and 1720 (VAM; Holburne of Menstrie Museum, Bath) but the rapidly expanding trade in oriental porcelain, plus locally-made imitations like Dwight's and Nottingham stoneware, provided a more convenient and decorative alternative. The much travelled and sophisticated Elizabeth, Duchess of Lauderdale, drank her tea, as well as her coffee, from silver dishes; a bill for andirons and sconces of May 1672 includes '18 tea cups' at £18 or thereabouts. No weight is given but at the usual rate of five or six shillings the ounce for plate, each cup weighed three or four ounces. These dishes travelled with her; another bill refers to making cases for three 'tay' dishes and another to hold a dozen.[42]

The other hot beverages, coffee and chocolate, also required special vessels for serving and drinking, although the equipment was less complicated and in the case of coffee pots at least, often supplied to match a tea service. The first silver ones in the 1660s may have had the curving spout and globular body familiar from earlier water ewers; they are depicted on the trade tokens of contemporary London coffee houses. But the earliest to have survived was made in 1681 (VAM) and, like the teapot of 1670, was presented to the East India Company. Since coffee came from Turkey and was generally drunk in the Levant, Englishmen were more familiar with it than with the exotic and more expensive tea and the convenience of the Restoration coffee house as a club and meeting place undoubtedly encouraged a taste for the new drink. A coffee house hostess in an engraving of the 1690s is wielding a tapering pot which, although larger, is recognisably of the 1681 shape; this was to endure at least until the 1720s.[43] Coffee pots were made in standard sizes suited to individual needs – quart, pint and half pint since it was regularly drunk at breakfast time, which was not always a meal taken in company. Coffee pots, like vessels for chocolate and tea, became rather more common after 1700; examples of all three vessels can be seen at the Manchester Art Gallery.

Chocolate was served as a thick powder, boiled with hot water and sugar, which had to be milled up to make it drinkable and to give a froth; coffee and chocolate pots supplied en suite, like the early pair of 1706 made by Alice Sheen for the Ironmongers' Company, were virtually identical, except that the finial of the chocolate pot was attached to a plug which was lifted or hinged to give access to the wooden mill or stirring rod. Sometimes a later customer's preference for a coffee pot has entailed soldering-in this plug. Conversely, the antique market sometimes throws up an early (pre-1730) coffee pot altered into a chocolate pot, to satisfy current market demand, as the rarer article can command a higher price. Very few chocolate mills are preserved; one silver-mounted wooden mill or 'molinet' is in a pot by Crespin at the Ashmolean Museum of 1730. In June that year Crespin supplied a chocolate pot to the Earl of Dysart costing £14 10s. His charge for this thirty-eight-ounce pot included engraving arms, but not the wooden handle and mill, charged at a shilling a piece.[44] Chocolate never achieved the general acceptance enjoyed by tea and coffee.

For London-made silver, the categorisation of pear-shaped 'Huguenot' and tapering 'English' coffee pots does not last beyond 1700, if indeed it ever applied, although it is worth noting that in Exeter, with less Huguenot influence, pots evolved a distinctive shape as can be seen in several made by John Elston between 1700 and 1720. So did the Boston-made coffee pots. Perhaps this apparent Anglo-Saxon taste can be attributed to a shortage of continental, or at least French, models to follow in those communities which were relatively self-contained and remote from London fashion.[45]

Punch Bowls and Monteiths

Punch, too, required silver utensils; one of the earliest is a handsome gadrooned bowl with a cover, on four feet, presented to the town of Stamford by its MP in 1685 along with a ladle (see Fig. 128). This is similar in shape to a covered bowl of 1640 at Kings' College,

Cambridge and to Scandinavian drinking vessels but much larger. Its feet and its cover distinguish it from later punch bowls of the 1690s onwards. Another contemporary gift to a town council is the monteith, with an accompanying set of beakers, at Newark on Trent, given by the Hon. Nicholas Saunderson (1689). This group rather contradicts Anthony à Wood's explanation of the origin of the monteith's notched rim, 'that it was to let drinking vessels hang there by the foot, suspended in cold water'. These beakers could not hang in the notches.

Monteiths had only a brief popularity; the earliest reference, to pewter ones, occurs in a 1677 inventory and the latest recorded is of 1720. The goldsmiths soon combined their function with that of the punch bowl by supplying a detachable notched rim. Punch bowls, as distinct from monteiths which have lost their collars, can be found from 1680, although references to this concoction occur from the 1650s; a later example, made by De Lamerie for Sir George Treby, is in the Ashmolean Museum (1723).[46]

Silver Furnishings

Perhaps the most spectacular aspect of Stuart silver, although the rarest now, is their furniture. The fashionable French triad of a console table with pier glass above, flanked by a pair of candlesticks or gueridons, was briefly adopted here at court; Charles II had two sets and maybe more and gave at least two of his mistresses silver furniture. Nell Gwyn had a bed and the Duchess of Portsmouth two rooms full of silver furniture, as John Evelyn noted in 1683. The City of London gave another set to William and Mary about 1690. This is still at Windsor Castle, with an electrotype copy of the table at the Victoria and Albert Museum. Another complete set may be seen at Knole, purchased in 1680; one made for the first Duke of Devonshire for Chatsworth about 1700 exists only as an engraved table top. In both style and design, these sets closely followed French originals and Paris was still recognised as the prime source in 1697. When William III needed silver furniture for one of his Dutch palaces he ordered it direct from Paris.[47]

More commonly found are hearth sets – andirons, tongs, shovel and fire box – which are either entirely of silver or have silver knobs or openwork panels applied to the iron case. In 1619 Anne of Denmark, wife to James I, had two sets of silver andirons at Somerset House, one with the arms of Denmark and the other without. With the increased use of coal rather than wood by 1700, silver andirons were becoming, as Randle Holme put it, 'for ornament more than profit' but were popular in the period between about 1670 and 1720. Several sets of hearth furniture, including chased silver strips to define the front edge of the hearth stone, were supplied for the Lauderdales in the 1670s and at Burghley a little later, both for reception rooms and for smaller private rooms like the Green Closet at Ham, where they may still be seen. They were normally supplied not by goldsmiths but by specialists retailing brass, silver and other metal lighting and fireplace equipment, although curiously enough one such order also included silver teacups.[48]

Most late Stuart andirons follow the standard baroque design of scrollwork topped by a ball finial. Some have figure terminals, like the putti with baskets of fruit on their heads on a set of andirons made by Andrew Moore for William III, which bear his royal cypher.

Fig. 26 **Candelabrum**
*c.*1670–90. Unmarked. H.48 cm. Several of this form are known, some by Anthony Nelme. The source
was probably a design by le Pautre, published first in Paris: Fig. 96.
Chicago Art Institute

Unusually, these are hallmarked; Andrew Moore is known also to have supplied the City's gift of silver furniture for the king. Other fireside equipment, like the fire screens with silver poles necessary to protect the clothes and complexion, is now very rare. Bellows of marquetry or mother-of-pearl with silver garnitures accompanied these hearth items, particularly in ladies' chambers. They are rarely marked, however, indicating that they were specially commissioned rather than stock items produced in large numbers for sale.[49]

After the Restoration, the French custom was introduced here of standing silver braziers or cassolettes in eating rooms to perfume the air, explaining the existence of silver openwork stands (one by Bodendick is in the Hermitage; *c*.1670).

Lighting appliances – candlesticks, sconces and chandeliers – were particularly popular, or have survived in disproportionately large numbers. Pepys's pleasure in the sailmaker's gift of 'two large silver candlesticks and snuffers and a slice to keep them upon' (1661) indicates their importance in the Stuart interior. Clustered columns with cast acanthus detail characterise those made by Bodendick in the 1670s; a decade later, figure sticks were popular. A set of candelabra with two single sticks of this type is known, unmarked but attributed to Anthony Nelme (Fig. 26). Other examples are in the Ashmolean and in the Bank of England Collection. The Duchess of Lauderdale had a pair of sticks with 'byes', presumably putti, in 1684.[50]

Late Stuart sconces adopted one of two basic designs; the simpler in construction, and presumably the cheaper, sits the candle socket on a semi-circle of metal soldered to a flat reflector plate, which is either undecorated and merely engraved with armorials or embossed with typical late baroque amorini or foliage. Behind the reflector plates are silver rings to hang up the sconces (VAM). But rather more elaborate, often embossed with foliage and putti or cast with devices appropriate to the purchaser, and substantially heavier, are the sconces made in sets of up to twenty-four for the state rooms of the Stuart aristocracy (Fig. 27). Eight from a set of twelve made for the royal family about 1670 (now at Colonial Williamsburg) weigh almost 1,000 ounces. Apart from the royal arms and cypher, altered subsequently to fit the sconces for William and Mary, they also originally had cast swags of oak leaves and acorns. These sconces have, as in so many cases, been fitted later with a second branch, in this instance by Garrards's in the 1850s. The Huguenot goldsmiths specialised in narrow upright sconces, directly following French designs; sets by Rollos and Willaume of about 1700 have the characteristic small-scale ornament, formally organised, which can be seen in a pair from Belton House (VAM).[51]

Chandeliers were always rare in England. One ten-branch chandelier made by Daniel Garnier for William III is now at Williamsburg and a second by George Garthorne hangs at Hampton Court, but there were only five in the royal palaces, as listed in the 1721 plate inventory. Cheaper alternatives in brass and gilt wood were available both from Holland and from English braziers and the amount of metal required (between 700 and 1,300 ounces in surviving examples) probably explains their comparative rarity. The history of a later chandelier, made by William Alexander in 1752, illustrates the practical problems associated with such massive constructions. A chandelier was purchased for the Fishmongers' Company in 1751. However, when it required repair, it was discovered to be close-plated over copper, a piece of blatant fraud on the part of the goldsmith entrusted with the original contract.[52]

Fig. 27 **Wall sconces**
*c.*1670. Unmarked. H.44 cm. From a set of four. The pierced monogram EAE below an earl's coronet
and within palm branches is for Anne Rich and John, Earl of Exeter, who married in 1670.
Burghley House, Stamford

The demand for silver in Stuart England was enormous and almost any household article, from a pudding basin to a shaving brush, was made in the metal for those wishing to afford it. Some of the new types – such as race prizes, sugar and pepper casters, mustard pots, forks, teapots, snuff boxes – which emerged at this time are still household objects; others like *trembleuse* cups, chocolate pots, silver toys and perfume burners are now merely interesting antiques with no practical function except as museum or collectors' pieces. But even this short selection serves to remind us of the almost universal application of silver; virtually every part of the house from the kitchen to the bedroom, and pre-eminently the dining room, had its complement of silver vessels.[53]

Apart from its obvious use as an expression of status among those wealthy enough, silver had certain practical advantages. The metal could be burnished to a hard surface and so was easily cleaned; it retained heat well, which was convenient both for cooking and serving food and for washing and shaving, and it could be readily engraved to record armorials or the occasion of a gift or presentation. No other material combined all these qualities and also conferred status through its ownership. Around 1700 could be taken as the high water mark for the use of silver throughout the home.

Notes

1 Boston MFA 1983, Vol. 3, 480–1. For silver discussed in this chapter see Oman 1970; Davis 1976; Hackenbroch 1969. For the Dysart/Lauderdale references, see Tollemache MSS.

2 Queens' College inventory 1642. In the 1640s plate production slumped only very briefly.

3 Oman 1979, 299–301; Hayward 1983, 260–5.

4 Mrs E Powys 1897, 377.

5 Pepys 1930; Girouard 1966.

6 Greenwood 1930, 2–3; Girouard 1966. Their original intention, to replace with copies, was abandoned; the new plate was to be of 'such pieces and parcelles as are now most fashionable.' These were themselves melted in 1674.

7 Oman 1970, 5.

8 Pepys 1930. For glass, see Charleston.

9 Oman [Kremlin] 1961; Jackson 1911, 244.

10 Penzer 1949, 48–52.

11 Mercers' Plate.

12 Jewitt and Hope 1895, Vol. 1, 392. The salt was given to Catherine of Braganza by the town of Portsmouth; she presumably sold it before her return to Portugal.

13 Hayward 1975, 22, pl. 16.

14 Tollemache MSS.

15 Younghusband.

16 Oman 1950, 45-8. One given to Witham Church in 1617 is in VAM.

17 For example, Oman 1970, pl. 218. Probably the 'dram cups' which crop up in smaller inventories. Slightly larger 'boate saucers' were popular in the 1630s.

18 Oman 1970, pl. 51A–52B. The sugar box 'chest' or 'tronk', essential for preparing spiced wine, was popular with corporations too; Coventry bought one in 1648; Jewitt and Hope 1895, 393.

19 Oman 1971, 10; Oman 1970, pl. 7B. The Eton cups were called 'Grace Cups' in 1772.

20 Greenwood 1930, 13–19, frontispiece.

21 Oman 1961, pl. 36.

22 Hackenbroch 1969; Wark 1978, 18–19.

23 The term 'Magdalen fashion' described several cups in the 1561 Pembroke inventory, one a gift from the queen. Their weights varied from 18½ to 49 ounces.

24 Collins 1955, 554, 558. Oman 1970, 12–13. The posset pot with a spout occurs in silver, glass and delft, and 'spout pots' presumably were of this shape. One at Burghley House, Stamford, in Chinese porcelain, was called a 'Syllabub Pott' in 1688: Lang 1983, 71 and Charleston 119.

25 Butler 1970, no. 9. For other instances, see Christie's 1955.

26 In S. Nicholas Church Museum, Bristol. Oman 1970, pl. 15A.

27 Nightingale 1891, *Church Plate of Wiltshire*.

28 For example, several Gloucestershire and Essex churches had them.

29 [Middle Temple].

30 Tollemache MSS.

31 Oman 1978, 76–8, Banister 1981. Gold salvers made from freedom boxes, were popular later, for example, Al-Tajir Collection, 80–2.

32 Tollemache MSS; Hernmarck 1977.

33 Thornton 1978; Hernmarck 1977; Gruber 1982.

34 Captain Willett (d.1674) had a 'wrought mustard pott with a silver ledd'. Boston MFA, 481. In the 1630s mustard pots of porcelain were ordered from China by the Dutch East India Company.

35 Oman 1970; Hernmarck 1977.

36 Grimwade 1963. Inventory of James II.

37 Cooper-Hewitt 1984; Penzer 1956. A pot by Harache at Burghley is a direct copy of a *blanc de Chine* pot. Wine pots like modern teapots in the load of the *Witte Lieuw* demonstrate that the form was known in Europe from at least 1613 or so.

38 Cooper-Hewitt 1984; Oman 1970.

39 Oman 1970. Teapot designs of great elaboration were published in France from the 1650s.

40 Tait 1972; Banister 1983.

41 For example, Hayward 1959; Wark 1978, 41–2. Ashmolean Museum, pl. 6.

42 Tollemache MSS.

43 Copies are in the Print Rooms of the British and Ashmolean Museums. For early coffee pots, see the Folger Coffee Company catalogue.

44 Tollemache MSS; Banister 1984.

45 For example, Safford 1983; Royal Albert Memorial Museum, Exeter, 1978; Kent 1980 and 1982. For Exeter see p.181.

46 The Weavers' Company had three pewter monteiths in 1677 and delft versions are known too. Lee 1978; Hayward 1959; Goldsmiths' 1952.

47 Thornton 1978, 1984; Oman 1970, 59–63; Penzer 1961; Rowe in *National Trust Studies*, ed. R Fedden 1978.

48 *Furniture History Society* 1971, Vol. V. Fire furniture from Ham is now in the Untermyer Collection.

49 Jones 1911. A pair of bellows, silver-mounted, is in the Ashmolean Museum; Hernmarck 1977, pl. 539. In 1984 a warming pan arrived as a gift.

50 One from the Nelme set is in the Chicago Art Institute. Oman 1967, pl. XXIV; Ashmolean Museum, pl. 5.

51 Hayward 1959; Davis 1976. An important set (unmarked) at Burghley is elaborately embossed and chased.

52 VAM 1984, 119–20. Three late Stuart lights at Williamsburg came from the Royal Collection, probably in 1808: Davis 1976, 13–19 and p.279.

53 Almost all were imitated in miniature as toys or to train young housewives; Poliakoff 1985.

FOUR

EARLY GEORGIAN

In spite of all the Refinements which the English have undergone . . . Eating and Drinking are still the Groundwork of what ever they call Pleasure

(*The Champion* 5 August 1742)

THE sixty years after 1700 saw both innovation and consolidation in the silver used by the English and can be taken as a consistent period, without drastic changes. We can document quite closely both the pattern of purchases, among aristocratic families at least, and how the craft operated. Both dining and tea silver became more complex and more uniform in design, as the concept of the service decorated to a common theme emerged. By about 1760, alternatives were competing for space – porcelain and, increasingly, plated wares were acceptable at the highest social levels.[1]

When a run of bills has survived, we can see the order of priorities in acquiring plate. A bachelor coming into money or marrying (often the same occasion) like Benjamin Mildmay, Earl Fitzwalter in 1724 or Lyonel Tollemache, fourth Earl of Dysart in 1729, immediately bought a silver shaving set of a notched basin and a hot water jug, a 'wash ball' (pierced soap box) and toothpaste boxes for himself, with perhaps a chamber pot.[2] On their wedding day, the husband customarily presented his wife with a set of dressing plate (a toilet service). One early Dysart chamber pot supplied by David Willaume, in 1731, is exhibited at Ham House, simply engraved with the family arms.

Where the plate itself still can be identified, our picture is fuller and the documents far more informative. On the marriage between Lyonel Tollemache and Grace Carteret in 1729, dining plate and candlesticks became another immediate necessity, along with a tea service. The next six months of bills from Willaume show a steady stream of purchases of tableware – two heavy soup spoons, a marrow spoon, a cruet frame and a set of casters. After this initial flurry of expenditure amounting to some pounds, the Tollemache family settled down to a more routine pattern of dealings with this silversmith. Willaume supplied, predictably, a three-ounce pap boat in May 1732, but the bulk of expenditure with him in the 1730s was on repairs – mending a child's toy, a glass for an ink horn and 'boiling and burnishing' are typical entries.

David Willaume's 1727 account ran until 1741 before it was settled, when it had reached over £550, although admittedly the goldsmith had received £200 on account in 1729, the year of the Tollemache marriage. These were of course by no means all the family's purchases. Willaume charged separately for that fashionable item, the 'brade basket' and two wrought sauce boats in 1734. Their fashion added considerably to their cost; the basket at almost thirty-seven ounces cost £10 14s 9d but fashion added £5 2s 6d. The boats were £13 19s 2d, with an additional £10 for fashion. These were apparently made by Crespin; they tally with a pair sold by the family in 1955.

Silver purchased for the Tollemache family between 1733 and 1748 was dispersed only in 1955. From the dinner plate sold then, covering some fifteen years, and from his goldsmith's bills, although the ornament of tureens, baskets and centrepiece was uniform, Lyonel Tollemache did not attempt to purchase an entire dinner service all at one time, as the Prince of Wales and the Earl of Kildare did in the 1740s. This entailed an outlay of capital, or a capacity to turn in old plate, which was beyond the reach of all but the wealthiest families, and both the prince and the earl were well placed in this respect. The former turned over to George Wickes 4,000 ounces of old royal plate, to the value of £1,100 or so towards the cost of his new service, and the latter had the good sense to marry an extremely wealthy heiress.

But the Tollemache dining table was furnished in stages, over eighteen or so years from 1729. After the purchases noted already, there was a gap until the early 1740s when Paul Crespin supplied the most costly part of any dinner service, silver plates for soup, meat and dessert and serving dishes. A second pair of shell-festooned sauce boats, to match the pair bought thirteen years earlier, followed in 1746. The centrepiece, the largest (259 ounces) and most expensive individual item, came from Crespin only in 1748. Judging by surviving plate supplied by Willaume and by Crespin for the family, the larger items were elaborately worked and chased in the rococo manner but to standard designs. None of the silver had more than engraved armorials; the additional cost of modelling his crest or supporters as finials or handles did not appeal to Lyonel Tollemache.

Frequent casual purchases of plate from shop stock, particularly from William Deards and Paul Daniel Chenevix, characterised both the Tollemaches' and the Fitzwalters' annual expenditure. In 1747, for example, Chenevix at the Golden Door, Suffolk Street, Charing Cross supplied Lyonel Tollemache with a nutmeg grater of gold, a silver salt and a large silver spoon, at a total cost of just under £10, a flea-bite when compared with the hundreds of pounds paid to Willaume and Crespin in the 1730s and 1740s. Peter Taylor, of the Golden Cup at the corner of Cecil Street, in 1743 supplied a 'can' weighing twenty-three ounces for £9 0s 4d; engraved arms added a further 5s. Chenevix was a regular retailer of fancy goods and 'toys' to the nobility. He supplied Earl Fitzwalter with a sugar caster in 1743 and in 1748, a half pint silver mug 'for my Lady Fitzwalter to drink her asses milk in' for £1 13s. A Tollemache running account with William Deards for three years from March 1737 includes 'a neat oval silver snuff box with a spring' for £2 12s 6d, silver penknives, mathematical instruments, to cutting a seal, putting new hair to shaving brushes and 'to a large silver corkscrew' costing 15s 0d.

The range of dress, writing, riding and other domestic accessories made in the precious metals was of course enormous and retailers specialising in fancy goods and curios, items usually produced by outworkers, or by specialist small-workers without a shop, formed a large section of London's luxury trade. Deards was clearly a large retailer of silver, as the Newdegate family's dealings with him in the 1740s show; he and William Shaw supplied all their plate, although probably made in other workshops. The Newdegate centrepiece (VAM) is by Paul De Lamerie.[3]

Fig. 28 **Inkstand**
Gilt 1738. Mark of De Lamerie. L.30 cm. An exceptional example of rococo silver: the stand is modelled
as a cartouche and chased with suitable references to the theme of communication – Mercury's bag of
wind and staff, scenes of travel on the inkpot and sand caster and a sealed letter under the inkpot.
Duke of Marlborough

The accounts of George Wickes, the London goldsmith, whose clients' ledgers between
1735 and 1747 have been so carefully analysed by Elaine Barr, contain many of the small sales
of luxury items – filigree toys, buttons, serjeants' rings, seals and chatelaines. In addition,
repeated entries for small repairs, boiling and burnishing old plate or engraving armorials
demonstrate the continuous and repetitive demands on workshop staff for maintaining,
rather than creating, plate. The output of Wickes's workshop cannot be estimated from the
clients' ledgers, since no statement of over-the-counter sales is included. Annual totals for
plate supplied to ledger customers, excluding flatware, produce perhaps three hundred
individual items, ranging in size from a tureen to a pap boat, although many of these were
probably bought-in from specialists, as Wickes's successors Parker and Wakelin are known to
have done.

The most interesting and useful aspect of Wickes's ledgers is that they can so often identify
plate currently on the market, where the weight agrees and the armorials of the original
purchaser have not been erased. Wickes had his fair share of the nobility; among his firm's
customers between 1750 and 1754 were forty-five members of the peerage with a further
thirty-three opening accounts by 1760. This is not to say that any, or all, of them confined
their patronage to his Panton Street shop. Few sets of accounts have yet been analysed to set

against the Wickes's ledgers but those noblemen whose goldsmiths' bills are still extant or whose plate is available for study clearly dealt with several goldsmiths at any one time. Sir Robert Walpole ordered plate from Paul Crespin, William Lukin and Paul De Lamerie before placing an order with Wickes in 1737; George Booth, Earl of Warrington, dealt with all the leading Huguenot goldsmiths, and between 1724 and 1754 Benjamin Mildmay dealt continuously with De Lamerie (until he died in 1751), to the tune of several hundred pounds, finally settling with his executors in 1752. During those years he also dealt on a large scale with Henry Hebert, who actually assisted his butler in preparing an inventory of plate at Schomberg House in 1739, and at least nine others are named in his accounts.[4]

Dining Room Silver

The difference between Henry Percy's purchases of dining plate for 1617 (see Chapter 2) and those made by Frederick Prince of Wales from George Wickes in 1738 is not one of bulk but of content. The earlier order comprised merely huge quantities of serving dishes in varying sizes and plates, reflecting old established English habits, whereas by the 1730s soup, sauces and

Fig. 29 **Cruet stand**
1721 Mark of Paul Crespin. With double spice box, casters and cruet. The elaborate ornament includes four hunting scenes chased on the tray rim and Aesop's *Fables* cast on the octagonal casters. A rare and early example of Crespin's skill as a chaser. See Fig. 65.
Colonial Williamsburg

79

the refinement of a central unit incorporating successively condiments, candles and dessert had arrived, under French influences. As the whole structure of the meal changed, so the form of the tableware required was quite different. Soup needed a tureen and ladle, sauces, sauce boats and smaller ladles and at the centre of the table was now an epergne or surtout, in which might be incorporated, at various stages of the meal, casters and cruets, candlesticks and dessert dishes (see Figs. 29 and 30). This shift in usage affected corporate dining too; the city of Norwich replaced its 'belly pots, salvers and pottingers' in 1735 with new salvers, sauce boats and salts, and the newly built Mansion House in London was completely equipped with dining plate, acquired in the 1720s and 1730s; for its origins, see pp.314–15.

For all these innovations, France was the source. The French court goldsmiths evolved a silver centrepiece, with one or more tiers, for Louis XIV in the 1690s. This could be dressed with cruets and casters around a large *pot à oille* (tureen), replaced with candle stands and dessert dishes at a later stage of the meal. All this was set on an immensely heavy and impressive silver table, oval in shape which, like virtually all French silver of this period, has vanished. Its appearance is preserved in the drawings ordered in Paris by Nicodemus Tessin and his son between the 1690s and 1740s; a Swedish nobleman, the elder Tessin was recording French court practice and design so that the Swedish court could follow it. Although the transmission process across the channel is less well documented, a pale imitation flourished here too, and to study English silver of this period it is essential to look also at the French situation, as the recent exhibition on the rococo in England (VAM, 1984) showed.[5]

Epergnes, Surtouts or Centrepieces

A centrepiece tureen with candlebranches was engraved by Massialot in a French cookery book (1716) and another by Ballin is depicted in a painting now in the Louvre; this is clearly the model for the English centrepieces of the 1720s and 1730s. The earliest with English hallmarks date only from the 1720s and it is rare to find one which retains all its component parts. These were in any case not uniform, although they normally comprised a frame or 'ring' with notches for four or eight branches, dishes for the branches which could be alternated with candle nozzles, sets of casters, salts, spice boxes and cruet frames and a large central basin. An epergne listed in the royal inventory of 1721 had a basket and cover in place of a central basin; this set also included sauce boats. The handsome effect was achieved by uniformity; centrepieces were set out with each quadrant matching the others, even in the more fanciful rococo ones by Roettiers made for French clients. The type was clearly well established here by 1720 and it is probable that many of the cruet frames and caster sets on the market originally accompanied epergnes which have been melted down. In the same year as the royal inventory the Hon. George Treby ordered an epergne from De Lamerie. It consisted of 'a fyne polished surtout with cruets'. He also had double salts and the whole assemblage weighed over 500 ounces. The central basin was covered with an elaborately chased shallow dish but had no cover (Fig. 30).

The centrepiece made by Paul De Lamerie in 1743 for Sir Roger Newdegate is a later example (VAM) and another very similar one by Augustin Courtauld (1741) is in the Hermitage. Not all have the subsidiary branches; one by De Lamerie of 1733 sits on four mask feet. The central basins in this one and the Newdegate epergne are fixed but in others it can be lifted out; it was presumably intended to contain some semi-liquid dish, which could be kept hot if necessary by putting a lamp underneath. The Fitzwalters' butler, listing the Fitzwalter plate at Schomberg House in 1739, noted 'an Epargne being two rings, four buttons, four saucers, one round bassin, four branches, one Trivett and lamp weighing in all 202 oz.'; clearly, to him the epergne was equipped with the means of keeping food hot.[6] Their popularity is obvious from the Wickes' ledgers; George Wickes supplied thirty-one epergnes or surtouts to his account customers between 1735 and 1745. They were interchangeable vessels, useful at both dinner as a set centrepiece and at supper as a serving dish.

Because table presentation at dinner precluded a central serving dish, the central basin could be more easily used at supper (a less formal meal) for the popular ragout or for soup, when the candles would replace the dishes and so give light to the table. The term epergne (not used in France) has two possible original meanings; it could be a 'treasury' bringing together in one place all the necessities and pleasures of the table. Alternatively they were so-called from their function of 'sparing' or saving service; to have all the condiments to hand centrally, on a table only seating perhaps ten to fourteen people, made dining both more intimate and less formal than the older linear seating pattern with servants bringing

Fig. 30 **Epergne**
1738. Mark of Paul De Lamerie. The branches and dishes can be removed for a simpler, less formal table setting; this was probably supplied with matching cruets, casters and salts. Note the restless ornament, broken border and helmeted putto, all typical of De Lamerie's silver *c.*1735–42.
New York, Metropolitan Museum of Art. Gift of George D. Widener and Eleanor W. Dixon 1958

everything to the table at once. Contemporary table plans, like those of Charles Carter (1730), show a central epergne and tureens but also salts disposed among the massed entrée dishes in the old manner.

In most epergnes in the rococo style of the 1740s and later the covered central basin has become a pierced basket to display fruit although composite centrepieces like the one by Sprimont (VAM 1745) and others in Toledo and the Museum of Fine Arts, Boston show a brief taste for another solution, a covered basin resting on animals which again came from French models.[7] The fashion for china figurines and other table ornaments, linked by hanging greenery, isolated the centrepiece and limited its function to display; the term 'dormant' implies that although the baskets on the typical Pitts epergne of the 1760s could easily be detached and passed round the table at dessert, this was not apparently customary.

Components of the Dinner Service

Pairs, or larger sets, of tureens were popular from the 1720s throughout the century (see Fig. 42). While plain ones were available from stock at the relatively low price of 4s 8½d the ounce (Wickes, 1742, for Sir Lester Holte) a handsomely chased pair like those supplied to Brownlow, ninth Earl of Exeter in 1756 by Edward Wakelin cost £277 9s 6d (for 500 ounces) with the cost of fashion bringing the charge per ounce to more than 11s. Soup ladles could be almost equally costly for their size; the Brownlow pair cost £10 17s. The earliest tureens were round, following the *pot à oille* model, but oval tureens were the normal English form by 1740. Sauce boats at first followed French models, with two lips and two handles; later they were elaborately modelled, often with wildly fantastic handles and shell bases; the Sprimont mermaids and shells are the most striking.[8]

A curiosity of the Georgian dinner service is the pierced strainer dish called a mazarine, normally oval (for fish) but sometimes round. The term *à la mazarine* in Restoration England described a set of small dishes used together, a French innovation, on a larger one. But either this term was transferred to another vessel or another ran concurrently. By 1700 mazarine apparently meant a distinctive piece of serving plate, deep but not pierced. At any rate, by about 1750 it had acquired its modern meaning, although a reference to a mazarine might include, silently, the underdish too. One is in the Queen's Collection, Wickes supplied 'fish plates' among the three serving dishes in the Prince of Wales's dinner service and a De Lamerie service of the late 1740s, still more or less intact, retains both mazarines and their matching under-dishes.[9]

By looking at an order for a complete dinner service, such as the one supplied by George Wickes for the Earl of Kildare (later Duke of Leinster) which, unusually, has survived more or less intact (170 out of the original 240 pieces) and with its accompanying account, we can discover and identify firmly the terms used by contemporary goldsmiths. For example, a fluted dish on three or four feet is sometimes now called a dessert or epergne dish (and some later epergne dishes are found with feet), but before 1750 for George Wickes and his customers these were 'sallat dishes', sometimes with covers, to accompany the main course.

The term box to Wickes and his contemporaries meant any small footed container with a cover, hence sugar boxes, but the condiment urns in the Leinster service are of particular

Fig. 31 **Tureen**
1734. Mark of David Willaume. A sturdy Huguenot version of this fashionable vessel, strongly
indebted to French ornament of twenty years earlier. Note the ball and claw feet and gadrooned rims.
By 1734 De Lamerie was already at ease with rococo asymmetry.
Spink's

Fig. 32 **Condiment vases**
a) Two 1757, one 1762. Mark of Parker & Wakelin. Popular design: note the twisted handles of the
ladles. Glass liners held the pepper, sugar and mustard.
VAM
b) 1771. Mark of Louisa Courtauld and George Cowles. H. 19.5 cm. Made for Nathaniel Curzon, first
Baron Scarsdale for Kedleston, Derbyshire. Their shape is copied from a measured drawing of a Greek
urn, published by D'Hancarville (1766–7) from Sir William Hamilton's collection. The engraved deities
are also taken from D'Hancarville, based on his redrawing of the Meidias Hydria (now in the BM).
Boston, Museum of Fine Arts

interest, since this shape has so often been described by collectors and the trade as a tea vase. Apart from those in the Leinster set, whose purpose can be firmly identified, in the State Historical Museum in Moscow a centrepiece (formerly the property of Count Bobrinsky, made by Paul De Lamerie in 1734) retains all its component parts, including condiment urns, shells (perhaps for butter) and salts. In the 1740s, the urn-shape for pepper and mustard replaced the older caster, still in sets of two or three but with the addition of ladles and stands or frames. In early designs these presumably sat inside the box but condiment urns of the 1750s, and later under neo-classical influence, are designed with loop handles.[10]

Because until lately they were thought to be for tea, these vase-shaped condiment urns have been highly collectable items and relatively few remain as intact sets. The ladles, whose use was quite forgotten, are rarely found still associated with their vases. One shape popular either side of 1760 by John Parker and Edward Wakelin shows strong French influence (see Fig. 32a). As goldsmiths' accounts make clear, they were supplied with glass liners too, although these too have almost always vanished.

Normally these urns were en suite with the rest of the dinner plate. Two sets made for the Kedleston dining room, by Louisa Courtauld and George Cowles in 1771, were apparently a conscious departure from the watered-down classicism of the rest of Curzon's dinner service, ordered from Philips Garden some years earlier. One of the sets (Boston, MFA, Fig. 32b) is not only directly copied from a Greek urn in Sir William Hamilton's Collection but also engraved with gods and goddesses from other Hamilton vases, so as to reflect the latest phase of neo-classicism. On these vases, the arched handles (copied from the ceramic model) are vertical and, therefore, impractical for attaching ladles, so the silversmith has added small subsidiary loops in order that the ladles could hang in the normal position.[11]

As with the condiment vases, so with the rest of the service; many of the pieces of plate now dispersed individually among collectors and museums were originally made to match up with a whole or part-service. Sauce boats had ladles and under-dishes, as in the shell-shaped sets by Nicholas Sprimont of 1746 (Boston, MFA), and tureens almost always had under-dishes and ladles too. A handsome tureen still retaining both can be seen in the treasury at Christchurch, Oxford, one of a pair made by George Wickes in 1744. It was presented by Frederick Prince of Wales to his physician Dr Matthew Lee; it bears the prince's arms and a commemorative inscription added by the doctor's widow who gave the tureen to the dean and chapter of Lee's college. In this instance, as so often happened, Wickes made up the order with an under-dish by another goldsmith, Peter Archambo, made about 1740. Either Archambo was working for him as a subcontractor or, more probably, had supplied him at trade rates from stock. Alternatively the dish was secondhand and refurbished.

Before the eighteenth century, mustard was served as a coarse powder, dry, to be mixed with vinegar on his plate by the individual diner. Early in the century the concept of selling mustard as a powder, finely milled like flour, was commercially exploited. This new product is linked with the name of a Mrs Clements of Durham but certainly by the 1720s it was generally available, as an advertisement in the *London Journal* for 1723 makes clear. The flour had to be mixed up and left to stand; as the advertisement said 'a mustard made of this flower will be fit to eat in 15 minutes'. Although the term pot had been applied to containers for dry mustard at least from the 1670s, when in sets of casters, the earliest distinctive mustard pots are barrel-shaped examples made by Jacob Margas and Paul De Lamerie in the early 1720s.[12]

Rococo taste required something less monumental and baroque; almost always France supplied the model, as in the service that Jacques Roettiers made for Augustus, fourth Earl of Berkeley in 1735–8. Here the Paris-made spice box is trefoil-shaped, chased with waves and the covers formed as cast shells, a design published by Germain in 1748. Lyonel Tollemache, fourth Earl of Dysart ordered a similar trefoil spice box from Paul Crespin in 1746, in which each section is cast as a shell, but this unfortunately has lost its covers. English noblemen frequently ordered their silver from Paris; the Duke of Kingston bought a French service in the 1730s, from which ice-buckets (Hermitage) and two extraordinary tureens survive and London goldsmiths matched-up French tableware as a matter of course (Fig. 31).[13]

The Berkeley Castle service, sold in the mid-1960s, is interesting as stemming from a Paris workshop, source of the designs which were stimulating London goldsmiths both at the time, when published in England in 1752 and as late as 1760. The tureens have crayfish and cauliflowers on their covers, taken from Meissonier's *Livre de Legumes* (1734). These designs were quickly picked up as is demonstrated by John Edward's crab tureens of 1737. Well into the 1760s English tureens are found surmounted by artichokes or other vegetables and by turtles, following the 1730s models and, incidentally, indicating their normal contents. A set made for Lord Holdernesse about 1760 has celery legs and handles and turnips on their lids, probably popularised through the English reissue of the *Livre de Legumes* in 1757. However, not all tureens made in the 1730s and 1740s were aggressively rococo in appearance. Apart from the cost of such 'curiously carved' work, some customers felt the incongruity of mixing it on the table with formal silver in the *Régence* taste. When George Wickes supplied tureens for Sir Robert Walpole in 1738, he was merely matching up a design supplied five years earlier by Paul Crespin, presumably to make four for large dinners. All four are in a style popular well before 1730.[14]

Another essential component of the dinner service was the bread basket. Since the sixteenth century silver bread baskets had been regarded as necessary, at least at refined tables. Before 1700 they are extremely rare, although one of 1597 is known. In shape, the early eighteenth-century silver basket conformed to its predecessors, 'woven' with straight sides on an oval or round flat base with two handles, exactly following baskets of wicker or straw. One by Thomas Folkingham of 1711 can be seen in the Victoria and Albert Museum, and a pair by Francis Nelme of about 1730 belonged to Lord Brownlow. In family groups by Arthur Devis, female sitters are often depicted with such baskets, perhaps dressed with embroidery materials or fruit. But this shape was to be supplanted in the 1730s, under rococo influence, by a far more fanciful pierced basket on four feet with a swinging central handle, and about 1740 by a scallop shell resting on three dolphins, a design in silver apparently originated by De Lamerie following Dresden porcelain of the 1720s. This shell basket proved so popular that it is still in production today. A disproportionate number of baskets have been preserved, because of their attractiveness and continued usefulness, when the more cumbersome and less adaptable tureens, which they originally accompanied on the table, have been melted down.[15]

The fashion for complete dinner services of silver which emerged from the 1720s was to have a relatively short life. Apart from the investment required, which effectively limited their use to the aristocracy and to the Mansion House, there were by the 1750s decorative and fashionable alternatives to silver on the dining table, notably porcelain from London's own factories at Chelsea and Bow but also imported from Dresden. Porcelain offered an alternative competitive in price and the silver service was in decline almost from the 1740s. Complete services with first and second course plates, salad plates and covered dishes are virtually never found intact, and undoubtedly many lost some components long before their remnant appeared on the open market this century. At its peak, silver under-plates retained their place on the table only to support the porcelain in which the host took greater pride. [16]

Designs for table layouts from the 1690s show a mass of circular and oval dishes closely packed together. A more elegant, and incidentally space-saving, innovation was provided by shaped dishes: a fan or cushion shape was popular from about 1700, since sets of four could be attractively massed together at either end of the supper table. These are rarely found in English museum collections, although two from a set by Lewis Mettayer of 1704 are in the Untermyer Collection.

The silver dishring, introduced at the Restoration to lift entrée dishes, sometimes used with a lamp, was to be supplanted in popularity by the adjustable dish-cross, by about 1730. One by Kandler of 1749 in the Queen's Collection is typical; it has a central spirit lamp with four revolving arms (to accommodate an oval dish) and adjustable feet. [17]

Some designs for tableware became so generally acceptable that they continued in production over many years. After the simple capstan salts of about 1700 with gadrooning and facetting, a version of the circular salt with applied leaf ornament on a solid base emerged about 1720. Thirty-eight years later, in the 1750s, Edward Wakelin was still making salts to this design. In about 1730 this was supplemented by a tripod salt with lion-mask and pad feet, festooned with shells, fruit or flowers. Examples with marks of most leading goldsmiths are known; it is likely that many were produced by outworkers supplying the trade although bearing the mark of De Lamerie or Wickes as sponsor. [18]

Sets of cutlery, including forks, were an innovation of half a century earlier, but apparently confined at that time to the wealthiest families, although of course dessert cutlery had a longer ancestry. In his informative recent study of English flatware, Pickford makes the point that before the 1770s there was effectively only one basic design for table cutlery in fashion at any one time – the trefoil end from about 1660 to 1700, the dognose to 1720 and the Hanoverian pattern between about 1710 and 1770. Knives were pistol-handled. Before the 1750s spoons, and three-tined forks, are normally plain, perhaps with a simple applied shell at the handle end, with the crest or armorials engraved on the back of the stem; the reason for this location is that cutlery after the Restoration was laid out in the French manner with bowls turned over and fork tines resting on the cloth. [19]

The renewed emphasis on soups and stews of the early eighteenth century brought a demand for silver serving spoons, commonly referred to in bills as soup, ragout or olive spoons, the latter being for lifting out of a tureen the popular beef or veal olives. These were normally cast with foliage or, in the case of some by De Lamerie and Wickes, with eagle terminals, but not yet made as part of the service of cutlery. Large spoons, apparently for kitchen use, also occur in bills, like the one of 3½ ounces which De Lamerie supplied to Benjamin Mildmay in 1733. A pair still at Woburn are described as bread ladles or servers;

although they are shallow enough to pass a roll or slice of bread, there is no contemporary evidence for this use and it is much more likely that they are ragout or veal olive spoons. Sauce ladles first occur in Wickes's ledgers in 1743.

Another new serving item was the trowel, for pudding or fish. Wickes supplied a pudding trowel to the Earl of Kildare in 1745 and four, two for fish and two for pudding, at the Goldsmiths' Company were presented in 1751; in Germany and Sweden they were in use by the 1720s. Fish slices are normally pierced with a geometrical design or, in the case of the Ashmolean slice by Paul De Lamerie (1741), with two fish; their handles are sometimes of silver and sometimes turned wood, with no apparent distinction according to function.[20]

Silver for Serving Wine

Silver for serving wine had, along with silver for personal adornment, probably the longest pedigree of any silverware. Although wine was now drunk from glasses rather than silver, the eighteenth century saw a rush of inventions to enhance the pleasures of drinking – tickets (labels) and stands for bottles, funnels, strainers and nutmeg graters for spiced wine, waiters and, for those wealthy and ostentatious enough to justify them, ice-buckets, cisterns and fountains for cooling wine and for washing glasses. None of these, apart from the bottle stands and tickets or wine labels, was a complete innovation but their widespread use, continued popularity into the nineteenth century and relatively small cost has made the latter extremely popular collectors' items, so that a disproportionate number survive. The Victoria and Albert Museum has, for example, over 1,600 silver bottle tickets and there are large collections at the Ashmolean Museum, at the Vintners' Company and elsewhere.

Wine and other labels, whether of silver, porcelain or ivory, have their own literature and long-established collectors' club which publishes articles on research and recent discoveries by members of the society. Bottle tickets for both wine and sauce, a purely English innovation, emerged about 1720 as a means of identifying the contents of green glass bottles. Once the value of storing wine in one's cellar to mature was recognised, some more elegant method of bringing it to the table than the common green wine bottle was inevitably required, and by 1750 clear lead glass decanters were common. Labels became increasingly elaborate. A predecessor of the decanter label may be seen in certain tin-glazed earthenware serving bottles of the mid-seventeenth century which are painted with 'sack' and other terms for wine; examples are in the Museum of London.[21]

Since the Goldsmiths' Company ordered a registration of new marks in 1739, it is possible to name three makers of early (pre-1739) bottle tickets whose marks have been recorded: they are James Slater, Sandilands Drinkwater and John Harvey. But clearly labels were widely available quite quickly; references to their purchase come in the accounts of Benjamin Mildmay in 1738; 'Paid Edward——, silversmith in Lombard Street, for 14 tickets silver, for wine bottles at 5s6d. each'. George Wickes included fifteen with a dinner service ordered for Frederick Prince of Wales in 1740 and George Booth had a set of ten in 1750, including champagne, methuen, red and white port, mild ale and strong beer, weighing between fourteen and sixteen pennyweight each.

Another shift in polite usage apparently drove out the silver punch bowl, as it had the monteith a little earlier; again referring to the Wickes ledgers, we find only one punch bowl listed between 1735 and 1745. Monteiths had effectively vanished by 1730, although a freak late order for Richard Bayley for the Corporation of Boston, Lincolnshire in 1739 shows a curious marriage of earlier motifs, like the guilloche-banded foot and female bust handles, with thoroughly fashionable asymmetrical reverse scrolls and cartouches on the body. More typical is a very plain punch bowl, which George Wickes supplied to Frederick Prince of Wales in 1750 (actually made by Thomas Whipham, VAM). The profusion of punch ladles, with marks of many different makers and dated between about 1730 and the early nineteenth century, demonstrates that the drink retained its hold, but porcelain or tin-glazed earthenware, as depicted in Hogarth's *Midnight Modern Conversations*, was more decorative and cheaper. Livery companies were not alone in taking advantage of the flourishing trade in export porcelain to order punch bowls from China personalised with their arms, mottoes and appropriate sentiments at this time. A punch bowl made by John Kentisber for the Chester town plate in 1767 shows how very plain and uninventive the silver versions had become.[22]

Bottle slides or plates, as coasters were originally termed, were a development of the eighteenth century, following inevitably on the widespread use of glass decanters and bottles. If a teapot or coffee pot had its stand so did a bottle and for much the same reason – to avoid marking the table surface. An early oval stand by Augustin Courtauld (1723) is in the Ashmolean Museum. A set of the familiar circular coasters (among the earliest known), by John Langford and John Seville (1763) with pierced sides incorporating labels for claret, port and madeira was shown at Goldsmiths' Hall in 1983 and inevitably the ostentatious George Booth had six at Dunham Massey in 1750.[23]

Although silver decanters were apparently not widely used, since George Ravenscroft's lead glass offered a handsome alternative in the late seventeenth century, there is a pair of covered jugs of 1697 at Temple Newsam, Leeds made by Pierre Harache, which are so similar in shape to contemporary glass decanter jugs as to imply a similar function. But wine was normally still served at the sideboard and brought to the drinker. Pilgrim bottles, as the tall sideboard flasks with chains are now termed, had ceased to have any function other than display but were still included in Jewel House issue to ambassadors and officers of state until about 1720. One by Pierre Platel was made for the first Duke of Marlborough between 1702 and 1714 (VAM), and a pair is displayed on a marble side table at Blenheim.[24] The vessels for wine depicted by Laroon and other artists are jugs and flagons but not necessarily of silver, rather pewter, although flagons continued to be used in churches.

The wine-cooler for a single bottle was a French refinement. Almost certainly the earliest to be used in an English home and certainly the most valuable are the pair of gold buckets formerly at Althorp. By family tradition these were made for the first Duke of Marlborough, although they bear no mark of any kind, either of the goldsmith or of an owner. These have been identified in inventories of the Marlborough plate of 1712 as 'two very large gold ewers' and in 1744 in the will of Sarah, Duchess of Marlborough as 'my two large gold flagons'. This uncertainty over proper title and function may be because a bucket for a single bottle was, until the middle of the eighteenth century, apparently rather less popular, and so less familiar, than the large cistern to stand under the buffet, which had a much longer ancestry. A pair of buckets at Ickworth, Suffolk made by Philip Rollos some time before 1720 for John, first Earl

Fig. 33 **Wine cistern**
1701. Philip Rollos. W.64 cm. Made for George Booth, second Earl of Warrington, whose heraldic
supporter, the demi-boar, forms the handles. A massive dining room piece, paired later with a fountain
(now at the Goldsmiths' Company).
National Trust, Dunham Massey

of Bristol, and others in the Metropolitan Museum and British Museum Wilding gift, and a
rococo pair at Blenheim (1733) demonstrate the heavy influence of French ornament on this
essentially alien form. It was only towards the 1760s, with the evolution of an English
neo-classical style, that ice-buckets became integrated with the rest of the sideboard plate
(Fig. 113).[25] Cisterns had a much longer ancestry than ice-buckets or coolers, as did
table-fountains, that is the fantastic creations spilling out scented water or wine like those
listed in the Jewel House of Henry VIII. Fountains were also popular medieval fantasies like
the fourteenth-century French one in the Cleveland Museum, but the cistern set out with an
accompanying fountain for water to rinse glasses and cutlery was essentially a late baroque
innovation (Fig. 33). Penzer listed thirteen cisterns before 1700 and twenty-four up to 1735;
the earliest dates from about 1670 and is exceptionally large, at four feet five inches tall. It
bears the arms of Philip Stanhope, second Earl of Chesterfield.[26]

Fountains were in effect statuesque tanks, with a tap to run off water; intended for rinsing
glasses, they were normally set on a marble buffet or side table in the dining room and so
designed to match the cistern which stood filled with ice and cold water under the side table.

Either might be ornamented with the heraldic supporters of the purchaser. The demi-boar of Warrington occurs twice as handles, both on the fountain made by Peter Archambo for Dunham Massey in 1728 and on the massive cistern which Archambo had supplied to George Booth twenty years earlier (Fig. 33). This cistern for bottles has a capacity of over 20 gallons and weighs over 1,100 ounces, almost twice the weight of its fountain. The largest ever made, the so-called Jerningham–Kandler cistern, has a capacity of sixty gallons (Fig. 132). It was in Russia by 1738, having failed to find a purchaser here because of its enormous size, and perhaps also because of the originality of its figure handles, modelled by the sculptor Rysbrack. Two others, by De Lamerie and Philip Rollos are also in the Hermitage. Another massive fountain and cistern, made for the earls of Exeter, may be seen at Burghley House, Stamford (Fig. 114).[27]

Although the fashion for cisterns and fountains died away later in the eighteenth century, as the concept of an architect-designed dining room, with tableware in the same taste and an adjoining pantry, became more common, their bulk and weight meant that they often survived (although old-fashioned in appearance), when the rest of the dining plate was overhauled and refashioned. A massive cistern with the royal supporters, the lion and unicorn, as handles, made by Thomas Heming for Speaker Cust in 1770, as part of Jewel House issue, can still be seen at Belton House. When Lord Scarsdale was equipping Kedleston in the 1760s he made up two sets of cisterns and fountains, to set in the niche in his Robert Adam-designed dining room: a Parisian fountain of about 1660 with an English copy by Ralph Leake of 1698 and a pair of cisterns, also by Ralph Leake, of 1698. These have now been split up and the French fountain is in the Getty Museum, one cistern in the Victoria and Albert Museum and the other belongs to the Goldsmiths' Company.[28]

Covered cups had always been a staple of the goldsmiths' trade. In the eighteenth century they became fossilised, no longer primarily intended as drinking vessels except on ceremonious occasions. They were the ideal grand gift, worthy to be presented by (or to) a prince, as in the case of the rococo cup and salver which Frederick Prince of Wales gave to the town of Bath to mark his visit there in 1738. This role is clear from their occasional presence in portraits. They might also of course reassume their original function as drinking vessels. Edward Tyng, a New England sea captain, was awarded a handsome two-handled cup by the grateful merchants of Boston after he captured a French privateer in 1744. From this, both then and since referred to as Captain Tyng's Bishop, the gallant Captain drank a mixture of mulled port wine, spices and sugar known as bishop. This was carefully engraved to order; the inscription cartouches is spiked with pikes, muskets, the Union Jack and cannon, all suitably bellicose devices.[29]

Because of its ceremonial function, a cup's ornament normally was formalised. Vines, Bacchic figures, panthers and putti were popular between the 1730s and 1760s. The Prince of Wales's feathers as a finial identified royal gifts, or cups commissioned to mark appointment to his household, as on the gold cup ordered by Colonel Pelham in 1736; cups were also a vehicle to express arrival in society, literally in the case of christening gifts, such as those given by George II and George III.[30]

A simple inverted bell was the standard form for cups from the 1720s into the 1780s, with only slight variations, for example in the flare or elaboration of the handles. Formal cast and applied ornament in the *Régence* style, combined with engraving, enlivened the basic shape until the 1730s. The surface of a George Wickes cup, a duty-dodger of about 1735 with the arms of Scrope, writhes with vine tendrils and reversed scrolls in the rococo taste, but its basic form remains solidly symmetrical. A cup by William Kidney (Goldsmiths' Company, 1740) has a superb cartouche of Bacchus and his donkey on a similar body.

Some cups were clearly *tours de force* in the rococo manner, copies lifted almost directly from designs by Germain and other Parisian goldsmiths. A series by Thomas Heming of the 1750s and 1760s are covered with vines, insects and flowers with Bacchic figures as handles. Heming was clearly proud of the design since it appears on his trade card of about 1765, but it had originated in France and was published by Germain in his *Elements de l'Orfevrerie* in 1748 (Fig. 97).

Such elaborately decorated cups did not lend themselves to the addition of inscriptions or large armorials and these are confined to a very small area indeed, such as the tambourine held by one of the handle figures. This no doubt accounts for the continued popularity of the earlier simple form for sporting prizes; one of 1769, which was twice won by a game cock called Red Spartan in 1770 and 1771, is engraved with an account of the bird's victories and a scene of a cock fight. Race cups too were normally plain; a neo-classical series starting in the 1770s had cast-applied plaques depicting racehorses with perhaps another left blank to engrave the date and name of the winner.[31]

Teaware

The tea equipage took shape fairly rapidly; its main components can be seen in a painting at the Goldsmiths' Hall of a family taking tea in about 1730 (Fig. 34). Other versions are in the Victoria and Albert Museum and the Paul Mellon collection at Yale. They depict a white silver teapot and lamp stand, sugar tongs and a spoon tray, a slop basin, tea canister and covered sugar bowl. One item, a covered jug, remains a query. Its wooden handle indicates that it was for something hot, presumably hot water, since tea was apparently drunk in the Chinese fashion, weak and without milk, by most people until the 1720s, and cream or milk jugs were not normally supplied with the rest of the equipage when a tea service was purchased, according to contemporary bills for plate. A 1729 bill from Charles Gardner for engraving a tea service for the Tollemache family itemised only a teapot, a square waiter, teaspoons and a sugar dish. Small silver jugs or pots for milk or cream are fairly common by about 1730; but Wickes sold only two 'milk boats' and six cream ewers to his account customers in ten years.[32]

In the 1730s and 1740s jugs were occasionally supplied in a boxed equipage with sugar nippers, strainer spoon, teaspoons, two tea knives, canisters and sugar box, as in a set made by De Lamerie in 1735, now at Temple Newsam, Leeds (Fig. 36). Twice Benjamin Mildmay bought a milk jug as a single transaction, in 1734 and 1745, the latter from Eliza Godfrey. Another time his wife bought six teacups and a milk jug 'of white Dresden china' (1744) to use with an existing silver pot. But jugs to match teapots are a later development; some people preferred 'novelty pots' like the heavy cast rococo examples of the 1740s (VAM), or John Schuppe's 'cow creamers' of the 1750s.[33]

Fig. 34 **Family taking tea**
*c.*1730. Note the covered sugar bowl, slop basin, tea canister and teapot on its heater; the wooden handle
of the other jug indicates that it was for hot water (or hot milk).
Goldsmiths' Company

Hogarth's *Marriage à la Mode* shows the cheaper, but still fashionable, alternative of a blue
and white porcelain teapot fitted with a silvergilt spout; Wickes's ledgers show only a dozen
or so teapots in ten years, suggesting a preference for porcelain. The extravagant George
Booth, Earl of Warrington, who lavishly and continuously spent on plate from the 1690s
until his death, left an extremely thorough inventory, prepared in 1750, in which the contents
of the tearoom at Dunham Massey were listed. This demonstrates the elaboration of tea
equipment by the mid-eighteenth century. Each of the four teapots had its waiter and the two
for Bohea had lamp stands, presumably because black tea can stand being kept hot, whereas
green tea tastes bitter if 'stewed'. These were all white silver, as was the 'pot for hot water to
the tea table' but the tea canisters (two of which were among his earliest purchases from Isaac

Fig. 35 **Tea kettle**
1694. Stand *c*.1700. The kettle, for cooking or boiling water, was far older than the rest of the tea service,
which emerged only in the later seventeenth century.
Norwich Castle Museum

Liger half a century before), spoons, strainer spoon, tongs and 'boats to hold the teaspoons' were all gilt (Fig. 81). Larger items such as the 202-ounce tea table made by David Willaume II in 1743 and the waiters 'to give tea on', were kept elsewhere, in the stillhouse.[34]

Waiters or stands to accompany teapots and kettles were customary from an early date, for obvious reasons. Some waiters were round, or facetted to match the teapot; in the 1730s triangles were popular; a handsome kettle and triangular stand of *c*.1735–9 by Kandler is in the VAM, and a magnificent set of tea and coffee wares by Sprimont and others is in the Hermitage. The service has a Chinese theme and the kettle sits on a salver with heads of the four continents around its border and is supported by the blades of a sugar-cane plant. The early 'tea tables' (large salvers) were relatively small and plain, normally either rectangular, with simple canted corners, or polygonal, until the rococo shapes hit London goldsmiths' shops in the 1730s. The tea table, often now described incorrectly as a tray, with its elaborately moulded border, was occasionally made to sit on top of a matching wooden table with edges notched for its feet. Only at Dunham Massey, Booth's home, does this original pairing survive intact, made in 1741 and described as '2 Mahogany stands to set the silver tea and coffee tables on'.[35]

Kettles with lamps were essential aids to elegant tea-making and a relatively large number have survived from 1700 onwards, their preservation due to their continuing usefulness (Fig. 35). Normally purchased at the same time as the smaller teapots, they were engraved with the owner's armorials to match, but few sets remained together. A teapot, chocolate pot and kettle at the Goldsmiths' Company of 1719 was made by Joseph Ward for William Ilbert of Bowringsleigh, Devon who married his second wife Catherine that year. Their arms are engraved on each of the three vessels and on the accompanying octagonal stands. The waiters for the two pots have four ball-shaped feet, as does a tray, with teapot, sugar basin and hot water jug, given by George I as a christening gift in 1721.[36]

Several items of teaware once part of a service belonging to David Franks of Philadelphia, a kettle and lamp, a slop bowl and a bread basket, bear De Lamerie's mark and the 1744 and 1745 date-letters. They have a common theme of putti, tea and coffee plants and flowers, chased on each piece. They were presumably ordered from England, although they might have been a gift from David's brother Naphtali, who was also one of De Lamerie's customers. The wealthiest families also had the convenience of a tall silver kettle stand, like the one of about 1725 (VAM) and another of the year before (Untermyer Collection) which retains its original kettle by Simon Pantin. One remained in use at Holkham until the 1760s.[37]

The 'canisters' (the term caddy is a later eighteenth-century innovation) were normally supplied in pairs, one for green and one for Bohea or black tea and often engraved with G and B to distinguish them. The earliest of the 1690s have simple pull-off caps which apparently doubled up as measures, and a sliding base so that the lead inner lining could be slipped out and refilled. Alternatively sometimes the entire top slides off. But this design was supplemented about 1720 by another, with a hinged lid. The hinges in the best examples are set flush, notably in a set by De Lamerie of 1735 (VAM). From their initial simple angular or facetted form, broken up only with some discreet engraving or flat-chasing, tea canisters broke out in a pot pourri of chasing on round or pear-shaped forms as the rococo taste caught on (Fig. 45). In sets of the 1730s and later they were usually accompanied by a covered sugar basin, sometimes chased to match (VAM; Wallace Collection).

In the tea equipage, strainer spoons were regarded as essential: this is clear both from surviving sets of teaspoons, boxed with a strainer spoon and tongs, or nippers for sugar, and from the goldsmiths' bills, such as that sent by David Willaume to Lady Irwin in 1726, in which he charged in all £3 19s for a gilt and engraved set, plus 3s for a case.[38] In 1759 Joseph Richardson, the Philadelphia goldsmith, ordered '6 dozen of silver tea spoons with tongs and strainer to each half Dozen in Shagreen cases' from his London supplier.[39] But collectors have confused the issue, both by terming the small pierced spoon with a pointed stem terminal a 'mote spoon' (not a term ever used by Georgian goldsmiths) and by debating its purpose. If the pointed stem was to clear blocked tea leaves from the teapot spout, as seems reasonable,

Fig. 36 **Tea equipage**
1735. Mark of De Lamerie. Made for the wedding of Jean Daniel Boissier and Suzanne Judith Berchere
in 1735, whose arms are engraved on the canisters and cream jug. The earliest complete English tea
equipage to be preserved intact, it remained in the Boissier family until 1954. The chasing on the
canisters is quite asymmetrical.
Leeds, Temple Newsam House

Fig. 37 **Chocolate frames**
Gilt with *blanc de Chine* cups 1718. Mark of David Willaume. Note the delicate chasing, alternately trellis
and panelled, characteristic ornament between 1715 and 1730.
British Museum

then the pierced bowl could have been to extract tea from the caddy; no other spoon shape
could pass the narrow necks of early caddies and it is significant that strainers drop out of use
at about the time that caddy spoons became popular. By this date, around 1760, access to the
tea was easier since caddy openings were more generously proportioned and a broad shovel
'tea shell' scoop easily manoeuvred within it. [40]

Tea silver was supplemented in the 1750s by the appearance of the hot water urn which
rapidly supplanted the kettle on stand. Its heating principle depended on a red hot iron rod or
block, sometimes cased in a silver cylinder within the body of the urn and sometimes, as in
urns of the 1760s, set onto the base so that the urn slotted over it. Both methods ensured that
the water surrounding the red hot iron retained a high temperature for a considerable time
without boiling away, a disadvantage of the earlier kettle. Normally these urns had one tap
only, but a handsome one of 1760 in the Courtauld Collection has three feet and three taps. Its
body is embossed overall with foliage encircling the Chinese scenes increasingly popular
from the late 1740s. Another by James Shruder of 1752, also with three taps, is chased with
ships and other marine motifs; his silver was often extremely inventive, not to say bizarre, as
can be seen in a coffee pot made in 1749 for Leake Okeover which has both handle and spout
twisting out of true. The spout is cast as a Triton riding a sea horse and the body is chased with
sea scenes emerging from scrolls (VAM). [41]

Whether chocolate fell out of fashion in the 1730s or whether it was simply served for preference in porcelain, by then available from Dresden, is not clear. George Wickes supplied only two chocolate pots to his ledger customers between 1735 and 1745, compared to the six to sixteen orders for coffee pots each year in that period. When James Boswell went to a coffee house for breakfast in the 1770s he drank chocolate, so that clearly it was still generally available. But chocolate pots are not found in silver after about 1740. This drink had never achieved the general acceptance enjoyed by tea and coffee and its use was largely confined to the wealthy, so it was not inappropriate that it should be drunk from *blanc de Chine* or Dresden porcelain cups set in silver frames on silver saucers. A few have survived, delicately engraved with trellis and shell borders (Fig. 37). The type continued into the 1740s and George Booth had a set of six 'chocolate saucers with frames to hold cups' in his tearoom at Dunham Massey in 1750. These were sent to London in 1821 to be exchanged for 'plate covers for larger dishes' (among other silverware), a neat illustration of how changing eating habits directly influenced the plate cupboard. Wickes supplied the Earl of Kildare, another big spender on plate, with six wooden-lined silver cups 'for tea or chocolate' in 1745.[42]

Another puzzle piece, but from the dining table rather than the tea table, is the small escallop-shaped dish, often on three whelk feet, popular from the late 1730s, although some of the 1670s are known. Several accompany the Augustin Courtauld centrepiece (1741) at the Hermitage, and George Wickes was supplying them in small numbers from the previous year – they are normally used today for butter or chocolates. At this time butter was served semi-liquid in basins and there are no references to knives for butter or 'spades' before about 1760. In the one case in which Wickes qualifies the 'escallop'd shells' he was supplying, he calls them 'oyster' shells. These shells survive in sets of three or so, not enough to allow one per guest. Their presence with a centrepiece suggest that they may have held a sauce or relish.[43]

Silver for Washing and Cosmetics

Toilet silver was, after silver for eating and drinking, the largest category in most collections of plate. For men, a shaving jug, bowl, toothbrush holder and tongue scraper, and soap box was the norm; for women, a complete set of 'dressing plate'. Their components, particularly boxes and jars, are still useful, which means that many are still about, albeit no longer associated with the rest of the set. Complete services may be seen at the Victoria and Albert Museum, the Ashmolean Museum, National Museum of Wales in Cardiff and at Waddesdon, Luton Hoo and Woburn (Fig. 18).[44] The toilet service, the customary gift for a woman at the time of her wedding, comprised up to thirty separate items, from a silver-framed mirror to a pair of candlesticks. The set which Paul De Lamerie supplied for Sir George Treby's wife Charlotte on their wedding in 1724 has survived, along with its bill. This set, 'finely carved all over and chased' cost 6s 2d an ounce for fashion and weighed over 637 ounces. It comprises now a mirror, three caskets, four round caskets, two whisks, two brushes, a ewer, four salvers, a pair of candlesticks with a snuffer and tray, two jars, two canisters and two glass jars, although a ewer and basin was supplied originally.[45]

These components were more or less standardised by 1700, and apart from the enormous contrast in style there is very little difference between the Calverley service of 1683 (VAM) and the Williams-Wynn service of 1768 in the National Museum of Wales. Both have caskets for jewels or gloves, pincushion, pomade bottles, brushes, trays for pins and covered bowls, whose use is disputed. These bowls may have been to hold an oatmeal face wash, a common eighteenth-century cosmetic treatment for both sexes. Certainly each of seven bedrooms at Dunham Massey was equipped with a silver oatmeal plate and an oatmeal box with a lid, along with chamber pots and basins of various sizes, graded for washing hands or mouths.[46]

There was of course another use for oatmeal; a handsome bowl with its accompanying stand (1725) formerly at Althorp was made by De Lamerie in 1723. It has always been described as Lady Georgiana Spencer's porridge bowl and bears the arms of Lady Georgiana who married into the family in 1733. Subsequently this bowl was adopted as a family baptismal basin. It is quite possible that the covered bowl with two handles, like a French écuelle, was regarded originally as a lady's cereal bowl, since in France the écuelle was the customary gift for a woman during her lying-in after childbirth. Queen Charlotte gave one, with an under-dish, to her infant son the Prince of Wales in 1763, identical with those in the Heming toilet service of 1766 which her husband, the king, presented to his sister Caroline Matilda when she married the Danish king Christian IV in that year, which supports the theory that they were sometimes cereal bowls.[47]

None of the surviving toilet sets is unique; although they are now rare (the demand for these lavish sets seems to have declined in the late eighteenth century), goldsmiths were clearly happy to re-use moulds for several customers and on occasion lend them to other members of the trade. Two services by Thomas Heming illustrate the first point; in the one ordered by George III in 1766 for his sister Caroline Matilda, the design of eighteen pieces is identical with those in the set ordered from the same goldsmith by Sir Watkin Williams-Wynn for his wife Henrietta on their marriage in 1768. Earlier in the century, some pieces in the Treby service of 1724, notably the pomade pots, are identical with those in a service with David Willaume's mark of 1725. The retailer often made up the set with other men's wares; a service supplied by Samuel Courtauld for the Empress Elizabeth of Russia in the late 1750s comprised thirty-five pieces; only seven bear Courtauld's mark and at least three other Huguenot goldsmiths had also supplied items. In the Heming services mentioned, Emick Romer made the snuffer trays.[48]

Caroline Matilda's thirty-piece toilet service still retains its original travelling case, so that we can be sure of its completeness. In addition to the jars, bottles, boxes and so on already noted as customary, it has a funnel, presumably for decanting cosmetic washes, and a bell. Curiously in neither of the two Heming services are the candlesticks in the late rococo floral style of the other pieces. Those now in Denmark are clustered columns, a form popular in the mid-seventeenth century, which reappears about 1760 (compare pairs of 1670 and of 1760 by Frederick Kandler, VAM) and those in Wales are straight copies of late Stuart figure sticks (as on Fig. 26) which may indicate a reviving taste for classical forms by this date. They are very different in feeling from the grotesque chinamen on candlesticks of the 1750s.

Boxes and jars from toilet service which find their way onto the market as individual items hint at the existence of many more services than the twenty-five or so still intact. Another late English service, now in Stockholm, was made by Daniel Smith and Robert Sharp in 1779.

Not surprisingly in view of its date and makers, this is markedly neo-classical in design and set with classical medallions after Tassie's gems, including the marriage of Cupid and Psyche. But after this the massive silver toilet service slipped out of fashion, to be replaced by smaller boxed sets for travelling and rather less elaborate dressing table sets. The charming portrait by Zoffany of Queen Charlotte at her dressing table shows almost the latest flourish of the silver toilet service.[49]

Notes

1 Grimwade 1959; Hayward 1975; Hernmarck 1977; Hughes 1957 and Ch. 12.

2 Edwards 1977, introduction. For Tollemache silver sold in 1955, see Trevor 1955.

3 Warwicks RO, Newdegate MSS.

4 For Wickes's customers, see Barr 1980.

5 The *Mercure de France* referred to a silver centrepiece as something quite new in 1692; Hernmarck 1977, 182–5. Thornton 1978, 401, discusses the drawings of French furniture and tableware collected for the Swedish court between 1687 and 1744.

6 Essex RO, Mildmay MSS. A complete epergne of this type was made by David Willaume in 1731. Derived ultimately from a design (for a salt) by Giulio Romano.

7 Hernmarck 1977, pl. 405 and 6.

8 In 1700 sauce boats with 'deux anses et deux becs' were made for Louis XIV, replacing the medieval 'saucers', Hernmarck 1977, 185–6; Buhler 1972, 2–7 and VAM 1984; Wickes supplied ten tureens in 1743, the busiest year of the decade analysed by Elaine Barr.

9 For a complete Kandler set (1751) at Ickworth, Suffolk, see Banister 1980, 792. For nomenclature, see Penzer 1955, 104–5.

10 Snodin 1977; Hayward 1975, pl. 33. Some heavily rococo condiment urns were made by Parker & Wakelin to match their handsome French-style tureens. Ladles were asymmetrical; Pickford 1983, fig. 295.

11 Hatfield 1981, fig. I.

12 The French barrel on foot, introduced about 1710, was popular here well into the 1760s; one is in the Ashmolean. Coleman 1979.

13 Trevor 1955, VAM 1984.

14 Grimwade 1959.

15 Davis 1976, 115–18. cf. a superb De Lamerie pair at Woburn, stolen (but recovered) in 1984. VAM 1984.

16 In the late 1740s a Frenchman commented on the small amount of silver tableware in use here; 'A choice of porcelain, more or less fine according to the taste and fortune of the master, supplies the place of a richer service' but the assay figures, and inventories, show that he was misled. Porcelain as a novelty was popular but had not the lasting investment value of silver.

17 Sir Edward Bagot had five dish rings in 1709; George Wickes was selling them in the 1740s and one of 1771 is at Williamsburg: Davis 1976, 164. A dragon-footed one by Kandler (Metropolitan Museum *c.*1735–9) perhaps paired dragon-handled sauce boats, for example VAM 1984.

18 At Althorp is a De Lamerie salt (1731) with lion mask feet. Rococo salts could be wildly fanciful, for example a mermaid and shell at Williamstown; Carver & Casey and VAM 1984.

19 Pickford 1983, 19. The new profile occurs as 'Turned back teaspoons' in Wakelin & Taylor's ledgers, 28 March 1760.

20 For fish slices, see Davis 1976, 189 and 190. Silver serving trowels were familiar in Germany and Scandinavia by 1730. On forks, see p. 65, 113.

21 Goldsmiths' 1983 includes a funnel and syphon, cork screws, bottle tickets and other drinker's silver. Davis 1976; Penzer 1947; Stancliffe 1986.

22 An equally plain example (Wickes 1726) see Davis 1976, 47.

23 Goldsmiths' 1983, 22.

24 A pair of about 1690 is in Hackenbroch 1969, 78.

25 Hackenbroch 1969, 125; Tait 1972; VAM 1984. As sideboard display plate, they were not replaced with the rest of the service; the unity lay in all being gilt, with a mixture of periods and styles.

26   Penzer 1957, 39–46. Another, at Belvoir Castle, cost £616 10s in 1682. A set from Althorp by Harache is shown in Hernmarck 1977, pl. 285.

27   Goldsmiths' 1978; Hernmarck 1977, pl. 284; Webster 1984.

28   Hatfield 1981, fig. 27; Wilson 1984.

29   Ward and Ward 1979. Mugs for ale were the drinking vessels in daily use.

30   Hayward 1969; the cup ordered for Bath also bore the Prince of Wales's feathers.

31   Young 1982; Ward and Ward 1979.

32   Penzer 1956; Tollemache MSS; information from Elaine Barr. See Museum of London 1982; Davis 1976; Hackenbroch 1969; Tait 1972 for tea silver.

33   For cream jugs, see Wark 1978; Davis 1976; Hughes 1956.

34   Dunham Massey MSS, Booth plate inventory 1750; photocopy VAM Metalwork Archives.

35   Ibid.

36   Goldsmiths' 1978, no. 82. The earliest English kettle (1694) is in the Castle Museum, Norwich. In 1709 Lady Bagot had a 'kitchin Wth 2 covers 1 chimney 1 stand 1 grate 1 table belonging to it', a fully-equipped chafing dish which could double as a kettle stand and heater.

37   McNab Dennis 1967; Hackenbroch 1969, no. 138. This was ordered for the marriage of George Bowes and Eleanor Verney.

38   Canisters could be boxed up with spoons, tongs and strainer spoon as in a set of c.1750: Pickford 1983, fig. 304.

39   Leeds RO, Temple Newsam MSS; Fales 1974, picture-back teaspoons were popular by 1740; Davis 1976, 177 and Pickford 1983, 210–12. Tongs replaced nippers for sugar in the 1770s: Pickford 1983, 194–6 and fig. 352.

40   Pickford 1983, 202–3.

41   For the Courtauld urn, see Hayward 1975, pl. 28. VAM 1984.

42   Tait 1972. Another pair is in the Philadelphia Museum of Art.

43   They might have held minced oysters but a sauce or dressing is more likely. A set of c.1675 is on loan to the Royal Scottish Museum.

44   Two incomplete filigree sets of about 1690 are at Burghley, plus a beautifully engraved third: Webster 1984. They were produced to standard designs across Northern Europe: Hayward 1970s.

45   Quoted in Phillips 1935. Services in France and Germany included breakfast pots and lamps too. A set of dressing plate regilt for the Earl of Egremont by William Cripps in 1762 included pairs of chocolate cups and stands. The 39 items weighed 423 ounces altogether.

46   Booth inventory 1750.

47   Grimwade 1974, pl. 1: Zahle 1960.

48   Grimwade 1970, introduction.

49   Hernmarck 1977, pl. 728.

FIVE

MID-GEORGIAN TO REGENCY

T HE 1760s saw a new phase for English silver, one in which innovations in both technology and design combined to produce a fresh product, appealing to new markets. Three factors – silverplating, neo-classicism and competition from new centres – combined to bring about this transformation. Because both more trade records and immeasurably more silver has survived from the later eighteenth century onwards, and because the shapes are familiar and in many cases still in production, we are no longer reliant upon contemporary documents to provide us with their names or functions.[1]

Curiously this plethora of both information and objects makes it harder to see patterns of spending and to distinguish the taste of social groups one from another. We know far more about the silver of the Prince Regent and the English nobility than about the preferences of the bourgeoisie, but broadly speaking mass production methods meant that all prosperous English customers enjoyed a certain uniformity in their silver, while at the upper reaches of fashionable wealthy society, the massive and intricately designed dinner service, wholly of sterling silver, apparently declined in popularity until 1800 or so. Then the great prosperity of agriculture, stimulated by the demands of the French Wars, stimulated a renewed demand. The duty payable from 1784, doubled in 1797 and increased again after 1800, stimulated the goldsmiths into cutting cost by cutting weight. By the 1830s it was quite possible for a miller's wife to own a silver teapot and spoons, bought from her earnings before her marriage, although as poor Mrs Tulliver discovered, nobody wanted her old fashioned silver teapot with its straight spout, when she fell on hard times. Fashion was the prime consideration rather than the value of the metal.

Innovations in metalworking techniques were characteristic of nineteenth-century industrial England; the earliest significant advance for the silver trade, setting aside the French mouldmaking and casting methods familiarised by Huguenot goldsmiths, was the flatting or rolling mill. First evolved in the 1720s, it rapidly became an essential craft tool for the working goldsmith, eliminating the slow and laborious process of beating out ingot silver into plate and ensuring a uniform surface which could then be raised or turned on a lathe, as the form of the finished article dictated.[2]

Quite apart from its dramatic effect on the cost of production, and so the selling price, of simple items, this invention was crucial to the spread of that other major technical advance of about 1740, the fusing of copper between two thicknesses of silver. This process created a sandwich capable of being worked as though it were silver, but at a much lower price (about one-fifth in the 1770s), given the reduced proportion of the more expensive metal.

Die-stamping was widely adopted about 1735, initially for picture-back spoons and lightweight boxes but with the arrival of harder steel made by the crucible method, dies improved and the technique was extended in the 1760s to components for larger wares, such as candlesticks and sweetmeat baskets; dies could be used equally well with silver as with silverplate, so that similar patterns could be common to several social groups.[3]

As neo-classical motifs such as guilloche, egg and dart and acanthus became popular, so the die-makers supplied variants which could be assembled in pleasing and diverse combinations to satisfy current demand and the retailer's claim to have plate 'of the newest fashion'. The steel dies produced effective relief ornament in thin sheet silver which was then, in the case of candlesticks, soldered up, filled with resin and the base loaded to give the whole stability. Sheffield-made sticks became highly competitive and London retailers, like John Carter, bought-in stock and overstamped the Sheffield maker's mark, even sending some wares to the London Hall for overstriking.

Fig. 38 **David Garrick's teapot**
1774. Mark of James Young and Orlando Jackson. From a seven-piece set supplied to the actor, probably for his new house in the Albany. Note the fashionable striped effect; the flutes are alternately burnished and matted.
VAM

103

With these technical innovations, Birmingham-made 'toys' or small fancy goods became cheap enough to supplant in popular taste the flimsy and crudely wrought silver so long supplied by London wholesalers to travelling chapmen. It was estimated that in 1750 Birmingham exported £500,000 worth of 'toys' a year. Although dies were expensive, the amount of metal used was rather less than by the traditional methods of raising from sheet, and designs for nutmeg graters, buttons, chatelains and other small silverware could be produced in hundreds of variations for a mass market.

In the next generation Edward Thomason made his fortune from these small wares, while at the same time dealing with aristocratic commissions costing hundreds of pounds and they are popular with collectors today, as are small toilet wares – bottles, toothbrushes and the contents of *étuis*.[4]

One characteristic of neo-classical silver was selective treatment of the surface to alternate burnished with matt or frosted strips, in imitation of Greek ceramic models. The tea/coffee service supplied for David Garrick in 1774 (VAM) is a handsome example of this technique; this may be compared with a 'strip'd silver sugar Bason and Milk Pail 2 colours and Snake handles' weighing nineteen ounces and costing £12 12s supplied by John Kentish of 18, Cornhill in 1777. These were presumably pierced since he supplied two blue glasses (5s) and a beaded milk ladle (16s) as well.

The stress on regular polite social intercourse – tea drinking in mixed company rather than all-male drinking sessions – and on correct usage meant that a new urban mass market for table and teaware emerged, to the benefit of the silversmith.

Extension of the Assay, 1777

In April 1777 the Goldsmiths' Company set out a revised list of rates to be charged for assay (from ½d to 2d per article), partly to recompense for the recent cost of building a new assay office and partly in belated recognition of 'various new invented articles of small plate' which had previously been assayed 'and inadequate sums taken for the same'.

This list of sixty-three categories of silverware is interesting as evidence that all these items were regularly passing through the assay office in large quantities. They were considered new by the Company only because they had become fashionable since the 1739 Hallmarking Act, an indication of that massive increase in middle-class consumption of silverware. The argyle, for instance, the mustard can, the bottle stand, the fish knife or the small wire basket were all now in common use; so were four different vessels for milk, the ewer, boat, pail (first mentioned as a novelty by Mrs Lybbe Powis in 1752) and inevitably, that novelty associated with John Schuppe, the cow, all innovations of the past thirty or forty years.[5]

Individual aristocratic orders did not justify a change in assay office prices; this was solely due to the pressure of great quantities of small machine-made silver arriving for assay. Another category, 'Pieces to garnish Cabinets or Knife Cases', was the characteristic silver trims found on boxes throughout the period 1730–90; they are far more often found unmarked, or struck with the maker's mark only, than fully marked, even after this date.

This list did not of course exhaust the small novel silver wares available from London shops; in the following month, May 1777, the wardens carried out one of their periodic fishing expeditions, buying gold and silver articles from shops in the City and Westminster to check on their silver standard and their marks. The list of offending silver adds several fresh categories – cases for pencils and for toothpicks, a 'Muffinger, two Mustard Tips and Covers, two Scissor Sheaths', each small but a reminder of the ubiquitous nature of silver as the most convenient, attractive and easily worked material for both tableware and small accessories.

The Company enforced its policy; five months later William Brockwell was fined 40s at the City Quarter Sessions and imprisoned in the Wood Street Compter for a week 'for a fraud in making teatrays worse than standard'.

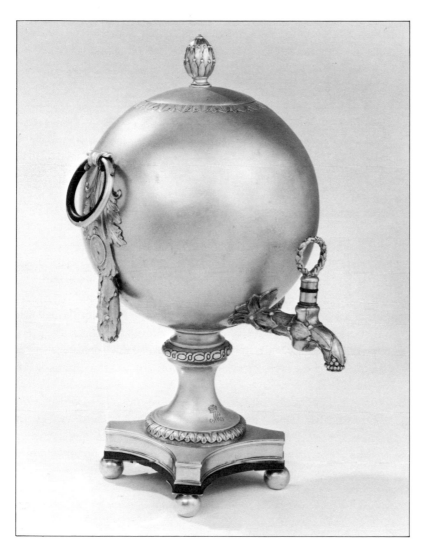

Fig. 39 **Tea urn**
Gilt 1773. Mark of Thomas Heming. H.31.5 cm. Engraved with Viscount's coronet.
Christie's

Among the innovations of the last quarter of the century were jacketed teapots, intended, like the argyle, to keep liquid hot for longer, eggboilers, and patent oil lamps.

Technical ingenuity was found in some special orders too; an urn by Thomas Heming (Cooper-Hewitt Museum, 1777) is designed as a figure of Atlas holding up the globe, its sphere set with four roundels chased with allegorical figures (the continents). Because a tap would detract from the unity of the whole, access to it is concealed behind a hinged medallion. When a key is inserted, water flows from a hanging garland into the pot below. Another tea-making device, or 'machine' popular about 1790 consisted of three globular urns on a frame, the central one for hot water, those flanking for tea and coffee; this design was executed on both silver and plate.

Competition from Birmingham and Sheffield

The long-running campaign, orchestrated by Matthew Boulton from 1766 until 1773, to establish a new provincial assay office at Birmingham, was not initially justified by the size of his orders for hallmarking. His first batch, sent in on 31 August 1773, comprised buckle-rims, spoons, tea vases and other small goods and weighed 841 ounces, perhaps a deliberately cautious testing of the new local assay arrangements for which he had pressed so hard.[6]

In 1779 the Birmingham assay office handled a peak of 61,000 ounces but this was still relatively small, given the number of manufacturing businesses sending wares to the Birmingham office; Sheffield reached its peak, 49,000 ounces, in 1776. Indeed, in London one of Parker and Wakelin's many suppliers, Sebastian and James Crespell, made up in 1778–9 more than 20,000 ounces of bullion, an indication of the overwhelming predominance of the London trade.[7]

Boulton's career as a silver manufacturer is interesting not so much for the quantity but the quality of his production. His inventiveness, in both design and manufacturing techniques, stirred the London firms into competition. He firmly resisted the Adam brothers' offer of a permanent London showroom in the Adelphi, fearing that the time and distance separating it from his Soho (Birmingham) manufactory would only lead to dissatisfaction among his London customers, apart from the danger of trade piracy.

Boulton was justified in fearing that his designs would be plagiarised by other less inventive manufacturers. In 1778 Patrick Robertson, one of two Edinburgh silversmiths whom Boulton and Fothergill were supplying with goods (largely plated wares, but some silver) from 1771, lifted for a tea urn elements peculiar to James Wyatt's designs for Soho, such as an in-curved base, guilloche moulding and fluted stem.[8]

Whether Robertson copied these details from his Soho wares or whether he noted details of Boulton's current production while on a visit to the manufactory in 1774 is not clear, but this unprincipled copying of fashionable motifs was so regular a practice that Boulton banned London goldsmiths from his exhibitions, inviting only the fashionable world. Certainly Boulton's self-publicising enhanced the general awareness of Soho's products. When Lady Beauchamp Proctor visited Holkham in 1772, she commented on 'a most elegant little

Birmingham vehicle to hold the rusks'. She made the footman tell her where it was bought, as she was determined to get one for herself.[9]

The problems associated with supplying luxury goods drove Boulton increasingly to concentrate on smaller mass produced items and plated wares. One case history analysed by Quickenden demonstrates vividly all the difficulties – both technical and financial – Boulton encountered in dealing with special commissions.[10]

In 1772 James Wyatt designed for Sir Robert Rich that fashionable piece of tableware, a silvergilt epergne or centrepiece with cutglass bowls (Fig. 100). He drew in the client during

Fig. 40 **Candlesticks**
1774. Mark of Matthew Boulton and John Fothergill. H.29.7 cm. Modified (from a design by James Wyatt) for large-scale production; the guilloche base (with another corner detail) was adopted for cups and perfume burners by Boulton.
Birmingham Assay Office

the creation of the design, which took some time to settle, although it is hard now to see how the finished object (hallmarked 1774; with Garrards in 1984) differed fundamentally from other neo-classical epergnes. But it was an application of Wyatt's characteristic etiolated and elegant forms.

The difficulties Boulton met in carrying out this order, from August 1772 when he was awaiting a final design, to December 1776 when Sir Robert finally agreed to settle his bill, and the eventual dissatisfaction of both manufacturer and client, demonstrates why Boulton turned his attention away from the special commission business to mass production and cheaper techniques. Constant letters between the partners Boulton and Fothergill and their London agent, the necessity to carry the epergne down to London for their client's approval before bringing it back for gilding and further alterations and additions, plus repairs subsequently ('Sir Robert was enraged at the many imperfections he finds in the epergne') made this a thoroughly unsatisfactory order.

The culmination was that Boulton and Fothergill had to accept a reduction in their price, negotiated by James Wyatt, since Sir Robert argued that a London firm could have produced it more cheaply. The fashion charge, at 5s 6d the ounce, was not unreasonable given that the design was an untried one, but one of Boulton's selling points was his constantly repeated claim to work more cheaply than the London trade. In June 1773 he wrote to Robert Udney Esq. about a coffee pot, to be made 'with Lamp and Hand supported by three Sphynzes, to a drawing we then had the honour of shewing you'; 'We shall only reckon you 3/– per ounce fashion although we are almost sure that no silversmith in the Kingdom would undertake to make such work as that under Double'.[11]

It was disingenuous of Boulton to argue, in a letter to Sir Robert Rich, that he had had to pay interest for two years on the value of the metal locked up in his epergne, but interesting as evidence that because he was both a newcomer to the silvermaking business, and operated at some distance from London, his clients did not necessarily treat him in the time-honoured way, by entrusting to him their old silver to melt, but left him to take the risk and expense of making the object before they paid.

The investment of both time and money required for special orders far outweighed the possible profit. Significantly, Boulton and Fothergill submitted only five epergnes in all to the Birmingham assay office, when one large London house, Wakelin & Tayler, supplied nineteen to their account customers in 1773–6. His smaller wares are crisply detailed but economically made, using wirework for lightness and economy, and die-stamped ornament, as on a sweetmeat basket in the Birmingham assay office collection of 1774. Boulton described himself as 'humbly copying . . . the most refined Grecian artists . . . and making new combinations of old ornaments without presuming to invent new ones'. This was not of course an accurate description of his products, and his 'Birmingham novelties' were eagerly sought after, and imitated by, the London trade. This problem of trade piracy was a constant irritation to Boulton. The private views of his new productions were ticket-only affairs, partly to exclude those potential copyists, 'all the dirty journeymen chasers, silversmiths etc.', and so enhance their appeal to his potential customers from the fashionable world.

This problem of copying was recognised generally by the trade; in a petition sent by Sheffield and Birmingham silversmiths in the campaign for their new assay offices, they

Fig. 41 **The Warwick vase**
Birmingham 1827. Mark of M. Boulton & Plate Co. H. 46.5 cm. Presented to John Foster of Brickhill,
Bedford by the Central Agricultural Society. The Warwick vase, found in fragments in 1770, was a
popular model for both silver and ceramics once reconstructed. For half a century at least after Piranesi's
publication (1774) tureens, ice buckets and centrepieces and prize cups, were all modelled after it. Note
the London retailer's name and address.
Birmingham Assay Office

argued that sending their goods to London for marking was commercially disastrous, 'the disclosure to rivals of inventions before the sale hath proved a sufficient reward to them'.

The assessment made of Boulton in 1809 as 'the first and the only one whoever made compleat service of silverplate, silver spoons and other large articles' gives probably a fair idea of his contribution to the history of English silver. Apart from stimulating his trade rivals, by supplying the London silversmiths, such as Brasbridge, with inexpensive and fashionable articles, he encouraged a taste for tableware and enabled his potential customers to emulate one another.

Plate versus Silver

. . . equal in everything but durability and intrinsic value to silver.

(Hirst MSS)

An early reference to Sheffield plate occurs in a letter written by Horace Walpole in 1760. He bought a pair of plated candlesticks in Sheffield for two guineas; 'they are quite pretty'. However, in 1774 he advised his friend Mann against 'Birmingham cover for dishes . . . All plated silver wears abominably and turns to brass like the age'; Mann persisted in his wish to investigate the 'propriety and duration' of his 'doubled plate' covers. Their appeal was twofold; they could not be distinguished from and for such a use would be as lasting as silver but their cheapness was the real attraction.[12]

Walpole encouraged Matthew Boulton by showing him the treasures of Strawberry Hill as potential design sources and, despite his doubts, the English upper classes gave a warm welcome to silverplate, especially for domestic objects in heavy use such as candlesticks and dish covers. It was not quite unfamiliar. Plating on iron had long been practised, particularly for fire furniture, and already in the 1750s John Legrix advertised that he made and sold the newest kinds of 'French-Plate'.

Successive masters of the Painter-Stainers' Company in the 1780s gave sets of candelabra, one pair plated and one solid silver, with no thought of the former being an unworthy gift.

In almost every page of Boulton's letterbook, the commercial appeal of plated wares, both to the trade and to the private customer, shines through. A letter to John Alston, the Edinburgh retailer, of 27 March 1773 refers to plated bread trays and bread baskets (at £4 4s a piece and 20 per cent discount), plated candle branches and nozzles 'to slip upon a square mahogany pillar', a travelling case and candlesticks. The only silver mentioned is a 'Teakitchen' or urn; these cost from £25 minimum, an indication of the price differential between the two materials.[13]

In London shops, plated wares were sold side by side with silver. Because the same dies could be used for both, many designs were identical and customers wishing to copy their friends' tableware had to check with the appropriate retailer as to material. Joseph Brasbridge, the late Georgian and Regency silversmith, described with glee how a trade rival and neighbour was caught when asked by Mrs Reboe 'for some silver corner dishes, which she wished to have like a set of Mrs. Hanson's, who had been supplied with them by me'. The shopman did not even know whether they had been silver or plated. Since 'she would have hers exactly the same as Mrs. Hanson's whatever they might be', she came at last to Brasbridge's shop next door.[14]

110

The design and finish of plated wares was virtually indistinguishable from those in solid silver. As the London trade complained in 1797, when the threat of an increase in the silver duty was growing, they felt the competition from these cheaper products very keenly; the plated manufacturers 'have been enabled to produce articles of the highest elegance and fashion, many of which are now made with solid silver – borders, shields and ornaments, finished in exact resemblance of real plate and which do cause injury . . . by curtailing the sale of wrought plate'.[15]

The struggle for customers was intense and the London manufacturers of wrought plate proposed that a duty of 6d an ounce be payable 'on all plated goods that have silver edges, bands, shields or any other parts of silver either for use or ornament'. This duty was not in fact extended to plated goods, nor was another request complied with, that the Sheffield makers of plated wares mark their wares and that a hall specially for plated wares be set up, to stamp each piece 'Plated' and with the arms of Sheffield. But their lobby was not strong enough to draw plated wares within the duty net.

The solid silver edges so objected to by the Londoners were introduced by Samuel Roberts and Cadman in Sheffield about 1785, to prevent copper grinning through at the point of hardest wear. Samuel Roberts is also credited with evolving a method of rubbing in a solid silver escutcheon, so that the gentry's demand for engraved armorials could be satisfied without the problem of the engraver's burin exposing the copper underneath.[16]

The platers identified their wares so closely with those of the traditional silvershops that in Sheffield, at least, they adopted marks like those of silversmiths. The shortlived Association of Silver Platers (1773–84) also attempted to control the trade by setting minimum discounts and selling prices, but less than a fifth of the platers known bothered to register a mark.

The thickness of the silver layer was undoubtedly reduced from Boulton's early years, to cut costs. Robert Hirst, in his account of the Sheffield plate trade written about 1829, commented that the plate 'was capable of being increased to any proportion, from 5 penny weights of silver to the Pound of Copper, to 16 ounces to the pound' and Brasbridge commented sourly on those unscrupulous manufacturers who so reduced the silver layer (so as to undercut their rivals) as to produce an inferior product and so undermine everyone's reputation for honest dealing. Other alternatives to Sheffield plate, such as silverplated Britannia metal, were popular from the 1830s.

From 1770 London retailers carried plated wares as a matter of course. In the 1790s John Bright ran a warehouse for Sheffield plated goods in Bruton Street, Berkeley Square, close to the fashionable world, selling epergnes with hanging baskets, hot water plates and tea equipages. In 1806 John Thomas of S. James Street advertised on his trade card that he 'Keeps an extensive variety of Best Plated Goods with Silver Edges'.

Silver in the Dining Room

Between about 1750 and 1790 gilding seems to have fallen from favour temporarily, except for sideboard plate. Often these ewers, basins and covered cups were older than the rest of the dining room plate, protected from heavy wear by their display status. At Holkham in 1760 the Earl of Leicester had 758 ounces of gilt plate, all for sideboard and dessert use except a standish, but over 9,000 ounces of white.

Fig. 42 **Pair of sauce tureens**
1769. Mark of Thomas Heming. Length of tureen 16.5 cm. Heming's familiarity with current French
design, so evident in much of his 1760s output, is apparent in these neoclassical tureens with their rams'
heads, ribbons and laurel wreaths.
Kenneth Davis

The English passion for displaying plate at meal times attracted surprised comments from
French visitors, who thought it barbarous. Both Rouquet, in 1747, and Moreau de
Saint-Mery nearly fifty years later, noted 'before dinner and all during dinner, as is the
English custom, all the silver one owns is displayed on the sideboard'. The Ironmongers'
Company were continuing this ancient tradition in 1783–4 when they accepted as the retiring
master's gift a set of three neo-classical (but gilt) ewers and basins. [17]

No doubt it was the current taste for heavy French gilt plate which stimulated a renewed
appetite for gilding about 1800. Several French émigrés brought or sent silver over to London
for sale after 1790 and services by the Paris goldsmiths Odiot and Auguste in a heavy
'Egyptian' classical style were available as models. The best documented is the service by
Henri Auguste (1778–9) of which part was sold by the Neapolitan ambassador on his
departure from England about 1801 and copied by Rundell's in 1803 and 1806 for the king and
for the Duke of York. [18] Another Auguste service (1776–85; sold by Sotheby's, Monaco
1979) described as having the royal cypher of George III seems never to have been in England;
it was apparently made for the king's use in Hanover, at Herrenhausen.

By the 1760s mahogany knife boxes were part of the dining room furniture, and were regularly displayed open on the sideboard, often with a full complement of table spoons arranged to show the decorative die-stamped bowls; London retailers often depicted these boxes on their trade cards. At Kedleston and Kenwood, according to Adam's sketch designs, sideboard dishes were to perch within the open boxlids.[19]

Several different patterns for forks and spoons became available, in addition to the basic Hanoverian popular since about 1710; old English was the first, in which the ends of handles turned up rather than down. Spoons were laid out bowl upwards and forks also differed in that they now had four tines; in 1773 Parker and Wakelin both altered spoon handles and supplied four-tine forks to many customers. Variations on cutlery border designs included thread, a continuous line following the outline, called in a bill of 1787 'double threaded each side', featheredge and bright-cut from about 1780. Dessert cutlery was lighter than the main course items and normally gilt, as were salts (inside at least), and their spoons, although glass liners were widely used – particularly once openwork designs became popular in the 1760s with the general availability of Bristol blue glass. Serving utensils for fish, asparagus and cheese became increasingly popular, and their manufacture more compartmentalised, so that a fish slice, for example, may have its blade marked by one of the Batemans and its handle by another specialist maker.[20]

Although aristocratic families had apparently been adopting silver table forks since the 1660s, the custom was slow to spread to the bourgeoisie, or at least to institutions. Although the Goldsmiths' Company was given three dozen in 1692–3, these were sent to the melt in 1711, to buy lottery tickets, and were not replaced and the Drapers' Company acquired their first six dozen silverhafted knives and forks only in 1782.[21]

About twenty years later Joseph Brasbridge, a City silversmith, expressed embarrassment when asked to dine 'at a fashionable hotel where the cloth was laid with a profusion of plate'. Taking up one of the silver forks, he explained to his host, Francis Eyre of Warkworth Castle, 'I know how to sell these articles but not how to use them'. Brasbridge sang the praises of that cheaper alternative, closeplating, as being more durable than silver; he had been using a set of silverplated forks for forty years and quoted the Duke of Argyll in support of their practicality. It is probable that many customers followed this course and saved the cost and temptation of the metal locked up in solid silver cutlery. As London retailers recommended in the 1830s, plated cutlery was ideal for the new hotels and other public eating places whose customers expected the sensation of eating with silver rather than steel or iron: 'to all those who are liable to be plundered of their plate, it will prove of great advantage'.[22]

Despite competition from porcelain and later from glass, the silver epergne or centrepiece flourished well into the nineteenth century. Its design reached its highest degree of fantasy and elaboration in the 1760s when one popular version incorporated a double pagoda hung with silver bells and surmounted by a pineapple. This Chinese theme, presumably echoed in the table candlesticks and certainly found too in the cast borders of salvers and bread baskets, was abandoned for the epergne's scroll branches and floral openwork base. These were made up of cast elements lifted from carvers' pattern books, like Matthias Lock's *Six Tables* (1746) and Lock and Copland *A New Book of Ornament* (1752), both frequently reprinted in the twenty years following.[23]

Although epergnes to this design are found with the mark of Thomas Heming, Whyte & Holmes and occasionally other goldsmiths, it seems to have been the speciality of Thomas Pitts. His successors, Pitts & Preedy, continued to supply epergnes to Wakelin & Taylor and their successor in trade, Robert Garrard, after 1800. One, or a pair, of epergnes was set out in a drawing room for dessert, to be enjoyed as a separate entertainment, although by the 1780s this long-standing custom was giving way to the more familiar modern formula, where guests remain seated at the table for dessert. Inevitably their design was influenced by this change, as much as by the fashion for lower, simpler table settings. A single long boat-shaped basket was sometimes set on a low stand; a set of a large 'chased epergne bason and table', and smaller baskets to match, was supplied by Wakelin & Tayler to the Earl of Chesterfield in 1792. These wide baskets have no subsidiary candle branches. A version of this design had been made as early as 1778, for George, second Baron Rodney.[24]

A somewhat cheaper alternative was the silver frame supporting cutglass bowls, popular from the late 1760s with the switch to neo-classical lightness; the Hennell family specialised in these (as in salts and cruets which combine glass and silver) and made effective use of bright-cutting as an economical form of ornament. Considerably cheaper were the baskets made from silverwire, sometimes with die-stamped leaves and other naturalistic motifs applied; components for these were sold from Boulton's London warehouse to the trade and the Batemans are only one well-known firm of silversmiths who assembled them for retail.[25]

Baskets from epergnes are frequently found for sale; it is probable that the epergne frame to which they belonged has been melted, since before the last war there was very little demand for them. A page from Matthew Boulton's pattern book (rearranged by Elkington's) shows eight basket variations but these were, like so much early neo-classical silver, very flimsy and not many have survived. Its practicality was reduced with its weight; Sir Robert Rich was probably not alone in demanding that the stability of the branches on his Boulton-made epergne be increased by adding two extra metal pegs at the point where the branch socketed into the frame.[26]

Within a decade of Lord Chesterfield's boat-shaped basket, a new shape emerged for the epergne, which is recognisably the forerunner of the popular nineteenth-century dessert stand. A classical figure, or a group of figures, supports a central basket, perhaps of cutglass resting in an openwork frame. Sets of these stands, often gilt, and with a larger central one flanked by a series of smaller matching versions, were set out on mirror plateaux. A dining table at Woburn is laid with a plateau and one made for the Earl of Belmore in 1810 is in the Al-Tajir Collection. A popular design, associated particularly with Paul Storr, it stands for many people as the archetype Regency object. When dressed with fruit and flowers, the effect must have been extremely rich, as visitors to Brighton Pavilion may bear witness (Fig.113).[27]

The silver plateau was originally a French refinement. It had its antecedents in the mid-seventeenth century, when pastry cooks published designs for temporary dessert sculptures built up on sheets of glass, gilt paper and pasteboard. These evolved into the 'tables' or large salvers which supported the centrepieces of the 1740s and 1750s; the Sprimont centrepiece (VAM) is an example. From 1770 this platform was often set with a sheet of glass; the taste for silver plateaux was partly a matter of fashion and partly in the interests of 'elegant economy'. Instead of filling the centre of the dining table 'with dishes of meat, which are

Fig. 43 **Marine salts**
Gilt 1820. Britannia standard. Mark of Edward Farrell. H.16.5 cm. From a set of eight with mermaid
spoons (1817, also Farrell). An example of rococo revival, these salts are cast, chased and textured; note
the sandy shell-strewn bases.
Burghley House, Stamford.

seldom or never touched', it was ornamented with 'a set of those waiters, salvers or whatever
they are called'. When President Washington needed a set in 1789, his agent Tobias Lear
ordered it from France; at that time there were only a handful of plateaux in use in the United
States.[28]

In England mirror plateaux flourished and became standard in the prosperous decades after
1800, at least in the grandest homes. Several are known to have a common design and bear the
mark of Paul Storr, presumably ordered through Rundell, Bridge & Rundell. In 1818
Edward Thomason of Birmingham supplied an elaborately gothic plateau to the Duke of
Northumberland. Its sides were cast as a frieze of lancet windows and the gallery was made in
the form of a pierced cresting; the Duchess was credited with this individual design which
was intended to harmonise with the dining room designed for Alnwick Castle in the 1760s by
Robert Adam 'in the Gayest and most elegant Style of Gothick architecture'.[29]

There is a marked contrast between dining silver of the late eighteenth and the early nineteenth century. Far more survives from just after 1800: this is not chance but attributable partly to the money flowing into the hands of landowners under the stimulus of a war economy. Also the sheer weight and size of the vessels fashionable during the Regency soaked up quantities of old plate.

The inventory of the plate at Holkham in 1760 makes the point quite clearly. The heaviest individual item was not for the dining room at all but a 'chased high stand for a Teakettle' (a piece of furniture already out of date). This, with its accompanying chased kettle and lamp, weighed over 400 ounces whereas the largest tureen (of 3) was a mere 169 ounces. The chased epergne was equally modest in size, at 150 ounces. This forerunner of the table centrepiece may be contrasted with that Regency standard, a Paul Storr plateau made in 1810 for the second Earl of Belmore; this, with its three dessert stands, weighed 536 ounces.[30]

The gilt dinner service, massive in both design and size, was a characteristic feature of Regency life. Rundell, Bridge & Rundell were responsible for three important royal services; the first, made in 1803–4, was given by the Jamaica Assembly to the Duke of Clarence, the second, the Egyptian service, was made for the Prince Regent, also in 1803–4 and the third, the Grand service, although initiated in that decade, was still growing twenty years later.[31]

The Duke of Wellington, as national hero, inevitably attracted presentations of plate; indeed the testimonial service was a characteristic mark of public esteem until the late nineteenth century. The gilt service presented to him by the army of the Deccan, and made between 1805 and 1807 by a combination of William Fountain, Joseph Preedy, John More and John Edwards (Fig. 101) may be seen at Apsley House, with a service presented by the Portuguese government, while more of his plate is displayed at Stratfield Saye.

The service he was issued with as Ambassador to Paris in 1814 contained 650 pieces. Although supplied by Rundell, Bridge & Rundell, at least six firms were involved in making up this order. Robert Garrard supplied flatware, Hennell and Pitts the dessert stands, William Fountain and Benjamin Eley Fearn and Chawner also flatware, Smith dishes, ice-pails and baskets. Paul Storr's contribution alone was 102 items, which weighed over 1,770 ounces, and may be compared with the Leinster service of 1745–7. Originally containing 240 items, this now consists of 170 pieces, weighing 5,216 ounces. The sheer bulk of these Regency orders is staggering, quite apart from their intricate designs and superb craftsmanship; some excellent examples, acquired within the past decade or so, are in the Al-Tajir Collection.

A service typically now contained a set of ice-pails as a matter of course (earlier many families had not troubled to replace their pails when refashioning the rest of the service, hence the existence of several *Régence* sets made for members of the English aristocracy in the 1720s, and the lack of later eighteenth-century examples), tureens in various sizes, dessert stands and massive candelabra, sometimes with the alternative of a central basket, plus sets of sauce boats, cruet frames, salts, mustard pots and the necessary ladles, tongs for fish or asparagus and serving spoons, running to several hundred items in all.[32]

The enormous weight of bullion locked up in these Regency services is almost certainly the explanation for their virtual disappearance in the preceding half century. They were simply melted down. A handful survive; inevitably, perhaps, the remnants of those ordered from Thomas Heming by Catherine the Great for three of her provincial governors in 1774–6.

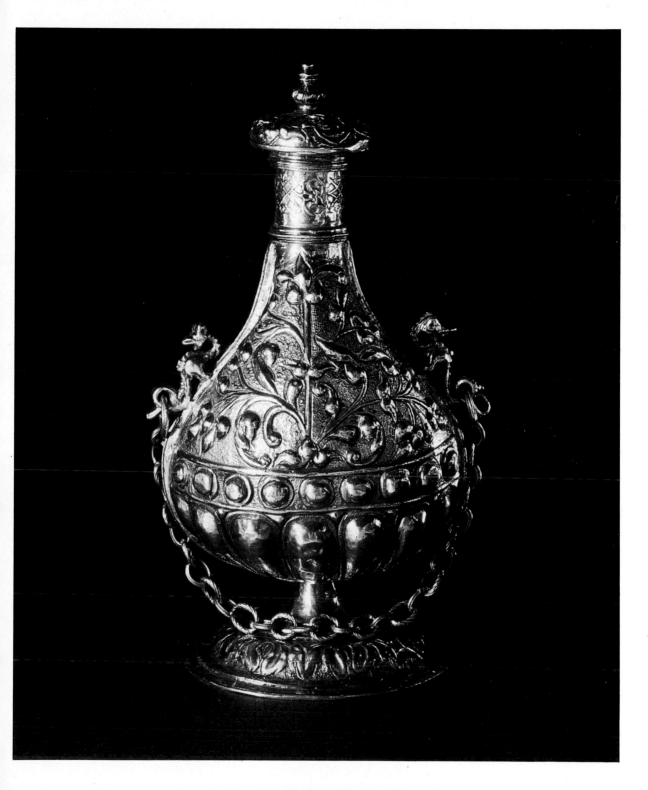

Plate 1 **Casting bottle for rosewater**
Gilt 1553. Mark a fleur de lis (?) H. 14.8 cm. Chased with foliage and with a die struck panel about the
neck. This Renaissance shape was fashionable for casting bottles at the Tudor court until the 1570s.
Sotheby's

Plate 2 The Paston treasure

Oil c.1660–70. A family collection of exotica; six of the mounted objects, and the shell-shaped flagons, still survive.

Castle Museum, Norwich

Plate 4 **Tea service**

Gilt and enamel 1851. Mark of Joseph Angell. This set, in the Moorish–Elizabethan taste, was shown at the Great Exhibition.

VAM

Thirty-eight candlesticks survive from one and salvers and dishes (at least) from the others, some to be seen in the Hermitage. But no intact dinner service of the early neo-classical period has been seen on the London market for many years, although occasionally individual items hint at their former existence (see Fig. 43).

Just one pair of candelabra made by Philip Rundell for George IV in 1821 weighed 482 ounces; each has a figure of Orpheus and a cupid, a goat and a dog below vine branches. The fashion charge, of 19s 6d an ounce, was unusually high and the two cost over £700. The design was not unique to the king; a pair had been made a year earlier for a private customer. Tureens could be equally substantial. A pair made for Rundell's in 1820 for the ex-actress Harriet Coutts (née Mellon) weighs 702 ounces.[33]

Ten entrée dishes, four sauce tureens and a cruet stand made for Sir Richard Sutton in 1819 weighed the astonishing total of 1,640 ounces. Add to these the plates, cutlery, salvers, wine coolers, coasters and other tableware and the service can be recognised as a phenomenon of the period. They were, and continue to be, popular; Norman Penzer, in an appendix to his book on Paul Storr, listed six Storr dinner services sold by Christie's before 1952. Ice-pails too have changed hands very frequently; forty-two sets, some of four or six, passed at auction before 1953. In the past thirty years, Storr silver has continued to command a premium, although Benjamin Smith was equally competent and worked to the same designs, often several years earlier than Storr.[34]

Where a family could afford to order an entirely silver dinner service, its design was carefully worked out so that all the components were en suite. A service supplied to Lord Bagot of Blithfield Hall, Staffordshire by Rundell, Bridge & Rundell between 1804 and 1806 followed the popular grapevine theme; satyrs supported the vine-entwined candelabra.[35]

Since these candelabra alone weigh more than 1,140 ounces, it is hardly surprising that many families preferred to use a mixture of silver and plate, at least for those items like liners to tureens, hot water stands, dish covers and entrée dishes which received heavy handling and were touched by servants rather than guests. A typical retailer's bill head of 1797 advertised all the components of a service including 'covers' and 'water-plates'. The bill was for a pair of 'New Pillar Candlesticks' which even with engraved cyphers cost only £1 17s. Joseph Brasbridge noted with pride in 1824 that some plated goods he had sold to Admiral Williams 'when I first went into business', that is about 1775, were still in regular use. But it should be noted that the thickness of the silver layer on plated goods varied and certainly was reduced by 1800 or thereabouts. In fact, the ledgers of Wakelin & Tayler and their successor Robert Garrard show how completely acceptable plated wares had become. A typical entry for Lord Robert Fitzgerald in September 1802 includes plated knife rests, 'patent nozle Bracket candlesticks' and snuffer trays. Another retailer, Philip Gilbert, goldsmith in ordinary to the Crown, also supplied the gentry from his West End shop with a mixture of new, plated and secondhand silver. In 1811 Frederick Booth Esq. bought there a plated taperstick for as little as 6s 6d and a plateau, also plated, for £11 two years later. But Gilbert was equally able to provide Booth with '4 Shell Double silver Dishes with chased Lion Crests' weighing 260 ounces. With separate charges for modelling and chasing the crests (an indication that they were made in Gilbert's workshop, not bought-in), these cost £193. In part payment Booth turned over an old silver mug and a tea urn, to the value of £38 7s.[36]

Smaller houses inevitably had to refer customers up the line sometimes, Brasbridge was proud of his occasional association with Robert Garrard, 'the first silversmith in London' who acted as referee when a client protested over a bill; 'I had frequently sent customers to this gentleman for services of plate, the orders for which were beyond my means of executing'.

In the foregoing account of dining plate, Paul Storr's silver has provided many of the examples; his work, especially for the royal family, is well documented and frequently on the market and so has attracted scholarly, as well as collectors' attention. Other London goldsmiths, notably Robert Garrard or Barnard's, followed a similar pattern; it has been markedly more difficult, however, to demonstrate the relationships between suppliers and retailers in the rest of the trade. John Culme's forthcoming study, for the nineteenth century, of the biographical dictionary of goldsmiths initiated by Arthur Grimwade will undoubtedly shed light on them. The ordinary retailers of the City and West End, houses like Joseph Brasbridge or S. Alderman of the Barbican (Fig. 72) catered to a different class of customer from Rundell's, Garrard's, or David Ellis of John Street, who supplied, 'Two richly chased wav'd Bottle Coasters . . . open work Chasd scrolls' for £187 19s 10d to John Samuel Wanley Sawbridge Erle-Drax in 1829. These extraordinary rich wagon wine coasters have the demi-lion and griffin crests of their purchaser cast on each end; made by Barnard's, they are of exceptional quality and changed hands in 1984 for £110,000.

The Antiquarian Taste

The eclecticism of the silver of William Beckford (1760–1844), collected for Fonthill and Lansdown Tower, sets him aside from the mainstream of English taste. But the highly finished 'revived Renaissance' gilt sideboard plate, or his gilt-mounted porcelain and hardstones, by no means dictated Beckford's choice of a style for his tableware, which was austere in the extreme. His elegant neo-classical dinner service of 1781 and his tea kettle with its triangular stand and draught-excluder is characteristic of the tea silver in aristocratic homes at the time; a similar design had been adopted by Parker & Wakelin eighteen years earlier, in 1763, for a kettle at Burghley House. A comparable handsome, almost cubist, travelling teaset made in 1786 by John Schofield for the fourth Duchess of Bedford may be seen at Woburn Abbey.[37]

The aspect of Beckford's silver which has attracted most attention from modern scholars, and indeed from contemporary visitors to Fonthill, is his extremely individualistic interest in Jacobean and earlier ornament. The strapwork, moresques and other forms of finely detailed overall engraving are quite against the prevailing contemporary demand for heavy architectural 'Roman' ornament associated with Benjamin Smith or Paul Storr. Integral to his silver were the heraldic elements of the families from whom he claimed descent, notably all the signatories of Magna Carta (Fig. 75).

Beckford patronised the royal goldsmiths Rundell, Bridge & Rundell from about 1800. In lighting, a renewed interest in silver sconces showed itself at this time, particularly since they were peculiarly appropriate to contemporary interior designs, whether in the ornate French 'empire' style or revived 'old English'. Beckford followed both lines, ordering in 1804, a set

118

from Paul Storr which hark back to Paris-made silver of the 1780s (although modified by the addition of Beckford's crest), and a set from William Burwash in 1818 (a single corded arm projecting from a double rosette) which are a curious mixture of late Stuart and Tudor idioms. Six years later Samuel Whitford copied for him a pair of about 1690 by Francis Garthorne, probably from the royal plate sold in 1808. Nearly twenty years later a Bristol retailer, Mr Short, made yet another pair for him, copying Andrew Moore's sconce of 1688.[38]

Beckford was by no means alone in seeking out earlier 'furnishing' silver. Despite the dispersals and melts in 1808, 1817 and 1823 which disposed of more than 50,000 ounces of old royal plate, the royal collection still retained some of its late Stuart furnishing silver – firedogs and creepers, sconces and chandeliers. Both categories were overhauled, altered and armorials added by Paul Storr for the Prince Regent in 1811, presumably to dress Carlton House. Many of the larger objects sold in 1808 can be traced down to the present.[39]

From as early as 1810, the royal household was re-acquiring antique plate, or plate made in the historic manner. Sets of massive gilt sideboard dishes embossed in seventeenth-century style were supplied by William Pitts in 1810 at the high price of £388 6s 4d; one pair of dishes was completely new, the others were set with plaques on the Apollo and Daphne theme, one

Fig. 44 **Sideboard dishes**
Gilt 1833. Mark of Robert Garrard. D. 56 cm. Engraved on back 'GARRARDS Panton Street London'.
Derived partly from eighteenth-century silver and partly from engraved ornament, these shellwork
dishes show great technical competence. Shell and foamwork was revived from about 1810.
Loan, VAM

dated 1678 and the other with the mark of Jacob Bodendick, a Limburg-born goldsmith who had settled in London in the 1660s. These and other antiquarian pieces were no doubt intended to dress the gothic dining room at Carlton House, for which 'large Mahogany Gilt Gothic ornaments' and two gothic sideboards (just visible groaning with plate in Pyne's view) were purchased in July 1814 (Fig. 113).[40]

Genuine antiquarian plate was already in demand and so expensive; in 1816 Rundell's sold the king an Elizabethan basin (1595) and ewer of 1617 for about £94. A Nuremburg nautilus cup and a Hamburg ewer and basin, all gilt, followed, plus a tankard set with a medallion of Henry VIII, which although recognised now as a confection, was probably purchased as, and considered at the time, a genuine Tudor object. Certainly Rundell's charged heavily for gilding it, £78.[41]

The function of these pieces of early plate had sometimes been forgotten over time; a pair of andirons of 1696, purchased by George IV at the Duke of York's sale on 21 March 1827 (they had originally been made for William III and were presumably among those sold in 1808) were described in the 1832 inventory of royal plate as 'two richly chased ornaments'. The andirons altered by Storr were similarly inventoried and listed under 'Sideboard plate'.

Fig. 45 **Matching-up by Farrell**
Tea caddies, two by Samuel Taylor 1761, one by Edward Farrell 1819. The chinoiseries theme was probably carried through into the teapot, its salver and breadbasket.
Christie's

However, two other Stuart sets of andirons with the cypher of Charles II were overhauled, given new feet and terminal figures and rebacked by William Fountain in 1827, when they were acquired by Lord Brownlow for Belton.[42]

This royal appetite for seventeenth-century ornamental, chased and embossed 'historical' silver could not be satisfied with existing pieces and George IV commissioned additions from Rundell, Bridge & Rundell. The rococo marine-theme dinner service supplied seventy years earlier to Frederick, Prince of Wales, was supplemented by John Bridge in 1826 with a tureen formed as a shell resting on three sea-horses; a few years later (1829) the original Crespin centrepiece was overhauled and raised on dolphin feet. But by this time the revival of interest in rococo naturalism was shared far beyond the royal circle (Fig. 44).[43]

The plateworker Edward Farrell made something of a speciality of 'revived Renaissance' and other historicist silver (Fig. 43). In 1816, for example, he produced a pair of lobed sideboard dishes, each with an inset relief apparently cast from a seventeenth-century original and chased around their borders with exotic animals taken from Bewick's *General History of Quadrupeds* (1785). This combination, of chased borders and inset plaques, proved popular with his customers well into the 1820s. But he made more straightforward tableware – salts, candlesticks and tea silver, in earlier styles too (Fig. 45).[44]

Farrell's association with that enterprising retailer Kensington Lewis, which started about 1816 and ran until 1834, is demonstrated by the inscription 'Lewis silversmith to HRH The Duke of York St James's St London', which is found stamped on a high proportion of Farrell's output, particularly the inventive pieces in revived baroque style. Lewis also advertised himself as stocking 'antique', as opposed to merely secondhand plate, a sign of the recognition the taste for earlier silver had achieved.

Kensington Lewis, from his first known appearance as a purchaser of antique plate at the eleventh Duke of Norfolk's sale held by Christie's in 1816, specialised in elaborately chased or embossed baroque silver. He also bought earlier pieces when he could. In 1826 he had at his S. James' Street shop the Aldobrandini tazze, a set of twelve standing bowls made in Genoa late in the sixteenth century. Ackerman described them in his *Repository* as 'twelve very very curious silver ornaments . . . by the celebrated Italian artist Benvenuto Cellini'. Cellini was the only goldsmith De Lamerie recognised at the time with the exception of 'Mr Delamere'.

Lewis was not alone in supplying a mixture of genuine old plate, refurbished old plate and modern pastiches of old plate, to his royal and aristocratic customers . . . Francis Lambert, who ran a retail business off Leicester Square, bought old plate as models, like a Flemish tazza of about 1660, which he copied for the Duke of Buckingham and Chandos. This firm flourished long after Kensington Lewis had collapsed in debt in 1834 and continued to sell a profitable mixture of genuine antiques, and new wares in imitation of them. In 1839, for example, Lambert & Rawlings ordered from their silversmith, Charles Fox, a silvergilt cup and cover in the German taste, with a Bohemian ruby glass beaker as the body, supported by a Moorish warrior.[45] Fox's mark and those of his successors appear on much inventive historicist silver between 1830 and the 1880s.

From their exhibits in 1851, Lambert & Rawlings were still heavily committed to historicism. Many of their objects were described in the catalogue as 'from the antique' or 'in the old style', a subtle distinction which is hard now to disentangle. Characteristic is the

121

Fig. 46 **Naturalism: writing set and teapot**

a) 1845. Mark of Robert Hennell III. H. 12 cm. Inkpots cast as a pomegranate and an apple, the bell as a pear. The taperstick is a tree stump, its branches a penstand.

VAM

b) 1844. Mark of Charles Thomas & George Fox. An apple (or a melon?) teapot, with stump-like spout and leaf base.

Shrubsole

122

massive silver parcel-gilt flagon in late fifteenth-century German idiom, purchased from the Great Exhibition by the Department of Practical Art (now the Victoria and Albert Museum). This is a supreme example of the non-functional, non-commercial exhibition product; two feet high, it and its pair took the Fox's workmen twelve weeks to raise and emboss by hand.[46]

Other fashionable retailers were not slow to advertise their capacity to produce historicist silver; a bell shown by R. & S. Garrard in 1851 was a curious mixture of applied lizards and house flies, in the style of Wenzel Jamnitzer, with rococo scrolls and festoons. This design had been in their stock production at least since 1845.

Notes

1   For silver pre-1800, Rowe 1965; Birmingham 1973; Museum of London 1982. For design, Ch. 12.

2   Its use was general by the 1740s.

3   Rowe 1965.

4   Goldsmiths' 1982; Birmingham AG 1973.

5   Prideaux 1896, Vol. II; Hughes 1957. An argyle or argyll by Crespell (1769) is in Museum of London 1982.

6   For Boulton see Seaby 1951; Dickinson 1937; Birmingham 1973; Quickenden 1980; Crisp-Jones, 1981.

7   Rowe 1965, 88; Grimwade 1961.

8   Baker 1973, 289.

9   Quoted in Ketton-Cremer, *Norfolk Assembly* 1957.

10   Analysed from the Boulton Letter Books by Keith Quickenden.

11   The argument used with the Admiralty over tureens in 1787 was that ten years earlier he had made identical pieces at less than cost, an indication of his desperate fight to win orders from London.

12   *Letters of Horace Walpole* ed. W. S. Lewis 1961.

13   Seaby 1951, 86.

14   Brasbridge 1824.

15   Prideaux 1896, Vol. II.

16   Hirst MS.

17   Rouquet 1755; Saint-Méry is quoted in Ward and Ward 1979.

18   Jones 1911, corrected by VAM 1954.

19   See p. 249–50.

20   Pickford 1983.

21   Prideaux 1896; Greenwood 1930. However, Liverpool acquired silver cutlery in 1733.

22   Brasbridge 1824: Alderman's price list, *c*.1830–40.

23   Grimwade 1974; VAM 1984.

24   Hughes 1955; for another Rowe 1965, pl. 66.

25   Seaby and Heatherington 1950, 116.

26   See p. 107–8 above.

27   Pl. 32 in the Al-Tajir Collection.

28   Fales 1973, 148.

29   Birmingham 1973a.

30   Holkham inventory 1760; VAM Furniture Archive (photocopy); Al-Tajir Collection, 32.

31   Bury *passim*; VAM 1954.

32   For example, Penzer 1954.

33   Now in the Al-Tajir Collection. E. H. Bailey's design had been made up by How in 1817.

34   See note 35 and wine coasters (1819) in the Al-Tajir Collection.

35   By Digby Scott and Benjamin Smith; sold Sotheby's, New York, December 1983, lot 118.

36   Booth MSS, VAM Library: ledger entries for Barnard's are similarly wide-ranging: Banister 1980.

37   For Beckford's silver see Snodin and Baker 1980; Baker, Schroder and Clowes 1980.

38   Baker, Schroder and Clowes 1980.

39   Jones 1911; VAM 1954; Davis 1976. Ch. 13 and 14.

40   Information from Geoffrey de Bellaigne.

41   Bury, Snodin and Wedgwood 1979.

42   Two are at the National Maritime Museum, their inscriptions erased. The other two were in the Clore Collection.

43   For example, Webster 1984.

44   For example, Al-Tajir Collection, pl. 48–50.

45   Smith 1974, pl. 3 and 4.

46   Culme 1977, 162.

SIX

FROM VICTORIA TO THE PRESENT DAY

Glaring, showy and meretricious ornament . . . disgraces every branch of our art and manufacturers.

(A. W. N. Pugin, 1834)

THE vitality of English silver in the 1830s and 1840s was derived almost entirely from reworking earlier themes. Elements from styles as diverse as the rococo, neo-classicism and the baroque, were mingled, to the horror of a growing body of would-be industrial designers. There is great charm in the naturalistic tea silver or chamber candlesticks of Joseph Angell, in which veined leaves cling together as the cast body and buds, or twigs form finials and handles, but even these have their ancestry in the late seventeenth century.[1]

Fig. 47 **'Gothic' teapot**
1830. Mark of John Wrangham and William Moulson for Lambert and Rawlings. H.16 cm. An exuberantly gothic communion set, supplied by Barnards for Mapledurham Church in 1831, is another early instance of this taste; compare Pugin's drawings for Rundell, Bridge & Rundell (1820s).
VAM

While the historicism of the Regency and 1820s had focused on late Stuart plate, by the 1830s taste had visibly shifted towards a heavier Jacobean or gothic style, in keeping with the artificial revival of the great hall and the general romantic concept of 'Old England' captured in Scott's *Kenilworth* (1821) or *Ivanhoe* (1819). The hall at Charlecote was reinstated in the Elizabethan taste by 1830, an occasion celebrated with a massive banquet, and new houses too adopted this look, with furnishings, including tableware, to match: Harlaxton, for instance, or Bayons Manor, the latter built by Salvin for Eustace Tennyson D'Eyncourt. A lithograph of 1842 shows a tenants' dinner in the Great Hall at Bayons, with the lord of the manor seated at a high table littered with 'gothic' crowned standing cups. At Merevale in Warwickshire, the dining room was furnished in 1844 entirely in Jacobean style with a 'Jacobean' wine cooler, plate warmer and other accoutrements, all supplied by Snell of Albemarle Street.[2]

Some silver at least closely matched these aspirations; a teapot of 1830 made by John Wrangham and William Moulson for Lambert and Rawlings (VAM, Fig. 47) has gothic or rather perpendicular tracery chased on its body, while the lid has a border of alternating lozenges and stiff foliage, presumably influenced by Pugin's enthusiasm for the period, although his first publications did not appear till 1835. Pugin was not alone in his distaste for these design excesses (although the workmanship – chasing in particular – was often highly skilled). As early as 1832 Sir Robert Peel commented on the superiority of English manufacturing techniques as compared with our inferiority in pictorial design.

Victorian Silver

Until 1837 the Mechanics' Institutes, founded in 1823, were the only establishments attempting to teach 'applied art' to artisans. They were seen as failing in this task, but given the general absence of public collections open for study, this was hardly surprising. As Matthew Digby Wyatt commented, the Great Exhibition showed the results, in design terms, of 'nearly a century's incessant copying without discrimination, appropriating without compunction'. English bourgeois taste has always been uneasy with unfamiliar forms, although liking novel ornament, and urn shapes, which had held sway on the tea and breakfast table since the 1780s, were universally popular at least until the 1870s.

The first government school of design (now the Royal College of Art) set up in 1837 at Somerset House, sent touring exhibitions of approved art objects and plaster casts by rail to provincial towns, for the benefit of the art training establishments, and through the 1840s the Society of Arts attempted to stimulate both design and research into little-used techniques, such as enamelling. Theophilus' treatise *De Diversis Artibus* was translated into English by Robert Hendrie in 1847, a sign of the renewed interest in what was seen as the silversmith's golden age, the Middle Ages. Enamelling received a further boost in the *Art-Journal* in 1850 when the enamel work of the Paris firm J. V. Morel was praised. Morel had moved to London in 1849, drawn, like so many contemporary French craftsmen, to the prosperity of London from the commercial confusion of revolutionary Paris. One English firm at least, Joseph Angell, was quick to pick up the suggestion.[3]

Angell showed to the Society of Arts in spring 1851 (and subsequently won a prize medal for it at the Great Exhibition) a tea and coffee service in neo-Tudor style with as many as

Fig. 48   **The Medieval Court, 1851 Exhibition**
Entirely designed by Pugin at the peak of public recognition for his long campaign for a purer gothic
style. John Hardman and John Keith exhibited church plate to his and Butterfield's designs.
VAM

sixteen separate enamelled areas on each article. His designer (unknown) did not escape the fashionable eclecticism; rococo elements appear also on this service, which is not only enamelled in translucent green and purple but also gilt. Angell claimed that 'the aim and object of every manufacturer' should be to produce useful objects which also showed 'talent, genius or mental capability'; this service shows technical skill, reflected in its high price of £120, more than three times an ordinary commercial product in silver. (By comparison a 'fluted pattern silver tea pot', purchased by Rev. W. Thornton in 1846, cost only £10.) Another 1851 service of Angell's, also on view at the Exhibition and now at the Goldsmiths' Company, is equally picturesque; each vessel has an openwork, frosted, silvergilt frame overlying the body; the case on each silver body illustrates one of Aesop's *Fables* (Plate 4).

The literalism of rococo revival, first noted about 1810 (if indeed it had ever fallen out of fashion) and vigorously attacked by Pugin in 1841, was running out of steam by the 1850s. In 1855 the *Art-Journal* deplored the obsession of English silversmiths with 'the incessant marrowbone scroll of that eternal Louis Quinze'. Designs in the early Elkington pattern books (about 1840 to 1868) show the commercial appeal of other styles, particularly formal figure subjects from Shakespeare's plays for dessert and salad stands, or modified neo-classical forms, particularly those incorporating piercing, an effective and economical technique (Fig. 102). A typically bastardised design was the coffee or tea urn castigated by Charles Eastlake; (a debased copy from some antique vase . . . in order to add to its attraction, the lid and handle are probably decorated *à la Pompadour* and to complete the absurdity, a thoroughly modern tap is inserted).[4]

It was generally agreed at the time that 1851, *annus mirabilis*, was a turning point for English design in the decorative arts, however little the mainstream of taste appeared to change its flow. Henry Cole (1808–82) has been claimed as prime mover in the long-running early Victorian campaign to improve English industrial design. Certainly his energetic support for the Society of Arts in the 1840s, his enthusiasm for the Great Exhibition (1851) and his concern later with the new Museum of Manufacturers, set up by the Department of Practical Art in Marlborough House in 1852 (subsequently transferred to South Kensington, and renamed in 1899 the Victoria and Albert Museum) each contributed to the genuine public awareness of, and interest in, design and the decorative arts. His attempt in 1847 to set up a company to commission designs for decorative art according to the best modern principles, the Felix Summerly's Art-Manufactures, was more significant for the ceramics that resulted than for silver design, although a popular christening mug was issued (Fig. 49).[5]

Fig. 49 **'Guardian Angel' christening mug**
Silver, London 1865–6. A reissue of a design by Richard Redgrave *c*.1849. In this piece Redgrave's literal application of the Summerly ideas on 'appropriate' motifs produced a shape which was hard for a child to drink from.
VAM

The new museum, for so it quickly became, purchased both new products and older objects as examples, with an initial investment of £5,000 to buy for the founding collection from the Great Exhibition. The Selection Committee included three leaders of the design establishment: A. W. N. Pugin, Richard Redgrave (whose christening mug of 1849 is referred to above, VAM) and Owen Jones. But the museum too was quickly captured by the antiquarian spirit and older objects rapidly overtook current productions in its accession books. The dealer William Chaffers was to the fore in silver, buying energetically at Ralph Bernal's massive sale of antiques in 1855. Two years earlier, the superiority of ancient craftsmanship was acknowledged when Elkington's received permission to make electro-types of historic silver in the museum, both for general sale and to act as models for schools of art and design.[6]

The stress on art education only fed the English appetite for derived styles and the national preference for what was familiar was reinforced by the choice of objects considered museum-worthy; it took a generation for silver to be generally saleable which was neither rococo nor 'Queen Anne' in inspiration.

A renewed interest in the simple angular shapes of the 1720s is apparent from the 1860s and straight copies, such as salts with three lion masks and paw feet, or faceted and melon-shaped teapots, were popular, often with additional engraved ornament. The variety of designs in the Elkington range was enormous; mustard pots, for instance, could be made in any one of fifty-seven designs, such as a French-derived monkey with a mustard barrel (originally put out by Odiot of Paris in 1819, number 3883), one embossed with a Teniers-style rustic scene,

Fig. 50   **'Mr. Punch' mustard pot**
1871. Mark of Robert Hennell IV. H. 9.8 cm. Design registered on 22 February 1868. A typical mid-Victorian tabletoy; Judy and pierrots were issued at about the same time by the Hennells.
Private collection

Fig. 51 **Church plate**
Designed for Skidmore of Birmingham and exhibited in 1851. A combination of a straight copy of a
medieval chalice and reinterpretations – the flagon and cup emphasising the revival of old techniques –
gemsetting, parcel-gilding and delicate floral openwork.
VAM

a pierced 'gothic lancet' design, an Elizabethan, fretwork and so on. Novelty tablewares
flourished until the end of the century and beyond and fresh designs for mustard pots, salts
and dessert stands were put out by Hennell's, as well as Elkington's, each season. An
interesting selection appears in the Colman Mustard Pot Collection (which tours provincial
museums) and regularly in the auction houses (Fig. 50).[7]

In May 1984, Sotheby's sold a set of figure salts, some of 1856 and some made a decade later
by Hunt & Roskell; the original models had been shown by J. V. Morel in 1851. Presumably
the Frenchman had sold his models, patterns or stock when he returned to France in 1852.
These were described in 1851 as 'in the Louis Quatorze style. They represent rustic children,
quite of the Watteau order'.

But these were not universally admired; Eastlake deplored the use of miniature versions of
objects originally in other materials such as wicker (a technique popular with Hennell's for tea
services, egg boilers and other small objects). 'Some of my readers may remember the little
gilt Cupid, wheeling a barrow full of salt, which once appeared in many an English dining
room and I have often been surprised that no ingenious Sheffield designer has yet adopted the
Martyr's Memorial as a pepper-caster.'[8]

129

A few years later *The Dining Room* (1880) attacked this prevailing taste for knick-knacks with heavy irony: 'There seems to be a painful poverty of invention when we see the same form employed to collect ashes from a cigar, to hold a Lady's thimble or to make a watch-stand. Yet all of these can now be had in the pleasing and graceful shape of a gentleman's hat!' Looking at the Elkington design books, which continue to be packed with both decorative and 'novel' designs, it is clear that these strictures on 'a hundred and fifty pretentious vulgarities fresh from Sheffield and Birmingham' had little effect; the alternative proposed, by Eastlake and others, was to turn back the clock and produce metalwork in the admired medieval taste, which was, in its own way, just as derivative. Only in the 1870s, with the designs of Dresser, was there anything approaching a new look.

The large firms, like Elkington's, Hunt & Roskell and Hancock's, emphasised their exhibition pieces, publicised by engravings in the *Illustrated London News* and *Art-Journal*; these were normally large thematic figure compositions, often made as presentation pieces, like the Sir Moses Montefiori centrepiece (1842, on loan to the Victoria and Albert Museum). One made by R. and S. Garrard for the Grocers' Company in 1842 incorporates the Company crest of a camel; two sit by a moss-grown wellhead with merchants in Eastern dress, a slice of realism probably designed by Edmund Cotterill, who had recently returned from a tour of the Orient, as the *ILN* commented.[9]

These testimonial pieces were rich in surface detail and their sponsors boasted of their literal accuracy. Rich contrasts were favoured, for example juxtaposed panels of frosting, burnishing and gilding. In 1853 the *Illustrated London News*, describing H. H. Armstead's Royal Yacht Squadron prize, praised the use of parcel-gilding which by 'producing a warm tone and reducing the glitter of the metal, gives that display to light and shade which only can develop the delicacies of such workmanship and design'. Technical excellence was all.

For half a century, table services showed the same literalism. In the Earl of Ellenborough's service, or the later Ismay testimonial (1882, recently at Christie's), the taste for exotic naturalism is seen at its best. In the Ellenborough service, rich in references to his military career in India, four different figure subjects were adopted for the dessert stands; typical was a 'Hindu girl depositing her lamp in the waters of the Ganges, under a Mango-tree'. Some of the handsomest services belong to English corporations, such as Bristol and Manchester.[10]

Racing and other prizes were a fruitful source of commissions for the leading firms too. The ornament of the 1842 Ascot cup alluded to the Battle of Crécy, described with great approval by the *ILN*, which first appeared in that year and continued to give prominence to prize silver and wedding presents in its reports. From 1844 the Emperor of Russia gave an annual trophy for the Ascot meeting, which Hunt & Roskell supplied. The 1846 design, of S. George and the Dragon below a thirteen-light candelabrum, was the work of E. H. Bailey.[11]

The self-conscious striving for ornament in presentation pieces, and the value set on it, is clear from a comment on racing cups in 1853; 'In former days what were called Racing Cups were . . . mere awkward vessels fit for rugged squires who contended for the possession of them; of so rude and inelegant appearance that . . . they excite curiosity at the rusticity of our ancestors and derision at their total want of good taste'.

The wheel of fashion has turned several times since then. The earlier cups so contemptuously dismissed in 1853, probably late Stuart embossed examples, like one owned by Lord Lonsdale of 1669, now fetch rather higher prices than their mid-Victorian replacements, which to late twentieth-century eyes seem somewhat overladen, pretentious and without a function, however technically ingenious. Charles Eastlake no doubt spoke for many people 'I for one, would rather possess a copper-gilt flagon of good design than a modern "trophy cup" of twice its weight in gold', although to him good design implied a restatement of a late gothic form (Fig. 51).[12]

Prize cups were pretty well standardised and virtually *de rigeur* to dress the sideboard; the 'county vicar of moderate income' whose sideboard and plate was described in *The Dining Room* would set out 'plenty of spoons and forks, perhaps a salver or two, or a vase given by grateful parishioners or cups won in athletic sports while he was at Oxford'.[13]

By contrast with this traditional sideboard display, to which a flower-filled epergne might be added, the magazines on household taste around 1880 recommended a sideboard dresssed, not to say crammed, with bric à brac, small antiques, old china and so on, in pale imitation of the superb collection shown in William Burges's dining room, described by Mrs Haweis in 1882 'Cup of jade, Knive-handles, goblets of silver and rock-crystal set with gems and quaint work, cameos, pearls, turquoises – cups such as that which Glaucus gave to the gambler Aodus . . . crowd the little shelves!'[14]

Popular taste can be gauged from a spate of publications on how to furnish appearing from the late 1860s. Their hints were aimed not at the old (or new) aristocracy but at the salaried classes, living in suburban villas. One of 1880, *Artistic Homes or How To Furnish with Taste*, published by Ward Lock in Sylvia's Home Help Series, illustrates how the tide of popular fashion was flowing away from ornament. 'If there be ornament let it be pierced or incised, not repoussé, or raised above the surface. Admit no realistic copies of natural objects, as butter coolers with staves and hoops to imitate milkpails and cream jugs modelled to a wicker pattern, or fish slices engraved with figures of fishermen.' However, these examples of debased design are lifted directly from Eastlake's comments twelve years earlier in *Hints on Household Taste*.

To overcome the problem of ugly overladen tableware, Eastlake recommended visiting 'the old jewellery-shops in Hanway Street and Wardour Street' for silver 'far better in design and at a cost rarely exceeding that which is paid for modern plate of the same intrinsic value'. He also stressed how much more attractive was antique cutlery 'seen in the windows of a curiosity shop' than modern plate 'cast in patterns which have no more artistic quality than the ornaments of a wedding cake'.[15]

As the status of old silver rose, stimulated by the exhibitions of antiques held from the late 1840s, so institutions commissioning presentation plate turned increasingly to copies of antiques, particularly those in their own collections, in preference to pretentious figure groups. The Queen's Gold Vase, made for the 1874 Ascot meeting, copied a Queen Anne pilgrim bottle. When a service with candelabra was ordered for Manchester's new town hall, designed by Alfred Waterhouse and opened in 1878, it was in the gothic spirit; as the *ILN* commented 'Gothic, of the Early English period, with a free use of ornament based on Byzantine examples'.[16]

At the lower end of the silver market, Sheffield firms, notably Martin & Hall and W. & G. Sisson, produced copies of mid-eighteenth century designs for baskets, chamber-sticks and

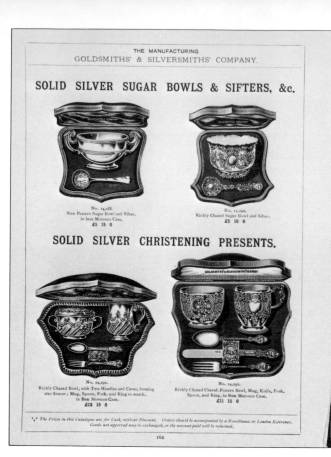

SOLID SILVER SUGAR BOWLS & SIFTERS, &c.

No. 14,288.
New Pattern Sugar Bowl and Sifter,
in best Morocco Case.
£5 15 0

No. 14,290.
Richly Chased Sugar Bowl and Sifter.
£5 10 0

SOLID SILVER CHRISTENING PRESENTS.

No. 14,291.
Richly Chased Bowl, with Two Handles and Cover, forming
also Saucer ; Mug, Spoon, Fork, and Ring to match,
in Best Morocco Case.
£12 15 0

No. 14,292.
Richly Chased Cherub Pattern Bowl, Mug, Knife, Fork,
Spoon, and Ring, in Best Morocco Case.
£11 15 0

. The Prices in this Catalogue are for Cash, without Discount.   Orders should be accompanied by a Remittance or London Reference.
Goods not approved may be exchanged, or the amount paid will be returned.

162

SOLID SILVER SALTS, &c.

No. 14,293.
Four New Hollow Fluted Salt Cellars, on three legs, with Pierced
Border, and Spoons, in best Morocco Case.
£7 15 0

No. 14,294.
Pair New Hollow Fluted Muffineers, in best Morocco Case.
Height, 5½ inches.
£4 10 0

No. 14,295.
New Hollow Fluted Sugar Dredger,
Height, 6½ inches.
£4 10 0

No. 14,296.
New Hollow Fluted Sugar Bowl and Cream Ewer, with
Pierced Borders, Six Teaspoons and Sugar Tongs to match,
in best Morocco Case.
£11 0 0

. In Ordering, it is not necessary to cut the Catalogue ; mentioning the Number of the Illustration and the Price will be sufficient.
☞ PLEASE READ TERMS OF BUSINESS ON PAGE 1.   Telegraphic Address : "ARGENNON LONDON."

163   L 2

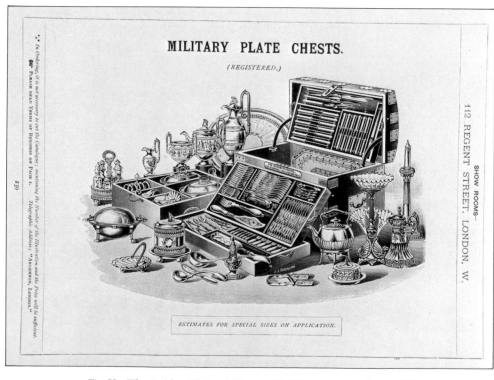

MILITARY PLATE CHESTS.

(REGISTERED.)

. In Ordering, it is not necessary to cut the Catalogue ; mentioning the Number of the Illustration and the Price will be sufficient.
☞ PLEASE READ TERMS OF BUSINESS ON PAGE 1.   Telegraphic Address : "ARGENNON, LONDON."

239

SHOW ROOMS—
112 REGENT STREET, LONDON, W.

ESTIMATES FOR SPECIAL SIZES ON APPLICATION.

Fig. 52   **The Goldsmiths' and Silversmiths' Company catalogue 1896**
Note the continuing dependence on indeterminate scrolls and 'Queen Anne' fluting: novel touches
include the Greek helmet finials on a tea/coffee service.
VAM

teaware. By the 1890s reproductions of earlier English silver, particularly the forms and ornament seen, however inaccurately, as 'Queen Anne', were bestsellers. That thrusting young retailing business, the Goldsmiths (and Silversmiths) Company of Regent Street, which had swallowed up the older firm of A. & B. Savory, may be taken as a touchstone of middle-of-the-road taste in silver (Fig. 52).[17]

An 1896 catalogue of this company, described in an advertising puff as 'a veritable work of art . . . you could keep it on a boudoir table', is packed with novelties, presentation plate and tableware which is almost entirely derived from earlier periods. This was seen as desirable; 'Many of the Designs are reproductions of the Antique at about one-sixth the cost of the original'. Despite the catalogue's claim to 'the advantage of improved art-education and modern ideas', there is no hint of Arts and Crafts motifs nor of Dresser's functionalism. The solid silver cigar lighters came in nine designs; apart from a kettle, a drum and a grenade (so suitable for the officers' mess) there were three versions of Roman lamps, one Greek and a design called 'Antique' which vaguely recalls a rococo two-handled cup.

Copies specifically acknowledged as such in the catalogue were few, although one prize bowl, offered in a price range from £8 to £72, reproduced a 1702 monteith at the Vintners' Company and a coffee pot, no.14534, was 'copied from an original in the South Kensington Museum', while a set of cutlery was based on a drawing by Holbein in the British Museum.

Fig. 53 **Silver and plate designed by Christopher Dresser**
Plated toast rack, Hukin & Heath; wine jug, Hukin & Heath 1888; sugar basin and spoon in the form of a coal scuttle and shovel, Hukin & Heath 1881.
Spink's

133

Tea services came in a rather short range of eighteenth-century patterns – Queen Anne, Georgian, Irish, Wedgwood and Grecian, the latter engraved with a frieze and capped with a Greek helmet finial. The Louis Quinze, for £28, offered the perennial rococo so criticised by Eastlake thirty years earlier while the Louis Quatorze had shaped feet, bird spouts and flyaway handles more familiar to an Augsburg silversmith. Another service, the Burmese, with its horizontal bands of close-packed relief ornament derived from Burmese carvings, clearly owed its appeal to the successful campaigns in Burma in the previous decade.

At the time this catalogue was published, the shoppers continuing to wander up Regent Street were able to buy at Liberty's commercial interpretations of the handcrafted silver produced by the various guilds, publicised through the Arts and Crafts Exhibitions Society (1888 onwards) and Ashbee's Mayfair showroom and reproduced in the *Studio* magazine (1893). But these were more expensive and always confined to a coterie of collectors whose lifestyle and philosophy they suited. Compare Figs. 52 and 54.[18]

A refreshing and truly original alternative to the excesses of historicism had emerged rather earlier, in the 1870s, through the silver designed by Dr Christopher Dresser for Hukin & Heath and from 1880, for Elkington. His simple angled shapes, seen for example in an electroplate tureen and ladle (VAM), offered a complete contrast and had an immediate and long-lasting commercial appeal, not least because they were made up in sheet silver rolled as thin as possible, to keep the price down – a sensible cost-cutting device urged by designers and ignored (largely) by silver manufacturers since the 1850s (Fig. 53).[19]

The Twentieth Century

The characteristics of Arts and Crafts silverwork – enamel, semi-precious stones, an unburnished surface so that the hammermarks rippled, 'Celtic' flowing forms – were those which appealed to A. L. Liberty's customers. In the two decades from 1895, people wanting a contrast to the prevailing rococo revival, or to historicism in the commercial silver of Mappin & Webb or Elkington's, had a choice of shopping at Liberty's, already popular for their household goods. Alternatively they could select, at other retailers specialising in silver and glass, those interpretations of Arts and Crafts themes by the Birmingham Guild of Handicraft or the even more commercial firm of E. A. Jones.[20] Liberty's started importing Japanese silver teaspoons, cream and sugar bowls and other small wares about 1890, marking them with L. Y. & Co. in addition to the import mark and in some cases the Yokohama maker's mark. This fashionable retailing company in Regent Street apparently took the commercial initiative in commissioning a range of English Arts and Crafts-inspired silver. By the summer of 1898 Liberty's were in touch with the Birmingham manufacturers W. H. Haseler and although the first few months' production in the 'Cymric' range of silver bears London marks (and no manufacturer's mark, only L. Y. & Co.), Haseler undoubtedly produced all the designs in the Cymric range until the Cymric Company was wound up in 1926. By then the style was falling out of favour, although a manufacturer of biscuit tins did copy a Tudric (pewter) box in 1926. But from 1900 to 1910 Liberty silver, stamped CYMRIC and with 'L & Co.' in three conjoined triangles, was extremely popular. In 1902 *Queen* magazine wrote up the season's novelties 'Blotting books of chamois leather with silver

Fig. 54 **Chafing dish and stand**
Silver and applied gold, London 1908–9. H. 30 cm. Designed and made by Henry Wilson (1864–1934).
Wilson is better known for his jewellery, which has the rich detail and fine wirework of this dish.
VAM

corners in Celtic interlacing . . . are among the latest productions in the Cymric silver'. Archibald Knox, Rex Silver, Bernard Cuzner and Oliver Baker each designed for the range.[21]

It should be emphasized that the manufacturing techniques adopted by Liberty's were those standard in the trade; holloware was spun or die-stamped, complete with its ornament and even its hammermarks, and then shaped and seamed.

W. R. Lethaby's criticism (1902) of the contemporary taste for 'merely capricious originality, a striving for exaggerated elegance' which was aimed at those silversmiths whose work showed 'violent curvature of form . . . unrelated splashes of enamel and the overinsistence upon hammermarks and chemically treated surfaces', was justified, in that Liberty's were quite cynically achieving a 'hand-made' appearance almost entirely by machine processes. Given the moral value attaching itself to the craft worker, and by extension to the purchaser of his creation, under William Morris's influence, Liberty customers were getting their uplift dishonestly!

135

Fig. 55 **Plate by Gilbert Marks**
1897. Signed 'Gilbert Marks '97'. Meticulously chased flowers and the sinuous lines of Art Nouveau distinguish Marks' work. His workman Latino Movio followed his style but their total production was well under 900 objects, made between about 1885, when he set up a workshop, and 1902, when he fell ill. He died in 1905.
Private collection

Liberty's suppliers, W. H. Haseler of Birmingham, and W. Hutton of Sheffield, were aware of the appeal of 'New Art' and their designs for tea and coffeeware around 1900 are noticeably sinuous. The influence of craft workshops went far beyond their actual output, which was tiny; but journalists ensured that their work was publicised, at least until the outbreak of the first war, through *The Studio*.

The style called Art Nouveau took its name from the Paris shop Maison de l'Art Nouveau where the first salon or exhibition of paintings and decorative art had been held in 1895. Characterised by a flowing, undulating line with a double bend or whiplash, its potential appeal to those already sympathetic to the organic, almost playful silver of the Arts and Crafts movement, was obvious. At the Exposition Universelle (Paris, 1900) the Goldsmiths' and

Silversmiths' Company exhibited a pierced plant stand and a silver clock, and Huttons had already in production a sensuously decorated tea and coffee service, with which they won a prize, the only English silversmiths to do so (Fig. 103).[22] Commercial firms continued to exploit the style until the First World War although artist-craftsmen and designers like Archibald Knox were moving away by 1905 or so. The postwar generation were happier with the romanticism and traditional forms with which Omar Ramsden satisfied his clients.

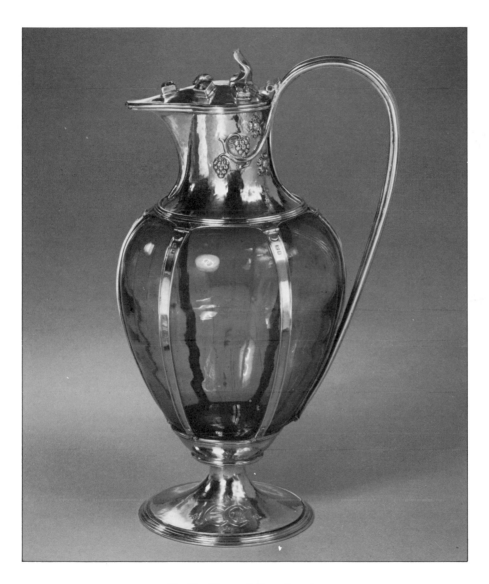

Fig. 56 **Glass and silver claret jug**
1922–3. Mark of Omar Ramsden. H. 20 cm. The four citrines set in the lid and the Celtic letter forms are characteristic of Ramsden. The hallmark on the straps are carefully positioned to add interest.
Hancock's

The partnership of Omar Ramsden and Alwyn Carr between 1898 and 1919 capitalised strongly on the turn-of-the-century admiration for the hand-made look in silver, that is for a gently-textured surface and no 'Birmingham-bright' burnishing.[23]

Quite apart from their use of Arts and Crafts-approved finishes such as enamelling, setting with semi-precious stones or mixed materials, these two Sheffield-trained silversmiths, who came to London on scholarships to the Royal College of Art, recognised the commercial appeal of personally signed work. The inscription 'RAMSDEN & CARR ME FECERUNT' appears not only on all their commissioned work but also on their cheaper lines, which were normally made from Birmingham-produced blanks. Indeed, despite Ramsden's commercial reputation and his much-emphasized image as an artist-craftsman (expressed for instance through his carefully arranged studio at S. Dunstans, Seymour Place, and the smock in which he dressed to receive potential clients) 'What is virtually certain is that from a very early date Omar Ramsden never participated in the actual execution of any of the pieces which bear his signature'. Like De Lamerie or Paul Storr, he found a successful formula – in his case, he took a wealthy partner with whom to set up, employed skilled designers, chasers and engravers, adopted methods to simplify and reduce the cost of production and satisfied the taste of his customers with reassuringly traditional shapes; the mazer and the rosebowl are both typical of this firm's output. He also incorporated other materials apart from wood; glass for claret jugs was popular (Fig. 56).

Ramsden's orders came not only from private customers but from English institutions – Anglican and Roman Catholic churches, livery companies, colleges and corporations, all with heraldry to supply appropriate ornament in the traditional manner. The Honourable Artillery Company purchased ten condiment sets in 1928, with pierced friezes composed of portcullises and ostrich plumes taken from the regimental coat of arms. A set of communion plate made by Alwyn Carr for S. Mark, North Audley Street in 1926, after the partnership was dissolved, is set with enamelled plaques depicting S. Mark. But their designs often referred back to early English silver; a christening cup given to Charles Cockayne in 1912 has the seven-cusped foot and rope mouldings of a late gothic chalice, while the spirally fluted stem, shaped bowl and pierced cresting are paralleled in Oxford college silver of the period 1490 to 1530, published by Moffat a few years before.

Ramsden's major contribution to English silver lay in persuading customers that 'craftsman-made' silver was preferable, for some purposes at least, to the commercial concentration of die-struck antique reproductions. But the brochures of the long-standing mass production companies offer only slight evidence that they felt the need to respond to this taste.

The London firm of Mappin's had been retailing silver and plate since 1862, when their wares were illustrated in an exhibition supplement to the *Daily News* (29 April 1862) and their trade catalogues between 1862 and 1928 show little evidence of fresh design influence. The Arts and Crafts movement, Art Nouveau and the slightly earlier taste for exoticism of the 1870s quite passed them by; while the firm's customers were content with Queen Anne tea and coffee sets, or rococo revival models with 'Gadroon Mounts' and shell-and-paw feet or vaguely neo-classical shapes (their three main designs), there was no need for innovation. Their 1925 catalogue shows a series of Pyrex dishes in tureen-shaped frames; although these were made in 'Princes Plate', not silver, they were available 'with hammered body' at slightly higher cost, a hint of one firm's limited commercial response to the handcraft revival.

Mappin and Webb reacted in 1935 to the repeated complaints of 'the general benumbing of the aptitude for design' by commissioning a series of designs for teaware from Arthur Hatfield, Keith Murray and others. A souvenir brochure produced to coincide with, and draw attention to, their prize-winning exhibits in the Royal Academy exhibition of British art in industry (VAM 1935), illustrated the simple curving or angular unornamented 'modern' forms popular at the time. There is a sharp flavour of Art Deco in the vertical, architectural forms of Keith Murray's ridged cocktail shaker and beakers (Fig. 57).

Fig. 57 **Cocktail shaker and beakers**
*c.*1935. Designed by Keith Murray for Mappin & Webb.
Goldsmiths' Company

Fig. 58 **Sauce boat**
1957. Designed by Eric Clements and made by L. W. Burt for Wakely & Wheeler.
Goldsmiths' Company

It must be admitted that this brief flurry of interest in contemporary design was not carried through into Mappin & Webb's later production in either silver or plate, nor is it evident in the wares of the manufacturing company Walker & Hall whose brochure (VAM 1938) has a depressingly 'revived' air. A large fruit dish with a vine border, costing £20, was described as 'of Handsome Modern Design', having 'Decoration of Artistic Merit'. Both forms and ornament would not have been out of place at any point in the previous three-quarters of a century; the economic climate in the 1930s was not encouraging to innovators. After the war it was essential to revitalise British industry and to restore our export markets although the prohibitive tax on gold and silverwork (110 per cent) meant that domestic demand was slow to pick up. The Council of Industrial Design encouraged young designers in both practical and luxury goods, and the first postwar exhibition *Britain Can Make It* was held at the reopened Victoria and Albert Museum in 1947.

After this hesitant start (the 1940s was virtually a lost decade for English silver) the 1950s saw a burst of exhibitions, competitions and institutional orders, coinciding with the emergence of a talented generation of designers and silversmiths from the Royal College of Art. Eric Clements (Fig. 58), Gerald Benney, David Mellor and Robert Welch were lucky in their time; as G. B. Hughes commented, 'Patronage in the arts grows with exhibition enthusiasm'. Certainly Hughes, on behalf of the Goldsmiths' Company, was a prime mover in this decade's run of exhibitions of both historic and contemporary silver.

Starting in 1950, with a modern show at the Fitzwilliam Museum, Cambridge, through to 1954, the Hall enabled the public to see civic, college and livery company plate from the fifteenth century to the present, and the Goldsmiths' Company continues, through its craft fairs and competitions, to give young craftsmen a shopwindow.[24]

Leslie Durbin, a silversmith trained in Ramsden's workshop and at the Central School in the 1930s, is a link with the last flickering of the Arts and Crafts tradition. He was to maintain a steady momentum between 1950 and 1977 when he sold his workshop to Hector Miller and retired. His work is notable for its superb finish and for his deep-rooted interest in symbolism, expressed for instance in a series of inkstands commissioned by the Bank of England from 1952 onwards. Durbin's pieces, seen recently at a retrospective exhibition at the Hall (1982) have been described as 'like a breath of spring in their innovative quality'.[25] They are in marked contrast to the cleancut forms, machine finishes and heavy texturing popular with his erstwhile pupils in silversmithing at the Royal College of Art. There, a common taste for texture, drama and eye-appeal is evident in the silver of Stuart Devlin, and Louis Osman too. A centrepiece by Devlin (1972) combines a ring of baskets containing clusters of gold openwork spires, alternating with candleholders, the whole a delight for a rich man's table.

The past decade has seen a continuing decline in manufacturing silversmithing, with old firms not only in London but also in Birmingham and Sheffield closing down or being taken over. A number of factors have contributed: with changing social habits, as fewer households have servants and more women work outside the home, the silver teaset, that centrepiece of English middle-class for two and a half centuries, has virtually disappeared. Simultaneously

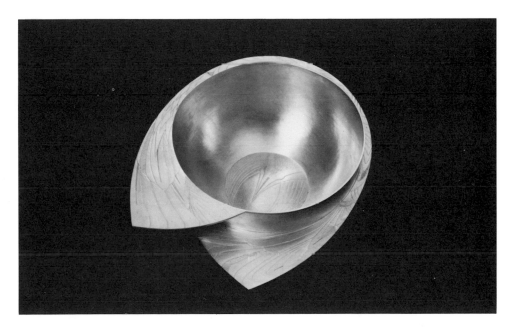

Fig. 59 **'Hawk' bowl**
Silver and two-coloured gold 1982. Designed and made by Rod Kelly. Note the careful chasing to
texture the surface and to define the wing feathers.
Private collection

141

the risk of burglary has so greatly increased that people are reluctant either to buy new, or to replace their silver, once stolen. While students continue to study silversmithing, the outlets for their work are extremely limited and few survive to make a living by their craft. One of London's few remaining manufacturing companies, C. J. Vander, depends on overseas orders for its comparative health.

In 1985 its workshops in London and Sheffield consumed or rather 'fashioned', five tons of silver hollowware and cutlery; other long-established London manufacturers are Naylor Brothers, now in-house suppliers to Garrards, Barnards (with the longest continuous history of any company, since the 1690s) and Comyns.

Notes

1   Shirley Bury attributes this taste to French influence, specifically to designs published in the *Art-Union* from 1845. See her useful essay 'Silver and Silver Plate 1830–60' in *Connoisseur Period Guides* (1968), 1388–9. Also Wardle; Culme 1977 and Ch. 12.

2   See Collard 1985 for the Elizabethan revival.

3   Bury 1983.

4   Eastlake 1867, 250–60.

5   It was reissued in the 1860s. Bury 1967a.

6   Ch. 13 and 14; Oman (VAM Bulletin); Smith 1974.

7   Colman Collection, for example nos. 125–8.

8   A direct copy of a cupid and mustard barrel made for Mme de Pompadour in 1750. For more table toys, see Colman Collection, 108, 111.

9   Al-Tajir Collection, pl. 51.

10   Birmingham AG 1973. A handsome marine theme service presented to Brunel in 1845 (launching of the *Great Britain*) is in the Al-Tajir Collection.

11   Al-Tajir Collection, pl. 55.

12   Skidmore of Coventry did well with gothic plate; Bury *Connoisseur Period Guides* (1968) 1391–2.

13   Almost every Sotheby and Christie sale has one or two.

14   H. R. Haweis. *The Art of Decoration* (1881).

15   For illustrations of these Victorian patterns, see Pickford 1983. Many are still in production, although more expensive than the originals to buy.

16   Birmingham AG 1973.

17   Culme 1977 and Ch. 12. Hughes 1967.

18   Anscombe and Gere 1978, chapter 1.

19   Bury 1962b.

20   Goldsmiths' Hall: E. A. Jones Exhibition.

21   VAM 1975.

22   *Art-Journal* special supplement 1901.

23   Birmingham AG 1973; Spinks 1984.

24   Described in Goldsmiths' Company 1965. Such a programme would be considered impossible now, both on security and cost grounds.

25   Goldsmiths' 1982.

PART II

CRAFT, COMPANY AND CUSTOMERS

SEVEN

'TOUCH', ASSAY AND HALLMARKING

HALLMARKS, invaluable aids to the study of English silver, have been understood by the non-goldsmith only for a little over a century. An exhibition at Goldsmiths' Hall in 1978 on the history of hallmarking *Touching Gold and Silver* may be taken as the latest, if not the last, word on this complex subject, which will therefore not be described in detail here, since the catalogue says it all and gives examples.[1]

The French, rather than the English, can claim to be the originators of hallmarks; the first town marks were mentioned in 1275 and maker's marks (at Montpellier) in 1427. The first mention of a mark for English silver was in 1300, when the leopard's head or king's mark was specified as evidence that the worked silver was up to sterling (coinage) standard; the guardians (or wardens) of the craft were to go from workshop to workshop, assaying and marking before the wares left their maker's hands. In 1363, the maker's mark was introduced: 'each Master Goldsmith shall have a mark to himself'.

In 1478 the Company was made specifically responsible for the keeper of the touch (or royal officer). To ensure that they could police his activities, they appointed a salaried common assayer on 17 December 1478, to work at the Hall only and mark all wares with a date-letter, the basis of the modern system.

One more mark joined these three in 1544, the lion passant crowned. In the 1540s the silver content of English coins was sharply reduced which led to sneering references to Henry VIII as 'Old Coppernose' whose shillings and sixpences were 'glowing for shame', as Latimer described in a famous sermon. This is almost certainly why the Goldsmiths' Company introduced the new mark. It indicated their adherence to the sterling standard for all hallmarked wares, no matter that the silver content in the coinage was by then only 50 per cent! The crown was dropped in 1550.

Changes in, and additions to, the hallmarks since then have occurred for various reasons. In 1697 the Crown required a higher silver content for wrought plate (95·8 per cent) to protect their newly issued milled coinage from clipping and melting, so new marks, a lion's head erased (torn away at the base) and a figure of Britannia, were substituted for the sterling mark and lion passant. New maker's marks were required as well, with the first two letters of the goldsmith's surname.

After the 1697 Act, provincial goldsmiths were left in an anomalous position, with no assay offices, no authority to sell sterling standard plate and no official Britannia standard mark. In Norwich, two goldsmiths, James Daniell and Elizabeth Haslewood, enterprisingly marked their wares with a stamp 'F:SIL' for 'fine silver', with repeated impression of their maker's marks to give four in all.[2] New assay offices were authorised in 1700 in York, Bristol, Exeter, Chester and Norwich and in Newcastle in 1702; two more, at Birmingham and Sheffield, opened in 1773.

When the Britannia standard was made optional (in 1719, operational from June 1720) several goldsmiths continued to work in the higher standard, notably Paul De Lamerie (first sterling mark 1733) and Augustin Courtauld, and some do to this day. Later additional marks have been connected with the duty levied on wrought plate. In December 1784 this was reimposed, at 6d an ounce, and a duty mark struck, with punches supplied by the Board of Stamps (later Revenue). The first mark, the sovereign's head incuse, was changed two years later to the more familiar sovereign's head in cameo, facing right, which was dropped in 1890 when the duty was removed. Since then, sovereign's head marks have been introduced in 1934, in 1952 (for two years) and in 1977, with the object of stimulating sales among collectors.

The foregoing summary omits the provincial assay offices, whose respective histories by no means parallel London's; they are too large a subject for this book.

The London Assay Office

Both assay and hallmarking procedures in London were described very fully by William Badcock in 1677 in *A New Touchstone for Gold and Silver Wares* after a revision at the Hall the year before. Although he recommended the touchstone method to would-be purchasers of silver, it is clear from his diagrams that the official assay procedure, whereby samples filed from an unobtrusive place on the object were wrapped in paper before testing by cupellation, was well established. Indeed, the wardens were assaying by cupellation early in the fourteenth century.[3]

Fig. 60 **London marks, 1579**

Sterling, lion passant, date letter B and maker's mark, a bird in a shaped shield. Typically deep and
clearly struck. The mark of a bird is found on high quality English work of c.1550–80. Although
unnamed as yet, he was almost certainly a court supplier. Note the high relief embossing, seen here from
the underside.

Loan, VAM

146

The steel dies used by the assay workers came in a number of sizes suitable for all types of silverware and, as Badcock explained, it was always possible to arrange with the assay master to mark intricate or hollow objects, such as sword-hilts or buckles, with especially small punches, 'the Work being first marked by the Worker with marks of Ink on every place'. Because striking the marks along spoon and fork stems or steels distorted the shape the assay office changed its practice about 1780, resorting to marking the upper part of the handle.[4]

Sometimes, on an elaborate display object, the hallmarks were deliberately placed unobtrusively on plain surfaces, as in the case of the Elizabethan Vyvyan salt. More often they were struck across a surface which was subsequently embossed or chased; only in the eighteenth century did their placing become more discreet. Recently hallmarks have assumed a decorative quality in their own right, for example on silver and silvergilt 'ingot' pendants, where they are struck with a set of large punches.

The official punches, of hardened steel, were carefully kept under lock and key. In 1511 Robert Amadas, already a court supplier and soon to be the leading English goldsmith of his generation, was fourth warden of the Company, with the duty of being touch warden; he casually removed the punches, and the keys to their chest, to his home and then left town. He was made to pay a substantial fine and the beadle, to whom he had delegated the task of 'touching' in his absence, was sacked.[5]

The Company has always taken the trouble to keep samples of false hallmarks, as in 1531 when John Dyamond of Exeter sold spoons 'marked with lettres and portcoylises (portcullis) . . . for touched spones'. 'Two Skantlyns (drawings) with their sayes and marks were taken and remain for example in the treasure house of this fellowship.' The same wish to protect their unique system lay behind the pamphlet on the Lyon and Twinam forged marks, which the Company published in 1889.[6]

Maker's Marks

Referred to, more accurately, since 1973 as sponsor's marks, this is one area of English silver which is constantly coming into new focus as diligent research appears in print. Grimwade, Culme, Taylor and Kent have corrected many of the misattributions of London marks in Jackson's classic *English Goldsmiths and their Marks* and no doubt the revised edition of Jackson will extend this process of reassessment to provincial goldsmiths too.[7]

Maker's marks of the later seventeenth century are clearcut and notably well-struck, a characteristic of later provincial silver, so much so that their marks could be quoted as identification in cases of theft. In 1759 and 1780 local silversmiths advertised in the *Newcastle Courant*, one offering to return stolen goods 'whoever has lost the same by giving in the marks . . . may have their own again', the other a retailer quoting his mark to identify two large tablespoons.[8]

MAKER'S MARKS PRE-1697

Occasional Tudor references to touchplates indicate that a version of the system described by William Badcock already operated; for example in October 1534 the Company required all smallworkers, 'Workmen of smallgear', to bring in their old punches 'to have them dampened' or defaced. Having cut out new punches, the workmen were then to bring them to the Hall 'to be sett into plate in the Sayhouse (assay office) therfor assigned'.[9]

For London goldsmiths, any hope of identifying firmly any individual's mark before 1697 is fairly small. Sometimes, by the happy survival of a distinctive piece of silver which can be tied up with a given order, this is possible; so the mark of the Elizabethan Robert Tayleboyes appears to be the stag's head caboched, since this mark occurs on the communion cups he supplied to S. Margaret's Westminster in 1551 and their purchase from him is recorded in the churchwarden's accounts. Similarly, a ewer and basin known to have been made by Simon Owen for the Goldsmiths' Company, and embossed with their badges, in 1611, pinned down to him the mark of so above a pellet; this was reinforced by the large number of ewers and basins marked by him, and by the wardens' criticism of his shop window that it was more befitting a barber than a goldsmith, because of his huge assemblage of toilet plate.[10]

Very occasionally the mark of a partnership, such as I M over F B for John Middleton and Francis Brown, who were partners in 1614, ties up so closely with its occurrence on hallmarked silver as to be indisputable. In Restoration Norwich a composite mark indicates another partnership, that of Arthur Haselwood with William Edwards. Robert Sanderson from Norwich, free of the London Company in 1632, emigrated to New England in 1637. He took his maker's die with him, and from documented silver made for his Boston customers it has been possible to identify both pieces made before he left London and others made in New England, marked in each case with R S under a sun.[11]

However, the sheer quantity of goldsmiths named in the court books and apprenticeship registers of the London Company and the many versions both of initial letter marks and of shield shapes on surviving silver makes manipulating this information difficult. Many of the older London attributions (about sixteen between 1545 and 1600 are quoted in Jackson, *English Goldsmiths and their Marks*) do not remain true once the working life of the man is set against the date-spread of the mark assigned to him.

Biographies of each goldsmith can help, indicating, for example if and when a man was excluded from touch and assay for a few months because of trade offences. After such an episode, the goldsmith had to register a new punch so that his old work could not be confused with his new; this identifies two versions of the T F mark attributed to Thomas Flint the second, active between the 1580s and 1622, and the G S of Gabriel Stark or Strick, who was free in 1613 and changed his mark, at the Company's insistence, in 1617.

Disputes with the Company are, from the historian's point of view, very helpful in pinning down individuals. Clement Punge, 'pulley salt maker', whose 'C P over a rose' mark appears on several scroll salts, for example the Innholders' salt bequeathed by Richard Reeve (in 1657, made in 1639) was in trouble the year before for using too much solder in his salts, and so increasing the weight of metal, but not of silver.[12]

Where the goldsmith's name was one in common use, or where his initials were shared with many other goldsmiths, such as I H (or J H), several potential candidates might be active and marking their wares at any one time. A recent exercise on the I H combination demonstrated that in the 1590s there were forty-four goldsmiths active in London with those initials and so potential users of them. So far, only three versions of the I H mark are recorded on silver of this period and for common combinations like this it is hopeless to attempt attributions, with one exception. A few years earlier, John Harrison kept his shop at the sign of the Broad Arrow in Goldsmiths' Row, Cheapside; he may reasonably be claimed as using the punch in which an arrow bisects the letter H to make a monogram.[13]

If, added to the initials, there was a device, perhaps a rebus on the man's name like the crook between G S of Gilbert Shepherd (active after the Restoration) or the W S flanking an arrow of Walter Shute (1630s), then a certain identification becomes more feasible.

The mark of Thomas Maundy, associated by collectors with his embossed sweetmeat dishes, which for many people epitomise mid-Stuart silver, occurs also on the mace he supplied to the city of Leicester in 1651. Because several letters he wrote about this order have been preserved, his mark has been identified and he has received perhaps unjustified attention in the sale room.[14]

Specialist goldsmiths are easier to track down, because they are often separately identified

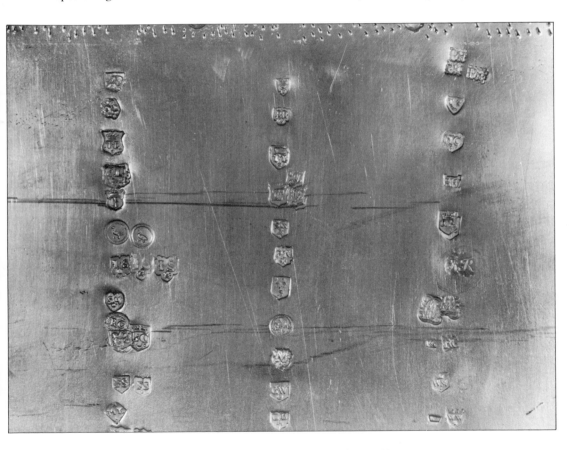

Fig. 61 **Copper mark plate, begun about 1680**
(Detail) After assay office practice was overhauled in 1676, London goldsmiths came in to strike their new marks onto a copper sheet and sign a parchment strip which hung alongside each row of marks. These have disappeared and very few can be identified. Note the variations in shield-shape and the one device mark, a goose in a dotted circle. Initials became compulsory in 1697.
Goldsmiths' Company

in craft and town records. Spoonmakers were a distinct group from the late Middle Ages, with certain families continuing active in the craft and taking one another's apprentices for several generations. A recent publication by Tim Kent *London Silver Spoonmakers 1500–1697* attributed marks to fifty-two workshops; he is now working on a much larger study of provincial goldsmiths, running to hundreds of names.

Because the retail goldsmiths acted as intermediaries in placing orders, the name of the maker is not often mentioned, even in well-documented cases. It is clear from the quality and weight of certain Restoration pieces that they were special orders, probably placed through the Jewel House whose orders were handled by Sir Robert and Sir Thomas Vyner; several bear the marks of the hound sejant (found from about 1646 to 1666) and the orb above a mullet (found from 1660). These are associated almost invariably with work of high quality and original ornament, such as the Thirkleby flagon (1646) or the Ashley-Cooper porringer and salver (*c.*1661, both VAM). Whether these two goldsmiths were responsible for the chasing and embossing too is not clear, but another Restoration goldsmith, the Zurich-born Wolfgang Howzer, who specialised in superb embossing, did register a mark, probably W H over a cherub (Plate 3).[15]

By the 1690s, more marks can be certainly attributed; because the names are known of those already active who registered new marks in 1697, it is possible sometimes to trace back to their earlier marks, as has been done with Thomas Jenkins, George Garthorne, Francis Leake and Philip Rollos.

The procedure for registering makers' punches at the Hall was fully described by William Badcock (incidentally himself not free of the Goldsmiths' Company) a member of the Longbowstringmakers' Company who produced silver weapon-fittings. His *Touchstone* illuminates the function of the one early copper plate remaining at Goldsmiths' Hall, struck with marks of the decade from 1680 (Fig. 66). This originally had strips of parchment attached, which each goldsmith signed by his punched mark; the marks on the plate are mostly initials but there are still some devices such as the goose in a dotted circle, a mark found on high quality silver of the 1670s and 1680s, particularly chinoiseries-chased items.[16]

Before the late eighteenth century, English goldsmiths very rarely signed their work. Occasionally engravers' signatures or initials are found, like Simon Gribelin or Joseph Sympson (p.218); this practice was carried over from their business of issuing engraved plates. A goldsmith using the mark P B in monogram was responsible for some of the more elaborately embossed and chased work of the Restoration, notably a dessert dish with a removable foot (formerly in the J. P. Morgan Collection). This is chased with plaques of putti symbolising the elements, between four clusters of fruit and vegetables, with a chased central scene of Venus and Adonis. Most unusually, the signature is engraved on the foot 'Paul Beuren Ao 1683' perhaps that of the maker himself, proud of a particularly skilled confection. Since it is fully marked, for London 1683, it is likely to have been intended for stock rather than being a special commission.[17]

Special commissions sometimes carried signatures, although whether as a sign of the creator's pride (as with Christian van Vianen) or as a means of identification to conform, however loosely, to the Goldsmiths' Company requirements, is not clear. The inscription on a mace at Wilton signed 'Ric Grafton fecit', should not be taken literally but rather that

Grafton had had it made, by a Salisbury goldsmith. Another Wessex mace, at Marlborough, was purchased as part of the general Commonwealth replacement programme in 1652. Perhaps to advertise his identity, the maker Tobias Coleman of London engraved both his name and his occupation.[18]

From the 1770s retailers regularly engraved their names and addresses on prestigious orders, as on the plinth of the Drapers' Company staffhead, signed 'Coyte fecit'. In fact the staffhead was made and marked by Thomas Pitts, but George Coyte was paid £63 for supplying it. Rundell, Bridge & Rundell are the best known followers of this practice, adding also that they supplied plate to the king himself: 'AURIFICES REGIS'. Kensington Lewis and David Ellis, who also supplied the royal dukes in the 1820s, copied them in engraving their names on orders, as the antique dealer and silversmith George Lambert of Coventry Street did later in the century.[19] The designer Christopher Dresser took care both to advertise, and to protect the copyright in, his designs by having a facsimile of his signature engraved, along with the Patent Office design registration mark. When the manufacturer's mark and retailer's name appear too, as on the 1880 teaset made by James Dixon, there is a formidable battery of documentation![20]

PROVINCIAL GOLDSMITHS

In provincial towns, identifying goldsmiths before the 1690s is somewhat easier. Local archives are more manageable and the number of men to be identified far fewer and, therefore, the possibility of confusion is less. Also a large number of spoons, the commonest item owned, have been preserved, providing a body of makers' marks. A convenient summary of the situation in the major provincial centres was written by M. Holland.[21]

Since goldsmiths were expected to be freemen, of whom a register was normally kept by the town, and since references to individual goldsmiths are easier to track down in parish records and through their wills, many more marks have been attributed. In Norwich, for instance, seven of the eleven found between 1565, when the assay mark series started, and 1600, have been identified. All but two, the C T for Christopher Tannor and I V over a heart for Valentine Isborne, are devices, such as the orb on a cross (with three different shapes of shield) for William Cobbold, a sun in splendour for Peter Peterson and a flat fish for Thomas Buttell. Devices remained popular in Norwich until the middle of the seventeenth century. Timothy Skottowe (T S) and Arthur Haselwood (A H) with one unknown W D were the only users of initial marks. Richard Shipden, their contemporary, used a ship as his mark but devices are normally harder to pin down.[22]

So much silver has vanished that we certainly do not have the mark used by every known goldsmith. For example, there are seven hundred pieces of Norwich-marked silver, made between 1565 and 1702; 27 marks are represented but about 60 goldsmiths were at work through this 150-year period. Even allowing for the fact that some were makers of small wares, this leaves a large number still unrepresented by surviving pieces. At King's Lynn, goldsmiths occur among the freemen from the early fourteenth century, with six named in the prosperous late Tudor period. One, James Wilcock, used not only an initial mark but also a punch with the Lynn town mark – three dragon heads with cross crosslets – but only four pieces can be firmly attributed to him.[23]

Fig. 62 **Laceback trefid spoon**
*c.*1680. Mark WR conjoined, probably for William Rowe of Liskeard and struck three times, probably
to satisfy the customer's expectation of multiple marks. From a set of six spoons to the pattern
introduced from France about 1660.
Timothy Coward

In Exeter the situation is rather different. Many more goldsmiths were at work there; the
names of over a hundred are recorded between the mid-sixteenth and mid-seventeenth
century, with a large number elsewhere in the West Country, notably Barnstaple, Taunton,
Liskeard and Plymouth, and there is a quantity of marked silver, largely spoons, to link with
the documents (Fig. 62).[24]

At Exeter devices had more or less fallen out of use by 1600 and several goldsmiths used a
full-name punch, such as John Edes, John Jones, Richard Osborne and Jasper Redcliffe. The
Barnstaple makers, John Quick and Thomas Mathew both added a mark like a berry which
is sometimes found with another, perhaps a retailer's, mark. Several West Country towns
had one or two goldsmiths who either used no town mark or adopted the Exeter mark,

presumably as a guarantee recognisable to the customer. One notorious Stuart spoonmaker, Thomas Dare senior of Taunton, went further and punched his wares not only with his own initial T and a town mark for Taunton (tau over a ton) but with a version of the lion passant mark. When the wardens of the London Company discovered these spoons among his stock on their 1633 visit, he claimed that the lion was his shop sign! He pleaded ignorance of any offence but since he had served his apprenticeship with a London goldsmith, Arthur Redcliffe, this was merely a face-saving defence.[25]

Exeter was not named as a town with its own touch in 1423 and the appearance of a town mark and (briefly) date-letter system in 1575 was the result of an agreement among the town goldsmiths themselves, without any evidence of official sanction from the mayor and aldermen. Each man had his own punch for the town mark and there was no local assay office, although the town mark of Exeter was sometimes adopted by other makers in the region and, therefore, was presumably a recognised guarantee of quality for retailers of silver. It is clear also that there was a considerable wholesale trade in wrought plate and that a working goldsmith in an out-of-town community might well supply a retailer in the larger regional centre; Salisbury goldsmiths, for example, were sending stock to Winchester retailers in the 1630s.[26]

Goldsmiths not only sold their wares retail in their shops but also to other goldsmiths for resale and at booths at the county fairs which dominated regional shopping until the mid-nineteenth century. The wardens of the Goldsmiths' Company included these fairs on their tours, to catch out men selling wares of less than sterling standard. At Stourbridge Fair, held at Michaelmas at Cambridge, six Norwich goldsmiths were fined in 1568.

On their 1635 visit to Norwich, the wardens reported that inspecting six shops took all Saturday. Monday was given over to making 'assays and trials' of plate and other goldsmiths' wares seized, 'as well by the fire as by the touch'. All the goldsmiths were fined, as was one haberdasher, who was selling thimbles, 'civet boxes', seals and jewels. The wares tested and found wanting comprised beer and wine bowls, scroll and other salts, porringers and spoons. John Howlett was fined the most, £10, and had the widest range and quantity of plate. Apart from tableware he had '12 papers of silver small wares being tags, whistles, bodkins, seals, toothpicks, clasps for hats, fan handles and corals garnished' plus rings and thimbles. Over two thousand ounces of plate were seized, plus thirty-seven ounces of gold rings. The silver goods tested were presumably representative of the goldsmiths' normal stock, if not their actual capability. There are no plates, sugar boxes or flagons, although all these were available to fashionable customers in the London shops.[27]

The shop stock might well include other makers' plate. At his death, Peter Peterson of Norwich had plate struck with the mark of William Cobbold in stock. On their 1631 visit to Salisbury, Simon Owen and his fellow warden took plate for assays from six shops; Thomas Hooper yielded sixty-three spoons plus rings, one at least marked by a poor working goldsmith, George Batter. So persistently did the Salisbury and other provincial goldsmiths work below sterling standard in the 1630s that in December 1637 the Company considered taking the advice of Salisbury's recorder Sir Robert Hyde and hauling the offenders before the next Sessions. The Salisbury goldsmiths were perhaps unfortunate in their relative accessibility to London and to the Company's watchful jurisdiction.[28]

The Company's interest extended also to the improper use of marks. John Dyamond of Exeter was brought before the wardens in 1531 with 'two spoons of his making with a round mark set in the cups (bowls) deceitfully where the touch should stand and were marked with letters and portcullis on their steales (stems) which he offered for sale as touched spoons'. The offence was that the marks imitated the London touch and date-letter. The spoons were not found to be below sterling standard but Dyamond was imprisoned none the less.[29]

Provincial goldsmiths were expected to swear to observe the sterling standard, to register their marks with the London Company and not, as we have seen, to imitate the London touch. When the Company visited Exeter in 1571, they took bonds for true workmanship from nine of the City's goldsmiths; this was perhaps to ensure that those goldsmiths, leading businessmen in the town, were ready to carry out the programme of converting West Country church plate. A close link between the church authorities and the Company in co-ordinating this enormous exercise is indicated. The shape of surviving communion cups, which is surprisingly uniform across the country, implies that the Company, or perhaps the church, supplied models for the local goldsmiths to follow.[30]

Such regional differences as are apparent in these locally-made communion cups – for example, the bucket-shaped cup of East Anglia is markedly shallower and broader than the Exeter version, which also had an in-turning rim – may well be features which reflect disparate local tastes in wine cups, but so little late sixteenth- or early seventeenth-century regional silver has survived that we have virtually no domestic plate with which to compare these church pieces. Spoons alone exist in such number as to permit one to distinguish, for example, a distinctive Salisbury knop as against, say, the 'Buddha' knop of Barnstaple.[31]

A common characteristic of plate from provincial goldsmiths is simplicity of form, especially when compared with elaborately worked London plate, and a lack of embossing. This does not indicate a want of skill but a want of demand. Workmanship or 'fashion' of course added to the cost without increasing the quantity of metal (and so the melt value) of the piece and may reflect the relative lack of interest in changing shapes and 'keeping up to date' of the provincial customer. Samuel Pepys's irritation at the high cost of fashion and its low resale value strikes a familiar chord.[32]

Generally speaking, the stock of even the London-apprenticed goldsmith comprised plain wares; customers requiring something more elaborate either had it made to order locally or sent to London for it. The inventory of Griffith Edwardes, a Chester goldsmith (d. 1637), is closely comparable with the stock of the Norwich smiths quoted earlier.[33] Apart from trencher salts, beer and wine bowls, porringers and spoons, he had in stock only one sugar dish, but quantities of cheap rings, '40 with beads', ten with stones and one with a diamond. His workshop yielded old lace, burnt silver and nine ounces of filings, indicating that he was not merely a retailer of other men's wares. Sometimes a London piece was copied; this presumably explains the Torrington goldsmith John Dagg making two crude examples of chinoiseries for adjacent Devon parishes.[34]

Outside London, every town of any size numbered at least one goldsmith among its tradesmen and in some at least goldsmiths, like cutlers, expected or preferred to mark their wares, following London practice. So of course did pewterers, and some leather workers chose to do so as did armourers. Despite a lack of references, local purchasers were by no means ignorant of the value of a town mark or maker's mark to indicate quality control. A late fifteenth-century spoon is the first example of the York mark of half a leopard's head and half a fleur-de-lis conjoined, although the fact that goldsmiths used the town mark is established from a reference of about 1411 to 'le comune touch de la dite cité'.[35]

There is no correlation between the seven assay towns named in the 1423 Act 'to have diverse touches' (York, Norwich, Newcastle, Bristol, Lincoln, Salisbury and Coventry) and surviving marked silver of the fifteenth and sixteenth centuries from provincial towns, and it becomes possible to associate references to goldsmiths' names with surviving pieces only from the later sixteenth century when both documents and objects become more numerous. In Bristol, the happy recovery of a maidenhead spoon, stamped R HARSELL, illustrates the output of just one late sixteenth-century goldsmith. One hundred or so are known to have been active in the town from the late Middle Ages to 1700.[36]

While there was no concerted, country-wide, campaign to force all goldsmiths to adopt versions of the London hallmarking system, both the goldsmiths and their customers recognised the advantages and gradually more and more towns joined in. 'Touched' plate was always valued more highly, since it had a guarantee of silver content; although few of the provincial towns operated an assay procedure, the makers' marks at least identified the maker within his region and so satisfied the need to identify workmanship.[37] Town authorities were responsible for controlling the quality of locally made wares, just as they were for weights and measures. Where the freemen had grouped themselves into a guild or company, as at Newcastle (in 1536), Hull (1598) and Salisbury, goldsmiths were always listed. The mayor gave at least tacit approval to whatever marking system was agreed and was expected by the Goldsmiths' Company to assist them in enforcing co-operation on their periodic visits with their cupels and touchstones.[38]

The policy of bringing conformity to Protestant worship in the 1560s and 1570s gave a tremendous boost to the goldsmiths' craft both in London and outside and several towns authorised the adoption of a local mark in addition to a maker's mark at about this time.

In Norwich the date-letter system and town mark started, with the approval of the Corporation, in 1565 and seems to be directly linked with the sudden demand to convert a large number of local communion cups in response to Bishop Parkhurst's campaign. The London system of date-letters was imitated in York from 1559 (although no letter A has yet been recorded), in Norwich from 1565 to 1571 and in Exeter, by certain goldsmiths only, from 1575 (even more briefly).[39]

One of the earliest surviving pieces with an identified Exeter maker's mark is a font cup made by Richard Hilliard (RH conjoined) of about 1560, in a private collection. Those of the Exeter goldsmiths who adopted the town mark (a Roman X crowned) had each his own punch, since there was no assay office in Exeter before 1701. At Hull goldsmiths are recorded from the fourteenth century. About 150 pieces of Hull-marked silver are known, the earliest a communion cup of about 1580 with H. Many belong to local churches or to Trinity House, Hull, which owns thirteen pieces, cups, beakers and tankards presented by past Brethren. From 1620 the town mark in use was three coronets, which is easily confused with the Dutch mark for Sneek in Friesland.[40]

The Chester goldsmiths had formed themselves long before the sixteenth century into a

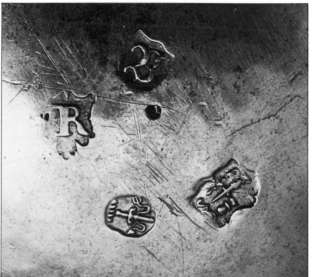

Fig. 63 **Chester spout cup**
a) *c.*1690. Mark of Thomas Robinson. H.11.2 cm. A typical provincial form, bottom-marked.
b) Town sterling mark (introduced in 1686–7) overstruck with Old City of Chester coat of arms in use from 1690; Chester Sword of State, date letter B for 1690–2; TR monogram for Thomas Robinson. Possibly old stock overstamped for sale after the 1690 reform.
Grosvenor Museum, Chester

company; a minute book of 1554 includes a regulation that all brethren should mark their plate with a personal punch, but no other marks were in use there before 1687. In that year the goldsmiths agreed to revise their arrangements in line with London practice and settled that all plate should be assayed and touched by the wardens, whose punches were to be the arms and crest of Chester, plus a letter identifying the assay master.[41]

The freemen of Newcastle had incorporated themselves into an associated company in 1536, with five goldsmith members, but the earliest known piece of firmly identified silver by a Newcastle maker is a communion cup, engraved 1583 and marked only with the initials VB for Valentine Baker. He had been a member of the Company since 1560. Newcastle goldsmiths in the later seventeenth century also felt the need to give their wares a mark of regional significance; John Wilkinson (d. 1664) adopted a single flower and William Ramsay a three towers punch for his town mark about 1670. By 1680 several Newcastle men used a crude three towers device. John Wilkinson had also adopted a lion passant mark in which he was followed by other local goldsmiths; the mark was struck twice, to make four in imitation of the London hallmarks, but the lion was reversed, pacing to the right not to the left.[42]

Lincoln, although named in 1423 as an assay town, appears never to have adopted a town mark. One goldsmith, John Morley, who was free of the London Company, is known to have made many of the local communion cups for the diocese between 1568 and 1570, but little other silver can be even tentatively attributed to Lincoln goldsmiths and there is no evidence that the city authorities ever required a mark. Jackson's attribution of the fleur-de-lis to Lincoln is no longer accepted.[43]

The Bristol 'common punch of a bull's head', authorised in 1462, has never been recorded and even the mark BR conjoined, also used as a mint mark there, in 1643–5, is extremely rare.[44]

It must be emphasised that the only substantial documented body of provincial silver before 1700 is the Elizabethan communion plate; these cups have formed the basis for many attributions of marks to goldsmiths of the Elizabethan period. William Mutton of Chester, who cornered the bulk of the post-Reformation conversions in his region from 1570, used the rebus mark of a sheep's head in a shaped shield. While this is found on many communion cups, there is no secular silver which can be attributed to this maker, although presumably he was capable of working for the domestic market too. Nicholas Goston or Gorston of Nottingham also is known only from his mark on communion plate – NG flanking a maiden's head.[45]

LONDON MAKERS AFTER 1697

Before 1697 there is no evidence that any books were kept by the Goldsmiths' Company to record makers' marks. The earlier system described by Badcock, whereby names on parchment strips were pinned alongside the punch marks, was presumably in use long before, but this system was abandoned for books in which the new standard marks were first entered. From 1697, when the Britannia standard was introduced, goldsmiths had to register new marks in two volumes, one for large- and one for smallworkers. Each maker dipped his punch or punches into lamp black and stamped the column by his name and address, which was then countersigned by the touch warden.[46] Metal plates for makers' marks were

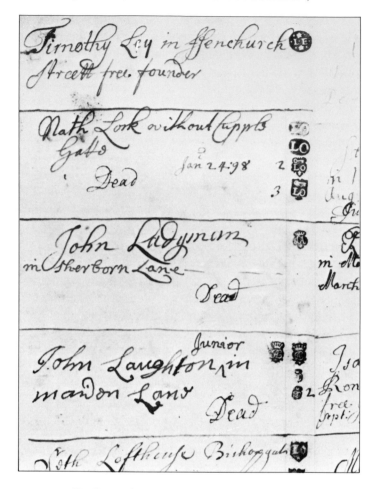

Fig. 64 **Marks entered in the large workers' book**
Detail of p. 30, vol. AI, 1697–1739. Note the rebus key mark of Nathaniel Lock and John Laughton's
unusual combination of three letters JAL. Punches of varying sizes were regularly needed.
Goldsmiths' Company

reintroduced after a House of Commons report criticised procedures at the assay office (1773).

The Britannia maker's mark was made up of the first two letters of the surname, sometimes both in capitals and sometimes with an additional device. Before street numbering was introduced in London (1760s) prominent houses, especially those with shops below, were given names, often with painted boards suspended outside; goldsmiths had frequently adopted their property-sign as an alternative or addition to their maker's mark. The Elizabethan William Denham took the sign of the golden cup from one house in Cheapside to another and apparently used that mark too. A century later William Atkinson of New Fish Street Hill, entered his Britannia mark surmounted by a two-handled cup, to indicate his house name.

When George Wickes was setting up his new premises in Panton Street off the Haymarket in 1735, with the Prince of Wales as his most distinguished customer, he not only adopted the king's arms and Prince of Wales's feathers as his shop sign but also incorporated first the crown (on 30 June 1735) and then the feathers when he registered his new mark in 1739. Later other royal goldsmiths used the crown too.

There was of course some duplication; the mitre, the golden cup and the crown each featured on several goldsmiths' marks simultaneously, since these were obvious names for goldsmiths' premises and easily recognisable as devices. Heal noted sixty instances of the golden cup as the address for London goldsmiths of the eighteenth century.

Both John Bodington and William Bellasyse entered a mitre as part of their Britannia marks; each man worked at the Sign of the Mitre. Sometimes the mark incorporated a rebus, as had been characteristic rather earlier. Andrew Raven had a bird, Nathanial Lock in 1699 a key and in 1759 William Bell, a smallworker, registered his mark as the initials WB flanking a bell. Since the mark had to be personalised and differentiated from all other goldsmiths with the same initials, it was important to find some individual element; this could of course also appear on or be incorporated into the trade card. Many of the first generation of Huguenots personalised their marks by incorporating a fleur-de-lis or a crown with the two *grains de remède* characteristic of Paris. These were not unique to them; Francis Leake also adopted a fleur-de-lis above his FL mark.

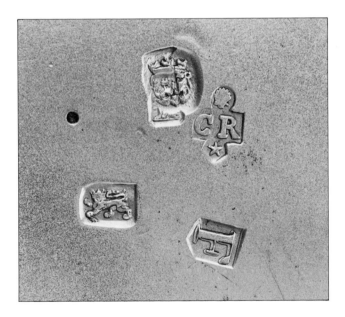

Fig. 65 **Overstruck mark on Crespin cruet stand**
1721. The sterling mark is struck over the Britannia mark; presumably within a year of the restoration of the old (sterling) standard, the assay officer still picked up the Britannia punches occasionally. De Lamerie, among others, continued to send in Britannia standard silver for some years. Note the setting-out point, indicating the centre of the sheet before raising and shaping.
Colonial Williamsburg

After the Britannia standard came in, several makers registered monogram marks: John Laughton junior in 1699, Matthew Lofthouse in 1705 and James Gould about 1734. The outlines for punches varied enormously; a simple rectangle was always popular and, when combined with a common combination of initials such as WC or IH, makes firm identification of a worn mark rather difficult. More interesting are the lobed marks, hearts, double ovals, indented shields and so on, characteristic of the eighteenth century. One maker, the inventive and original Aymé Videau, adopted an asymmetrical surround for his punch, in response to the prevailing rococo style of which he was a distinguished exponent. Although women goldsmiths often adopted a lozenge-shaped punch, the heraldic convention for a widow's or spinster's coat of arms, this was by no means the universal practice. To take three names from Grimwade, Mary Chawner, Mary Hussey and Margaret Harrison each used conventional masculine forms.

Joint punches were not necessarily recut when a partnership broke up; when Richard Carter left the trio of Carter, Daniel Smith and Robert Sharp in 1778, his initials were simply trimmed from the top of the punch, leaving a trace behind. An object bearing this curiously imperfect punch is William Beckford's gold teapot at the Barber Institute, Manchester.

The workmen making flatware for large manufacturing businesses in the later eighteenth and nineteenth centuries each had their own mark, often an incuse device such as a crescent, star, portcullis, triangle or line of dots. Smaller than the hallmarks and main maker's or sponsor's punch, these had no retail significance but were an aid to quality control, enabling the employer to identify substandard work once the finished batches had been brought in.[47]

Other marks are sometimes found engraved on large or complex objects. The twelve-branch silver candelabra made for the Fishmongers' Company in 1752 is engraved with a series of notches, to enable each of the branches to be married up with its correct slot. On tureens or condiment vases of the rococo period, where the irregularly shaped covers could sit happily in one position only, small location marks were engraved on both cover and body. On the feet, stems and covers of Tudor standing cups, components which were normally cast separately and slotted on to a central rod, location marks – crosses or double lines – are frequently found (for example, Fig. 10).[48]

MARKS ON NON-LONDON SILVER POST-1697

Copper mark plates survive at Chester, begun in 1701, and at Newcastle, begun in the following year. Jackson referred to the 'small brass plate from the Assay Office at York' but this is now lost. At Exeter the London system of books was followed. The practices of the major provincial assay offices are relatively well documented after 1701; their occasional anomalies, like the right-facing lion found struck on Newcastle silver in the 1720s and on York silver in the period 1793–1808, can be explained as a local engraver's error, in that he took as his model the impression rather than the punch itself. Another oddity, the double impression of the monarch's head found on Birmingham and Sheffield silver briefly from July 1797, is explicable as a convenient means of witnessing that double duty had been paid. Most provincial goldsmiths' marks are recorded in local assay records, or can be identified from directories; the new edition of Jackson will correct and supplement his original lists of provincial makers. One assay office, that at Exeter, took its regional role seriously and in the first half of the eighteenth century encouraged West Country silversmiths to register their marks.[49]

The demands of the London retail market led in the 1770s to Sheffield marks being overstruck. Sometimes the maker's mark only is obliterated; more often, as in the case of neo-classical candlesticks made by John Winter in Sheffield but sent down for sale to John Carter, the London man overstruck all four marks, only the varying shield shapes peering out from behind the London punches betraying their place of making. Another set of Sheffield candlesticks die-struck and loaded, has the mark of the London retailers Makepeace and Carter (1778). In Plymouth the retailers regularly overstruck the manufacturer's marks in the eighteenth century; Tim Kent quotes four distinct combinations, of which Samuel Willmott's is most commonly found.[50]

Matthew Boulton recognised the commercial appeal of wares bearing a retailer's punch and agreed to send the Edinburgh silversmith, Patrick Robertson, some candlesticks unmarked. Although it was illegal, 'we are willing to strain a point to oblige you'.[51]

A generation later the London firm Barnard's, which had a large overseas and provincial wholesale manufacturing business, provided a similar service for the York silversmith James Barber. Either his London-made stock was sent up 'to be hallmarked in York' or he could have it stamped at Barnard's with his own punch.[52]

The growing export trade in silver in the second half of the eighteenth century brought its own complications. Although the Hall was not concerned with duty marks until December 1784, silver parcelled-up for export was required to be assayed and marked in the normal way. An incident in April 1783 concerned a Quaker silversmith, William Stevenson of Lombard Street. He was caught by the customs officer exporting a box of silver wares 'which have no Hall Mark upon them' and were worse than standard. His defence, that he had bought most of those worse than standard 'at public sales', was accepted by the Company and he suffered the relatively light penalty of having the offending articles broken and returned to him. The problem of substandard wares recurs in the minute books of the Company through the eighteenth century; exporters without their own manufacturing businesses were dependent on acquiring their stock as cheaply as possible and no doubt thought the risk worthwhile.[53]

'Duty Dodgers' and Counterfeit Marks 1720 to 1800

Quite apart from the traditional offence of working plate worse than standard but selling it at sterling prices, the imposition of duty at 6d an ounce in 1720 led to a new temptation, that of duty dodging, and a new difficulty for the Company in policing the craft.

The splendid tea and chocolate set (now belonging to the Goldsmiths' Company) made by Nathaniel Ward in 1719 is the earliest example of transposed marks. Before the introduction of the duty on plate (on 1 June 1720) Ward apparently sent in three waiters for marking. He then cut a marked strip from one and set it into the lamp stand; another he set into the base of the kettle. By so doing he avoided the duty which was about to become payable which at 6d an ounce was to be a considerable burden on large orders. Another example, also in the

Goldsmiths' Collection, a massive wine fountain, has a false base inserted by Peter Archambo in 1728.[54]

The practice of transposing marks was quickly taken up by the trade who inserted marks from old plate too and in January 1730 the wardens were considering how to remedy this 'ancient evil practice, amongst ill-disposed goldsmiths of cutting out the Company's marks from old plate and soldering the same into new pieces, which had never been tried at the Hall and may possible be very coarse'. A coffee pot (in a private collection) made about 1730 has marks of 1645 and a teapot, also of about 1730, has marks of 1692.[55]

In order to prevent this, the assay officers were ordered to strike their marks on the plate as far distant from each other 'as the same conveniently may be struck, so that they may not be cut out together'. The practice of transposing marks flourished until about 1750 but examples are found only occasionally after that and it has been suggested that the Company and the craft achieved some form of accommodation. The ledgers of George Wickes and his successors Parker & Wakelin demonstrate that this large business house certainly did not pay duty on every item made and sold.

Since the duty was levied at the point of assay, it was tempting for the goldsmith to obtain illegal copies of the official punches, strike the 'hallmarks' in his workshops and pass the plate off as legitimately marked. Presumably this temptation to evade the duty lay behind the sudden concentration of cases of counterfeit hallmarks in the 1730s and 1740s. Indeed these offences were probably a large part of the impetus towards the 1739 Act on hallmarking and the concurrent revision of assay procedures. In November 1737, for instance, Humphrey Payne was rewarded for his help in prosecuting Kirk Ryves, who had made and sold buckles 'worse than sterling' with marks resembling the Company's marks.[56]

On 20 June 1739 (a week after the Bill received royal assent) to impede further counterfeiting, Thomas Long, an engraver, was ordered to 'alter all the [Hall] Markes by working or scolloping the Escutcheon of each mark'; the twenty replacement punches he made for the assay office were delivered a month later. At the same time every goldsmith had to register a new mark, a convenient means of dating for pieces bearing a maker's mark only. But the problem of counterfeiting continued. Within two years David (or Thomas) Moulden was sentenced to twelve months' hard labour in Bridewell for non-payment of a £900 fine for this offence and two men were prosecuted by the clerk in February 1743, one for selling, the other for making counterfeit punches.[57]

An alternative method of avoiding assay was for the goldsmith to strike just his maker's mark four times; pieces so marked are called duty dodgers. This presumably was to reassure the customer who at a quick glance would see the normal four marks and perhaps not examine it more closely. At least where the piece was for a major client, like George Booth, the metal was well up to sterling standard so that it may well have been the customer who winked at this tax-avoidance device.

Where secondhand plate was concerned, plate that was untouched achieved a lower price than pieces which were fully marked, so that the trade at least was not deceived. An interesting instance in the assay office collection is a caster, with the maker's mark struck four times and no other marks. Much later, presumably in the late nineteenth or early twentieth century, when the flourishing collectors' market made it worthwhile, someone has cut out a fully-marked base from another piece of silver and soldered it over the original marks. This of course is an offence and the piece was withdrawn from circulation by the Antique Plate Committee of the Goldsmiths' Company.

The value of hallmarks as guarantee of quality to potential customers was generally recognised; a provincial goldsmith, Robert Windsor, wrote from Lymington on 12 February 1751 to Mr Nash, the Company's junior weigher, to provide him with a stamp; 'twill save the writer expense and trouble'. Presumably he planned to mark his wares for sale without the inconvenience of sending them to London. In another case a buckle-maker, John Innocent of Little Newport Street, was accused of casting hallmarks from marked buckles 'to buckles moulded in sand' but this was apparently a false accusation by a disgruntled apprentice since no evidence against him was found in his shop or workshop.[58]

Because the tax on wrought plate was unpopular and hard to collect, the system was changed in 1758. All those selling, trading or vending silver had to buy a licence costing £2. In 1784 the direct tax on silver was reintroduced, and doubled in 1797, although the system was tightened up and a duty mark struck, with punches supplied annually by the Board of Revenue. But the licence system continued and the fee to working goldsmiths was doubled.

Pseudo Hallmarks

Pseudo-marks (a category distinct from forged marks) are attracting interest in their own right as they come to be recognised as an aspect of colonial silversmithing. Since the silver normally follows current English styles and turns up fairly frequently in England, I make no apology for including a short description of their main characteristics, drawn from the useful account published by Wynyard Wilkinson in 1975.[59]

Sometimes attributed in the past to the smaller Scottish towns or described, more vaguely, as 'provincial English', these marks echo current or recently current English sterling marks. They are a curious mixture of devices, initials, right-facing lions, and out-of-period monarch's heads, usually in blocks of four or five, only now being correctly allocated. That silversmiths of the English-speaking overseas territories – Canada, Australia, India, Malaya – found it worthwhile to strike marks in imitation of sterling demonstrates how widely the English hallmarking system was recognised, by both workman and customer.

In pre-Revolutionary America there was no assay office, despite the repeated requests between 1756 and 1770 from the Philadelphia silversmiths that one be established there. Colonial silversmiths sometimes struck their maker's mark four times and several New York makers used a N:YORK punch in addition to their punchmarks. After the Revolution, in 1792, the silver content of coin was set at 892 parts per thousand, a lower standard than sterling. To identify silver made from locally-minted coin, a number punch was sometimes used. From 1837, when the standard was raised to 900, the word COIN is found exclusively struck on American silver, or the letter C or D, standing for Coin or Dollar. But in the 19th century sometimes punched letters were merely pseudo-date letters. About 1830, Frederick Marquand of New York used four marks: FM, a right-facing lion, a king's head and a 'date-letter'.

Canadian-made pieces were sometimes struck with a crown or an anchor, a reminder of the large export trade in plate from Birmingham and Sheffield through Liverpool; Canadian customers were at least as familiar with these marks as with the London ones.

Two Australian silversmiths, Alexander Dick of Sydney and Henry Steiner of Adelaide used full-name punches plus 'London' marks between about 1825 and 1841. Their flatware turns up occasionally in London.

In Calcutta there was a flourishing silver industry, producing in the English style for English customers. Pittar and Company used three marks between about 1831 and 1848; the marks of other large Indian firms such as Hamiltons were recognised and discussed by Jackson. A complication of so-called China Trade silver is that some silver with Chinese makers' punches was undoubtedly made in the China Bazaar in Calcutta and there given local Indian retailers' stamps.

Silver had been made in China proper, in Canton, for English customers at least since the early 18th century. East India Company merchants, like Richard Scattergood, ran accounts with the Canton goldsmith Buqua, who repaired watches and jewellery and sold in 1714 a 'silver teapot to keep tea water warm'. From the late 18th century, the export trade in Chinese silver for the European and American market is well-documented. As an English traveller in 1811/12 noted 'The articles in silver were executed many with English cyphers and coat of arms upon them. The engravers have books of heraldry which they consult and copy with great accuracy'.[60] Chinese silversmiths had adopted the English conventions for marking fairly widely by 1830 or so; their wares normally carry a Chinese ideogram, indicating the maker's name, as well. The best-known is probably the capital C and reversed S of the Canton silversmith Cumshing.

In the late nineteenth century there was a steady demand for Chinese and Japanese silverware; Yokohama jugs and teaspoons over stamped by Liberty's and other retailers, and bearing the F import mark (introduced 1867, altered in 1904) are fairly common.

Notes

1 Goldsmiths' 1978; Morgan 1853 and Ch. 13.

2 Norfolk 1981. Roe of Plymouth did the same, and some Chester men. Grosvenor Museum 1984.

3 Assay procedure: Reddaway and Walker 1975.

4 Badcock 1971, 96; Pickford 1983.

5 Goldsmiths' Company, minute book D f77; Glanville, *Proceedings of the Silver Society*, 1985.

6 Goldsmiths' Company, minute book E f4r; Goldsmiths' 1889.

7 Grimwade 1976; Culme forthcoming, Taylor, *Proceedings of the Silver Society*, 1984; Kent 1981.

8 Gill 1980, 261. See also 150, 254–5, 263, 284ff.

9 Goldsmiths' Company minute book E/F, f67, 15 October 1534.

10 *Goldsmiths' Review* 1969–70, 16–18.

11 Barrett 1981, Boston MFA 1982, Vol. III 'Robert Sanderson and the Founding of the Boston Silversmiths Trade', 491. Gerald Taylor is making a special study of late sixteenth/early seventeenth-century London marks; *Proceedings of the Silver Society*, 1984.

12 Goldsmiths' 1978, no. 48.

13 Glanville 1984; indexes at Goldsmiths' Hall.

14 Jewitt and Hope 1895, Vol. II, 59–61; Goldsmiths' 1952, introduction.

15 Oman 1970, 33–5.

16 Badcock 1971, 27, although he describes the touch plate as 'a Table artificially made . . . one column of hardened lead, another of Parchment or Velom'.

17 Sold Christie's NY 1983; now Al-Tajir Collection.

18 Jewitt and Hope 1895, Vol. II, 42–6; Kent 1983. Robert Tite marked (and presumably made) the former.

19 Greenwood 1930; Culme 1975 and 1977, p. 100.

20 For example, Goldsmiths' 1978, 166.

21   Holland 1971. Provincial silver often belongs to the local town council and to local churches; Chester, Norwich, Exeter and Hull museums also have good collections.

22   Norfolk Museums 1981; Barrett 1981 for objects, marks and goldsmiths' biographies.

23   'The Kings Lynn Goldsmiths' in *The Arthur Negus Guide to British Silver*, Brand Inglis 1980.

24   Royal Albert Memorial Museum Exeter.

25   Kent *Proceedings of the Silver Society* 1984.

26   Kent 1983, 210.

27   Barrett 1981.

28   Kent 1983, 211–12. The copper content of Salisbury spoonheads is often so high that they glow with colour; no wonder they were gilded originally!

29   RAM Museum Exeter (Corfield).

30   Oman 1957.

31   West Country variations are best seen in the Corfield Collection: RAM Museum, Exeter.

32   William Fitzhugh, ordering silver from his London agent in 1688, stipulated that it 'be strong and plain, as being less subject to bruise, more serviceable and less out for the fashion'.

33   Ridgway 1968.

34   Near Torrington, West Putford and Merton. Information from Tim Kent.

35   Lee 1978, 15 and pl. 1; Goldsmiths' 1978, 32.

36   How 1974

37   Badcock stressed the need to look for marks and to ask the seller if it was standard, since many kept 'both of the standard goodness and of a coarser Allay, ready for sale'. He also suggested taking an unobtrusive filing, to see whether the surface had been silvered.

38   Goldsmiths' 1978, 28. Kent 1984,

39   Goldsmiths' 1978, 27.

40   Alec-Smith 1951; Kingston-upon-Hull 1951.

41   Goldsmiths' 1978, 25.

42   Gill 1980, 15.

43   Jeavons, *Church Plate of Nottinghamshire* (1965) 12–13.

44   Goldsmiths' 1978, 24.

45   Ridgway 1968; Jeavons, *Church Plate of Nottinghamshire* 10–11.

46   What follows is drawn from Grimwade 1976.

47   For example, Culme 1977, 23–4 and 121.

48   Fallon 1980, 147–8.

49   Jackson forthcoming, Kent 1975, 1980, 1983. Exeter marks are noticeably well and deeply struck. Bristol continued to mark in small quantities until the mid-eighteenth century.

50   Kent 1983, 62.

51   Baker 1973, 290 and Ch. 9.

52   Gubbins 1983.

53   Prideaux 1896, Vol. II.

54   For example, Goldsmiths' 1978, 82, 86. A helmet ewer by De Lamerie (VAM), marked on the base, was taken apart in 1944 to reveal the extra plate soldered in, with marks of 1736. See Ch. 13.

55   Goldsmiths' 1978, 90; Holbourne of Menstrie Museum, Bath.

56   Goldsmiths' Company committee minute book 7, f146.

57   Goldsmiths' Company committee minute book 7, f206; book 8, f117.

58   Prideaux 1896, Vol. II.

59   Gubbins 1974; Wilkinson 1975. Ch. 9, No. 4 for Jamaican practice.

60   Quoted in Irons 1982, 48, 49–50.

EIGHT

TECHNIQUES OF THE SILVERSMITH

THERE are three basic methods of forming silver – casting the molten metal in a mould, hammering or raising an ingot (or sheet) of silver into the desired shape over anvils of different profiles, or assembling the completed object from smaller elements (cast, raised or seamed) soldered together. Finials, handles and feet were normally cast, several at a time, in sand moulds formed by the silversmith from lead or brass patterns. Simple hollowware objects, such as casters, beakers or spouts, were seamed up from a strip of silver, and the bases cut out with shears and soldered in. The lathe simplified and speeded-up production by making it possible to spin holloware; surface decoration, engraving, chasing or embossing was added after the object had been planished (hammered smooth) and polished with pumice or water of Ayr stone (Fig. 66).

The rolling mill, which produced silversheet of a uniform thickness without the effort and monotony of hammering it out, had come into general use in London by 1747, when Campbell published his guide to careers; 'formerly goldsmiths were obliged to beat their metal from the ingot into what thickness they wanted; but now are invented Flatting Mills which reduce their metal to what Thinness they require at a very small expense'.

Patents had been taken out from the 1720s, although the real value of the rolling mill, originally hand-turned and then horse-powered, came when it was harnessed to the steam engine. Sheffield led the way here but the London manufacturers fairly quickly installed steam-powered mills, to keep their products competitive.[1]

The economy of metal made possible, by using lighter-gauge rolled silver, undoubtedly stimulated the popular demand for silver tableware in the second half of the eighteenth century, a demand whose growth can be traced in the assay office records from 1740, when a new method of keeping records was set up. Between 1740 and 1760 the weight of silver brought in for hallmarking more than trebled.[2]

A very clear description of casting metalwork, chasing and other techniques common to the makers of silverware and jewellery was written by Henry Wilson, the eminent Arts and Crafts silversmith in 1902. This handbook *Silverwork and Jewellery* is still in print and has the added interest of comparing traditional methods, as described by Theophilus in the twelfth century, with current practice in the small craft workshop. But essentially the techniques and the simple tools required by the silversmith remained the same until the nineteenth century; 'the use of punches, moulds and dies are all primitive methods of enduring utility'.[3]

Beading tools, cutting punches and iron stamps are all described by Theophilus; as today, the true contrast is between the artist-craftsman using largely hand methods, and factory

Fig. 66 **Stuart goldsmiths at work**
To the right, three men are hammering out the rim of a plate. The seated man is weighing old and
broken silver while behind him the master applies his punch to a completed object. Frontispiece of
Badcock, *A Touchstone for Goldsmiths 1677*
Goldsmiths' Company

production, especially of flatware and simple cups and teaware, which are stamped out or
spun. A useful description of factory methods, drawn up by Henry Mayhew in 1865, was
based on his visit to Hunt & Roskell's factory off the Gray's Inn Road, which employed
between eighty and a hundred men.[4] For earlier workshop layout and equipment, there are a
few illustrations, such as the frontispiece to Badcock's book and an invitation to a
Goldsmiths' Company gathering, plus Diderot's *Encyclopedia* for the later eighteenth
century. Probate inventories of tools and equipment, and surveys of workshops for insurance
purposes, demonstrate the preponderance of heavy iron implements; equipment auctioned in
1829 after the death[5] of the Newcastle goldsmith James Hamilton comprised pairs of bellows,
sugar tong, fork, table- and teaspoon punches, spoon moulds, spring, melting and forging
tongs . . . anvils, hammers, a polishing lathe, cutting shears, ingots and so on (Fig. 67).

Training

The normal route into the craft was through apprenticeship, a seven-year term starting at about fourteen, during which the apprentice boy was trained but received little or no pay. On completing his indentures, the boy then worked as a journeyman for two or three years to get experience before setting up on his own account. A busy workshop might have up to seven apprentices at any one time, as William Denham, of the Gilt Cup, Goldsmiths' Row in Cheapside did in the 1560s although the Company imposed restrictions.[6]

Although this system operated throughout the nineteenth century, and indeed still operates today, a likely lad might work himself in through the shop, counting house or workshop. Joseph Brasbridge recalled the early days of the spoonmaker Richard Crosley of Giltspur Street: 'He came originally to London as a boy and was employed by Chawner, the spoon-maker in Paternoster-row, to carry charcoal to his men; hence he was known by the name of Charcoal Dick but being a smart lad and writing a good hand, he was soon promoted to a place in the counting house.'[7]

Stephen Gilbert and James Ansill had worked their way up in the Wickes/Wakelin partnership from the same basis. An alternative was to bring in capital and selling ability, as John Bridge did at Rundell's.[8]

A recent retrospective exhibition of the work of Leslie Durbin brought out the mixture of art-school training and direct experience enjoyed by this twentieth-century silversmith. Apprenticed as an engraver to Omar Ramsden, he spent several years engraving 'OMAR RAMSDEN ME FECIT' onto the firm's products while attending classes in the evenings and on Saturdays. Winning prizes in two competitions by the Goldsmiths' Company gave him a chance to travel and to break away from Ramsden, although he later acquired many of his moulds and casting patterns after Ramsden's death (Figs. 56 and 78).[9]

Apprentices were expected to be capable of draughtsmanship and to be able to copy and to make working drawings for their own use. Their sources were printed pattern books and perhaps the master's portfolio of sketches prepared for past customers. However, virtually none of this visual evidence of workshop practice survives and we are forced instead to reconstruct the patterns of production and, through these, the range of sources with which the workshop staff were familiar.

In their textbooks, Stuart writing masters emphasised the value of their techniques for apprentice-goldsmiths. A neat hand, with or without calligraphic flourishes, was essential for potential masters. Also essential was a training in draughtsmanship and apprentices sometimes specified that they should attend a drawing master.[10]

It was normal practice for the goldsmith to submit a sketch design for a commissioned piece. Nicholas Sprimont made a drawing of a silver tureen with ostrich feet, presumably for the Coke family, earls of Leicester whose crest was an ostrich and whose principal house at Holkham has ostrich-supported tables (VAM) and another drawing attributed to him, for salt spoons and a salt, has been recognised as a design for the royal marine salts made by Paul Crespin in 1741–2. Sometimes a model of lead or wood was prepared too, although this added considerably to the cost if the modeller was a distinguished artist. A 'fine chaised candlestick' ordered by Lord Mountford in 1748 was returned to its maker George Wickes at cost, but the dissatisfied patron had still to bear the expense of the pattern, which at £70 represented a substantial element in the total price.[11] But Sprimont is unusual, in being both a designer and a businessman capable of running first a goldsmith's shop and subsequently a porcelain factory. Most goldsmiths had to buy their designs and modify as necessary (Fig. 91).

In the 1730s a new centre for studying design was established. William Hogarth set up an academy in S. Martins Lane for artists, sculptors, wood and metalworkers. Here he brought together those wishing to study the new ideas from France; sheets of engraved designs by the innovative Meissonier were published from 1734 in France and from 1737 reissued in London. Both Georg Michael Moser, the Schaffhausen-born gold chaser and modeller, and Hubert François Gravelot, the French engraver, who had come to London in 1732, taught at the Academy, in addition taking private pupils. So familiarity with the various strands of the rococo style spread quickly even to those unable to travel to Paris; this first phase, from about 1735 to 1745, was a unique period of vitality and originality for the designs of at least some English silversmiths.[12]

The 'Masterpiece'

In the German towns the workman was expected to produce a masterpiece to show his fitness to pursue the craft but in England this practice was not consistently enforced. There were occasional sporadic attempts, notably in 1444, when the proposal came from alien craftsmen in London more at ease with the practice, and again in 1572; the young men of the company 'shall not set up to work for themselves till they have made their masterpiece to show their skill in the work in which they were brought up'. Intermittent references in the Company's records suggest that the procedure was not always enforced; but the low standards of craftsmanship prevailing in the early seventeenth century attracted critical attention and several cases of enforcement occur in the minute book in 1606–8. For example, Robert Gunning, late apprentice of William Aldersley, was bound in £10 to make his masterpiece before setting up shop for himself. The order on the masterpiece was read out to the whole Company in 1607 to remind them of its provisions, a campaign which coincided with the building of a workshop attached to the Hall, in which the piece should be made under, as it were, examination conditions. However, when the Hall was rebuilt by Nicholas Stone in the 1630s, no workshop was provided, so the practice had presumably lapsed again.[13]

This requirement on the masterpiece was introduced, or revived, at Newcastle a few years later. The 1634 ordinances of the Newcastle Company specified that the master certify that the masterpiece was his apprentice's own unaided work. But later Newcastle ordinances omit this provision.[14] There is no equivalent in England to the collection of masterpieces presented to their guilds by the Nuremburg or Augsburg goldsmiths, although sometimes London goldsmiths followed this procedure; on 16 October 1607 William Hole presented to the wardens a silver bowl engraved with the Company's arms 'which is allowed to be his masterpiece whereupon he is to bring in his mark and have assay and touch'.[15]

169

Chasing

A Youth designed to be a chaser must have a good Genius for drawing and ought to be early learned the Principals of that Art.

(Campbell, *The London Tradesman*, 1747)

The art of the chaser is that of the sculptor or carver on a smaller scale. Chasing is the technique of modelling the surface of cold metal with hammer and punches into relief designs. Embossing is chasing done from the reverse side of the metal. A third term, flat-chasing, describes designs created within the plane surface of the metal by striking with a chasing tool; on thin-gauge silver this reads on the reverse as a series of bulges, unlike engraving which removes a sliver of metal but makes no impression on the reverse. Flat-chasing was popular in the last twenty years of the seventeenth century, used then for chinoiserie figures, birds and scenes. For the history of chasing and engraving, see Chapters 10 to 12 (Figs. 90, 92–5).[16]

The chaser of gold or silver (or base metal) was regarded as the aristocrat of the craft. Because he worked freehand, he had to have a trained eye, as Campbell explained, and chasers were regarded as artists rather than mere workmen. One, Georg Michael Moser, was elected the first keeper of the Royal Academy in 1768. Moser, Augustin Heckel and George Daniel Gaab, all active in London in the mid-eighteenth century, signed their small goldwork but the identity of silver chasers is rarely recorded.[17]

The high prices paid for chased work by Edward Seymour in the mid-sixteenth century are discussed elsewhere. In the seventeenth century, chasing and embossing in the auricular manner attracted great admiration but a century later the style peculiarly suited to it, the rococo, saw the highwater mark of chasing in England. The heavy use of cast ornament, characteristic of the period 1700 to 1730, was supplemented by *tour de force* chasing, as may be seen on the silver by Wickes, De Lamerie and James Shruder in particular. When De Lamerie supplied the Goldsmiths' Company with their ewer and basin in 1741, he made the usual fashion charge, but submitted an additional bill for £44 2s for chasing 'with curious ornaments'; he had the services of an exceptionally skilled modeller and chaser from about 1735 to 1743, whose identity is not known.[18]

For Campbell, whose handbook to the London trades came out in 1747 at the height of the rococo, it was natural to class the goldsmith with the sculptor, because he had to model before using casting techniques; 'All works that have any sort of Sculpture, that is raised figures of any sort, are cast in Moulds'. The goldsmith's education had to include draughtsmanship, he 'ought to be a good Designer', and be 'possessed of a solid judgement as well as a Mechanical Hand and Head'.

Sixty years later, Tatham re-emphasised the importance of a training in modelling: 'Good Chasing may be considered as a branch of Sculpture . . . it is constant application to Modelling alone that will form a good Chaser.'[19] From their different standpoints, both men were stressing that marriage of trained hand and eye without which no craftsman could flourish. Chasing was indeed sculpture in miniature.

Engraving

The technique of setting out a design on a piece of silver was simplified by the invention of carbon paper, allowing the engraver to transfer his design directly from the original with a pointed tool.

An older method was to spread a thin layer of wax and whiting over the warmed metal, lay on it face downwards a tracing of the design and rub hard all over. Alternatively the design could be drawn freehand into the slightly roughened surface. Then the engraver took up his burin and followed the lines at an angle, cutting away a fine sliver of metal to produce a V-shaped groove.

Occasionally the setting-out marks were not obscured by the subsequent engraving or burnished away in the finishing process. The commemorative inscription on the early Stuart ox-eye cup at the Mercers' Company sits on clearly-ruled lines. Engraving on large and important orders was relatively expensive. The plateau to the Prince of Wales's centrepieces, supplied by George Wickes in 1745, is richly engraved with scrolls and the prince was charged £23 for the engraving alone. Another object supplied by the same firm fifteen years later, a tea tray with scrolling foliage interlaced with garlands and a magnificent cartouche from Jacques de La Joue, cost £1010s for the engraving, the charge for metal and fashion of this 'large oval Nurld Table ornamented with vines' was £119 18s 6d.[20]

In earlier times the engraver was not necessarily literate, or at least not capable of an exact transcription. A stoneware mug in the Museum of London, fitted with mounts about 1560, has on the cover a merchant's mark and an inscription; several letters are reversed as they are on the mug given by David Gittings to the Vintners' Company at this time.

Make-up of the Craft

Makers' marks identify only the more successful of the craft, specialists such as spoonmakers or those who ran largish businesses. There was a much larger submerged membership, men who had passed out of their apprenticeship but remained employees – journeymen – to other goldsmiths. Those whose business was wholly retail, with the inevitable element of money-lending also, did not necessarily register a mark, and nor did specialists such as refiners, and gold and silver wire-drawers.[21]

The Company struggled to control the activities of men such as William Wheeler, a Jacobean goldsmith who was progenitor of the family banking business which, through a series of intermarriages, evolved by 1700 into Child's Bank. Despite his necessary association with the Company, and later with the Mint, he was a businessman rather than a practising goldsmith, as was the goldsmith John Thompson who acted as agent for Thomas Ingram of Temple Newsam in the 1650s. He handled bills of exchange, organised loans, paid postage and supplied the odd silver item such as 'a silver penne for Mr. Arthur'.[22]

In the next generation, Pepys's goldsmiths, alderman Edward Backwell and Sir Robert Vyner, were still able to supply plate, but it was no doubt bought-in; Child's and Hoare's also organised silver and had it engraved for their banking clients in the 1690s.

Demarcation of the craft was nothing new; specialisation was already evident in the fifteenth century and the names of royal goldsmiths conceal a mass of other craftsmen actually raising, chasing or embossing part of any order. In the records of the Drapers' Company, their suppliers of plate are named from the early seventeenth century, but when compared with the goldsmiths' marks on their surviving plate there is no correlation. In eighteenth-century trade directories the term 'Plateworkers' was used to describe those goldsmiths supplying the retail trade; Daniel Smith and Robert Sharp, for example, made superb race cups, on which their mark appears, but the retailer, William Picket, advertised himself on the Richmond Race cup (1770) by stamping 'W.P. fecit' prominently on the base, assuming a clear distinction between his role and theirs in the customer's eyes. [23]

Overstriking by the retailer had a long ancestry and as long as the plate conformed to sterling standard (and was fully hallmarked) this practice was acceptable to the Company. The pre-Britannia mark of Thomas Jenkins, one of the handful of late Stuart goldsmiths to be firmly associated with his mark, has been identified because in 1698 he made a pair to a jug of 1685 struck with his earlier mark (T I between two mullets or stars). More interesting still, the later jug bore the Britannia mark of the leading Huguenot silversmith Philip Rollos, just visible underneath that of Jenkins. This fact, and the very wide range of Thomas Jenkins's output, as illustrated by the two hundred-plus pieces known by him, from a cistern (VAM) to a mace, suggests that he too had a retailing business. However, since a fifth of the pieces with his mark are not hallmarked, he presumably had some special customers for whom he worked, or placed orders, directly. [24]

Earlier in the century, London retailers were overmarking silver imported from Nuremburg which had great appeal here, and 'in regard of the fashion is uttered [sold] before English plate'. By the Sterling Standard Act of 1576, selling unmarked wares had become an offence, hence their action, but they were at fault because the standard for Nuremburg silver was considerably lower than sterling, at 870 to 890 parts fine. The Company was brought in in January 1607 because six disgruntled workmen complained about the unfair competition these superior imports (in fashion at least) offered to their products. [25]

A ewer and basin (1617) belonging to Norwich Corporation has been described as foreign-made and marked here for retail (because of its very high quality) and a Nuremburg-type cup with London marks in the Kremlin is presumably also an import. However, aliens were at work in London who could have produced these pieces. Certainly the English royal collection was well stocked with recognisably German plate. When John Acton bought 'the Great Gilt Cupboard of Estate' from Charles I in 1626, his purchase included eighteen German double cups (two described as 'Nuremborowe') and five Nuremburg cups and covers. The surprisingly high proportion of German cups among gifts to London churches at this time suggests that they were not readily saleable on the open market. At King's Lynn in 1634 the borough acquired a cup standing over three feet tall, made by Martin Dumling of Nuremburg, with a bequest from Thomas Soame, thrice mayor. The parish women of Bromley by Bow presented a Nuremburg cup to their church in 1617, as an inscription on it records. The role of aliens is discussed in Chapter 12. [26]

Because clients dealt only with the high street retail goldsmiths, the working goldsmiths who supplied them remain shadowy figures. They had a distinct role and identity within the

Company, although their names are only mentioned when there was a dispute; for example on 22 January 1607 James Whaffe, a Scot, was charged with his 'deceitful work'. His defence was that the goldsmiths who supplied him with 'base and bad silver' were to blame 'which if he refused to take, others will receive and work the same for them to his hindrance'. There was some sympathy among the court for his difficulty. But the workmen were expected to take reasonable precautions as to their raw materials.[27]

Half a century later another workman, Whittingham, called the Company in to settle a dispute with Archer, a refiner, who had supplied him with eighty ounces of silver. When he made it up, it was found to be four pennyweights worse than sterling standard and his wares were broken by the assay office. The refiner argued that since Whittingham had not assayed the silver before using it, he refused to reimburse him 'for the loss of the fashion', that is his time working it up. The Company ordered that the refiner should pay just 8s to the workman, the bare value of the shortfall in the silver.[28]

As working men, these goldsmiths were referred to by surname only or by Christian and surname rather than by the more courteous distinction of Mr and surname, and their social standing was of course considerably lower. Samuel Pepys showed his sensitivity to this social gap in September 1667 when he enjoyed an evening's singing with the musician Benjamin Wallington who 'did sing a most excellent bass and yet a poor fellow, a working goldsmith, that goes without gloves to his hands'.[29]

In the eighteenth century, and probably earlier, the Society of Working Goldsmiths annually booked the Hall for an entertainment; several invitation cards to these festivities are preserved, stamped in gold with the current date-letter, a token whose significance was known only to the fraternity (Fig. 67). Their interests were distinct from those of the retail goldsmiths, as their occasional corporate appearances in the Company records demonstrate. In 1668, the working goldsmiths went beyond the Company, petitioning the Lords of the Council to take action against alien workmen, a recurrent grievance. Again, in 1725 they presented a remonstrance to a committee of the livery, complaining against the evil practice of plating brass, iron, copper and other metals with silver.[30] However improper, close-plating to deceive certainly occurred, as the sad case of the chandelier made for the Fishmongers' Company by William Gould in 1750 shows; the technique was commonly referred to as 'French-plate' in the classic chauvinist term of disparagement.[31]

Subcontractors and Suppliers

The complex network of relationships within the craft can rarely be documented but the fortunate survival of a series of workmen's ledgers from the house of Wakelin & Tayler demonstrates their dependence on nearly seventy specialist firms, with whom they had accounts running sporadically from 1766, but clearly commencing earlier. The accounts show that two firms, the Crespell brothers between 1773 and 1786 and James Ansill and Stephen Gilbert a little earlier, were subcontractors; other firms supplied them with their speciality. All the familiar names are to be found; Ebenezer Coker and John Carter for candlesticks and waiters, James Tookey for salt and tea-spoons and William and Thomas Chawner for other flatware, David and Robert Hennell for saltcellars, Emick Romer for

Fig. 67   Invitation to the Goldsmiths' service 1701
Britannia and sterling marks appear on the shields held by Britannia and S. Dunstan at the top while the
1701 date letter, F, is below the workshop scene, all symbols whose significance was known only to the
craft.
Goldsmiths' Company

sugar and cream baskets, Walter Brind for mugs and cream jugs and Thomas Pitts for epergnes. They also ran accounts with makers of plate chests, knife boxes and pocketbooks and 'Plated Goods Makers', quite apart from the various specialist firms supplying jewellery and related products.[32]

No census of the craft exists before the late eighteenth century; the missing registers for largeworkers (1758–73) and for smallworkers (1739–58) mean that no totally comprehensive list can now be reconstructed. But in 1773, as an appendix to the parliamentary report in the assay offices, all the 'Goldsmiths Silversmiths and Plateworkers' with marks registered at the London Hall were listed, with their addresses, and sometimes their trade speciality. Those with London addresses numbered 668. Excluding goldmakers, spoon, buckle and watch-makers and others unspecified, 164 described themselves specifically as goldsmiths or plateworkers. Given that retailers and journeymen need not or would not have a mark and so are not included, the number is very high.[33]

For the first half of the nineteenth century a further series of trade records exist, ledgers for the firm of Edward Barnard & Son, plus some stock books from 1825 to 1863. In 1825 engravers listed included Hobdell and Jackson and Donne, plated goods were supplied by Boulton and three other firms. Merryfield was a modeller, Clarke and Holland were named as chasers.[34]

An incident recounted by Joseph Brasbridge, whose memoirs on his career as a silversmith appeared in 1824, shows how dependent the retailer was on his suppliers; needing to match a pair of candlesticks for a client, Mr Pemberton, 'I took them to Mr. Whipham a silversmith, to get the corresponding ones made'. But Whipham misread the scratchweight on one as the weight for the two and so sent a very lightweight pair 'exactly similar indeed in point of pattern but as thin as paper, so light that I could not offer them'. This commission brought more trouble since the original maker, Mr Makepeace, was on bad terms with Brasbridge and refused to supply a set from stock at trade rates.[35]

Partnerships

Dick Whittington's proverbial route to success in the city, by marrying his master's daughter, has a considerable smack of truth, as far as goldsmiths were concerned. Boys taken as apprentices were by no means poor, or poorly educated, since a goldsmith had to be a good businessman, on easy terms with his noble or gentry customers (the major silver-buying groups) and a man of standing and honour, able to attract capital, the essential raw material for his business above all. These qualities were well tested by the seven-year close family contact resulting from the apprenticeship system.

A pattern of marriage/business connections, often through two or three generations, is evident from the late fifteenth century. In 1496, for instance, Robert Amadas, son of a London goldsmith, married the granddaughter (and heiress) of Sir Hugh Bryce (d. 1496). He also, shortly afterwards, followed in Bryce's footsteps as an officer at the Mint and as supplier to the court. The son of one of Amadas' apprentices, Martin Bowes, married his granddaughter, and carried on the family link with the craft.[36]

Through this continuity, capital was not drawn out of the business, and goodwill was retained. This family cohesion and mutal confidence is particularly evident in the well-studied Huguenot community; one such goldsmithing dynasty was the Courtaulds. Philip Rundell was expected to marry his senior partner's (and former employer's) daughter, Miss Picket. Failing this, he paid her a thousand pounds a year from the business.[37]

Partnerships are often found, sometimes expressed by a joint mark but more often documented rather through trade directories and other business records. The pattern was for a trained silversmith to take as his partner a businessman with access to capital or useful connections.

The career of George Wickes and his successive partners is well understood. He became free in 1720 and registered a mark in February 1722. In 1730 he set up shop in Norris Street with John Craig, a partnership which broke up in 1735 when he opened at the King's Arms and Feather in Panton Street. In 1747, he took Edward Wakelin (a former apprentice of John Le Sage) as a partner. Samuel Netherton, apprenticed to Wickes in 1738, joined the partners in 1750; he never registered a mark and probably specialised in the jewellery side of the business. John Parker, a former apprentice with the firm, became a partner about 1760 and Stephen Gilbert, starting as a workshop boy, was apprenticed in 1752 and free in 1764. After two years as a journeyman he joined with James Ansill, supplying the Wakelin & Parker partnership with stock. John Wakelin entered a joint mark at the Hall with William Tayler in 1776, in 1792 Robert Garrard joined John Wakelin and so the firm passed into the hands of the Garrard family, which kept it until the 1950s.[38]

Paul Storr's career took a slightly different pattern, in that he was briefly a partner of William Frisbee on becoming free in 1792. He then worked alone until 1807 when he moved to 53 Dean Street, Soho and registered a new mark, an indication of the change in his status arising from his association with Rundell's. Unlike Wickes, he did not open a retail establishment until much later in his career in 1821, two years after he broke away from Rundell's. But he had to take a partner, John Mortimer, for his New Bond Street business. In 1826 the partners were joined by John S. Hunt and in 1838, after a legal wrangle between the partners, Storr retired.

The best documented working partnership of the Regency is that of Rundell, Bridge & Rundell, goldsmiths and jewellers to George III and George IV. Philip Rundell, founder of the firm, was first a shopman for and then in partnership with William Picket, alderman, a leading City retailer with a showroom at the sign of the Golden Salmon, 32 Ludgate Hill, from about 1768 to 1785. His junior partner, John Bridge, bought himself in with a loan from his Dorset cousin of the same name, a wealthy farmer with a special interest in breeding sheep. Possibly through this cousin's friendship with George III (also an enthusiast), the royal patronage was transferred to Rundell & Bridge in 1797. This brought so much business, both from the king and from the rest of the royal family, that a third partner was introduced, in or before 1803, Philip's cousin Edmund Rundell.[39]

Between 1799 and 1803, the firm set up two large workshops, one managed by Paul Storr in Air Street, Piccadilly and later at 54 Dean Street, Soho and Benjamin Smith's at Lime Kiln Lane, Greenwich (Smith was working in partnership with Digby Scott between 1802 and 1807). At their peak in 1806–8 these three houses together employed over a thousand workmen although many were concerned with the jewellery side of the business rather than silver. The output of Storr and Smith was entirely absorbed by the needs of Rundell's many customers until Smith broke away in 1814. Between 1807 and 1809 Rundell's contract with the Storr workshop specified 10,000 ounces of silver to be supplied every month which did not, however, prove adequate for the consumption required. Casting moulds were apparently shared by the two workshops and despite the kudos now attached to Storr's name, there is no discernible difference in the quality of their output.

Large manufacturing businesses are well documented from the 1840s, and their commercial and design policies can be traced both through their own statements in trade and exhibition catalogues and in the comments of the *Art-Journal* and other periodicals concerned with design and the decorative arts. Elkington's, for example, was one of the most innovative technically and quickly outstripped its competitors after the introduction of electroplating in 1840.[40]

Specialisation

The typical bread-and-butter products of the Elizabethan and Stuart goldsmith were spoons, drinking vessels, mounted wares and salts. The commonest items to be mentioned in contemporary documents, they are sometimes discussed by historians of plate as though each were a unique example of a particular goldsmith's inventive skill. A more realistic view of the craft's organisation recognises that rather more than 90 per cent of the surviving antique plate represents standard items, available from any one of London's retail goldsmiths' shops, often produced either by another independent master or put together from components made by outworkers specialising in that particular line.

Plate with provincial marks might actually be London-made, the local man overstriking with his own mark, as John Peard did in the 1670s, to reassure his local Devon customers. A century later, American silversmiths also overstruck the London maker's mark, and John Carter, a leading London retailer, bought from Sheffield candlesticks in the neo-classical style and overstruck the provincial marks with the full London ones, to reassure his metropolitan customers. A hundred years earlier, Badcock noted that because of the reputation of the London Hall, provincial makers sent their wares up for marking rather than to one of the regional assay offices: 'by reason the Marks of those Places are little known, they bear as little credit'.[41] Marks are by no means always a reliable guide.

Components were made as cheaply and conveniently as possible, using casting where appropriate (for finials, stems, handles, applied elements and feet) and stamped-out friezes and figured borders which could then be applied to covers, rims or feet as needed. An early Stuart coconut cup given to Trinity House, Hull, bears the Hull town mark and maker's mark of a local goldsmith on its mounts and foot. But the distinctive wide punched strips of Tudor roses and ovolo are identical with those on London-marked work of the early seventeenth century; either the Hull goldsmith was marking as a retailer or he had purchased ready-made strip for his mounts from a London supplier.

Modelling in wood, making moulds of clay or casting patterns and making-up handles, finials and spouts were all specialist branches of the craft. The apostle spoons of the sixteenth century have their finials apparently individualised, but actually the basic figure was cast from one of a limited range of moulds; only six were used in the Benjamin Yates set of 1626 belonging to the Goldsmiths' Company. The attributes of the twelve apostles were then cast separately and applied to distinguish between them.[42]

Lead models for casting were also in use here. There is no description of goldsmithing equivalent to Cellini's *Trattato del Oreficeria* but the benefits of casting had been recognised for centuries. 'This is a particularly good way, because when the Master has his lead model and has finished it to suit his purposes it can serve ever so many more times than a single casting.'

A lead scroll handle found in the workshop debris of James Geddy in Williamsburg (active 1750 to 1770) indicates that this colonial silversmith was making, as well as selling plate.[43]

Across Europe in the late seventeenth century, cast plaques were set into the lids of toilet jars, bowls, salvers and caskets. At least three toilet services were made by the goldsmith WF with a knot in the early 1680s (one the Calverley set, 1683, VAM) which incorporate plaques cast in the same set of moulds. Versions occur with both classical scenes and with figures in contemporary dress, indicating their wide appeal in Restoration England, although France was the source of the original design, if not the actual plaques.[44]

Paul De Lamerie introduced the scallop-shaped bread basket with mermaid handle about 1740, probably basing it on a French design (at least twenty are known). This quickly became a standard item, although not peculiar to his workshop; Thomas Gilpin marked one, with a horsehead handle, in 1747. Philips Garden apparently purchased these moulds, which were among the workshop equipment auctioned in 1751 on De Lamerie's death; shell-shaped baskets continued to be available with mermaid handles and dolphin feet cast from De Lamerie's moulds but with Garden's mark. Later other goldsmiths, such as Parker and Wakelin, were to mark these baskets, presumably as retailers, having purchased stock from a working goldsmith.[45]

When Thomas Heming made a toilet service for Sir Watkin Williams Wynn in 1768, he re-used moulds (for side panels on the boxes) which he had prepared for a royal order of two years earlier. Returning to De Lamerie's casting patterns, certain designs for candlestick stems and basket handles are common to him and to Henry Hayens and Robert Tyrell in the 1750s; it is likely that Hayens and Tyrell also purchased items at the 1751 auction.[46] This was the normal means of disposing of tools, patterns, moulds and so on, which constituted valuable equipment, unless a son or a widow intended to continue in business. Workshop staff would follow a well-established design, using existing casting patterns, with only minor variations dictated by the customer's whim or an expressed wish to incorporate a personal device or armorials. This question of customer-preference is crucial in any discussion of antique plate up to the early nineteenth century. From that time, if not earlier, the market's division into the mass of standard items and the occasional special commissions can be clearly seen.[47]

Even where a special one-off order was concerned, the goldsmith inevitably drew on his past experience and streamlined production by re-using casting patterns. When the dean and chapter of Durham ordered a new altar service for their cathedral in 1766, the goldsmiths had no obvious precedent to follow. No cathedral or chapel royal had ordered new plate for almost a century and the baroque embossing of the Restoration sets was inappropriate as a model. But Francis Butty and Nicholas Dumee adapted from their recent domestic output;

the cathedral's flagons, with cast handles and flutes and floral swags in the current rococo manner, are merely enlarged coffee pots, and the massive pricket candlesticks follow the design of a pair made for a private customer years earlier. Equally the patens and almsdish have the frilly edges of contemporary dinner plates, although the former are set on trumpet feet, following normal practice for church plate.[48]

From the sixteenth century at least, cutlery or flatware (spoons, forks, knife hafts and blades) was made by specialist firms; the 1773 appendix to the parliamentary report on hallmarking names thirty-six spoonmakers, with haftmakers separately identified. A century earlier, thirty-odd spoonmakers in partnership were noted by the Company.[49]

This branch of the trade was dominated from about 1730 until 1840 by successive generations of the Eley, Fearn, Chawner and Smith families who took one another's apprentices and operated in partnership from time to time. Pickford has traced these trade networks back to the early eighteenth century, when Joseph Smith I had four apprentices, all of whom became spoonmakers, in addition to Ebenezer Coker, who is more frequently described as a maker of candlesticks and salvers. However, it seems that he ran a workshop producing flatware too. His mark, a cursive EC, has sometimes been taken for that of Elias Cachart, another plateworker who made flatware also. As Tim Kent has demonstrated, these family trees of apprentices, not unnaturally following their master's speciality, can be traced in the sixteenth century and probably earlier, where the documentary evidence survives.[50]

Another specialist craft was candlestick-making. The Gould and Cafe families intermarried and worked in partnership during the eighteenth century and a design by James Gould of 1729 is found with his former apprentice John Cafe's mark twenty-six years later.[51]

The shifting pattern of partnerships obscures the essential continuity of certain manufacturing businesses, such as that run between 1808 and 1829 by Rebecca Emes and Edward Barnard. This firm had formerly been known as Chawners and traced its continuous existence back to Anthony Nelme, active around 1700.

Although Paul Storr had to leave models and casting patterns behind at Rundell's when he set up on his own, he certainly passed on some to his successors in trade Hunt & Roskell; John Culme noted a pair of candelabra of 1844 with dolphin stems and branches identical to those on a Storr centrepiece of 1822. By the 1860s the firm of Hunt & Roskell was one of the three leading manufacturing silversmiths in London, with between eighty and one hundred employees at their Harrison Street works, although cutlery was made for them by Chawners and Francis Higgins & Son. Our picture of this London firm is extraordinarily distinct, thanks to a visit paid by Beatrix Potter in 1881. Her acute eye recorded for her diary a vivid series of impressions too long to quote in full but clearly the full range of processes was carried out there. She was shown die-stamping, wire-drawing, the process of sandcasting 'small twirls, chiefly belonging to candelabras', raising and subsequently shaping a cup by spinning. She then visited the engraving shop where 'Each old man had a bit of brown paper pinned between him and his neighbour' and the design studio where a model was sitting as Vasco da Gama for the centrepiece of the White Star Line presentation service. She was very struck by the dust, by the pattern room and the adjoining die-store with its pigeon holes stuffed with innumerable steel dies.[52]

Miss Potter's precise account of the set-up at Hunt & Roskell's confirms the earlier description by Henry Mayhew in 1865. He was also very struck by the passage 'hung with innumerable plaster-moulds for coffee pots, teapots, candlesticks and various ornamentations'. Conservatism of design in the manufacturing houses is largely a matter of practical economics; dies and casting patterns are expensive and must earn their keep by repeated use.

Notes

1   Campbell 1947; Culme 1980.

2   VAM 1984, 324.

3   Theophilus (the Benedictine monk Roger of Helmarshausen) used dies for repeating patterns.

4   Culme 1977, 45–6.

5   Culme 1980; Williamsburg 1966; Gill 1980. Apart from the spoon moulds all these tools could be found in Robert Amadas's workshop 300 years before.

6   Hare 1984.

7   Brasbridge 1824, 142–3.

8   Grimwade 1961; Anon 1827.

9   Goldsmiths' 1982, introduction.

10   The Englishman Alexander Neckam (1157–1211) stressed the importance of drawing: 'Let his untaught apprentice have a waxed tablet . . . so that he may portray and draw little flowers . . . in various manners'. Quoted Lightbown 1978, 5.

11   VAM 1984, 114–15; Barr 1980.

12   VAM 1984, 64–74; Girouard 1966.

13   Goldsmiths' Company minute book, quoted Hayward 1976.

14   Gill 1980, appendix.

15   Goldsmiths' Company minute book.

16   Maryon 1954, 113–16; Dauterman 1964. For chinoiserie silver at Polesden Lacey, see Clayton 1965, with his warnings.

17   VAM 1984, 126–37.

18   VAM 1984, 111–12.

19   Udy 1975.

20   Ch. 11. VAM 1984, 12.

21   Culme 1985 and Grimwade 1976 emphasise this point.

22   Leeds RO, Temple Newsam MSS.

23   Sitwell 1962. Greenwood 2–3; Rowe 1965.

24   Grimwade and Banister 1975.

25   Goldsmiths' Company minute book. The Queen, Anne of Denmark, took an interest, an indication of the appeal at court of these imported cups.

26   Oman, 1964 and 1961. Hayward 1976. The King's Lynn cup is on show in the town's Regalia Room, the Bromley cup in S. Paul's treasury.

27   Goldsmiths' Company minute book.

28   Prideaux 1896.

29   Pepys's *Diary* 1667, Vol. 8, 437.

30   Prideaux 1896.

31   Fallon 1980; Hughes 1969.

32   Grimwade 1961.

33   Grimwade 1976. A century later, in 1870, it was estimated that a thousand people were employed in the London silver industry, Culme 1977, 42.

34   Banister 1980 and 1983.

35   Brasbridge 1824.

36   Reddaway and Walker 1975; Glanville, *Proceedings of the Silver Society*, 1985.

37   Evans 1933; Anon 1827; Museum of London 1985.

38   Barr 1980; Grimwade 1961.

39   Penzer 1954; Bury 1966; Culme 1977, summarises the firm's history, 57–65.

40   Culme 1977; Birmingham 1973 illustrates their output.

41   Badcock 1971, 206.

42   On this see How and How 1952. Identical castings were adopted for many purposes, for example the figures on Foxe's crozier at Corpus Christi, Oxford. Wilson 1981.

43   Noel Hume 1970, pl. 19.

44   Oman [Caroline] 1970; Hernmarck 1977.

45   VAM 1984, 115–16.

46   Grimwade 1956.

47   Culme 1977 emphasises this.

48   VAM 1984, 124; Oman 1957, pl. 83.

49   Kent 1981; Royal Albert Memorial Museum, Exeter, n.d., for West Country makers.

50   Pickford 1983; Kent 1981.

51   Fallon 1980. For the Hennell family, see Hennell 1968 and 1973.

52   Culme 1977, 47–8, 53.

LONDON, THE COUNTRY
AND THE COLONIES

A LTHOUGH we have particularly rich evidence for the carriage-trade of Wickes and
other leaders of the craft, we can also reconstruct the framework whereby provincial
and overseas goldsmiths acquired their stock.

In Tim Kent's recent analysis of the Exeter trade after the Britannia Standard Act of 1696,
he described how a contract between a manufacturing goldsmith, John Elston, and a group of
local retailing goldsmiths, operated. Exeter, and the West Country towns generally, were at a
peak of prosperity between about 1660 and 1750, thanks to the woollen industry, and the
region supported a large number of goldsmiths. But because the 1696 Act had not specified
Exeter as a town with the right to mark the new standard, the local men were both working
and marking illegally (below standard) until, under the 1701 Wrought Plate Act, an assay
office was set up there. This gave Elston his chance. Setting up a workshop with
London-trained journeymen familiar with the new standard, he made an agreement with the
wardens of the Exeter Company that he would manufacture plate 'in twentyone days from
ye time of its bespeaking' and that he would work to certain fixed prices; in return, seven local
silversmiths (several whom had been caught out by the London Company in their 1696
campaign) agreed to buy only from Elston, not from London, to bring him silver to work
with and that they would not attempt to undercut him by making-up the commoner objects
in their own workshops. This agreement was extended to three out-of-town silversmiths,
Philip Muston of Plymouth, Henry Servant of Barnstable and Francis Servant of Bideford in
1708. Undoubtedly many goldsmiths, in London as in the country, had similar discount
suppliers.[1]

Discount Suppliers

The rates for fashion agreed by Elston incidentally show what was most in demand locally:
tankards, belly porringers, two-handled cups, mugs, trencher salts, salvers, casters, spoons
and forks. There is no tea or coffee ware (although Elston is known by one superb chocolate
pot of 1707, on loan to the Royal Albert Memorial Museum in Exeter, Fig. 68) and one puzzle
is the reference to 'sucking bottles', which were charged at 7s apiece for fashion. Whether this
was what is now called a syllabub pot, that is a narrow-spouted vessel, is not certain; this
vessel seems to be a regional speciality, produced also at Chester and Norwich and by New
England silversmiths.

Wholesale orders for plate, jewels and watches sent to his London agents by the

Philadelphia goldsmith, Joseph Richardson, between December 1759 and 1762 specify a range of fairly lightweight and standard items, such as 'Plain and Chast Cream Pots' to weigh about three ounces, ten pennyweight, apiece; or in another letter 'Plain Milk Pots or Ewers' from 3½ to 4 ounces apiece. The distinction between them, if any, was not one of size. Tea silver was the largest part of Richardson's orders, with an occasional coffee pot and the inevitable sets of 'Double Bellied Pepper and Mustard Casters Neatly chast', with glass liners to the mustard casters, and salts with glass liners and shovels or ladles. No one item weighed more than twenty-five ounces, an indication that they were intended not for the aristocracy of Philadelphia but for a less wealthy bourgeois public.[2]

Fig. 68 **Exeter chocolate pot**
1707 Mark of John Elston. This combination of cutcard panels with punched ornament and fluting is not found on London-made plate, which quickly echoed current French designs. Late Stuart provincial silver is normally plain, depending on form rather than ornament.
Loan, Royal Albert Memorial Museum, Exeter

The orders, which were put together for him by a clockmaker, Thomas Wagstaff of the Ship and Crown, Nagshead Court, Gracechurch Street, also included fancy goods and jewellery of low value, such as silver boxes, corals with bells for babies, men's and women's watch chains, shoe and knee buckles, crystal buttons 'set in silver, half with Cyphers' and coral beads. To ensure that whatever he ordered was saleable, and in the current taste, was extremely difficult for Richardson. Apart from stating the weight of each item required, his letters specify that the double-bellied teapots with stands or waiters should be 'neatly chased', with covered sugar dishes to match. We cannot say what this meant but it is contrasted with other plain teapots and sugar dishes 'of a middling substance', a term presumably indicating a retail category familiar to both men. Normally, however, we cannot get behind the brief references to export business, such as the London goldsmith John Fossey's claim in 1747 that his business in secondhand plate and jewellery went back twenty years 'both in the Home, as well as in the Foreign Trade'; he too gave wholesale discounts.[3]

A 1759 order for 200 pairs of shoe buckles of specified versions and sizes from Richardson were to be 'of the Neatest and Newest Version of Different Patens'. A distaste for his agent's choice presumably forced him to ask Daniel Mildred in London to 'Procure a few Puter (pewter) Patterns from the work man Numbered and Noted by him . . . that I may choose my patterns for the buckles'.

There was of course no official assay procedure in the American colonies and that essential back-up, the refiner, was missing too, so Richardson had to send his waste silver, shop sweepings and clippings to London for refining. Although Richardson worked up silver from ingots in the traditional way by hammering, he ordered steel rollers from London in 1759 to ease his labour by producing sheet silver.

It is probable that Richardson overpunched the London-made stock with his own IR mark. In Jamaica, where the colonial sugar planting aristocracy was prosperous enough to support as many as twenty goldsmiths at its peak of prosperity around 1745, some island goldsmiths overpunched London silver and others made up stock by casting from London-made pieces. From 1740 Jamaican silver is sometimes marked with the Jamaican assay master's punch of a cayman's head, the assay master's initials and the goldsmith's initials. But some pieces bear also the impressions of four London hallmarks, faithfully transferred from the original in the casting process.[4]

Similarly, New York silversmiths both copied fashionable London shapes and overstruck stock imported from London. Myer Myers marked cast candlesticks so close to London-made pieces of the 1760s that they are either from identical moulds or direct casts. A basket by William Plummer with a date-letter in the mid-1760s came into the stock of William Whetcroft of Annapolis. This American silversmith attempted to obliterate the London marks by overpunching and then struck his own mark boldly inside the basket, in full view, a most unusual position; perhaps he was responding to the growing pressure not to import English goods.[5]

The export trade in silver to America reached a peak of £4,700 in 1760 and 1761; despite American consumer-resistance during the Revolution it continued on a large scale until the 1790s. An English object could serve as a model immediately it arrived with its American purchasers; a flagon with the mark of the London makers W & J Priest (1767–8) purchased for the First Church, Salem, Massachusetts, was copied exactly in 1769 by the local maker, John Andrew.[6]

With this farflung trade, travellers' catalogues were becoming necessary. The trade cards of the 1750s and 1760s undoubtedly sometimes served as a convenient means of showing current stock; George Ritterdon sent his very detailed sheet to Richardson in Philadelphia in 1758. Matthew Boulton was surely not alone in preparing sets of engraved catalogues for the overseas market, although those of his that survive (two are at the Victoria and Albert Museum, with a collection of Sheffield plate travellers' catalogues of between 1792 and 1810) are for plated wares. Their text is sometimes in French as well as English, with the retailer's discount of about 30 per cent normally quoted too. The first of the two Boulton catalogues was issued in the 1770s and contains small images suitable for cutting up and posting to customers; the second, dating from the 1780s has full-sized images and was described in 1803 as 'such as he generally sends abroad for Correspondents to order from'.[7]

Although often overstriking the London manufacturer's mark, as Thomas Ollivant of Manchester did on a 1790 cream jug made by Peter and Jonathan Bateman, provincial retailers emphasised on their billheads and trade cards that their stock represented the latest in

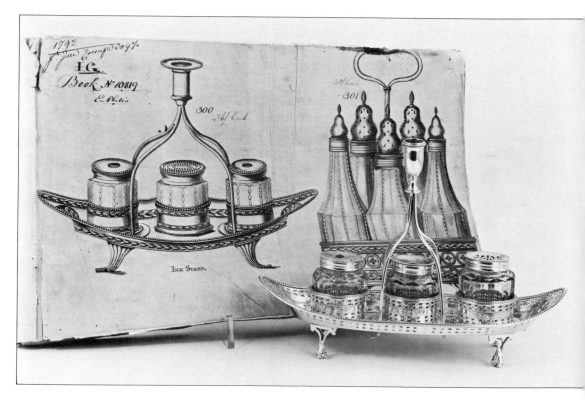

Fig. 69 **Inkstand**
1784. Mark of Robert Hennell. Its design remained popular for a decade or more; a very similar inkstand
is figured in the export trade catalogue, annotated with prices and references.
Bristol Art Gallery/VAM

metropolitan taste. Hampton and Prince in York in 1772 advertised their 'large assortment of all kinds of elegant large and small chased and plain plate'.[8]

This partnership had taken over an older York business (in which they had been employed respectively as workman and apprentice) two years earlier, and their first announcement in 1770 quotes an interesting list of currently fashionable items: 'Tea kitchens, Tureens, cups with covers, Bread Baskets, Candlesticks, Waiters of all sizes, Coffee Pots, Casters . . . also a large assortment of Sheffield and Birmingham Plated goods'.

The 1770s saw the commercial appeal of plated wares sweep the provincial retailers' shops. By this time Matthew Boulton was well into his stride, producing economical versions in plate of all the items listed (as indeed was the Sheffield firm of Henry Tudor and Thomas Leader) and his letters frequently quote the standard wholesale rate for plated objects. Pierced baskets, for example, were £44s, with 20 per cent for quantity discount, in 1773. The Edinburgh silversmiths in the 1770s advertised that they sold a variety of London, Birmingham and Sheffield goods at the lowest prices; particularly a 'neat assortment of plated Candlesticks, Cruet-frames, waiters, snuff-dishes (a local speciality), cream-jugs and handsome tea urns of an antique form'.[9]

No wonder the provincial workshops following traditional practices fell into decline; they could compete neither in price nor in quality with these factory-produced goods, which had the added cachet of fashionable approval. By the mid-eighteenth century the London shops were largely dependent on manufacturing businesses for their stock. Those, like Philips Garden, who had workshops capable of more than repairs and simple copying were in the minority and emphasised this aspect of their business on their trade cards: 'N B work perform'd in my own House'. Wickes also, when setting up in Panton Street, in 1735, advertised that he made, as well as sold, silver plate.[10]

Shop Layout

The Company required that no plate be uttered for sale except by daylight, which virtually dictated the appearance of London shops. Wide windows were essential and tourists from the fifteenth century onwards commented on the generously filled window displays along Cheapside. Their security apparently depended on the apprentice standing beside the doorway.[11]

Wooden 'showglasses' or cases, glass-fronted, were used for jewellery from the sixteenth century. The frontispiece to William Badcock's *A New Touchstone for Gold and Silver Wares* (1677) shows a typical Stuart shop interior, with shelves reaching to the ceiling crammed with plate, protected by wire-framed doors, and a large goldsmith's scales on the solid counter. Eighty years later Philips Garden's shop looks very similar, except that his display units are glazed and the woodwork fashionably gothic. The contents of small glazed cases were always at risk; Joseph Brasbridge (d. 1831) once lost the entire contents of one, gold buttons and trinkets 'even to the cotton that they lay upon'. His shopman had been distracted.[12]

The importance of good display was well understood and a visit to the large Bond Street shop of Mr Jefferys, royal goldsmith was a highlight of Sophie von la Roche's visit to London in 1786. She was struck particularly by the bright lights, the lavish display of stock and the special room devoted to antique plate. Sometimes the showroom was taken over for a special exhibition; when Rundell's showed their newly completed order of a dinner service for the Prince of Wales in 1807, Ludgate Hill was jammed with the carriage-folk coming to view. Hancock's in Bruton Street was the first shop to install electric light, in 1885.[13]

Although Badcock shows three smallworkers at a table under the shop window, the workshop was always behind the scenes, upstairs or even in another building nearby. As George Wickes's business expanded, he bought a second house in Panton Street to house his workmen.

The Company attempted to keep track of workshops 'so that men may see they work truly' and disapproved of 'garrets, chambers and other secret places with doors locked upon them' but this was futile, as the 1651 survey of Goldsmiths' Company properties makes clear.[14] In a crowded city, workmen were crammed into garrets or backyard extensions.

Insurance policies taken out in the later eighteenth and early nineteenth centuries with the Sun Fire Office (exhaustively analysed by John Culme) include a most interesting plan of Messrs Bateman's premises at 107 Bunhill Row, on the outskirts of the City, made by the insurance company's surveyor in 1802, which shows the layout of a medium-sized manufacturing business. Facing a central yard was one three-storey block of workshops, with a further three lower buildings ranged round a smaller yard, all with long windows. The firm had a newly built steam engine house with the older power source, a horse mill and flatting (rolling) mill above. These facilities for flatting metal had apparently been added in 1791; the initial investment was no doubt recouped by their ability to supply other firms with sheet.[15]

Cleaning and Repairs

Among the services the goldsmith offered his customers was instructions on cleaning their silver. The advice given by Paul De Lamerie in 1737 with the church plate he supplied for Stinsford in Dorset is well known; an earlier instruction, also preserved with an order for liturgical silver, was written in 1680, presumably by the goldsmith I N over a star from whom Dean Smith purchased a new set of plate for Carlisle Cathedral. The silver was to be washed and dried thoroughly; then 'Rub the flagons and chalices from the top to the Bottom, not crosswise, but the Bason and patens are to be rubbed roundwise not across and by no means use either chalk, sand or salt'.[16]

Some goldsmiths, at least in the American towns, were prepared to provide a boy to come and clean plate periodically; an advertisement inserted in 1760 in the *South Carolina Gazette* by John Paul Grimke, stating that he had lost his plate-boy with the smallpox, suggests that his customers' servants brush their plate 'with whiting dissolved in rum or any other spirits; which will restore to it its former beauty and brightness again . . . without spoiling the chased work'.[17]

In London the larger firms made a regular business out of boiling and burnishing their customers' worn plate. Indeed, it was possible to take refurbishing much further, without actually going to the expense and delay of a complete refashioning. In 1778, the Earl of

Egremont spent £75 with Wakelin & Tayler on his four tureens, table candlesticks and their branches and twelve pairs of salts, 'taking off the Matting, Boiling and Burnishing and rechaising'. He had some plated salts repaired at the same time and by spending a relatively small sum had a handsomely equipped dining table again. Gilding also wore away and had to be renewed periodically; William Cripps charged 1s 9d an ounce for regilding a toilet service in 1762; since the service weighed over 450 ounces, the cost was considerable, Thomas Harachè, 'gilding a parcel of Silver Dressing Plate' for Curzon in 1755, charged even more, 3s an ounce, or £69 altogether, a reminder of the enormous gap in spending power between the wealthy aristocracy and the merely comfortable gentry. [18]

Repairs were also frequently necessary; cups were dropped and bruised, handles broken off and sometimes alterations were needed to make a large piece more stable. A helmet ewer was given to the Fishmongers' Company by Sir James Bateman in 1706, 'Being too small in circumference that it is continually falling and bruising the silver bason belonging to it, it is ordered to enlarge the foot' (in 1739). [19]

Frequently the goldsmith was requested to match-up with an earlier object, either to replace something lost or to extend a service, or possibly to provide a series for gifts to children. Wickes copied Crespin's tureens for the Earl of Orford in 1738, to make a set of four, and it is probable that some of Paul Storr's copies of De Lamerie and Crespin candlesticks were to make up sets. But this practice was largely confined to the wealthy families whose silver was of high quality and intricate workmanship in the first place (Fig. 45). [20]

Repairs, or rather additions, were supposed to be hallmarked. Sometimes these can date successive overhauls of an old piece, for example a Nuremburg cup of about 1650, given to Christ's Hospital by Thomas Poynder in 1840. When unscrewed, this reveals three phases of repair, all marked. The first is a plate inserted by Walter Brind in 1736, the second a new lining to the cover (Joseph Taylor, 1840) and the third is undated. [21]

When enamelling was popular, as in the sixteenth century, it was easier and more effective for the craftsman to enamel onto gold plates rather than directly onto silver. Armorial finials too were sometimes cast in gold and then applied to a silver body; this practice may explain the large number of sixteenth-century cups which have replacement finials in silver, since the more precious and softer metal was doubly vulnerable. When Sir Martin Bowes gave the Goldsmiths' Company the Bowes cup he referred to his arms as being enamelled on gold, and several finials on plate at the Clothworkers' Company are of gold. The royal inventory of 1574 lists many objects, from Edward Seymour's plate in particular, with gold elements. [22]

Unusual finishes could be applied temporarily to plate for special occasions; the Duchess of Devonshire, in her recent account of Chatsworth, refers to the man who came up from London when a great set piece dinner was planned. Locking himself into the dining room for a day, he laboured to create frosting on the banqueting service by a secret process.

Pricing and Credit

The largest element in the cost of silver plate was always the raw material. The fashion charge, per ounce, varied according to the complexity of the design from a few pence for very

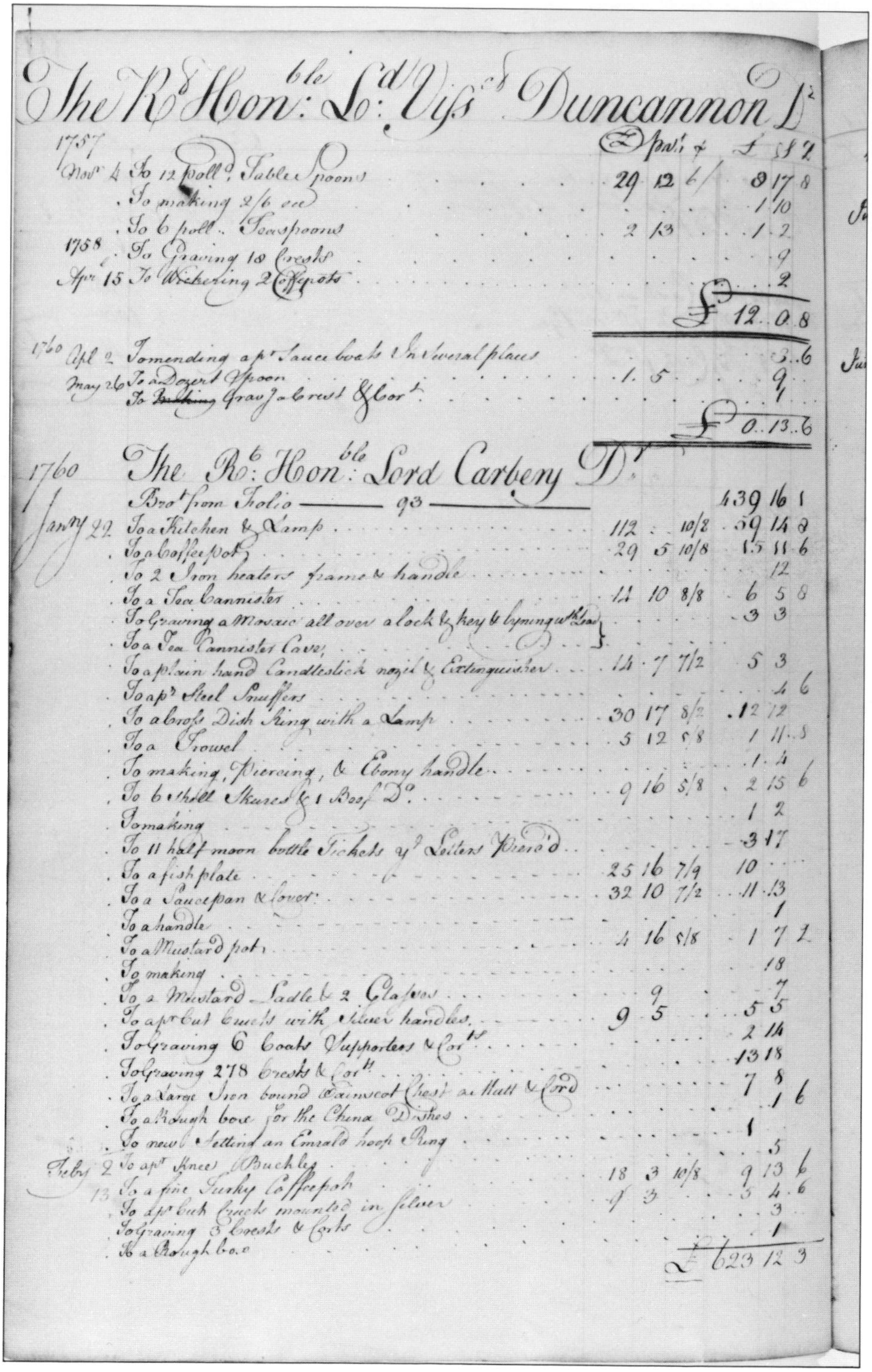

The Rt Honble Lord Viscount Duncannon Dr

1757
Novr 4 To 12 poll'd Table Spoons .... 29 12 6/ ... 9 17 8
        To making 2/6 each 1 10
        To 6 poll'd Teaspoons .... 2 13 ... 1 2
1758   To Graving 10 Crests 9
Apr 15 To Newleting 2 Coffeepots 2
                                                         £ 12 . 0 . 8

1760 Apl 2 To mending a pr Sauce boats & in several places .... 3 . 6
May 26 To a Dozert Spoon .... 1 . 5 ... 9
        To Graving Crest & Cort ....
                                                         £ 0 . 13 . 6

1760 The Rt Honble Lord Carbery Dr
Jany 22 Bro't from Folio ——— 93 ——— 439 16 1
         To a Kitchen & Lamp .... 112 : 10/2 ... 59 14 9
         To a Coffee pot .... 29 5 10/8 ... 15 11 6
         To 2 Iron heaters frame & handle 12
         To a Tea Cannister .... 11 10 8/8 ... 6 5 8
         To Graving a Mosaic all over a lock & key & lyning with Lead .. 3 3
         To a Tea Cannister Case ....
         To a plain hand Candlestick nozel & Extinguisher ... 11 7 7/2 ... 5 3
         To a pr Steel Snuffers 4 6
         To a Cross Dish Ring with a Lamp .... 30 17 8/2 ... 12 12
         To a Trowel .... 5 12 s 8 ... 1 11 3
         To making, Piercing, & Ebony handle 1 4
         To 6 chill Skures & 1 Beef Do .... 9 16 5/8 ... 2 15 6
         To making 1 2
         To 11 half moon bottle Tickets & Letters Eng'd 3 17
         To a fish plate .... 25 16 7/9 ... 10
         To a Sauce pan & cover .... 32 10 7/2 ... 11 13
         To a handle 1
         To a Mustard pot .... 4 16 s/8 ... 1 7 2
         To making 18
         To 2 Mustard Ladle & 2 Glasses .... 9 ... 7
         To a pr Cut Cruets with silver handles .... 9 5 ... 5 5
         To Graving 6 Coats supporters & Cort 2 14
         To Graving 278 Crests & Cort 13 18
         To a Large Iron bound Wainscot Chest at Hull & Cord .. 7 8
         To a Rough box for the China Dishes 1 6
         To new Setting an Emerald hoop Ring 5
Feb 2   To a pr Knee Buckles .... 18 3 10/8 ... 9 13 6
     13 To a fine Turky Coffeepot .... 9 3 ... 5 4 6
         To a pr Cut Cruets mounted in Silver 4 3
         To Graving 3 Crests & Corts 1
         To a Rough box ....
                                                         £ 623 12 3

Fig. 70   **Parker & Wakelin's gentlemen's ledgers**
c.1760. On 22 January 1760, Lord Carbery purchased a complete set of cutlery plus ragout spoons,
mustard pots and ladles, skewers, bottle tickets, sauce boats and waiters: 278 items were engraved with
his crest and coronet. The most expensive was his condiment 'vases' at 11s 8d per ounce for fashion, the
figure given in the third column, while the weight in ounces and pennyweights appears in the first two.
Lord Carbery had not settled his account three years later, when he was charged interest on a bond to
cover it.
VAM

simple items to 4 or 5s an ounce in the mid-sixteenth century for chased pieces (from the goldsmiths' bills of Edward Seymour, 1540s). Additional work, such as engraving and gilding, was charged on top as the Wickes Wakelin ledgers show. The customer paid in secondhand plate, credited almost always at its melt-value unless the piece was exceptional, or in cash; a large order might take several years to complete and deliver, which suited both goldsmith (who thus spread the work and the cost of the metal) and client, who had extended credit. The Duke of Leinster's dinner service was made over a two-year period, 1745–7 and a century later Hunt & Roskell took three years over the Ismay testimonial, a massive service. For a bill, see Fig. 70.

The ability to wait for payment was crucial, particularly when dealing with members of the royal family and the aristocracy, who notoriously would let a tradesman wait two or three years for payment. In 1544 Nicholas Trappes had the fortitude to refuse to hand over some silver to Edward Seymour's agent until he was paid. Only the agent's proposal to his master that Trappes could be influenced by Seymour's offer 'to be his good lord' unlocked both credit and the goods in dispute.[23]

From time to time the Company attempted to regulate both the prices to be charged by goldsmiths and the rate to be paid per ounce for old silver and silver gilt. In 1516, a committee of seven leading goldsmiths including Robert Amadas and three other royal suppliers, set new rates which were read out before an assembly of the whole company at their hall. The prices set as trade rates were from 3s 2d to 3s 7d the ounce. These are interesting for the various categories quoted. Apart from the usual distinction between white and gilt and the old and new touch (presumably the former refers to plate made before the date-letter came in, in 1478, nearly forty years earlier) three quality levels were recognised for gilt 'swags, coffins of salts, haunces (handles) of pots, bottoms of cups, mazer bands, girdle harnesses, chalices, cups, salts, spoons'. Minimum selling prices were inevitably higher and had a wider range; no man was to sell white plate under 3s 8d, parcel-gilt, graven or chased, under 4s, gilt plate chased graven or pounced nor crosses for churches under 5s and hooks, 'disents', wreaths or other small gear under 6s. A constant complaint against the aliens working in London was that they undercut the native English and it is significant that the 'stranger' goldsmiths were called to this assembly too. However, the melt price was the only one to which virtually everyone adhered.[24]

Silver warehouses, retailing a wide range of other makers' goods, can be identified from the late eighteenth century. One, the London Silver Plate Manufactory, run by Thomas Daniell at the Silver Lion opposite Goldsmiths' Hall, issued a stock list in 1788. Daniell claimed to keep '20,000 ounces of every Species of Silver goods' in stock with 'Embellishments of the latest and best Designs and at the Workman's Wholesale Prices . . . at least a third cheaper than the usual'. Goods are quoted at standard weights such as 'Greek Cream Ewers' at four to six ounces (Fig. 71).[25]

Advertising

Trade cards and newspaper advertisements are a rich source of information on both the shop stock and working practices of retail goldsmiths. Three members of the Briscoe family, John,

LONDON SILVER PLATE MANUFACTORY,

Oppofite Goldfmith's-Hall, Fofter-Lane, Cheapfide;

Carried on by Thomas Daniell and his late Father upwards of 40 Years.

TWENTY Thoufand Ounces of every Species of Silver Goods kept ready finifhed in the higheft Elegance of Patterns, of peculiarly ftrong and excellent Workmanfhip and Embellifhments of the lateft and beft Defigns, at the Workman's Wholefale Prices, which will be found, at leaft, one third cheaper than the ufual Charges for Fafhion or Making ; Advantages none but real Makers can give, and which the unqueftionable Services of Ready Money very juftly Claim.

Cuftomary Weights, viz.

Epergns with 6 and 8 Branches 80 oz. Coffee-Kitchens 36 oz. Coffee-Vafes, Ewers, and Pots 24 oz. each. Sauce-Boats with covers, and Ladles, 12 oz. to 20 oz. a Pair. Rummers Gilt Infide, 6 oz. Chamber Candlefticks, 6 oz. each. Difh-Croffes with Lamps, 14 oz. Pint Canns and Mugs, 12 oz. Pierced Salts, 3 oz. Tureen Salts, 6 oz. Silver Snuffers, 3 oz. a Pair. Tureen-fhaped, Pierced, and Engraved Bread-Bafkets, 20 to 30 oz. Boat-fhaped Snuffer-Pans, 4 oz. Bottle Stands, 2 oz. each. Oval Sugar and Cream Pails, 10 oz. Oval Pierced and Gondola Eight-Glafs Cruet-Stands, 8 oz. to 20 oz.

Round Five-Glafs Cruet-Stands, 6 oz. to 15 oz. each. Pierced Muftard Pots, and Ladles, 4 oz. Bright Engraved Tea-Pots 10 to 15 oz. Double Beaded and Engraved Waiters Beaded Gallon Tea-Urns, 80 oz. Table-Spoons, and 4 Pronged Forks, 2 oz. Skewers and Scoops. Oval Pierced Sugar-Bafkets, 5 oz. Bright, Engraved, and Beaded Tea-Spoons, Tongs, aud Strainers. Silver Handled Knives and Forks. Beaded Soup-Ladles, Ragout-Spoons, and Butter-Ladles. Greek Cream Ewers, 4 oz. to 6 oz. Rich Fancy Silver Buckles. Silver-Hilted Drefs Swords. Wine Funnels, Bottle-Lables, &c.

Pillar Table Candlefticks, of the lateft Defigns and Models, 14 to 20 oz. a Pair.

Brilliant Pafte Shoe and Knee Buckles, Gold Enameled Bracelets, Lockets, Rings, Pins, &c. ornamented with Pearl and Hair Devices, Diamonds, &c. Engraving on Plate and Cornelians, with Arms and other Subjects, in the moft exquifite Manner. Motto Rings with the utmoft Expedition: alfo the ftrongeft Plated Goods. Ivory Knives and Forks. Bronze Tea-Urns.

N. B. New Silver is charged 5s. 6d. per oz. and the fame Money allowed for Old Silver in Exchange. The Prices charged for making the various Articles in Plate may be had at the Warehoufe and Workfhops as above. A Sett of Elegant pearl Jeffamine pins. A pair of Brilliant Slides, and a Clufter Ring, Second Hand. Alfo feveral extraordinary good fecond hand Ladies and Gentlemen's Watches. Crefts and Cyphers Engraved at 4d. each. A very capital Silver Tureen and 2 dozen Table 4 Pronged Forks.

Fig. 71 **Thomas Daniell's trade card *c*.1780**

His London silver plate manufactory offered standard items in both silver and plate. He stamped his address 'SILVER LYON FOSTER LANE' on his wares, as on a 1785 teapot (Holburne Museum, Bath).

Guildhall Library

Stafford and William, advertised in London papers between 1748 and 1751, describing at length their current stock of secondhand plate, an aspect of the trade which sounds modern but which occurs as an advertising feature on trade cards from the late seventeenth century. Although the London papers carried advertisements of thefts and occasional trade announcements in the late seventeenth century, this form of advertising flourished particularly from the 1730s. Newspapers were invaluable too as a means of attracting customers to the occasional closing-down sale, like that held by John Hopkins of Fleet Street in 1755 'having succeeded in Business to his utmost satisfaction . . . therefore intends to dispose of his remaining Stock cheap' (*Public Advertiser*, 2 January 1755).[26]

Some years earlier (1747) Hopkins had on offer 'A very neat Epargne – a Handsome Surtout', an unusual distinction which almost certainly differentiated between an open framework like the Newdegate centrepiece (VAM 1743) and the closed tureen-like composite group such as the Sprimont centrepiece (VAM 1747). Hopkins's stock was apparently of high quality; items like 'A Pair of Curious Ice Pails' or 'a Large and Useful Tea Table' were not carried in the normal goldsmith's stock, at least judging by their trade cards.[27]

The same year John Fossey at the Gold Ring, Ball Alley, Lombard Street, issued a price list of new plate 'made in the newest Taste, and by the best workmen'. Tea kettles and teapots were the most costly per ounce, at 7s 6d; candlesticks 'polished, of the newest Patterns' were 2d an ounce less. This list is an interesting glimpse of those items most in demand; the only flatware is 'Large Table Spoons' polished or burnished at 18s per dozen for fashion. There are tankards, round-bottomed or 'Strait', pint mugs, waiters, sauce boats, cruet frames, casters and 'leg'd' salts; in other words, just exactly the tablewares depicted on trade cards.[28]

Stolen goods were sometimes advertised too. In 1749 Frederick Kandler publicised the loss 'since the month of October last, out of a family, three Silver Teaspoons of a very large size of foreign Silver, with two stamps (hallmarks) and a Scroll'. Five years earlier in October 1742, Paul De Lamerie announced in the *Daily Advertiser* that a heavy silver tankard had been stolen 'out of a back room in the House of Christian Claus' in James Street, Covent Garden. This was an elaborate object, probably foreign, with 'Shell and Rock Work on the Handle' and a cupid on the cover above a medal of Gustavus Adolphus. 'Three Guineas Reward and no Questions asked!'[29]

The alternative, of the tankard turning up in the hands of a pawnbroker, was the favourite route for disposing of plate improperly acquired. The temptation was sometimes too much for workmen entrusted with home-working orders; the *London Evening Post* reported on 1 October 1743 that the 'Workers in Gold, Silver and Jewels' intended to petition for an act to stop pawnbrokers taking in unfinished plate from workmen 'by which they know it is not their Property'.[30]

In England the demand for low-cost silversmiths' work away from the large provincial centres was fulfilled by chapmen, travelling hawkers who were notorious for selling substandard or rather below standard silverware. One is depicted in Marcellus Laroon's *Cries of London* (1711) with his travelling box open to show needle and pencil cases, small boxes, bodkins, almanac holders and the like. Itinerant goldsmiths or chapmen sometimes inserted advertisements in provincial newspapers; in 1717 S. Haughton announced to the 'Gentlemen and Ladies' of Stamford that during his visit they 'may be furnished with all sorts of Goldsmiths' Ware as cheap as if they were in London'. These chapmen, who bought their stock wholesale in London, were notorious for passing off light-gauge silver; William Badcock in 1677 complained 'the great part of what is made by the London workers and sent into the country is exceedingly Adulterated and Debased'.[31]

An advertisement in the *Newcastle Courier* (1729) shows the local goldsmiths acting in concert to drive out of the area a chapman who was undercutting them. This 'common raffler' had in stock tankards, oval snuff boxes, casters, porringers, tea tongs and spoons and punch ladles, all small portable objects whose possession nevertheless would give an air of gentility to their owners. With vastly improved communications and the constant anxiety to emulate London fashions, provincial goldsmiths lost their regional identity and became mere retailers.[32]

Trade cards are a rich pictorial source for goldsmiths' stock and for what each man felt would appeal to his particular customers; although they cannot always be taken as evidence for current fashion, the leading houses certainly changed their card designs frequently. Another card of John Fossey (1748) of Lombard Street, shows a sauce boat with scrolling handle, a tureen, a pear-shaped kettle and shaped waiters, all in the forefront of rococo taste. George Wickes, for example, showed that fashionable piece of tableware, an epergne with candle branches, on his 1735 trade card. Picture-back tablespoons are displayed in open knife boxes, with their decorative backs visible, on cards of the 1760s. The rapid and general popularity of pear-shaped flower-chased tea silver is evident also at this time. Rococo was the essential ingredient for the golden age of English trade cards (*c*.1730–70). In the 1760s Thomas Heming, the royal goldsmith, certainly had his card altered to show three of his outstanding recent lines, a cup, a tureen and a ewer, all known from surviving pieces (Fig. 97).[33]

Occasionally a shop interior appears, as on Philips Gardens's card of about 1750, although another on the card of Peter de la Fontaine is probably a fantasy. The cards of 'toymen' like Daniel Chevenix and William Deards demonstrate the range of small fancy goods such as gold boxes, spectacles, mathematical instruments and so on sold in the equivalent of the modern stationer's shop, along with larger silverware. Chevenix's window, depicted in a 1750 engraving, has a piece of silver by every pane of glass. But trade cards cease to be as informative in the late eighteenth century, the goldsmiths confining their text to simple statements such as 'Buys second-hand plate' or 'plate in the newest fashion' with no or very little presentation of their wares; sometimes a small selection of neo-classical silver appears on a bill head.

In 1824 Joseph Brasbridge explained in his memoirs the principle he followed in his advertisements; 'expose enough to excite curiosity and conceal enough to leave curiosity ungratified', a sentiment more readily associated with a stripper than a silversmith. He chose the *St. James's Chronicle* (familiar to readers of *Cranford*) as his medium, since this paper was read especially by the clergy; the Archbishop of Canterbury was among his customers, a happy chance which he was careful not to conceal.[34]

Advertising became far more general in the nineteenth century as the opportunities offered by cheaper printing techniques were recognised. Also the larger houses, from 1841, received

Fig. 72 **Price list issued by S. Alderman *c*.1833–40**
Alderman offered prices 'LOWER than at any other House in the Trade'. He offered to design
presentation plate and had a large stock of christening presents in silver.
Guildhall Library

publicity in the *Illustrated London News* where royal and aristocratic wedding presents were often described and illustrated. The international exhibitions of 1851, 1861 and so on were widely reported and interesting current productions of manufacturing goldsmiths from London, Sheffield, Birmingham were discussed in the daily press too. But the twentieth century has seen a rapid decline in the general English awareness of contemporary silver design, with more people spending money on old silver, or copies of old silver, than on innovative work.

Advice on window dressing for silver shops quoted in the *Goldsmiths' Journal* in 1937 sounds a slightly desperate note: 'the most important idea to convey is that the silver itself is as smart and modern as the newest of the new homes'. The retailer was advised to reinforce this impression by standing his stock on glass bricks. 'Most Sunday newspapers have a section devoted to pictures of new residences . . . Put it in the window. You might have one of your own advertisements of silver enlarged to superimpose on the page . . . Grouped around this page should be a selection . . . chosen for their importance in entertaining'. *Plus ça change, plus c'est le même chose*; in 1742 a French visitor commented in disgust 'Eating and Drinking are still the Ground-work of whatever they call Pleasure'. Only silver designed for the dining table can be sure of a steady market in England.

Notes

1 Quoted and discussed in Kent 1982.

2 His papers are at the Henry Francis du Pont Winterthur Museum and quoted at length in Fales 1974.

3 On his trade card: Heal 1935.

4 Information from Robert Barker, who is shortly to publish on Jamaican goldsmiths in the *Proceedings of the Silver Society*. Fales 1974.

5 MFA Boston 1982; Davis 1978.

6 For the export trade in silver, see Fales 1973 *passim*; fig. 143.

7 VAM 1913; Goodison 1975.

8 Goldsmiths' 1978, 84; Gubbins 1983, 12.

9 Seaby 1951; Baker 1973.

10 Heal 1935. Barr 1980.

11 It had a long ancestry: Reddaway and Walker 1975, 234 (1368 ordinance) and 222 (the 1327 charter).

12 For Philips Garden, Heal 1935; Brasbridge 1824.

13 See p.267, Sophie von la Roche, quoted in Grimwade for 1976; Anon 1827.

14 Goldsmiths' Company MSS: 1651 Survey. The ordinances on working 'in open shop' were read to the assembled Company from time to time, as in May 1729, a clear indication that they were being broken.

15 Culme 1980.

16 De Lamerie's advice is quoted in Nightingale 1891, *Church Plate of Dorset*, 120. For Carlisle, see Ferguson 1888, 29.

17 Fales 1973, fig. 227.

18 Petworth MSS: Goldsmiths' bills, VAM: Kedleston MSS, information from Lesky Harris.

19 Goldsmiths' 1951, no. 104.

20 Barr 1980, 24–5; Christie's 1984. Ch. 11.

21 Penzer 1960.

22 For example, Collins 1955, no. 368, a cup, and 501–2, bowls with covers.

23 Seymour MSS, Longleat; Vol. IV, 100. Grimwade 1961.

24 Goldsmiths' Company, minute book.

25 Daniell was clearly an enterprising man; he advertised in the first edition of *The Times* on the front page.

26 Wills 1983; Burney Collection, BM.

27 Burney Collection. Heal 1935.

28 British Museum, Print Collection.

29 Burney Collection.

30 Burney Collection.

31 VAM Metalwork Department archive; Badcock 1971, 108–9.

32 Gill 1974.

33 Heal 1935. For Heming, Young 1982.

34 Brasbridge 1824.

PART III

DESIGN AND ORNAMENT

HERALDRY AS ORNAMENT

Armorials 1200 to 1500

D ESPITE the scarcity of examples, a clear division may be seen between goldsmiths'
work of the early Middle Ages, before about 1200, and later. This change was fuelled
largely by the English appetite for heraldry. Once the concept of inheritable personal devices
was accepted in the late twelfth century, both noblemen and the king adopted arms rapidly
and used them lavishly in every aspect of their surroundings – on textiles, in wallpaintings
and on their plate and jewels, although tomb-decoration is now almost the sole surviving
visual evidence. Seals, the first manifestation of this new personal emblem, were in general
use by the early thirteenth century and supplied a whole new range of raw material for
decorative art. The English royal arms, three lions passant, first found on a seal of Richard I in
1198, remained unchanged until the 1340s and Edward III's French claims.[1]

Once ordinaries of arms became common (Matthew Paris prepared the earliest known
compilation of blazons before 1259) goldsmiths could reproduce them as the customer
required, whether in the form of plaques enamelled and applied, or engraved directly on to
the object.

Badges became popular at the court of Edward III as a means of demonstrating allegiance
and were rapidly taken up by the goldsmiths, retaining their popularity into the sixteenth
century and falling out of favour only with the death of bastard feudalism. They were cast,
like the miniature Bainbridge squirrels which form handle-terminals on the early Tudor
snuffers of Cardinal Bainbridge or the sickle terminals on Sir Robert Hungerford's spoons.[2]

Until the sixteenth century, cups, as the most intimate, most valued, and so most carefully
decorated of a man's silver, bore his arms as a matter of course, whatever the rest of the
ornament might consist of. Most of the forty-four silver goblets left by Edward II at
Caerphilly Castle in 1327 were enamelled inside both bowl and cover with the leopards of
England, as were basins, pots and ewers. Three of the finest goblets were silvergilt and
enamelled; the largest was engraved with 'divers baboons', an example of a typically
complicated expensive piece. It was priced at over £12, three times its weight in silver, an
indication of the premium set on highly skilled craftsmanship. Two other goblets, one chased
or 'chiselled without', the other 'chiselled' inside, were valued at twice their weight in
sterling.[3]

This obsessive use of armorials had a valid political justification and one which is most
clearly expressed in an early fourteenth-century piece, the Bute or Ballatyne mazer.[4]

Although made for a Scottish family, the Bute mazer perfectly embodies the feudal relationships which operated also in England. Its boss bears in the centre a cast lion, emblematic of Robert the Bruce, surrounded by discs enamelled with the arms of six Scottish noble families. The family for whom it was made were hereditary high stewards of Scotland and their arms lie symbolically between the paws of the lion, a delicate reference to the prevailing relationship of king and noblemen. The mazer was probably made to mark a celebration (perhaps post-victory over the English at Bannockburn in 1314), at which the king was to be present.

No English equivalent to this now exists, but Hans Holbein's drawings of Tudor royal plate demonstrate the continuing popularity at court of both personal and royal heraldic ornament two hundred years later. When Henry VIII assumed the crown imperial, he ensured that it appeared also on the finials to his drinking vessels; open-arched or 'imperial' crowns occur in several designs, as also on the coinage, from the late fifteenth century.[5]

Heraldry was not confined to plate for domestic use. One has only to look at the Ramsey Abbey incense boat (VAM) with its terminals of rams' heads arising from the waves, or the copper-gilt morse with the Virgin and a shield enamelled with warden pears, the arms adopted by Warden Abbey, Bedfordshire, to appreciate that churchmen, major patrons of decorative art throughout the Middle Ages, shared its prevailing passion for brand images. The incense boat, found in Whittlesea Mere in 1850 with a silver censer (also in the museum) had presumably been stolen, a mischance which preserved it since all other English examples vanished in the mid-sixteenth century; some pewter plates, presumably for domestic use, found with the censer and incense boat also bore the ram's head device as a mark of ownership.

Gifts to churches frequently bore the donor's arms, even before the Reformation; later they were often old plate given from the donor's home or private chapel and so engraved as a matter of course (Fig. 115).[6]

In domestic plate, heraldry was ubiquitous. Every one of the gold cups described in the Holland inventory of 1447 (see p. 10) had the earl's shield in the bottom; at each gulp, the guest was reminded of his host's colours. This constant reinforcement of the visible signs of feudal lordship was to break up quite rapidly in the sixteenth century, once Henry VIII had established the monarchy as supreme and so downgraded livery badges as ornament. Of the handful of important fourteenth- and fifteenth-century cups to survive, almost all are enamelled with arms inside, and some also on their covers. The covered beaker-shaped cup left by William Bateman to Trinity Hall has his arms in a trilobed frame in the bottom, in translucent enamel. Another simpler armorial roundel is set inside the cover.[7]

The same requirement did not apply to the plainer, simpler cups sold to those without arms, or for the use of retainers, or necessarily to mazers, which often have bosses or silver engraved with religious subjects such as S. George and the Dragon, or the Virgin, perhaps with some personal or fraternity significance to the owner, now lost. Generally speaking, no cups had arms enamelled within after 1530.

The badges of the donor, his ancestors and of the king appeared as significant elements in virtually every piece of medieval plate, whether secular or ecclesiastical. Even the gilt bronze processional crosses carried by Richard III's men at the battle of Bosworth had the sunburst

Fig. 73 **Foundress's cup**
Gilt 1507. Mark a fish in an oval. H. 24 cm. Engraved with fleur de lis, portcullis, Tudor rose and marguerite, each a badge of the donor, Lady Margaret Beaufort. The foot, originally gemset (compare Fig. 108), is shaped as a Tudor rose and the finial repeats the portcullis and marguerite theme.
Christ's College, Cambridge

199

badge of the Yorkist kings.[8] The Foundress's cup at Christ's College, Cambridge is typical. Left to the college by Lady Margaret Beaufort, mother of Henry VII, it had been made over sixty years before. It has a print enamelled with the arms of Humphrey Duke of Gloucester impaling those of his second wife and is embossed with sprays of oak, rose and vine leaves in reference to his heraldry and reminiscent of a cup belonging to John Holland, which was 'chased wreathwise with vines and roses'. Bishop Foxe's gold salt has the pelican badge and his initials, and the Anathema cup (1481) is enamelled in the bottom with a seeded rose and foliage, probably a device associated with its donor Dr Thomas Langton.[9]

Sometimes these personal devices effectively dictate the ornament. The Leigh cup, presented to the Mercers' Company in 1569 by Sir Thomas Leigh, is covered with cast maidenheads, pilgrim bottles and Tudor roses in a diaper pattern. It bears the London hallmark for 1513 (formerly read as 1499) and the diaper design is very similar to that on another beaker, presented by the foundress to Christ's College, of 1507, although here the marguerites and roses of Margaret Beaufort are engraved, rather than cast and applied. In the latter piece, the form of the foot itself, a double Tudor rose, recalls the badge of greatest significance to her family (Fig. 73).[10]

The constant reference to badges in Sir John Fastolf's inventory is discussed in Chapter I but he was by no means unusual; Sir Robert Hungerford of Heytesbury, who died in 1459, had, among his other plate, spoons with sickle terminals and basins 'pounced' with his family badge of the sickle; virtually every item had his arms engraved. Whatever the vagaries of changing taste in ornament on plate between 1200 and 1500 (we know so little that it is unwise to be dogmatic) this one element remained constant.[11]

Armorials from 1500

Those who could afford silver at all were a small minority, perhaps five per cent of the population in the sixteenth and seventeenth centuries. Many of them were armigerous and those who were not, the prosperous urban aristocracy of London and a few other towns, and the lesser gentry with no arms of their own, could use personal devices, rebuses like the eye and 'slipped' branch of Abbot Islip, or if retained, might take the badge of their lord. Devices are frequently found on jewellery, notably seal rings, and could be adopted to identify plate as well. Merchants' marks, which came into use in the late thirteenth century, appear on the mounts of some stoneware mugs, such as David Gittings's gift to the Vintners' Company of 1563 and another, undated, in the Museum of London, and the Elizabethan lawyer John Bowyer used his and his wife's initials in cypher. Outside London merchants' marks remained acceptable, even for men of some standing, well into the seventeenth century; a standing paten and a flagon given to S. Margaret, King's Lynn about 1640 both bear the marks of local men, in a central cross-like device within the conventional laurel wreath.

An alternative, for those who were members of livery companies, was to adopt their Company's arms or badge; a large quantity of silver exists engraved with corporate armorials, but many were originally private orders. Others were gifts, or plate sold by institutions at times of hardship to their members and retained in the purchaser's families. Objects made at corporate expense as gifts for their members were normally engraved with

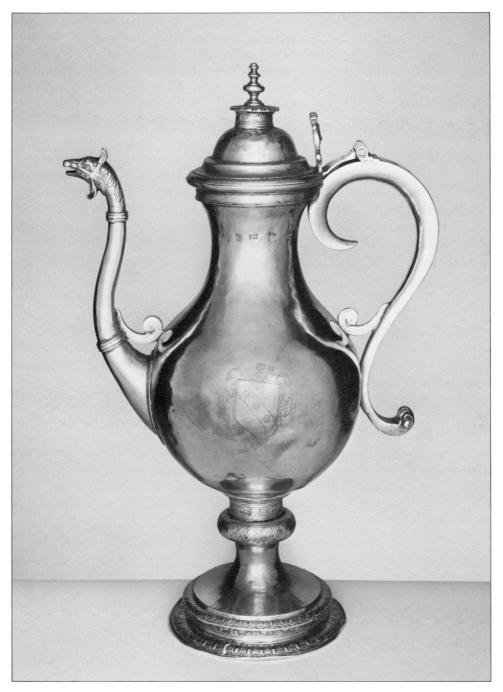

Fig. 74 **Ewer for rosewater**
Gilt 1609. Mark RM below a harp (?). H. 20.5 cm. Pounced (stippled) with arms of Emerson, who gave
it to his parish church in 1619: perhaps as a baptismal ewer. In use until 1980; now S. Paul's Treasury.
S. Mary, Monken Hadley, Herts

201

the corporate arms, a subject discussed in Chapter 14, in 1897 the Salters' Company presented each of the livery with a pair of gothic salts, copying those on their coat of arms.

Silver seized in battle was automatically engraved with the victor's arms too, as occurred in 1666. When Admiral Sir George Ayscue's ship the *Prince Royal* ran aground in a four-day battle with the Dutch, his plate was divided between Vice-Admiral Sweerts and Lieutenant-Admiral Tromp; the arms of Sweerts and his wife appear on candlesticks and boxes from the English ship, alongside those of Ayscue. Even when the plate was refashioned by its captor, he kept the association by engraving not only his own arms but those of the old owners, in triumph, as in the plate seized at the battle of Newport. The dish made from this is now in the Metropolitan Museum.[12]

Royal arms are of course no indication of personal use by the king or even within his household; those men engaged on the king's service, whether ambassadors or officers of state like the Speaker of the House of Commons, were issued with plate (from the early sixteenth century to the early nineteenth century) engraved with the royal arms or a Garter badge; a ewer and basin by Philip Rollos (VAM 1705) was issued to Lord Raby as ambassador in Berlin. A Jewel House service issued to Lord Methuen in 1703, well known since its release on to the market earlier this century, is a typical assemblage of fashionable dinner plate, including a set of fan-shaped serving dishes.[13]

From the sixteenth century the most consistent use of armorials, whether engraved, cast and applied or enamelled on bosses, was on sideboard plate intended for display throughout the meal: ewers, basins, flagons (Fig. 17).

In the early seventeenth century another technique became popular for simple armorials and crests; 'pouncing' or punching dots to define the outline, occurs on a gilt ewer of 1609 at S. Paul's treasury (Fig. 74), and a group of 1630s wine cups found buried at Stoke Prior are pounced with a wolf's head, presumably the owner's crest (VAM, see Fig. 118).

Pouncing was a cheaper and quicker method than engraving, but did not give as rich an effect and because it barely scored the surface, has often been obliterated by heavy polishing over the years. A beaker (VAM *c.*1640) has faint traces of pounced ornament and initials beneath later engraving; initials and dates are often found also on seal-top spoons and on spoon bowls, objects typically prized by the non-armigerous but prosperous classes in Stuart England. Enamelled armorials are very rarely found after about 1600, although occasionally a flagon or basin now in church hands retains its enamelled boss; some may be later antiquarian additions.

The skilful execution of personal heraldry, on utilitarian plate at least, was not given high priority. The Virginian William Fitzhugh, ordering his new plate from London in 1698, saved himself the expense; 'have no letters engraved upon them nor Coats of Arms, having a servant of my own, a singular good engraver, and so can save that money'.[14]

The surrounds to armorials became increasingly elaborate from the late seventeenth century, when simple mantling (crossed palm branches indicating conjugal love, often tied by ribbons below the shield, for example Fig. 80) gave way to baroque scrolls and architectural frames around circular shields. From about 1710, a brickwork background is sometimes found running behind the shield. A design popular in the 1720s and early 1730s was an intricate but symmetrical scrollbordered frame on which pastoral figures and pots of flowers perched in apparently casual disarray; this can be seen on a salver of 1733 with the arms of John Shales Barrington (VAM). This design was apparently the speciality of one engraver, employed by Simon Pantin, Thomas Farren and other leading goldsmiths.[15]

Asymmetrical cartouches, breaking out of a formal border of shells, trellis and scrollwork, were the first evidence of the rococo style in England. Not only on silver by about 1730, but also in book plates, trade cards and other engraved sources, these developed into full-bloodied irregular openwork frames entwined with flowers. These are sometimes found cast rather than engraved on large silver of the later 1730s and 1740s, since the new fashion

Fig. 75 **The Beckford dish**
Gilt 1814. Mark of Samuel Whitford and William Burwash. D.57.7 cm. Engraved with badges of the families – Hamilton, Douglas and Latimer – from whom William Beckford (1759–1844) claimed descent. Here the heraldic message dictated the ornament although his (spurious) armorials, on a removable disc, occupy the central boss in the traditional manner.
VAM

203

carried with it a demand for relief enrichment which extended to armorials as well. An early example of these rich relief armorials are those of Sir George Treby, cast and applied to his dish in the British Museum (1723) and to the salver in the Ashmolean Museum. Roses also entwine around the cast armorials of the Goldsmiths' Company on their De Lamerie ewer and basin of 1741–2. On the silver baskets at Woburn, made in 1737 when the fourth Duke of Bedford remarried, his cypher is incorporated into the pierced design.[16]

Later in the century, heraldic engravers occasionally adopted settings drawn from a romanticised antiquity, part-classical, part-gothic – ruinous ivygrown buildings, tombslabs or milestones – within which to place the coat of arms. A condiment urn by Louisa Courtauld and George Cowles (VAM 1771) depicts an aged Roman soldier leaning on his shield, on which the client's arms are engraved. The round shield, the soldier's beard and his companion's plate armour are all from quite another epoch (see Fig. 84). Thomas Bewick's inventive compositions of natural, not to say wild, settings for his North Country clients around 1800 are more familiar in the form of book illustrations, a further reminder that engraving was not compartmentalised.[17]

In the nineteenth century heraldic engraving, often elaborate and pedantically precise in its quarterings, becomes somewhat lifeless. There are of course exceptions, although their vitality is often derived from earlier sources: William Beckford adopted not only an elaborate coat of arms (to endorse his claim of descent from all the barons signing Magna Carta) but also all the badges of his reputed ancestors (Fig. 75).

The better Stuart and Georgian engravers, working for their most demanding and status-conscious customers, the aristocracy, followed the heraldic conventions fairly accurately, distinguishing the various tinctures of a blazon by cross-hatching. Gold was denoted by dots, and a plain surface indicated silver or white; horizontal hatching stood for blue, vertical for red, diagonal left to right green. Engravers also were expected to adopt the correct marks of cadency, the eldest son being identified by a label, the second by a crescent, the third a mullet and so on. George Booth, Earl of Warrington (1675–1758) had his coronet and cypher engraved, as the minimum mark of rank possible, even on his silver chamberpots![18]

For a woman, it was correct practice to blazon her arms in a lozenge or diamond-shaped shield; the diamond punch adopted by women goldsmiths such as Louisa Courtauld, Eliza Godfrey or Mary Lofthouse illustrates the general contemporary acceptance of this convention. A woman's personal plate, that is her toilet service and breakfast bowls, chocolate cups, milk or ale mug and so on, was often engraved with her cypher, as may be seen on the superb toilet service at Burghley House, Stamford, supplied to the Cecil family by Pierre Harache in 1695. On the covers of the boxes two trumpet-blowing cupids support a lozenge, with a coronet above, containing the cypher (Fig. 76).[19]

Another technique popular in the late seventeenth century was to cast and gild the cypher and apply it onto a plain silver box. This method was used also for furniture mounts; some of the silvergilt panels applied to tables of the 1670s at Ham House carry the cypher of the Duke and Duchess of Lauderdale, and a set of sconces in the royal collection made for Charles II had his cypher removed and that of William and Mary substituted about 1690.[20]

That status was indicated by armorials, or at least by initials as marks of identification, is

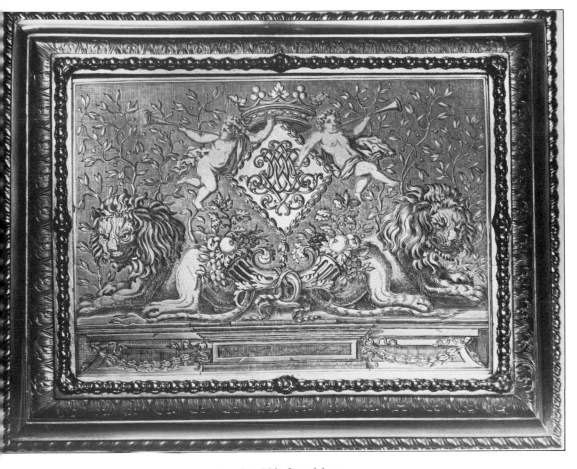

Fig. 76 **Lid of comb box**
Gilt 1695. Mark of Pierre Harache. L. 26 cm. From a toilet service, each piece engraved with a cypher
within a lozenge, an earl's coronet above. The engraver's name is unknown, but his technique is familiar
from other pieces.
Burghley House, Stamford

evident from the order book of an Annapolis firm, Wallace Davidson and Johnson, in the
1770s. One customer, William Lux of Baltimore, was quite explicit in his instructions (in
1771) and incidentally demonstrates the continual turnover of secondhand plate. 'All of the
above [tea and coffee ware] are requested to be bought at second hand and if Any Arms
should be engraved on either of them to be taken out and Cypher W.A.L. put on each as me
think it looks better for Little Folks than their Arms'.[21] One of Benjamin Rhodes's customers
in the 1690s, 'Admirall Russel's man' asked for a coat of arms 'so obviously bogus that a
reference to a textbook would be merely a waste of time', as Oman put it.

A series of embossed sideboard dishes in the seventeenth-century taste supplied by
Kensington Lewis to the Fetherstonehaugh family in the 1820s (and made by Edward Farrell)
were beautifully engraved with the family arms within a cartouche lifted from Stefano della

Bella's *Raccolta di Varii Capriccii* (1646). The wild sea-horses surmounting the cartouche had appealed to heraldic painters a century earlier when they supported the arms of Leake Okeover on a porcelain plate (and see Chapter 11).[22]

A careful examination of the engraving on old silver is always wise since armorials have often been erased and those of a later owner substituted, as on the Wickes or the Simon Owen ewer and basin (see p.316). Armorials should not be taken as necessarily a reliable guide to ownership unless the suggested provenance has independent support. Another reason for caution is that from the seventeenth century at least, those aspiring to coats of arms, but without entitlement, sometimes adopted a convenient approximation from such guides to heraldry as Gwylim's. Secondly, the coats are often so simplified as to suggest that no heraldic advice was provided and they could apply to any one of a number of people; thirdly, there is the problem of the improving hand of the last hundred years or so, enhancing objects for the antique trade. Indeed, it may have been happening already in the eighteenth century; a salver and porringer in the Museum of Fine Arts, Boston, has the arms of Cromwell, added about 1720. William Cripps commented on the 'improving' activities of dealers in the 1870s and one late Victorian at least, Charles Twinam, added reasonably convincing rococo armorials to his fake Georgian sauce boats; thus the whole value of armorials as contemporary evidence is thrown into uncertainty.[23]

Three-dimensional Heraldry

Engraving, although quite suitable for utilitarian plate, was not always considered sufficiently handsome for presentation pieces; the ornament of these, particularly cups, was often modified to incorporate some personalised reference appropriate to donor or recipient, or both. When the Phoenix Fire Office gave a cup to the Drapers' Company in 1796, they commissioned the goldsmith to model their crest, a phoenix rising in flames, for the finial. A cup at the Saddlers' Company of 1661, now with a cover of 1657 – presumably there were originally two – has as its finial a saddled and bridled horse, the crest of the Company.[24]

Inevitably most additions or alterations to standard designs were heraldic in origin, for those without personal arms, a play on names was permissible. In 1642 the Skinners' Company was given a piece 'in the form of a colt' as a bequest from Coulte.

Feet, finials and handles all lent themselves to being cast as crests; on a flagon of 1597 given by three brothers to Christ's College, Cambridge the heraldic message is duplicated. The body is engraved with their family arms and crest within a scrollwork incorporating the badges of the college foundress, Margaret Beaufort, and the family crest of the griffin's head is cast as a finial. Another Cambridge piece, a cup given by James Bertie, Lord Norreys, in 1669, has its two handles cast as bearded crowned men, in reference to the D'Eresby crest and a raven finial, the crest of Norreys.[25]

Sometimes the decorative scheme was more elaborate still and extended to panels of chasing on the body reflecting the occasion for the order. Two ewers and basins ordered by the Goldsmiths from Simon Owen in 1611 were chased with their buckles, covered cups and leopards' heads around the border. A cup at the Master Mariners' Company is one (of at least two) made by Thomas Whipham in 1748 to celebrate a successful privateering voyage against the French three years earlier. Its cover is surmounted by a stern light and its body is embossed and chased with a sea fight, in which the three British ships are identified.[26]

The enormous gulf in purchasing power which lay between the wealthier aristocrats – the Earl of Warrington, the duke of Rutland, the Spencers, the Howards, the Cecils – and the country gentry is reflected in both the bulk and the nature of their respective plate holdings.

Silver in gentry families was more likely to be in standard forms, personalised only by engraved armorials, or possibly a crest as a finial, added at the time of purchase. Few commoners could rise to the ostentatious splendour of George Booth's wine fountain, made by Archambo in 1728. This massive piece is conventionally chased with male and female masks, shells, palm leaves and strapwork, the normal repertoire of late *Régence* ornament, but the handles are designed as demi-boars, Warrington's supporters, and the cover is surmounted by an earl's coronet (Fig. 33).[27]

A cistern at Belvoir has four standard lion feet, but the Manners's peacocks support the

Fig. 77   **Handle and cover of cup**
1669. T M over a coronet. Presented by James Bertie, Earl of Abingdon. The crowned head of his arms
appears also cast on the handle.
Magdalene College, Cambridge

207

Fig. 78 **Goldsmiths' cup**
Parcel-gilt 1982. Mark of Leslie Durbin. H. 16.2 cm. Commissioned by Samuel Goodenough as
member of the Court of Assistants of the Goldsmiths' Company. The stem is based on the Goodenough
crest of a wolf rampant holding an escallop.
Goldsmiths' Company

handles. The charge per ounce for making this massive piece in 1682 was about 6s, very little above the standard rate for plate, although to raise a sheet large enough for this object must have been a long and expensive process. In the 1730s, tureens, the largest and most showy component of the dinner table, sometimes incorporated references to the owner's heraldic devices. A pair by Wickes have the griffin crest of the earls of Malton as finial and handles.[28]

Where presentation pieces were concerned and where money was no great problem, the commission might be laden with appropriate personal symbolism. A superb gilt ewer and basin made at the cost of the city of Bristol for presentation to their Recorder, John Scrope in 1735 is one example of a lavish personalised gift. The cast and applied symbols on these two display pieces refer to wine, water and prosperity by trade, justice, civic pride, a wholly appropriate range of references, given Bristol's maritime supremacy and the Recorder's judicial role. But the arms are those of a later owner.[29]

George Wickes's workmen, in carrying out the commission on behalf of Bristol's Lord Mayor, Lionel Lyde, surpassed themselves and it is sad that we do not know the identity of the chaser responsible. He was almost certainly French-trained, since at least two of the motifs are drawn directly from a book of cartouches published in Paris a year or so earlier; Wickes, and his successors Parker & Wakelin, were always very dependent on France for their design sources, although the insistence of the English aristocracy on their heraldry appearing in their tableware posed some interesting design problems for the goldsmith. A drawing in the Victoria and Albert Museum of a tureen incorporates ostrich legs as its feet, which sit rather curiously below the French-derived body and cover ornament. In this instance Nicholas Sprimont, the designer, was working for the Coke family of Holkham, Norfolk, whose ostriches appear elsewhere in the house as table supports.[30]

This obsession with heraldry as ornament was, however, confined to dinner and sideboard plate. Teaware was inclined to be both more decorative and more stylistically cohesive, following a theme such as chinoiseries or naturalistic foliage and flowers or, as in the case of a design used many times by De Lamerie, putti rioting among shellwork (Fig. 82).[31]

The pure line and archaeological consistency of the first generation of neo-classical silver also demonstrated the strength of fashion; tableware in the archaeological spirit, designed by Adam or James Wyatt, has none of this burdensome armorial reference, although the customary engraved armorials, or perhaps a small engraved crest, may be found. A superb pair of wine jugs, made by Storr for Thomas, seventh Earl of Elgin as ambassadorial plate, has royal crowns as finials (1799) (Plate 8).

In the nineteenth century manufacturers of both silver and plated tableware offered their customers a choice of finials; they could be supplied cast as lions, dogs and other semi-heraldic forms. Naturally heraldry as a source of ornament has never fallen entirely out of favour, as corporate commissions make clear today and the inventiveness of the small objects sold by Omar Ramsden, for instance, can be delightful.[32]

Private individuals too enjoy the opportunity to see some personal reference in the handles or stem of an object. Leslie Durbin is noted for using crests, particularly those representing animals. A bowl he made for the Ironmongers' Company has its salamanders as handles and a cup commissioned by Sam Goodenough when he joined the court of the Goldsmiths' Company had his crest of a bear as its stem (Fig. 78).[33]

Notes

1   British Museum 1978. Glynn 1983. Goodall 1977.

2   In the British Museum; *Somerset Wills* 1901.

3   Inventory 1327.

4   National Museum of Antiquities *Angels Nobles and Unicorns Art & Patronage in Medieval Scotland* Edinburgh 1982, 37–9.

5   Haywood 1976, pl. 41, 43 etc.

6   Sometimes a plate with arms of a later owner was soldered over the top, e.g. the Thirkleby flagons (VAM; Temple Newsam).

7   Goodall 1977, pl. 1 & 2.

8   Belonging to the Society of Antiquaries.

9   Campbell 1984; Fitzwilliam 1977.

10   Fitzwilliam 1977, frontispiece.

11   *Somerset Wills* 1901.

12   To the confusion of antiquarians.

13   Queen Charlotte had her cypher engraved on all the plate she ordered as gifts.

14   Quoted in Safford 1983, 3.

15   The Courtauld link with Sympson, the engraver probably responsible, is discussed in T. Murdoch 'The Courtaulds: silversmiths for three generations'. *Proc. Silver Soc.* III, 4, 1984, 88–97.

16   Grimwade, (Bedford) 1965.

17   Sold Christie's 25 June 1980, lot 87; Hatfield 1981.

18   Other owners certainly did the same; compare the chamber pot at Ham House.

19   Webster 1984, 18–19.

20   The bellows have cyphers too: Hackenbroch 1969, 55. Davis 1976.

21   Quoted in Fales 1970.

22   VAM 1984, 243.

23   Cripps 1878 (1886 edn) 146; Johnson 1983.

24   Goldsmiths' 1951, 43.

25   Fitzwilliam 1978, frontispiece.

26   Goldsmiths' 1951, 76–7.

27   It is a duty-dodger: see p. 161–2.

28   Davis 1976.

29   Barr 1984.

30   VAM 1984, 111.

31   For instance McNab Dennis 1967; Kaellgren 1982.

32   All his work, from salt and pepper sets to cigar boxes, capitalised on the English nostalgia for heraldry.

33   Goldsmiths' 1982; no. 140.

ENGRAVING AND ENGRAVERS

W HATEVER fashion might dictate in the way of chasing or embossing, engraving
was a constant source of ornament. Engravers were specialist craftsmen, sometimes
apprenticed in the Goldsmiths' Company but usually anonymous because they registered no
marks, although a body of work by one man can sometimes be recognised and attributions
are possible by analogy with his work for printers, as with Thomas Bewick.[1] The bulk of
silver produced was in standard forms, personalised only by the far cheaper alternative of
engraved armorials, which were the commonest form of ornament and could quickly be
added at the time of purchase, either from a heraldic engraver's textbook or from artwork
supplied by the purchaser (see Chapter 10).

Engravers

Between about 1567 and 1575 a craftsman, almost certainly an alien, was engraving silver in
England. His mark of P over M, with his distinctive style, link a group of four sets of gilt
dessert plates and two sets of a ewer and basin, which are tightly engraved with biblical scenes
adapted from the work of Vergil Solis (1520), Bernard Salomon (1553) and scenes from
unidentified sources. None can be associated with a contemporary patron. One set only
(VAM, Fig. 9) has English arms but these are a later addition. The ewer and basin of 1567 in
the Boston Museum of Fine Arts, with portraits of English kings from William I to Elizabeth,
was presumably made as a gift for the queen but there is no hint of the donor's identity.
Overall designs, whether from biblical or classical sources, were popular, as the description
of a basin and ewer in the 1561 inventory of the Earl of Pembroke's plate shows: both pieces
were 'faier graven with a print graving of Stories of the Bible'.[2]

   Another immigrant engraver active in Elizabethan London, who this time can be named, is
Nicaise Roussel, whose work is discussed in Chapter 2. He engraved curious designs of
monsters, hippocamps, flowers and other elements in panels of grotesque ornament which he
also published. These appear both on silver, such as a Magdalen cup of 1573 (Manchester Art
Gallery) and a pair of flagons of 1587 belonging to S. Mary Woolnoth (Fig. 79), and on the
case of a gilt brass clock (VAM).[3] Roussel had a later career making jewellery for James I and
Anne of Denmark.

   From the 1580s for about thirty years broad loose flowering scrolls were popular, engraved
all over the surface, comparable to contemporary blackwork embroidery and no doubt taken
from the same pattern books. The Maria Corbet wine cup (1587) at the Goldsmiths'

Company and a mother-of-pearl box (VAM) show the technique; a cup (Trinity College, Oxford 1603) incorporates thistles and roses, no doubt in reference to the new monarch. But by no means all Elizabethan plate, even presentation pieces, was elaborately engraved; the Vice-Chancellor's cup at Cambridge University, given by the Earl of Essex in 1598, alternates panels of matting with plain burnished metal. Elizabethan tankards and the beakers popular about 1600 have bands of floral engraving around the top, perhaps with pendent festoons of vine leaves or scrolls, and the body left plain. A tankard at Goldsmiths' Hall, another belonging to a Dorset church (VAM) and a group of beakers given to the vestry of S. Giles, Cripplegate around 1610 illustrate this effective technique, which was of Dutch origin (Fig. 127).[4]

Fig. 79 **Flagon**
Gilt 1587. Mark TS and a doubleheaded eagle. H. 38 cm. One of a pair engraved with grotesques in the manner of Nicaise Roussel (active in London *c*.1580–1620) which were acquired by the churchwardens a century later, in 1697, by exchange for old plate.
S. Mary Woolnoth, City of London

212

Plate 5 **King's Lynn cup**
Gilt and enamel *c*.1350. H.38 cm. Richly enamelled inside the bowl, over the body and at the foot with
hunting scenes. Although long called King John's cup, there is no basis for this; lovingly cared for by the
town since at least the 1540s.
Regalia Room, King's Lynn

Plate 6 **'Lady Emilia's Christening present'**
Tureen *c*.1720–30. Mark of Edward Feline, struck four times. W.37.5 cm. Inscribed 'Lady Emilia Lenos
Oct. 25th 1731'. Daughter of the Duke of Richmond and Lennox, and baptised at S. Margaret
Westminster, she was granted a Jewel House issue of 200 ounces of gilt plate as a christening gift. This
tureen, modelled on a French design of *c*.1715, was presumably already in the royal goldsmiths' stock.
Sotheby's

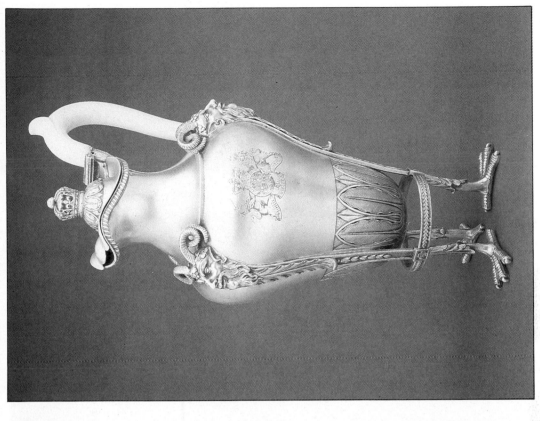

Plate 8 **Wine jug**

Gilt 1799. Mark of Paul Storr. Ambassadorial plate, part of a service supplied to Lord Elgin.

Sotheby's

Plate 7 **Rococo coffee pot**

1738. Mark of Paul De Lamerie. H.28 cm. An extraordinary design, in which the whole body is twisted. De Lamerie repeated this basic shape, always with superb chasing.

Christie's, New York

Plate 9 **Biscuit box**
Silver, mother of pearl and enamel. Birmingham 1901. Designed for Liberty's Cymric range by
Archibald Knox. H.19 cm.
VAM

The commonest Stuart commission was inevitably for armorials, initially set in roundels or simple shields but later in more or less complex surrounds; crossed palms, the symbol of conjugal love, became popular as a surround by the mid-seventeenth century (Fig. 80). Pictorial engraving was unusual; simple scenes from contemporary woodcuts illustrate the horrors of the Plague and Fire. Topographical prints provided the occasional subject but the most interesting engraving, of flowers taken from botanical books, appears on a series of peg tankards made by the York goldsmith John Plummer between about 1650 and 1670.[5]

From about 1680 to 1730 was a golden period for the goldsmith's engraver; he was a specialist employed on piecework by retail goldsmiths, as Benjamin Rhodes was by Sir Richard Hoare, or occasionally directly by the client. In a period of upward mobility, when

Fig. 80 **Communion cup and paten**
*c.*1621–4. Mark RB over a mullet. Engraved with the arms of Stuart impaling Howard within palm boughs for Ludovic Stuart, Duke of Lennox and Richmond (1574–1624) and Frances Howard, whom he married in 1621. His crest with an earl's coronet is on the paten.
Hugh Jessop

213

status was judged not only by the possession of armorials, but by their prominent display in tableware, the engraving was often the dominant ornament on everyday drinking and serving vessels. While the price for engraving an individual item was only a few shillings, a steady flow of orders ensured a good living. A list of plate given to master shipwrights between 1708 and 1736 (although the custom had a much longer ancestry) demonstrates a range of charges for engraving. The recipients were unlikely to have their own coats of arms, and an inscription and probably the royal arms or cypher, with the recipient's name, was the usual formula. Over a twenty-year period just one shipwright, Richard Stacey, was issued

Fig. 81 **Tea canister**
Gilt 1706. Made by Isaac Liger. H. 11.5 cm. Engraved (probably) by Simon Gribelin. One of a set made for George Booth, Earl of Warrington whose crest of a boar's head has been incorporated into the design. Gribelin's book of pulls in the British Museum includes two versions of Booth's arms.
VAM

214

with plate worth £303, of which the engraving accounted for £17 15s. He built up a complete service of silver – plates, cruet stand, flatware, sauce boats, punch bowls and tea and coffee ware.[6] A pair of candlesticks (1712) and a tankard are two of these gifts, to be seen in the National Maritime Museum.

Sometimes engraving was added later in another workshop; a footed dish now belonging to S. Margaret's Church, King's Lynn was hallmarked in London in 1619 by the maker Thomas Flint; presented to the church later, probably as a stand for a flagon, it made a pair with a similar dish, united by laurel roundels and the merchants' marks of the respective donors engraved on each. Both were presumably engraved locally as one order, perhaps at the cost of the churchwardens.

Neither the engraver nor the maker necessarily dealt directly with the purchaser. The Newdegate centrepiece (VAM) bears De Lamerie's hallmark for 1743. It was clearly purchased in that year but the cost of engraving the Newdegate arms five times on basins and dishes was charged by the family's main plate supplier, and William Shaw, the supplier, presumably had his own preferred engraver.[7]

Engraving, whether on silver or on copper, was a widespread skill not confined to goldsmiths; orders from America occasionally specified that the engraving was to be carried out by the purchaser's own man, perhaps a trained slave.

At the end of the seventeenth century we have a glimpse of a jobbing engraver at work. Benjamin Rhodes, employed by Hoare's Bank to embellish the plate which they were supplying to their customers, kept careful accounts of his commissions for four years from 1694 to 1698, with sketches of the arms, crests and cyphers he was engraving and a note as to the style of the inscription and the price to be charged. In the case of a cup presented to Magdalen College, Oxford in 1697, he received 13s 6d for two coat of arms and an inscription in script.

Charles Oman makes the point that Rhodes would have remained unknown but for the chance survival of this account book at Hoare's Bank. He was at work for at least forty-five years and must have been responsible for much of the surviving heraldic engraving, particularly on pieces by John Boddington (a goldsmith who produced many of Hoare's orders for customers) but never signed his work and had trouble getting his accounts paid, as did so many contemporary craftsmen. At the end of his career he issued a book of his designs, A New Book of Cyphers (1723), whose interlaced and reversed letters are in the style of the 1690s and can be found on a number of pieces, such as boxes from toilet services.[8]

The price charged by the goldsmith was not necessarily what the engraver was paid; De Lamerie charged six guineas for the arms on the Treby toilet service, considerably less per item than Rhodes's rate.[9]

Rhodes's designs were clearly assembled throughout his working life and entirely backward-looking. Goldsmiths in provincial towns and in New England, not directly in touch with the larger community in London, were dependent on printed books of engraved ornament for their sources; Joseph Richardson of Philadelphia sent to London for a cypher book in 1725. If the book he received was Rhodes's, it is not surprising that the engraving on Richardson's silver has an old-fashioned air.[10]

Armorials and crests were not intended necessarily to demonstrate ownership but merely to record a donor's or patron's identity. Dishes in a service made by Wickes in 1740 for the Earl of Scarborough were engraved with the full armorials of his employer the Prince of Wales, just as Lord North had the Prince of Wales's feathers engraved on candelabra in 1731.[11]

The superb ewer and basin which Samuel Pepys gave to the Clothworkers' Company in 1677 bears his arms along with those of the Company, its crest and a dedicatory inscription. The baptismal gifts made by George I to his godchildren, although usually purchased for the purpose rather than drawn from existing Jewel House stock, are all engraved with the royal arms and it was almost always customary, when replacing plate, to copy the original donor's arms again, as on the Hanbury and Feake cups at the Goldsmiths' Company.[12]

The most distinguished of the late Stuart engravers is Simon Gribelin (1660–1733). His assiduous self-publicising through several books of engraved ornament (the most interesting came out in 1697 and 1700), illustrations for botanical and other books, and engravings of old master paintings in the royal collection and the Raphael cartoons, means that it is not easy to distinguish his work, usually unsigned, from that of his imitators. However, two albums, one in the British Museum and another at Strawberry Hill, which he compiled in 1722 contain a collection of proofs, pulls and counterproofs from his past thirty years' output. These enable us to ascribe to him certain engraved plate from about 1690 to 1717. Examples are a comfit box and a set of waiters, and a tea canister made for George Booth, Earl of Warrington (VAM, Fig. 81), a seal salver in the Burrell Collection, Glasgow and two more at Chatsworth and a ewer and basin at S. John's College, Cambridge. An alms dish (signed with his initials only), made for the chapel at Dunham Massey in 1706, can still be seen there. The gilt tea canister, one of a pair supplied by Isaac Liger to George Booth in 1706, is unsigned but is clearly by the same hand; pulls of several versions of the earl's arms appear in the 1722 album.[13]

Bills from the engraver Charles Gardner among the Tollemache family papers show that he worked for them directly between 1729 and 1735, but he had also a large clientele among the goldsmiths. He had such a reputation in the trade that when he offered to engrave their new plate 'in the best manner with good despatch at reasonable prices', the court of the Goldsmiths' Company accepted; De Lamerie, Humphrey Payne, Thomas Farren and Richard Bailey supplied some items chased with arms while others went to Gardner for engraving. Gardner's skill is clear from the Company's arms engraved in a circle on the 'teatable' or salver, in which his meticulous hatching of the tinctures is unusual for the period. However, the design of the roundel is entirely conventional (and not unlike that on salvers of the 1720s) with no hint of rococo influence. He ran a substantial workshop with three apprentices at the time and was a liveryman of the Company.[14]

The dispute over William Hogarth's responsibility for engraving the Walpole salver (VAM, Fig. 82 made by De Lamerie in 1728 for Sir Robert Walpole) has moved back and forth for 200 years. Recently Charles Oman has concluded that it could be attributed to him, as Nichols originally stated in 1781. Certainly Hogarth was dismissive late in life about his apprenticeship to the silver engraver Ellis Gamble, he claimed that the tedium 'of the business determined me on engraving no longer than necessity obliged me to it' but at least one other piece of silver with an elaborate armorial cartouche, a tea canister (VAM) is said to be his work.[15] Like De Lamerie, his reputation flourished continuously and at exhibitions in the

Fig. 82 **The Walpole salver**
1728. Mark of De Lamerie. Engraver probably William Hogarth. Made from the silver of the two
halves of the Great Seal, whose design is reproduced in the centre. Note Sir Robert Walpole's cypher in
the shell and trellis border; as Keeper of the Exchequer, the old seals were his perquisite.
VAM

1850s and 1860s several pieces of engraved silver were attributed to him.

But none of these engravers, with the occasional exception of Simon Gribelin, signed his work. The solitary plate engraver in London permitted to declare his identity was Joseph Sympson, whose career can be illustrated through engraved plate from 1715 to the 1740s, in addition to the brief and disparaging biography given by Horace Walpole. Most of his known work is armorial, such as a gilt salver of 1717, engraved with the arms of Richard, fifth Viscount Ingram, surrounded by the Four Seasons. The goldsmith William Lukin used Sympson for several aristocratic commissions, as did Thomas Farren and probably Augustin

217

Courtauld; a triangular kettle stand of 1730 by Courtauld gives an early instance of asymmetry in the flyaway scrolls of its border.[16]

Although De Lamerie's engraved borders of trellis and shellwork, as on a tray of 1732 in New York, were among the first in English silver to show rococo influence, engraving became markedly less important between about 1735 and 1770 as a means of decoration except on tea trays and waiters.[17] Heavy emphasis on embossing and chasing, coupled with the current popularity of cast and shaped body forms, meant that in both table- and teaware, engraved armorials shrank to an insignificant place in the design. Indeed, some handsome presentation cups, like a series wreathed with vines of the 1750s and 1760s, had no space allotted for arms at all.[18]

There was, however, a marked revival of interest in engraving from the 1760s; two leading houses, Parker & Wakelin and Louisa Courtauld, sold silver in which the subject of the engraving was deliberately designed to enhance the whole. Parker & Wakelin sold a number of 'teachests', tea caddies marked with lines and Chinese ideograms to simulate the packing cases in which tea was imported.[19] High quality and intricate engraving was charged accordingly; a 'Tea Tub' bought in 1769 by Sir Roger Newdegate cost £7 3s 10d, plus two guineas for 'graving a Chinese border and characters'. Louisa Courtauld produced at least two sets of condiment urns which both in their form, and in the classical deities engraved

Fig. 83 **Plate from D'Hancarville's**
The couple struggling in the centre, redrawn from a Greek vase, were among the figures lifted by Louisa Courtauld's engraver for silver around 1771: compare Figs. 32b and 84.
VAM

218

Fig. 84 **Engraving on condiment urn**
1771. Mark of Louisa Courtauld and George Cowles. The couple now face left (compare Fig. 83). The honeysuckle border is lifted directly from pl. 22, vol. II of D'Hancarville. Note the 'gothic' stone block, with the arms of Curzon. Made for Kedleston.
Boston, Museum of Fine Arts

around them, were directly lifted from D'Hancarville's recently published three-volume account of Sir William Hamilton's collection of vases. But their engraver remains anonymous (Figs. 83 and 84).[20]

In Newcastle, Thomas Bewick was, like Sympson half a century before, an engraver on silver whose reputation has flourished, in part at least, through his signed work as a book illustrator.[21] In discussing the career of Thomas Bewick as a silver engraver we are exceptionally well supplied with information. In the 1820s he wrote a memoir, describing his career from 1767 when he was apprenticed to Ralph Beilby of Newcastle, and the account books of his long association up to 1800 with the Newcastle firm of Langlands & Robertson enables several surviving pieces to be firmly attributed to him. Although unsigned, his distinctive style identifies his hand even without a specific reference.

219

Bewick's peculiar skill lay in his natural history engraving. The earliest engraving on silver attributable to him, on a set of communion plate at S. Andrew's, Newcastle, is a wild and windy landscape in which the elderly saint leans against his cross, with fish and nets as further identification. The Newcastle firm sent a porter to Bewick with wares for engraving three or four times a month – anything from dog collars or hunting buttons to freedom boxes – his output was no doubt typical of the range expected of a competent engraver.

Styles of Engraving

'Bright-cutting', a technique of angled cutting with a polished curved burin which appeared about 1775, was immediately popular. It was cheap and simple to carry out and lent itself as ornament to objects of every type, from spoons to epergnes; its festoons, ribbon-swags and

Fig. 85 **Hawksley testimonial salver**
1880. Mark of Hunt & Roskell. D.50.6 cm. Part of a centrepiece commissioned by the Nottingham Water Company for Thomas Hawksley, designer of waterworks, pumping stations and reservoirs. Irises, bullrushes and other water-plants separate views of six projects, while the border is composed of watercress leaves.
VAM

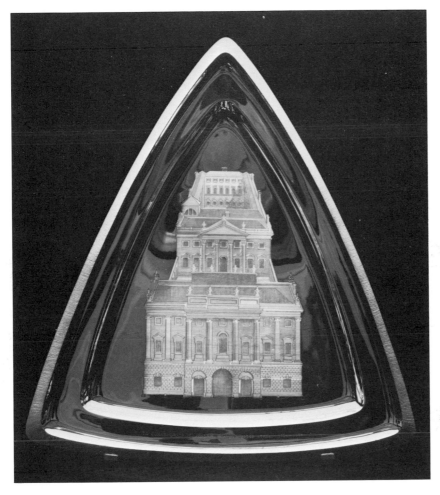

Fig. 86 **Bank of England salver**
1984. Mark of Christopher Lawrance. Engraved by George Lukes with a view of the old Bank of
England (George Sampson, 1734): a presentation piece.
Bank of England

bands livened up the somewhat dull shapes characteristic of small later Georgian tableware, particularly when combined with floral or scroll piercing. At its peak, in the hands of a skilled craftsman, it was extremely effective. The products of the Hennell family are noted for their bright-cutting, particularly on baskets and condiment pots. Paul Storr used it extensively in the 1790s before adopting the heavier Egyptian classicism with which he is normally associated. It was popular particularly at the cheaper end of the market, since the technique was easily learned. Craftsmen were paid accordingly; Langlands & Robertson paid Bewick only 12*s* a piece for bright-cutting teapots.[22]

The nineteenth century, heyday of the testimonial, naturally gave a renewed boost to engravers on silver, although often text, rather than pictorial engraving, dominated presentation pieces. A Sheffield tea tray (1844) bears twenty-five lines of text recording it as a gift 'from a contented Tenantry' to their Anglo-Irish landlord; banal depictions of the Four Seasons in the corners are subsidiary. The choice of images on testimonial plate – steam engines, waterworks and other urban and industrial objects – was new, but the engravers were not necessarily inventive, lifting their subjects from current lithographs or periodical illustrations like those in the *Illustrated London News*; for example, Fig. 86.

The rapid succession of historical revivals between the 1830s and 1880s stimulated a fresh demand for engraving on silver, although the subjects, notably the perennial 'Etruscan' style, were largely confined to friezes reinterpreted from antique sources.[23] Motifs were also taken from Owen Jones's influential *Grammar of Ornament* (1857), which was the principal source of stylised patterns for over twenty years, producing a 'genteel precision', as in the tea/coffee set by Samuel Smily (Goldsmiths' Company 1869), whose basic urn-shape is 'improved' with palmettes and waves from Owen Jones.

The Japanese style flourished from the later 1870s; Elkington's led the field in popular designs for tea silver in which fan-shaped trays, and vessels copying oriental ceramic and metal forms, were engraved with prunus blossom, cranes and insects. The Japanese effect was further enhanced by partially gilding the surface, to imitate the widely admired Japanese techniques of encrusting and mixed metals (Fig. 86).[24] To encourage higher standards in the craft, the Goldsmiths' Company offered annual prizes from 1871. Whether these had the intended effect, they at least ensured publicity for skilled engravers within the trade.

Notes

1 For engraving in England, see chapter 10 and Oman 1978, Hind 1985, Corbett & Norton 1964.

2 Oman 1978; VAM, Pembroke inventory 1561.

3 Oman 1978, 47–8.

4 Fitzwilliam 1975, SC10, cover. Goldsmiths' 1951, 29, pl. 27.

5 Lushington 1957; Oman 1970.

6 Jones 1920, 135–7.

7 Warwick RO, Newdegate MSS. When S. Benet Fink (City of London) was given communion plate in the 1650s, the donor's arms were added at parish expense, including the cost of buying a print of them for the engraver to follow.

8 Oman 1978.

9 Phillips 1935.

10 Fales 1974.

11 Barr 1980, 149–50.

12 Prideaux 1896 and chapter 14. And see Masters 1978; Greenwood 1938.

13 Oman 1978.

14 Tollemache MSS; Oman 1978; Goldsmiths' Company minute book 1741.

15 Oman 1978.

16 Hayward 1975, 15, 17, 18. A basin (De Lamerie 1722) in the Ashmolean Museum is perhaps by the same engraver. The kettle stand is in the Metropolitan Museum of Art 1977, 57–8.

17 For example, Barr 1980, pl. 70–2, 119. The cost of engraving these intricate and large designs could be as much as £10.

18 For example, Young 1983; VAM 1984, 112, 121.

19 Rowe 1965, pl. 26. A salver of 1770 is exceptionally skilled and pretty: pl. 79B.

20 Hatfield 1981.

21 Oman 1978; Laing AG.

22 Good examples of bright-cutting are mustard pots in the Colman Collection, 27–30, 32–3. For Storr, see Penzer 1954. For two approaches (one very fussy by Hester Bateman) compare Rowe 1965, 81 and 86.

23 Culme 1977, 161 shows an Elkington and Mason 'Arabesque' coffee pot, 1851.

24 Bury, S. *Goldsmiths Review* (1975).

TWELVE

ALIEN CRAFTSMEN AND IMPORTED DESIGNS

From Renaissance to Mannerist Ornament c.1510–c.1610

FROM at least the late Middle Ages, alien craftsmen have worked in London in large numbers, attracted by the prosperity of the capital and its accessibility to royal and noble customers at Westminster. Although wealthy, England was technically less sophisticated than its immediate Northern European neighbours and in return for exporting cloth was importing not only raw silver but quantities of luxury manufactured goods, particularly from the Low Countries and France. But this was contrary to Tudor economic theory and it was preferable to import the craftsmen instead.

Deliberate Crown policy under both the Yorkist and Tudor kings encouraged skilled artisans, such as printers, engravers and metal workers, to settle here. Engraving in particular was a skill in which the English did not excel and the newcomers were more in touch with, or had personal experience of, the sources for Renaissance ornament. Alexander Brucksal, a Badener, was appointed engraver of dies to the Mint under Henry VII. He is credited with designing the first Tudor portrait coins or 'half faces' in 1505 and appears regularly in the royal accounts until his departure about 1510. Another foreigner, John van Delf, ran a London workshop from 1418 to 1504, producing plate both for the Jewel House and for general sale, and employing at least twenty-one 'stranger' journeymen over this period. Of the 400-plus strangers licensed by the Goldsmiths' Company between 1479 and 1514, almost all took service with aliens already here and their names occur frequently in the royal accounts, often supplying specialised skills, such as garnishing a 'sallet' (helmet) with silvergilt or engraving and cutting new seal dies.[1]

While it is impossible to distinguish between their products and those of the native goldsmiths from the few pieces of surviving Tudor plate, it is significant that many of those supplying the court were of foreign origin and clearly retained their cross-Channel contacts. One instance can be quoted; a gold girdle book in the British Museum, enamelled with the biblical story of the brazen serpent, is attributed to the goldsmith Hans of Antwerp, Holbein's friend, who was already in London by 1511. By the 1530s he was well established and was receiving orders regularly for royal plate and jewels. In 1537 he was admitted to the Goldsmiths' Company and travelled abroad several times with royal despatches. On one such journey to Antwerp he apparently saw a design by his fellow goldsmith Hieronymus Mamacker for a book cover commissioned by the Abbey of Tongerlo. The brazen serpent scene on the book cover at Tongerlo and that on the miniature girdle book in the British

Museum are virtually identical, despite the difference in scale. It might be argued that such a piece is English only by courtesy of its having been made in London for an English customer, since both the design and the craftsmanship were from across the Channel.[2]

Classical ornament (coupled with heraldic references) dominated European art from about 1520, and fashionable English customers required plate incorporating these motifs. The phrase 'in the new fashion' crops up repeatedly in contemporary inventories and dealers ensured that there was also a good choice of imported plate available in London, in addition to the pieces made here following engraved designs. The purchases of Edward Seymour, Earl of Hertford, in the 1540s show that while Metcalfe, Trappes, Morgan Wolf and other London goldsmiths received some orders, his finest and most expensive plate – chased sugar plates, standing cups and bowls with antiques and moresques – came by Peter van de Walle, a Fleming.[3]

Van de Walle was regularly importing such luxuries as tapestries and glass for Henry VIII's courtiers; the massive standing cups (between 70 and 170 ounces each) with which he supplied Edward Seymour were chased with a boar hunt, a lion hunt, episodes from the classics and other subjects closely reminiscent of the contemporary decorative plaster schemes at Fontainbleu. These cups may well have been imported. Charged at 8s the ounce, they cost almost twice as much as the melt-value of the silvergilt from which they were made. As the normal allowance in the price for fashion, that is for the goldsmith's time and skill in working the metal, was only a few pence above the bullion price, the high figure set on them clearly indicates their great elaboration. However, since Francis I expelled many foreign craftsmen in 1542, and some certainly came over here to work for the court, perhaps an alien newly arrived from Paris made them. A survey of alien goldsmiths taken by the Goldsmiths' Company between the 1530s and 1562 shows a marked rise in 1542–3.

From about 1520 classical ornament, either cast or engraved, had become part of the repertoire of English goldsmiths too and 'naked boys', moresque bands, acanthus, mermen and rinceaux all occur in descriptions of plate in the following two decades. All these elements and the heads or 'targets', that is classical roundels in the style of Da Maiano's terracottas at Hampton Court and Whitehall, appear in a gold cup which Holbein designed for Queen Jane Seymour in 1535–6. Sometimes, as on the Howard Grace cup (1525) they are combined with gothic fretwork and sometimes as in a cup of 1529 (on loan to the VAM) or on the thistle cup of 1545 belonging to S. Peter Mancroft, Norwich, they are more sophisticated and integrated, in the manner typical of contemporary German goldsmiths' work.

Chasing, a technique enabling the goldsmith to create elaborate schemes or friezes as on the cup at S. Peter Mancroft in Norwich of 1567, was more expensive and is found only occasionally on surviving Tudor plate (for example, Fig. 87), although it occurs in designs by Hans Holbein for royal plate of the 1530s and early 1540s. Nothing of this quality exists today.

Whether imported, which is possible, or made here by a French-trained workman, which is also possible, elaborately chased cups were outside the normal run of work for English goldsmiths, whose response to the stimulus of Renaissance ornament was perhaps more typically expressed in the cover and foot of the covered standing bowl given by Henry VIII to the Barber-Surgeons' Company in 1543. Both surfaces are covered with entwining foliage,

Fig. 87 **Chasing on the foot of a cup**

From the Glynne cup 1579: Fig. 10. The hunting scene is chased on a matted background; the strips of
repeating ornament are stamped out and bent into shape. Note the little crosses or registration marks;
two sections slot above one another on a central tube and are then screwed tight, the normal
sixteenth-century method of assembling elaborate standing cups.

Loan, VAM

in which the ubiquitous badges used by the Tudor kings are incorporated. The design is very
similar to that used on Henry's Greenwich-made tournament armours, and also on a few
surviving textiles, and was to fall rapidly out of favour in the 1550s when engraved ornament
embodying Northern European mannerist designs swept the London goldsmiths' shops.

A further wave of foreign goldsmiths arrived in the 1560s, mainly driven from Antwerp;
although less well documented than the Huguenot invasion a century later, these newcomers
too brought fresh skills and new designs.[4] Chased strapwork and embossed fruit swags, the
characteristic decoration of Elizabethan cups, tankards and salts for half a century, directly
imitate Antwerp plate, or rather, English goldsmiths were working to a common source,
originating in the decorative schemes at Fontainbleau about 1540. Although a number of
collections of engraved designs for plate survive, mainly issued by Germans, Flemings and
Italians, these cannot usefully be compared with existing pieces to demonstrate a direct
influence upon English goldsmiths, since a published design often postdates a piece of
hallmarked plate. The Cirencester cup of 1535 is a type printed by Hans Brosamer of Fulda in
Germany, but not until 1543. It is clear both from contemporary paintings and from another,
Bruges-made, version, now belonging to an English church, that its form was generally
familiar across Europe well before his compilation appeared.

225

Few Englishmen issued sets of engraved ornament before the late seventeenth century, since the market here was hardly sophisticated or large enough to support such an enterprise and there was plenty of foreign-printed material available. Although Thomas Geminus published *Morysse and Damashin renewed and increased* in London in 1548, this was derived from designs published in Paris by Pellegrino in 1530 and Du Cerceau a decade later and panels of engraved moresques had appeared on English cups earlier in the 1540s, presumably copied from imported engravings or sketches.[5]

While we do not know which engravings were on sale in England, the designs of Pieter Flötner of Nuremburg (d. 1546) were circulating here a generation or so after his death. Two display salts, one of 1569 at the Vintners' Company and one of 1572 now in the Jewel House, incorporate chased panels after Flötner, although the goldsmith apparently misunderstood his source or had an incomplete set of subjects to copy from (Fig. 20). For the 1567 salt, he put a plaque of Venus with the Virtues. While a skilled craftsman would improve on his original source, designs could become utterly degraded, as is clear from an English salt in the Kremlin Armouries with lumpy figures of Mars, Venus, Mercury and Diana.[6]

Direct Italian influence on English silver is rarely found, but a ewer of 1583 (VAM) has a cast lion handle and ribbon-swags, clearly taken from a design by Agostino dei Musi, dated 1531. Under fashionable mannerist influence, the London goldsmith has added to the original strongly 'antique' ewer chased snails, embossed sea monsters and flowers and a cast and applied mask. Although skilfully done, this is overladen with ornament.[7]

Similarly decorated pieces were popular at court twenty years earlier although with the exception of the Wyndham ewer (Fig. 88; BM 1554) none has survived. An inventory of the first Earl of Pembroke's plate taken in 1561 lists, among the basins and ewers, a basin chased with bible stories 'in the middest a woman sytting upon a dolphin, the handell of the eware being of crotiske (grotesque) carrying a basket of fruyte upon his backe the crotiske standing upon an antique heade, the bodye of the eware chased with a band of antique with naked chyldren having whinges' (presumably putti). Another set was chased with figures of Justice, Prudence, Faith, Hope and Charity with the 'eware of cratistoes (grotesque) wurcke, the handell being borne up with a satyr'.[8]

The comparative rarity of north European plate makes it difficult to distinguish a regional style; plate might be made to the same design by, say, a goldsmith in Bruges and a goldsmith in London, and marked appropriately in each town. Because so little high quality English plate survives, pieces like the IV– marked ewer and basin in the Norwich civic plate are considered as imports; but they stand as rare examples of the top level of London work, as does the Rutland ewer and basin in an earlier generation.[9]

Imported ideas for ornament were often applied to distinctively English forms. The early Elizabethan squat alepot, bell and pillared salts, tankards, flagons and steeplecups, all shapes peculiar to English goldsmiths, are found with cast or chased ornament such as applied heads, shells and classical figure finials; only from the early-seventeenth century can specific foreign influences on form, first Dutch and subsequently French, be recognised.

The more elaborate the ornament and skilled the execution, the more likely that an alien craftsman, or a goldsmith using an imported design, was responsible. Caryatid straps occur on mounts of crystal and porcelain vessels with London hallmarks from 1554 (the Bowes

Fig. 88 **The Wyndham ewer**
Gilt. 1554. Mark intersecting triangles. H. 35 cm. Now paired with a later basin (Simon Owen, 1607).
British Museum

cup, Goldsmiths' Company) to about 1600 but a crystal cup, made in Antwerp about 1560 (Schroder Collection), illustrates the international dimension to Tudor plate design. This cup, like the Bowes cup, is a crystal drum in elaborate silvergilt caryatid mounts; the two are virtually identical in size, design and construction. Were both makers working to a common model, or engraved source? If the London goldsmith was employing alien workmen the similarity is explicable; alternatively this may be an imported piece, marked here for sale purposes.[10]

The caryatid was an element of classical architecture rapidly picked up by mannerist potters, goldsmiths, woodcarvers and embroiderers. Before 1600 engravings derived from Androuet du Cerceau published in France, and John Shute's architectural drawings, published in England in 1563, were generally available but their precise and delicate archaeological drawings were also translated into far cruder, perhaps woodcut, versions which then were copied as convenient new ornamental forms by craftsmen in the decorative arts. Because of the popularity of mounted exotica, discussed in Chapters 2 and 13, strapmounts were a standard element in plate until 1620 or so.[11]

For about seventy years from 1550 variations on marine subjects were popular both as form and ornament for European silver; these were sometimes engraved, as on the set of gilt spice plates in the VAM (Fig. 9) but more often these marine subjects were embossed and chased. A ewer and basin belonging to the Earl of Pembroke in 1561 followed this taste; the basin was chased with scallop shells and monsters of the sea, while the ewer was shaped like a gourd, with a scallop shell spout. Basins often picked up the marine theme; in two sets of 1611 (one VAM) the basin is shaped like a mussel shell and its companion ewer is the figure of a mermaid. When she is filled with perfumed water and tipped, the water pours from her nipples over the diners' hands and is caught in the shell-shaped basin below, a typical mannerist conceit more familiar in European than English silver (Fig. 89).[12]

Simon Owen, a maker of ewers and basins, is one of the few Stuart goldsmiths whose mark has been identified. He made for the Goldsmiths' Company a handsome gilt pair, with marine plaques on the basins and pear-shaped flagons in 1611. Another gilt marine set with his mark was sold to Eton College in 1613 by a fellow goldsmith, William Terry of Lombard Street. It was already secondhand, having been hallmarked three years earlier, and Terry added a central boss with the arms of the donor, Adam Robyns, and an engraved inscription.[13]

These Jacobean basins were to fall fairly rapidly out of domestic use, at least as dining room plate, and a number were given to churches as alms dishes; one at S. Peter le Poer (Muswell Hill, formerly City of London) given in 1625, sixteen years after it was made, was copied a century later, to make a pair, presumably one for each aisle. Basins, with their large surface area and watery associations, particularly suited these plaques of dolphins and more fanciful marine monsters sporting in the waves.[14]

The dolphin plaques occur also on flagons, such as the pair of 1618 by WR in the Norwich civic plate and on steeple cups, often sitting uneasily among scrolling foliage or, as in the case of a cup presented by Romney to its MP in 1627 (VAM), flanking panels engraved with the town's arms. They appear, with very little variation, on plate by many different goldsmiths, over half a century or more, and it is clear that a common printed design source was available

Fig. 89 **Mermaid ewer and basin**
1610. Mark TB monogram. The mermaid's tail unscrews; when she is tilted, the rosewater flows from her nipples. Note the skilful texturing of shells, waves and hair. At least one other set is known (Toledo Museum of Art).
VAM

229

to London workshops. Norman Penzer tracked back the origin of these monsters to the *Carta Marina* published first by Olaus Magnus, from which the English map publisher Christopher Saxton lifted them for his map of 1583.[15]

The scallop shell was taken also as a model for sugar or spice boxes, often standing on cast shell feet. An early example, of 1598, is now at the Middle Temple. Another shell was the nautilus (from the West Pacific) which made curious cups, often mounted up with a chased sea monster swallowing a man, representing Jonah. One of 1557, with its original shell later replaced by a silver body, may be seen in the VAM. Another, with an engraved shell, has York marks for 1600.

After Henry VIII's death, for half a century or more there is no evidence of great interest at court in the design or ornament of plate and there are no sets of designs for the later period comparable with those attributed to Holbein in the British Museum. Not until the early seventeenth century does it become possible again to identify the aliens working alongside English plate workers. At the same period new designs can be recognised.

Imported Ornament and Alien Craftsmen c. 1610 to c. 1680

The influence of Northern European mannerism on English decorative arts in the late sixteenth and seventeenth centuries was very marked and silver, as an essential element in the display of status, inevitably embodied mannerist symbolism and ideas. Ornament was appropriate to the function of the object, so that sugar boxes, which played an essential role in courtship, and the covered bowls in toilet services – a customary wedding gift from husband to wife – normally have handles in the form of coiled serpents, an emblem of warning against interference in marital quarrels. The widespread use of marine monsters and other sea motifs on drinking and washing vessels has already been noted.

Granulation and applied filigree work of a particularly refined and elegant nature is characteristic of a small group of silver objects made about 1610. These are both skills peculiar to the jeweller rather than the goldsmith; an anonymous (but almost certainly alien) craftsman was responsible. His work includes a standing cup at Christ's College, Cambridge, with its pair in the VAM (both 1611), small casters, a salt (BM) and a rock crystal covered cup belonging to Tong Church in Staffordshire. All are attributed to the goldsmith whose mark was TVZ or TYL, a combination of initials suggesting a Low Country origin although this technique is typical of South Germany and Hungary.[16]

A few years later three members of the Van de Passe family settled in London. The elder brother Simon received commissions from James I to engrave portrait medallions of members of the royal family in the Dutch manner for distribution at court. These silver plaques are unmarked but signed; each version is so similar in execution that it has been suggested that Van de Passe had the secret of casting the plaques. As an engraver, he was of course employed principally in copperplate engraving for printing and the family is best known for sets of gaming counters (apparently die-stamped) with portraits of English kings and queens.[17]

A more significant figure is Christian Van Vianen, who came from a family of distinguished goldsmiths in Utrecht. In 1630 he was given a royal pension by Charles I and

Fig. 90 **Chased panel from inkstand**

1639. Mark AJ: Fig. 16. To combine stylised dissolving scrolls and masks with finely detailed plaques was characteristic of Utrecht goldsmiths and specifically of the Van Vianen family. The chaser, if not Christian Van Vianen himself, was almost certainly a foreigner, working in his Westminster workshop.

Loan, VAM

quickly obtained commissions both from the king and from prominent courtiers, but he ran into the hostility of the native goldsmiths who were actively pursuing their monopoly interests in the 1630s. When submitting a bill for plate for Hatfield in July 1636 he agreed to have it 'marked and touched [at Goldsmiths' Hall] whereby it may appear to be equal to the standard' although his normal custom was only to sign his work. A superb inkstand embossed and chased in the auricular style associated with the Van Vianen family, bears a mark which is probably that of Alexander Jackson, assay master (Fig. 90). He apparently sponsored the piece for Van Vianen (or one of his alien colleagues); since the form of the standish is emphatically English and rectangular, it is likely that the individual panels and figure candlesticks were embossed by craftsmen skilled in the auricular technique and subsequently assembled by an English workman.[18]

This court style, in which elements melt one into another, with grotesque masks and fleshy lobes on vessels of markedly irregular and asymmetrical forms, had its roots in late sixteenth-century Italian mannerism but in silver was effectively the creation of Van Vianen's father Adam and uncle Paul.

Christian worked here, with some absences, from 1630 until the early 1640s and again in the 1660s, although only a handful of surviving pieces for English patrons can be attributed to him. One, a lobed bowl made for Henry Percy, tenth Earl of Northumberland, some time between 1636 and 1642 was so valued as to be specified as an heirloom in his widow's will in 1704, and one at Burghley in 1690 was attributed to 'Vienna' or Vianen.[19] The Percy bowl,

231

after a design of his father's (which Christian was to publish in 1650 in *Modelles Artificiels*), has the characteristic dissolving grotesque masks and fluid lines. However, Van Vianen's influence here was, following the practice of English goldsmiths, absorbed only slowly and as one element in the ornament. Flagons of 1646, from the workshop of the anonymous hound sejant maker, combine scrolling foliage from a French ornamental print and auricular dissolving masks around formal chased plaques, as on the standish of 1639. Several Restoration salvers incorporate auricular masks as border ornament (Fig. 133).[20]

The peculiar skill of the Van Vianen family lay in creating 'cabinet' pieces whose function was to excite the eye and stir the sense of wonder. Charles I so valued a candlestick 'curiously wrought' by Christian that he kept it in his cabinet of wonders and works of art at Whitehall. The sums the king laid out with Van Vianen for the chapel plate for the Order of the Garter at Windsor demonstrate not only the premium commanded by a highly skilled craftsman, but also the importance Charles attached to the forms of liturgical plate[21] which took a fresh direction before the Civil War.

William Laud has often been considered the driving force behind the new 'Gothic' designs for high Anglican church plate of the 1620s and 1630s. These were revivals of the last mass chalices before the Reformation, and their origins are to be sought a decade or so before Laud's preferences as Bishop of London and later Archbishop became apparent. When Eton College bought new chalices in 1613 and 1616 both had crosses as finials.[22] The cross was an essential element in the renewed emphasis on ritual and symbolism and cross-finials appear on all the high Anglican cups and covered patens made for members of the court circle, even those sets commissioned during the Commonwealth. The hound sejant maker cornered several important commissions, notably plate for the private chapel at Staunton Harold and another set (now belonging to the Bishop of London) both made in 1653 (Fig. 115). These include covered sacrament bowls or ciboria, and have beautiful detail, down to the cast angel heads at the points of their feet, and handle-beading, of which this maker was an early exponent, another feature derived from French ornament.[23] By the 1640s Paris was seen as the best source of ornament, 'Examples of ornament and Grotesks in which the Italians themselves confess the French excel', as Wren excitedly wrote promising to collect engravings there and 'bring you all France in paper'. The close links are evident already in the 1630s, when Inigo Jones used Callot designs (at the Queen's House) and Theodore Rogiers made plate for Charles I.

After the Restoration a fresh group of aliens came into prominence, equipped with the fashionable skills of cage-work, chasing and embossing. In 1664 Wolfgang Howzer from Zurich and Jacob Bodendick of Limburg presented a letter from the king instructing the wardens of the Goldsmiths' Company to assay and mark their work. Both had been at work in London for several years and were probably responsible for the embossing of various Jewel House orders such as the gift taken to the Tsar by the 1663–4 Embassy, although the marks on the plate now in the Kremlin are those of Henry Greenway, Robert Smithier and Francis Leake. The mark WH over a cherub has been convincingly attributed to Howzer; Bodendick, who apparently used the mark IB over a crescent between two pellets from 1664, is also noted for superb embossing, particularly on ginger jars, and for his candlesticks. Cage-cups and tankards by him are known, some with noticeably auricular handles.[24]

232

Fig. 91 **'Proper ornaments to be engraved on plate'**
By C. de Moelder, London. 1694. Mostly for ornate chased dressing plate, in Dutch and French styles
popular well before 1694, a reminder of the dependence of English goldsmiths on imported designs.
Compare the 'Chinese' panelled canister with the cups by Willaume, Fig. 93.
VAM

233

The Chinese Taste c.1680–1720

As always when dealing with decorative art, the work of innovators can be identified but the means by which goldsmiths translated from their design source into ornament are obscure. Take for example the chinoiseries flat-chased on so much London silver between about 1670 and 1695. The printed source of these picturesque scenes with their *mélange* of Turkish and Indian figures, Chinese birds and classical fountains and ruined arches is unknown; the technique, which used a stabbed line, is quite unlike that adopted for other chased work at the time, implying that it was peculiar to the original medium, but no sheet of comparable ornament is known. The designs for japanned work published by Stalker and Parker in 1688 are similarly exotic in general appearance but quite different both in line and in execution (Fig. 92).[25] A set of candlesticks by a New York silversmith, Kierstede, incorporates figures with astronomical instruments from another source, suggesting that the English designs were indigenous.

Fig. 92 **'Chinoiserie' cup and salver**
Gilt. Cup 1671. Mark not known. Salver 1691. Mark of Ralph Leake. Both pieces flat-chased with a carefully integrated scheme of chinoiseries about 1691 and engraved later with the arms of Oliver Cromwell as Protector, perhaps a deliberate attempt to create an association.
Boston, Museum of Fine Arts

234

Fig. 93 **Cups**
Gilt. 1711. Britannia mark of David Willaume. The six-lobed body and inset shaped panels with birds
and blossom are taken from Chinese models, although the handles are pure late baroque. Both are found
on English silver by the mid-1690s, but these cups are a rare instance of a blending of styles.
Mrs How

Although it has been suggested that a single specialist chaser was responsible for most of the chinoiseries on London silver of between 1670 and about 1690, variations in both design and technique make this unlikely. A salver and porringer at the Museum of Fine Art, Boston has a carefully planned scheme in which the figures and trees are subordinated to a quatrefoil layout, and contrasting areas have been burnished or matted, an effect reinforced by skilful gilding (Fig. 92).[26] This is a far cry from the naive out-of-scale figures and plants which romp crudely around so many tankards and mugs and it is hard to accept that one man could have produced both. These mock-Chinese designs were so popular that they occur even on church plate and some plain wares were apparently taken back to be 'beautified' well after they were made. Because chinoiseries have been regarded as an added attraction for a century or so, they have sometimes been added quite recently to enhance a piece of antique plate.

By the 1670s a wide range of Chinese, Japanese and Indian decorative art was available for the European market – wallpaper, textiles, ceramics, metalwork, cabinets. If the source book for the chinoiseries on silver was printed in England after an oriental original – these pictures are unique to English silver – then it is curious that no trace of it has been recognised in other media, and a further reminder of how little we know about the design sources of engravers and chasers before the nineteenth century.[27]

Another form of 'Chinese' ornament popular between about 1690 and 1720 in both England and Holland employed panels chased with figures and trees in high relief, imitating carving. Snuff boxes, small lobed cups by Willaume, tea canisters and cane handles in private collections and designs published by de Moelder in 1694 incorporate this encrusted technique. It has been argued that these are all Chinese-made for the European market, but the variety of shapes and the existence of fully marked Britannia standard pieces, makes an English source more probable. A recent analysis by X-ray fluoroscopy showed a much lower copper content in one piece at least, and a high silver content, suggesting that this (a teapot, VAM) came from a non-English source (Fig. 93).[28]

The Influence of France

The Huguenot influx in the 1680s brought a marked change to the character of London-made silver; the best French-trained craftsmen quickly attracted aristocratic patronage and so stimulated native goldsmiths to imitate their techniques, notably casting. In the longer term, by retaining their cross-Channel links, the leaders of the French goldsmiths circulated imported designs (Fig. 26) which swept aside current London design. However, in those towns such as Exeter, where there was no significant influx of immigrant craftsmen at this time, the cast elements and heavy baroque motifs characteristic of London silver of the 1690s are rarely found (for example, Fig. 68). Silversmiths in New England too, virtually ignored the first generation of 'Huguenot' styles. Fashion played its part too. From the 1680s designs for silver tea equipages, mustard pots, tureens, cruets and other new tableware were copied from Paris, not only in England but also in Sweden.[29]

A recent exhibition at the Victoria and Albert Museum (1982) brought out the significance of Stefano della Bella's etchings for later goldsmiths. Between 1620 and 1664 he produced eighty-two plates of ornament, which retained their appeal for a century and a half. His delicate friezes of dogs and putti metamorphosing into foliage are found on English silver of the 1690s (Fig. 94). Sheets of current designs, like those issued by de Moelder in London in 1694 (Fig. 91) circulated throughout Northern Europe, journeymen trained in workshops familiar with, for example, the refined French casting techniques, would be particularly well placed to carry out such work.[30]

The bitter complaint from English goldsmiths that they were undercut by the 'necessitous strangers' is true only in the sense that the newcomers, familiar with the cast and applied ornament currently or recently fashionable in France, were quicker and more skilled at executing orders. The Jewel House, recognising the Huguenot skills, rapidly drew them in as subordinate goldsmiths and close cross-Channel links are evident in royal orders of the 1720s (Pl. 6).

Where important commissions, such as the orders placed by successive tsarinas of Russia, or the King of Portugal in the 1720s were concerned, the second-generation Huguenots were still preferred and were able to charge well above the going rate for their work.[31]

To take David Willaume the elder (1658–1741), this French-born goldsmith supplied sets of helmet ewers with figure handles to adorn the sideboards of several aristocratic families; a handsome set of 1706 is at the Fishmongers' Company, a gift in 1717. Paul Crespin

(1694–1770) was another Huguenot who, although born here, corresponded with the agents of his aristocratic clients such as the Duke and Duchess of Portland in French and clearly, from his crisp response to French changes in style in the 1730s and 1740s, retained close cross-Channel links (Fig. 29).[32]

Piercing, enhanced by engraving, and cut-card work both make an occasional appearance before the main influx of Huguenots, the latter notably on the Dawes cup at Fishmongers' Hall (1671) and on a chalice made in 1675 for S. Andrew Kingswood in Surrey (on loan to VAM) although the goldsmith, Jacob Bodendick, had been trained abroad. Another

Fig. 94 **Hexagonal waiter**
Gilt 1698. Britannia mark of Benjamin Pyne. D. 12.4 cm. From a set made for Sir William Courtenay of
Powderham, Devon, whose arms were perhaps engraved by Simon Gribelin. The chased border of
putti and dogs is after a design by Stefano della Bella, *c.*1660.
VAM

237

technique – the use of heavy cast or embossed acanthus bands on tankards, porringers and standing cups – derived from current French practice. Baroque designs by Berain and Jean le Pautre for figure candlesticks, helmet ewers or harp handles were widely imitated here, a generation or so later than their first publication (and use) in France (Fig. 26).[33]

The disappearance of virtually all the important French silver made before 1720 makes it difficult to be certain how quickly their cousins in England responded to new designs, but English noblemen visiting Paris brought back not only designs but complete dinner or tea services. In the 1720s innovations were visible to those with the entrée to the homes of Robert Walpole, or William, Viscount Bateman, whose plate had been made by Germain. In the 1730s the Duke of Kingston and the Earl of Berkeley ordered complete services in Paris, and in 1732 the Duke of Marlborough had ice-buckets made by Paul Crespin which lift their form and ornament from one published in Paris a decade earlier in an engraving entitled 'Pour M. le Duc'; whether goldsmith or patron chose the design is not known. A Germain design was made up by Simon Pantin in 1740, for a set of casters for an English customer (VAM).

Design Sources and Origins of the Rococo

Sources of inspiration for goldsmiths' work are often easier to describe generally than to establish precisely; the rococo style is a good example. The first phase had its roots firmly in the sixteenth century and also in the chased and engraved ornament popular between about 1620 and 1650. By 1735 two strands were emerging as characteristic of De Lamerie's silver in particular: a revival of auricular motifs, the fleshy dissolving grotesque masks of the silver of Johan Lutma and the Van Vianen family, and inset plaques or putti which harked back to Nuremburg silver of about 1650. However, to look for a precise starting point for a style is to

Fig. 95 **Chasing on coffee pot**
1738. Mark of De Lamerie. Plate 5.
Private collection

238

ignore the realities of craft work. Sheets of engraved ornament, copied and reinterpreted, circulated in the trade; craftsmen practised a series of techniques in one European centre, then drifted to another, taking their ideas with them to refresh the repertoires of their new workshops, and customers played their part too by asking for something a little different and fashionable, or perhaps by insisting on the incorporation of personal motifs, whether heraldic or emblematic.[34]

But in the early eighteenth century, the happy combination of a relative plenty of surviving pieces, many associated with identifiable patrons or designers, and contemporary comment enables us to plot the routes by which the style permeated the goldsmiths' shops.

Rococo, or *rocaille*, derives its name from the shellwork which is so ubiquitous an element in the first two decades of its popularity here. This distinctive new look had emerged in France by 1720, initially in the cartouche designs of Toro and the silver of Juste Aurèle Meissonier, court goldsmith to Louis XV from 1724, and in the 1730s in the silver of Pierre Germain and Jacques Roettiers.[35]

Essentially the style was a revolt against the symmetrical forms and controlled ornament of late baroque silver. Writhing, fluid and sculptural, it is seen at its most characteristic in plasterwork and wood carving. But certain English goldsmiths took to it quickly: Paul De Lamerie, Paul Crespin and the only innovative goldsmith not of Huguenot descent, George Wickes, were all working in this style by the mid-1730s. The German-trained Charles Frederick Kandler also produced silver recognisably in the rococo manner in the 1730s but in a different tradition; his globular kettle on triangular stand supported by three tritons and the spout is a nereid blowing a conch (VAM).

Each man had his preferred sources; in the 1720s, Paul De Lamerie had used chased bands of lattice work and classical busts, as on the Treby family silver (Ashmolean and British Museums) or on the Walpole salver (Fig. 82). These broke out into asymmetrical cartouches, initially used merely as ornament on well established and regular forms, but by the late 1730s the irregular cartouche was itself occasionally taken as the form of an object. A collection of sixty sheets of engraved ornament deriving from Italian mural decoration was published in London in 1736; these conmingle shells, busts and dissolving masks, foam and swags of flowers in exactly the manner adopted in the following decade.[36]

An inkstand at Blenheim Palace of 1738 incorporates many of De Lamerie's new ideas; the base is shaped as a cartouche with one tip facing one way, the other the opposite way. The entire surface is modelled, with at one end the attributes of Mercury, the messenger god, and water plants and at the other a cornucopia of fruit and flowers. Only one section, the bellstand, is a regular circle, a form dictated by the necessarily round shape of a hand bell. The pounce and inkpots each sit in shell-shaped sockets and each container is set with delicately chased plaques. These would be curious enough, with their gently undulating forms and dimpled borders reminiscent of octopus suckers, but De Lamerie has interwoven a serpent around each container, whose body passes through and behind the chased plaques, a design deriving through Boucher back to sixteenth-century Italy (Fig. 28).[37]

This entwining of apparently unrelated elements is characteristic of the style; the serpent weaving in and out of the body is a motif used by De Lamerie as handles on several ceremonial cups, notably one at the Fishmongers' Company, at about this time. One to this design, 'a Fine cheased Gilt cup and Cover' supplied by George Wickes to the Prince of Wales in 1740 at a cost of £61 13s, is still in the royal collection. Its fashion was laborious and costly, as the price of 15s an ounce demonstrates.[38]

When De Lamerie made a commissioned piece, such as the ewer and basin for his own Company, the Goldsmiths', as part of a large replacement order in 1740, he worked out its design with great care so that each element in the imagery was peculiarly appropriate to the Company's activities. The rim of the basin is set with four plaques depicting putti dressed as Hercules, Vulcan, Mercury and Minerva, with the attributes of each wrapped around the edge. Between them are a lion, an eagle, a phoenix and a marine monster for the elements of earth, air, fire and water; each section of the border is busy with ornament, panels of shell and foamwork in four variations, trellis and flowers.[39]

By 1747 Rouquet,[6] 'a French commentator on English patronage of the arts' could refer disparagingly to the taste called 'contraste' a taste so ridiculous and whimsical which 'everyday produces as it does elsewhere, some new monster'; the style swept the goldsmiths' shops so that trade cards of the 1750s depict shell salts and sauce boats, chinoiserie-chased kettles and coffee pots and tureens encased with flowers in strong contrast to the clean formal shapes of the 1720s and early 1730s.[40]

The ewer and basin set had by now purely a decorative function, to enhance the sideboard display. It was regarded as suitable to present to public figures. The ewer and basin which George Wickes made for presentation to John Scrope, Recorder of Bristol in 1735, which was sold by Sotheby's in 1983, is also laden with imagery appropriate to the recipient, his city and his work, prosperity by trade, the sea, wine, justice – represented by profile busts of caesars, patriotism – Britannia on the ewer handle, each drawn from a different pattern book. The goldsmith's, or his draughtsman's, skill lay in selecting and then combining these elements into a harmonious composition; a successful and effective motif, such as the caesars in cartouches, might be used again immediately on another piece. These appear on tureens made for Lord North by Wickes the same year and were lifted from a collection of cartouches published in Paris two years earlier.[41]

The influence of Jean le Pautre (1618–82) on goldsmiths of up to a century later is easily demonstrated. His *Nouveau Livres de Termes* and other sets of etchings 'pour Embellir les Maisons et Jardins' was clearly the origin of the female figure candlesticks of the 1680s and 1690s in the Ashmolean, Chicago and Bank of England Collections. Other subjects of le Pautre's re-used later include blackamoors and Chinamen, picked up as costume figures for candlesticks in the 1740s.[42] Apollo's pursuit of Daphne, a theme which was a potent source of imagery for European artists from the time of Bernini, was adapted by G. M. Moser, the Swiss-born goldchaser and enameller, about 1740–5 for a set of four candlesticks, made for an English customer and now in the VAM. Moser altered the laurel bark of Bernini's metamorphosing Daphne, an engraving of which was clearly his starting point, into typically rococo scrolls; her pose was based on a contemporary print by Oppenordt, drawing again on a sixteenth-century original. The triangular bases of these and other figure candlesticks owe much to designs for silver by Meissonier, publicised before 1739 by the French artist Louis Desportes. The essence of the style was its use of elements drawn from the classical repertoire combined with monstrous beasts, exotic figures, flowers and other naturalistic elements (Fig.

Fig. 96   **Design for stand or candelabrum**
Etching by le Pautre *c*.1660, republished *c*.1674 in England. The theme of flower-draped caryatids was
taken up by London goldsmiths in the 1680s (Fig. 26) and again in the 1740s and later; le Pautre's design
was clearly the stimulus.
VAM

241

28). Philips Garden supplied Curzon with four candlesticks 'with historical figures' in 1759 at the high cost of 18s an ounce. These had a shepherd and shepherdess and a cupid under trees, perhaps from a Germain design.[43]

While Paul De Lamerie's design sources are not so easily established, his sets of garlanded male and female figure candlesticks of the 1740s are clearly in the same line of descent. Flowers and putti recur on candlesticks in both silver and ormolu. A chamberstick by Paul Crespin of 1744 was made up in both materials; a reclining putto holds up a flower in which the candle sits, also derived from a near contemporary French design by Thomas Germain (VAM). But Peter Archambo in 1746 produced an original candlestick design, not French-inspired, in which bulging Solomonic columns rise from swirled triangular rocky bases.[44]

Some French commentators scorned English goldsmiths for their treatment of 'contraste'. Certainly the relentless layering of apparently unrelated ornament on tea-silver of the 1750s can seem indigestible and even repellent to an English eye, more at ease with plain burnished silver or a minimum of controlled and localised ornament such as engraving. But the rococo is essentially a sculptural style, to be seen and enjoyed; Moser's Apollo and Daphne candlesticks are designed to be viewed from several points and were probably made as part of a large set on the same theme for a dining table. Nicholas Sprimont, the Liège-born goldsmith who turned after 1747 to making porcelain in London, modelled all his silver, from centrepieces to tea and coffee ware, as pieces of sculpture, as a coffee pot from the 1740s (VAM) demonstrates.[45]

The marine dinner service (in the royal collection) made for Frederick, Prince of Wales in the 1740s has as its centrepiece an oval tureen surmounted by Poseidon, resting on four dolphins and two mermaids. Although this has the mark of Paul Crespin, it has been suggested that Sprimont was actually responsible for it since he was a near neighbour of Crespin's, in Compton Street, Soho and did not enter his mark at Goldsmiths' Hall until January 1742, whereas the centrepiece is hallmarked 1741. Whichever man was responsible, it is clear that the salts and sauce boats in this service, which continued the marine theme, are Sprimont's work. Between 1742 and 1745 he supplied salts to four different designs, a lobster on rocks and shells, a crab with shells, a shell on two tritons and a shell on a dragon; the sauce boats are shells on dolphins, one with Venus and the other with Adonis.[46]

The heavy sculptural quality of this service is in strong contrast to the delicate centrepiece supplied by George Wickes in 1740. This was to a design by William Kent and is equally decorative, despite substantial additions in the nineteenth century.

Engraved designs for silver by Englishmen are extraordinarily rare but a set of William Kent's was published by John Vardy in 1744, *Some Designs by Mr Inigo Jones and Mr William Kent*. These not only enable us to attribute some surviving silver, since Vardy identified the customers for whom the designs were made up initially, but also show that Kent's designs were clearly influential, for a generation or so after their first publication.

Not all patrons were swept along in the rising tide of rococo. Several pieces by George Wickes follow Kent's designs, such as a cup made up in gold for Colonel Pelham in 1736 and a mug he produced in silver for Sir Charles Hanbury-Williams in 1745. Both are late baroque in feeling, the cup personalised for the Hon. James Pelham by its finial of Prince of Wales's feathers. He was private secretary to Frederick Louis, Prince of Wales at the time he commissioned it. Kent was the designer, and Wickes the goldsmith, favoured by the Prince of Wales so Pelham's choice of their work is understandable.[47]

William Kent's published designs included several of Wickes's current commissions, a centrepiece for the Prince of Wales (in the royal collection) and a pair of horse-head tureens ordered by Lord Mountford, both supplied by the goldsmith during 1744–5 and listed in his ledgers. Other designs by Kent were presumably made up by Wickes in the 1740s but examples do not survive. Later versions by his successors, Parker & Wakelin, notably a set of

Fig. 97 **Trade card of Thomas Heming, royal goldsmith**
*c.*1761. At least four of the objects perched around the frame, the two-handled cup, the tureen and the ewer (on the right) are well-known Heming lines. The tableware shows his close attention to French silver design, reflecting his aristocratic customers' preferences: compare Figs. 39 and 98.
VAM

243

owl candlesticks made for the Duke of Newcastle in 1775, show a renewed interest then in Kent's heavy classicism, which was an alternative to, but quite in keeping with, the contemporary demand for classical ornament.[48]

Kent's designs, once published, continued to appeal to other leading goldsmiths for half a century. Henry, Earl of Lincoln, who married in 1744 Katherine, a niece to the Duke of Newcastle, ordered a year later a set of candlesticks from Paul Crespin whose husks, foliage and shells would be recognisably Kentian even without the evidence of the printed design and caption.

Fig. 98 **Candlesticks**
1769. Mark of Thomas Heming. A direct response to French neo–classical silver. Like all Heming's
output, crisply detailed and well finished.
New York, Metropolitan Museum of Art

By 1750 we can identify some other English designers and even match-up pieces of silver to surviving publications. John Linnell (1723–96) was principally a furniture designer but a set of his engraved designs for silver, published by 1760, are clearly the immediate source for an unusual and beautiful set of three covered boxes for tea and sugar made by the goldsmith Arthur Annesley (VAM 1758). Each has an irregular fluted body and fluting conical cover and stands on openwork bases of vine branches set with cast insects. Others were more derivative; in about 1760 Robert Sayer in his *Ladies' Amusement* included a page of vases originally published by Stefano della Bella in *Raccolti di Vasi diversi* a century earlier; this was a convenient source used by John Parker and Edward Wakelin too whose condiment vases from the late 1750s (VAM) follow one of the antique forms in della Bella's sheet.[49]

Another collection of rococo designs for craftsmen was issued by Thomas Johnson, a carver and teacher of drawing and modelling, in 1758 in parts and in 1761 as *One Hundred and Fifty New Designs* but only five are specifically for goldsmiths. But the influence of French engraved designs for silver continued to predominate. Thomas Heming, royal goldsmith from 1760 to 1783, was so conscious of his debt to the designs of Pierre Germain, published in France in 1748 as *Elements d'Orfevrerie* and in England four years later, that one, a ewer, appears on his trade card, and another, a tureen, is close to silver made by Jacques Roettiers in the 1730s (Fig. 97). Both designs were popular with his English customers; presumably this breadth of sources was an essential part of his commercial stock in trade. The tureen was made up by Heming as part of a Jewel House order as late as 1770 and Heming was producing the ewer, covered with entwining flower sprays, throughout the 1760s. One of these ewers is in the Williams-Wynn toilet service (1768).[50]

Another piece on Heming's trade card, a covered cup, is unusual both in form and in ornament. Cast figures of Pan and a Bacchante form the out-curving handles, while the body is covered with vine stalks rising from a foot cast as a rock, with applied insects and marine life. Six cups to this design are recorded, although not all are marked. One is at Manchester Art Gallery and another at the Victoria and Albert Museum. For the figure handles at least, Heming was apparently drawing on his knowledge of rococo silver of the 1730s and 1740s, notably an engraving of the massive wine-cooler designed by George Vertue and made by Kandler in 1734, now in the Hermitage (Fig. 132).[51]

Heming was clearly a resourceful and talented goldsmith, using an eclectic range of sources, as the candlesticks he supplied with two toilet services of 1766 and 1768 demonstrate. While the services are conventional late floral rococo, one set of candlesticks is a direct imitation of a late Stuart design, indeed so close to a pair at the Ashmolean that they were thought to be seventeenth-century work, while the other is a gothic clustered column, a design also popular briefly in the 1670s and revived in the 1760s; (loan, VAM) Fig. 98 shows his awareness of contemporary French silver.[52]

Neo-classical Designers

It becomes considerably easier to name designers (or identify design sources) with the advent of neo-classicism, partly because the style continued popular for a generation or more, ensuring the preservation (and renewed use) of designs by Robert Adam, James Wyatt and others (Fig. 99), and partly because the trade itself has left fuller records. Birmingham Reference Library and the Victoria and Albert Museum have pattern books and trade catalogues of Matthew Boulton's firm. Ledgers exist of both London and provincial businesses, such as those of Parker, Wakelin, Tayler and their successor Robert Garrard and in Newcastle, for Langland's and Robertson.[53]

From the early nineteenth century even more has been preserved; many papers concerning Rundell, Bridge & Rundell are at the Public Record Office, some of the firm of Barnard's ledgers and a series of Elkington pattern books from the 1840s are in the Victoria and Albert Museum (for example, Fig. 102). In all these sources, designers' names are occasionally noted or can be associated with marked products. For instance, when William Pitts made up a candelabrum in 1800, the base was engraved 'Tatham Archt', in acknowledgement that C. H. Tatham had provided the design, and both at the Splendens sale (1810) and the Fonthill sales (1822, 1823) attributions to designers were given for a few pieces.[54]

Those silversmithing firms supplying the fashionable world had to be aware of the same innovations in style as their clients expected of their upholsterers, decorative painters or garden planners; designers were often retained over many years. The architect concerned with all details of an interior, from tableware to door furniture, can only be clearly documented from the 1760s. The perennial reputation of Robert Adam, a phenomenon for his business skill as much as for his ability to translate classical motifs into acceptable

Fig. 99 **Design for an epergne**
English, *c.*1780. Pen and ink and grey wash. A preliminary idea to show a client, this sketch would be redrawn with measurements and an estimate of the metal required for the plateworker.
VAM

246

ornament for the English aristocracy, has been reinforced both by the handsome visible evidence for his career, as at Kedleston, Kenwood and Osterley House, and by the general attribution to him of designs for the decorative arts and particularly for silver.[55]

The idea that plate, like furniture and interior decoration, should be consciously designed to complement an interior rather than merely drawing from a common repertoire of ornament, emerged later in England than in France. Whereas Berain and le Pautre had published designs in the previous century, the English only in the 1740s saw the first designs published by an architect (William Kent 1684–1748), both for his patrons' interiors and for their silver. Inevitably the designs were almost exclusively of large, or at least highly visible, display plate, for public formal use, whether centrepieces, sideboard urns and dishes, or tureens and candlesticks for the dining table.[56]

Although Robert Adam has received credit generally as the first to design silver appropriate to his interiors, the idea was not unfamiliar. Chippendale included a handful of silver designs in later editions of *The Director*. Those people uneasy about employing an architect could now select a design in the goldsmith's shop, or at home in their own library, but this moulding of taste and preference is much more influential as far as the craftsmen were concerned. Crucial were the books of engraved ornament and designs issued in London from the 1730s. Gaetano Brunetti's *Sixty Different Sorts of Ornaments . . . Very Usefull to Painters Sculptors . . . Silversmiths etc* (1736) included shells, broken pediments, dolphins, grotesque masks and so on, set asymmetrically and available to any craftsman willing to spend a guinea. Single sheets also circulated widely and were reissued, copied and adopted for trade cards and other printed ephemera, so familiarising both craftsman and customer with the elements of the style.[57]

A decade later the Chinese figures, dragons and temple bells and pagodas of Lock and Copland's designs for tables, mirrors and stands were quickly picked up right across the board, from engravers of trade cards to goldsmiths; the latter used them for cast borders, feet and handles of salvers and bread baskets. Lock's curving table feet were used on epergnes by Heming and Pitts well into the 1760s, a continuity explained by the repeated reissue of his plates under different titles.[58]

But there is a difference between those fashionable echoes, made up from generally available components, many of which were cast from patterns, and specific commissions. Here Robert Adam (1728–92), followed by James Wyatt his near contemporary, effectively interposed a new stage in the design of their clients' silver through their ability to reinterpret classical forms. The sixty years from 1775 was a golden age for those designers skilled in translating classical motifs to other media and possessing the necessary personal knowledge through travels in Italy, Greece or Turkey.

The unique feature of Robert Adam's architectural practice was his unusual degree of control over every detail of an interior. The dining plate at Kedleston was remodelled on his instructions, to better fit it for his atrium design. The influence of his ideas was immediate. As Sir John Soane commented, 'Manufacturers of every kind felt, as it were, the electric power of this revolution in Art'; inevitably designs were rapidly pirated. In 1767 at least two firms, Daniel Smith & Robert Sharp, and David Whyte & William Holmes produced versions of candlesticks to his design, the latter possibly pirated (Fig. 98).[59]

The enormous collection of Robert Adam's design drawings, many for named clients, at Sir John Soane's Museum deserves fuller treatment. Designs for silver by Adam or Wyatt, which are often somewhat sketchy, were presumably merely for the client's approval, to be then made up by the goldsmith from a more precise annotated drawing prepared in the workshop. A punch bowl, now in the National Museum of Wales, was made up to Adam's design for Sir Watkin Williams-Wynn in 1771; for this two drawings survive, the second showing adaptations for stability.[60]

The widespread use of standard neo-classical ornament undoubtedly simplified this task of translation. Components such as drapery swags, acanthus, bound reeds and masks were already within the goldsmith's competence and needed only a regular neo-classical framework and form. Drawings for silver in James Wyatt's album (in a French collection)

Fig. 100 **Sir Robert Rich's epergne**
Gilt. Birmingham. 1774. Mark of Boulton & Fothergill. Designed by James Wyatt with his characteristic ram's heads and sphinx feet. Its swooping etiolated lines made the epergne unstable.
Garrard's

248

have a similar sketchy quality when compared to the silver actually carried out by Matthew Boulton and John Fothergill to his designs in the 1770s. A pair of candlesticks of 1774 in the Birmingham assay office collection shows how Wyatt's ideas were adjusted and simplified, to enable standard components to be used so that the sticks could be more cheaply produced. Wyatt's original design has acanthus feet and a pendent base which disappears from the Boulton and Fothergill pattern book version. The sticks as made retain Wyatt's characteristic etiolated line, as does an epergne of 1774 (see Fig. 100 and p. 108).

Other Boulton silver of the 1770s undoubtedly derived from Wyatt's designs too, such as an elegant wine jug of 1776 or the boat-shaped tureens and sauce boats of the mid-1770s (VAM; Birmingham assay office) although here again the lack of ornament around the foot suggests an economical modification. The sauce tureens in the Victoria and Albert Museum lack the massive central turret on Wyatt's original design.[61]

James Wyatt had a family connection with Boulton (his father had built the Soho Manufactory and his cousin was Boulton's London agent) but he supplied only some of Boulton's designs and indeed worked for other goldsmiths too. In 1774 he received two guineas from Parker & Wakelin for a 'Fine chased Sarcophagus' they were making up for Assheton Curzon of Kedleston.[62]

Matthew Boulton was exceptional in his well documented and assiduous search for novel design sources. He borrowed from friends through the introductions of his patron Mrs Montagu and subscribed to several archaeological publications of the 1760s and 1770s, notably the account of the discovery of Herculaneum by Martin and Lettice (1773) but he also collected printed designs. A sheet of tureens designed by Pergolesi, and published in 1782, is pasted into one of his pattern books, as are designs from the Sheffield firm of Tudor & Leader. He watched these trade rivals just as they and the London houses watched his current production.[63]

The style of Boulton's early silver is hard to document, since the contents of his pattern books were rearranged by Elkington's after they were sold in 1848, but there is a clear link between the design of a Boulton rococo candlestick, hallmarked at Chester in 1768, and a London-made Butty and Dumee stick of the previous year. This may not be merely a case of pirating but a direct commercial relationship, since Boulton had dealings with Nicholas Dumee some years later. A cousin of his came to work as a chaser at Soho, remaining until 1773. But Boulton preferred to train up local lads according to his own programme, rather than adopt the apprenticeship system.

Flaxman and other Regency Designers

The outstanding figure in neo-classical silver design, as in ceramics, is John Flaxman (1755–1826). His design sources were wide ranging, from D'Hancarville's Greek vases to gothic sculpture, and his long association (from 1805, the Trafalgar cup to his death) with the royal goldsmiths Rundell, Bridge & Rundell ensured that much of the prestige plate they supplied to their aristocratic and royal customers was to his design. His masterpiece, the Achilles shield, took fifteen years (1807 to 1822) to design and make. The first copy was displayed at the Coronation banquet of George IV; four royal dukes then purchased copies and one of these, belonging to the Duke of Northumberland, was sold in 1984 at a world record price of £440,000, an indication of the continuing regard for his quality. He may well have carried out some of the initial chasing himself, although William Pitts is known to have taken the main responsibility for this massive and skilled task.[64]

Rundell's also employed Thomas Stothard RA between 1809 and 1815; a candelabrum design by him (VAM) shows the influence of le Pautre's prints of Pan and Syrinx. But Stothard's design, like those of Robert Adam or Wyatt, is sketchy and had to be worked up. Edward Baily at Rundell's copied it about 1820 but modified it in the interest of practicality. A similar translation process was probably always necessary, since none of the artist-designers of the Regency had trained as goldsmiths.

Flaxman's near contemporary, Thomas Hope, preferred a gamey flavour of Egyptian themes in his classicism and had a greater interest in the complete interior than in individual tour de force pieces. He published in 1807 *Household Furniture and Interior Decoration Executed from Designs by Thomas Hope*, several of whose sixty plates included metalwork. He had designed silver for customers of Rundell, Bridge & Rundell and several Storr-made pieces are recognisably related to his designs, such as a snake-handled bowl and a tureen in the royal collection of 1803–5. Hope's Duchess Street house was much studied by contemporary artists and designers; Matthew Boulton sent his protégé John Philip there to make drawings. Rundell's had an in-house designer too, William Theed, from 1803 to 1817. Theed had worked for Wedgwood and was probably the link between that firm and Flaxman, whom they apparently commissioned to design the Trafalgar vase in 1805.[66]

Another designer who concerned himself with neo-classical silver was Charles Heathcote Tatham (1772–1842); employed by Henry Holland at Carlton House from 1789, he went on a buying trip to Italy in 1794, came under Piranesi's influence and published a much reprinted series of *Etchings of Ancient Ornamental Architecture* (1799). Seven years later his designs for aristocratic clients, such as the Lords Spencer and Carlisle and Earl Camden, were published as *Designs for Ornamental Plate*, remembered particularly now for Tatham's trenchant condemnation of the lightweight Adam-style silver as against 'Roman Massiveness . . . to the utter exclusion of all good Ornament'. A candelabrum centrepiece supplied to Lord Kinneard by Rundell's in 1806 closely follows one of Tatham's designs, which had been prepared for the Earl of Carlisle in 1801.[67]

Certainly solidity and grandeur, not to speak of archaeological exactitude, characterises much of the plate produced between about 1800 and 1830 (for example Fig. 101). The 1822 order for new church plate for William Inwood's church of S. Pancras was carried out by Paul Storr with great skill, despite the incongruity of adopting anthemium, ovolo and astragal beading from the north porch of the Erechtheumas borders for flagons, chalices and salvers for Christian use. The Warwick vase, brought to this country in 1774 and familiar through Piranesi's 1788 engraving, was copied from about 1800 for salt cellars, wine coolers and soup tureens. Paul Storr was using it as a model from at least as early as 1812. In 1827 Lady Blackett had two six-quart soup tureens made by Barnard's copying the vase and the same firm, who were largely manufacturers to the trade, produced in 1828–9 for the retailer David Ellis column candelabra 'of a mix't style . . . ornamented in the Greek and Gothic style . . . to a Drawg of an old Engravg of an ancient fragment in India' (Fig. 41).[68]

Thirty years earlier Paul Storr had put together motifs from Pompeii and from Egypt in a cruet frame supplied to Trinity College, Cambridge in 1800. Its four feet are Egyptian lotus flower capitals and the fluted pilasters are taken from a marble table found at Pompeii. Gastronomically this frame is elaborate too; the six bottles carry labels for soy, cayenne, chili, anchovy, lemon and ketchup. This could well have formed part of a large service on the same theme.[69]

Fig. 101 **Sauce tureen from the Deccan service**
Parcel-gilt 1806. Mark of John Edward. The Deccan service, presented to Arthur Wellesley by the Army of the Deccan, has an appropriately Indian design theme; note the finial. The weight of this sauce tureen is 84 ounces: a massive Regency order.
Wellington Museum, Apsley House

251

Historical Revivals c. 1810 to c. 1840

While the wish to match-up with an older broken set can sometimes explain direct copies of earlier silver, a voracious appetite for designs in the rococo style marked the period 1810 to 1830. Edward Farrell is particularly known for his reinterpretations of those marine themes associated with Nicholas Sprimont and Paul Crespin in the 1740s, as in a set of eight standing salts (1820) at Burghley. A sea king and his queen, one riding a dolphin and the other a sea-horse and holding conch shells, rest on rocky asymmetrical bases; the salts are Britannia standard, gilt and chased and have accompanying mermaid and mermen spoons of three years earlier, indicating that Farrell was working in this style by 1817 (Fig. 43).[70]

Of course the rococo had never gone quite out of fashion; in 1780 the fourth Duke of Rutland and another each purchased copies of the marine service made for Frederick Prince of Wales in 1741–2. But there was a marked demand for it among late Regency customers; on a set of candlesticks, also at Burghley, the stems are moulded Chinamen on elaborate rococo scrolled bases. Only two of the set are by Farrell (1816) the other, earlier ones by John Crouch (1812), suggesting that there was a wide demand for rococo revival silver.[71]

This feeling for the rococo emerged only a little after the heavy 'Egyptian' neo-classicism more commonly thought of as typical of the early nineteenth century. In 1808 Paul Storr made candlesticks which are a close reinterpretation of a Meissonier design, in 1811 shell-shaped double salts resting on shells with a dolphin handle and in 1812 a pair of sauce boats which in form and handle are typical of those made by Peze Pilleau in the 1740s, although Storr has added entwined serpents to support the bowl, a feature taken from rococo cream jugs rather than sauce boats. Whether these pieces of small tableware were used alongside the massive tureens more typical of Storr is not known. Sometimes he copied directly, as in a pair of candelabra at Woburn, whose stems are from a Crespin set of 1747, although the branches are from a design by Thomas Hope.[72]

Two other strands in this revival of earlier styles were the interest in Stuart embossed silver and in the panelled relief work associated with Chinese imports of around 1700. Apart from the large display plate made by Farrell and others in the 1820s, Storr is known to have embossed tea and coffee ware with flowers and acanthus within shaped panels, in the mid-seventeenth century Dutch manner. In 1825 Storr made a hexagonal teapot with shaped panels enclosing 'Chinese' scenes in relief work, imitating the encrusted technique popular about 1690–1700 in England, which were themselves imitations of Chinese silver vessels.

Turning to Edward Farrell again, we find that he shared this awareness of the fashion for seventeenth-century ornament. A massive mustard pot of 1818 on four lion mask and paw feet is chased all over the body with Teniers' style figures and flowers; Farrell continued to produce teaware in this taste well into the 1830s.[73]

The large businesses, such as Rundell's, could easily copy, or take motifs directly from, their aristocratic clients' antique silver; for instance, Paul Storr produced several pieces directly imitating De Lamerie's engraved shell and trellis borders, not a motif otherwise in use at the time. For smaller firms, their sources were more often reinterpretations from printed designs, such as the *Scroll Ornaments* published about 1830 by Frederick Knight, which included derivations from Le Brun, le Pautre, Meissonier and Gribelin, Fig. 44 shows a variant.[74]

Alongside the reinterpretation of rococo marine themes ran a taste for plant and insect forms cast from life, a technique Flaxman, among others, experimented with. In the designs of Knight (he also published *Vases and Ornaments* in 1833) a strong flavour of organic naturalism is evident among the more familiar baroque or rococo sources, and in the 1830s and 1840s several silversmiths were adopting plant models with enthusiasm. Barnard's, for instance, who were among the subscribers to Knight's *Vases and Ornaments*, made chamber candlesticks in the form of lilypads or harebells. A popular flower form in the 1840s was the convolvolus, adopted for condiment sets, writing sets and candlesticks.[75]

A riot of technically inventive products and competing styles characterised the 1840s onwards.

Elkington's and the London Firms from 1840

In March 1840 G. R. Elkington of Birmingham patented the process of electroplating, that is depositing a coating of silver onto base metal. This commercial foresight ensured the firm's predominance in the Birmingham silverplate business, within a decade effectively killing off the earlier method of plating on copper known as Sheffield plate.[76]

Earlier experiments with gilding by electrolysis had been unsuccessful; although the Rundell, Bridge & Rundell 'Galvanic Goblet' (Royal Collection 1815) has been claimed as the first example, a recent test at the British Museum showed it to be mercury or fire-gilt. Elkington's were the first to capitalise on the process, and expanded their silver production too. By 1851 they were able to compete on equal terms at the Great Exhibition with the London firms of Hunt & Roskell and R. S. Garrard; Rundell's had been in decline since the early 1830s, finally closing down in 1842.[77]

Examples of silver produced by Elkington's, Garrard's and the other leading manufacturers such as Barnard's, between the 1850s and 1914 were shown at the Royal Academy in 1972, before the Handley-Read Collection was dispersed; some were purchased for the national collection. Inevitably this collection stressed the unusual pieces such as the christening cup designed by W. F. Spencer, and supplied by Garrard's to Prince Albert in 1848.[78]

The significance of the Birmingham, Coventry and Sheffield manufacturers is the sheer bulk of their production. Their designs reflected, however fitfully, the slowly changing taste of the general public, as against the royal, aristocratic or institutional clients of Hunt & Roskell, Hancock's and Garrard's. Elkington's straddled this divide, managing to keep a presence at the international exhibitions long after other firms had ceased to compete.

At both the 1851 and 1862 exhibitions, the silver displays were dominated by Elkington's, whose stand was crammed with, to modern eyes, pretentious highly finished creations such as an enamelled and parcel-gilt dessert service, 'in the Graeco-Pompeian style' (1862). They retained as art director the French designer A. A. Willms, who remained with the firm until 1899, but their outstanding exhibition pieces were the work of Leonard Morel-Ladeuil, a French chaser and modeller who had been assistant to Antoine Vechte. A basin and ewer of 1874 is typical of his output; they incorporate chased figure plaques, each one expressing an

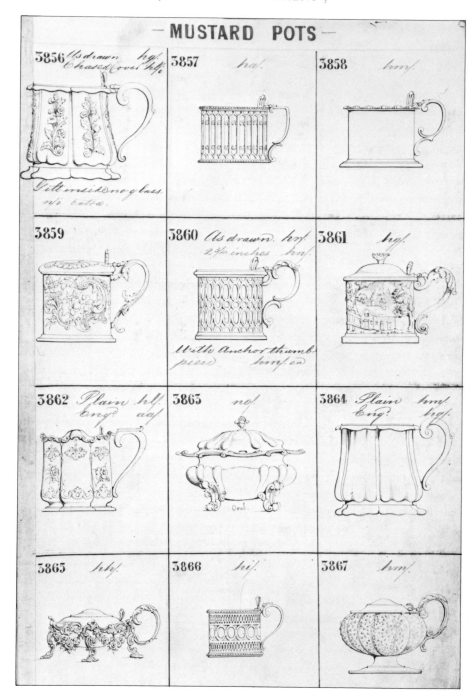

Fig. 102 **Mustard pots: Elkington's Design Book 3**
c.1840–1868. A few of the many designs they produced. The annotations are price-codes for supplying
retail silver.
VAM (Design Archive)

astrological sign, from a design by Morel-Ladeuil. But the firm's output in smaller goods in electroplate was the basis of its success; many of these are noticeably simpler in design and less banal than the 'artworks' and 'style of Cellini' pieces of which the firm was so proud (Fig. 102).[79]

The London firm of R. & S. Garrard were less prone to publicise their designers than Elkington's. Although the Frenchman Emile Jeannest was their principal designer from 1850 until his death in 1857, from about 1830 their studio was run by Edmund Cotterill who had trained at the Academy schools and whose speciality was large sculptural groups. His 1851 centrepiece in Moorish style, with figures illustrating a scene from one of Scott's novels, marked the shift away from heavy rococo or classical ornament and was awarded a £200 prize by the Goldsmiths' Company. Another of his 1851 exhibits was the Emperor of Russia's vase, which depicted in full relief the Labours of Hercules, an Ascot prize cup for 1850. In 1862 Garrard's showed a characteristic mixture of gems (including the Koh I Noor) and elaborate figure groups; the central feature was a table fountain with horses standing about a cupola-topped fountain (made a decade earlier) in whose design Prince Albert had taken a hand. This incorporated the much admired contrast in surface finishes, being parcel-gilt, enamelled and partly oxydised.[80]

These massive exhibition pieces often remained in the showroom for years, being taken round to one exhibition after another. The continuing demand, at a certain level of society, for large showy creations suitable as trophies or prize cups ensured their preservation, and their history can often be traced through inscriptions or the arms of later owners. For example, a centrepiece designed and modelled by Cotterill for Garrard's in 1831 and sold to the Duke of Buckingham, was sold at the Stowe sale (1838) to Richard Gunter, the fashionable caterer. This distinctive group, two horsemen engaged in a hand-to-hand fight based on an incident in Scott's novel *Old Mortality* can be seen in a stereoscopic view of a wedding party, part of a set issued in about 1865. It had presumably been hired out by Gunter's. The centrepiece turned up again as a race prize in 1893.[81]

Hunt & Roskell inherited from Paul Storr's studio the services of the sculptor E. H. Baily; as with all the leading concerns, they were eager to publicise their exhibition pieces but carried on a large trade in smaller goods too. These were always of good gauge metal, carefully finished and struck with serial numbers. Charles Frederick Hancock, formerly a partner in Hunt & Roskell, set up on his own shortly before the Great Exhibition. Like Hunt & Roskell's, Hancock's specialised in trophy and presentation plate of very high quality. 'Artists of celebrity are engaged as modellers of groups and designs for *surtouts de table* and the *dressoir*, presentation pieces, racing prizes . . .' Photographic albums still held by the firm show pieces designed by H. H. Armstead, Marochetti, Rafaelle Monti and Eugene Lamy. But the firm was and is better known for its superb jewellery; indeed, so familiar a figure was Hancock in the international world of society that Disraeli could write him into his novel *Lothair* (1870).

A speciality of certain firms was the production of church metalwork. Well before the 1840s, A. W. N. Pugin was firmly established as a passionate advocate of the gothic style; he had published in 1836 *Designs for Gold and Silversmiths* and from 1838 was collaborating with John Hardman of Birmingham to realise his designs for ecclesiastical orders. But his interest in archaeological sources for metalwork was evident already by 1827 when he was commissioned by Rundell, Bridge & Rundell to design two royal orders, chapel plate for Windsor and the Coronation cup (Figs. 47 and 48).[82]

In describing two embossed and enamelled chalices purchased from the 1851 exhibition, the first catalogue of the museum (VAM 1852) credited John Hardman with having made plate 'fully exemplifying the treatment of silverwork by the medieval goldsmiths'. These two chalices, designed by Pugin, stood for a distinct class of mid-Victorian metalwork, plate for churches both Roman Catholic and Anglican designed in the gothic manner.[83] A brief flirtation with baroque forms for church plate had been evident in the 1830s when, for instance, the newly opened Christchurch, Albany Street acquired a seventeenth-century Irish chalice. This, with its rococo revival embossed flowers, was taken as the model for the chalices for this church, but within a decade a typical gothic revival set of flagons and chalices by John Keith was acquired.

The next generation of designers after Pugin continued to satisfy the steady demand for church metalwork with designs in a broadly gothic taste. G. E. Street and William Butterfield had designs executed not only by Hardman but by Francis Skidmore of Coventry and in London, John Keith and the partnership of Barkentin and Krall.

Inventive gothic plate was characteristic of the designs of William Burges (1827–81), the architect who assisted Matthew Digby Wyatt in the early 1850s with *Metalwork and its Artistic Design* (1852, examples of historic metalwork) and *The Industrial Arts of the Nineteenth Century* (1851–3, a report on the Great Exhibition). This gave him a solid grounding in the design and techniques of historic metalwork. Although Burges's designs for silver were not produced commercially in large quantities, a recent exhibition demonstrated the range of his activity, from simple engraved soup plates to highly decorated claret jugs set with ancient coins, cameos and gemstones, the whole enhanced with parcel-gilding.[84]

By contrast, Christopher Dresser (1834–1904) is that oddity of the Victorian silver-smithing world, an innovative designer whose work was commercially produced in large quantities. On the staff of the School of Design from 1859, he designed silver (and electroplate) not only for Elkington's but also for James Dixon & Son of Sheffield and, from 1878, for Hukin & Heath of Birmingham.[85] His work is spare, angular and carefully thought-out so that, for example, teapot handles allow the maximum lift with the minimum of effort. These principles of ergonomics he propounded in 1873 in *Principles of Decorative Design*. But he was not afraid of rich ornament as long as it was linear and not figurative. He recommended the Elkington electrotypes of Saracenic damascened basins in the Victoria and Albert Museum; 'I strongly advise those who can afford to purchase these beautiful copies to garnish their sideboards with plate of this description, rather than with the meretricious electroplate which we often see in our shop windows'.[86]

His peculiar knowledge of natural, especially plant, forms (he held several professorships of botany), coupled with his interest in Japanese decorative arts, were entirely fresh sources of inspiration and his designs of the 1870s contrast strongly with the cluttered shapes, heavy with embossed and cast detail, familiar since the 1850s. His commercial sense led him to create designs that reduced the thickness of metal to a minimum and so made them accessible to the middle-class purchaser, rather as Boulton had a century earlier. Despite the general

256

decline in the English silver industry perceptible from the 1870s, the evidence of his design influence in both electroplate and sterling silver was clear until the First World War in the stock of both Elkington's and Hukin & Heath.

The Arts and Crafts Silversmiths

The silversmith's shop where serious work in craftsmanship is done, in distinction to the Trade Shop, whose only standard in saleability, possesses a stamp of righteousness which hallmarks both its productions and the men who make them.

(C. R. Ashbee)

The 1880s saw a rash of guilds or workshops, their founders motivated by the Morris ideal: the Century Guild (1882), the Art-Workers' Guild (1884), the Birmingham Guild of Handicraft (1890) and Ashbee's Guild and School of Handicraft. The Keswick School of Industrial Design Art, started by Canon Rawnsley about 1884, also included silversmiths. Their members were motivated not only by a passionate desire to involve themselves in every stage of production but also by the moral worth of the activity itself.[87]

Fig. 103 **Coffee service**
1898. Designed by Kate Harris for William Hutton & Son, Sheffield, and sold by the Goldsmiths' and Silversmiths' Company. A variant of this design won an award at the Paris 1900 Exhibition.
Oslo, Kunstindustrimuseet

257

The danger of low standards of execution peculiar to the guild concept was a real one. In commenting favourably on the superbly embossed and chased silver of Gilbert Marks (1861–1905), a maverick original who belonged to none of the guilds, the *Magazine of Art* (1893) praised him for his technical skill, by contrast with the 'vague indeterminate bumpings and exaggerations of empty spaces which characterize the simple tribe' of guildsmen and women (Fig. 55).[88]

One of the most successful of these craft workshops was the Artificers' Guild, founded in 1901 by Nelson Dawson. It ran until 1942, selling the work of Paul Cooper and Edmond Spencer among others. Spencer, having found an effective formula in combining mother-of-pearl and other materials such as shagreen or wood with pale gilding, continued to produce in this taste until the 1930s.[89]

Ultimately the Arts and Crafts movement ran out of steam, failing, as Ashbee recognised, to raise the general public understanding of design as applied to the decorative arts. Its participants would probably be astonished at the continuing and sometimes indiscriminate enthusiasm for their work today. At the time it appealed only to a minority of wealthy patrons (inevitably, given the low rate of output). Without resorting to trade methods to streamline production, their wares could never be either cheap enough, or available in large enough numbers, to flood the market.

The poor economic climate just before the First World War was discouraging to the luxury trades generally and only those silver firms with a commercial sense could prosper. Two firms capitalising on the Arts and Crafts tradition, Liberty's and Ramsden & Carr, managed to retain their customers but to satisfy the mass preference for the familiar rococo scroll or for Queen Anne was safer, as the early twentieth-century catalogues of Mappin & Webb and other manufacturing firms show. Art Nouveau silver, characterised by whiplash ornament and flower motifs, was widely popular; Hutton's won a prize at the Paris 1900 show for a teaset which blurred the lines between Arts and Crafts and Art Nouveau themes (Fig. 103).

Stylised forms, mixed materials and a general lack of glitter characterise the innovative silver designed between the wars, demonstrating the waning influence of the Arts and Crafts movement. One ornamental technique virtually ignored by Henry Wilson and his contemporaries in the years before 1914 was engraving. This was revived in the 1920s by H. G. Murphy (who had made up Wilson's elaborate jewelled objects before the war) and by Harold Stabler (1872–1945). Stabler had trained at the Keswick School of Industrial Art as a woodcarver and metalworker; he taught at the Royal College of Art from 1912 to 1926 and carried out many special commissions. His work predominated in the 1938 exhibition at Goldsmiths' Hall; one of the earliest industrial designers, he not only designed ceramics but also successfully in both silver and plate. His tea service (1935) was made by Adie Brothers of Birmingham in both materials.[90]

'Things are extremely bad . . . 90 per cent of British Industrial Art is devoid of any aesthetic merit' (Pevsner, 1937). Design standards in the trade were recognised generally in the 1920s as being very low. The English appetite for the antique or more often antique reproduction, raged still, virtually unaffected by recent design-thinking in Scandinavia or France. In 1925 an important exhibition of industrial art was held in Paris, and this was the light on the Damascus road for one influential Englishman, George Hughes, then assistant

Fig. 104 **Sideboard dish and covered beaker**
1938. Designed by R. M. Y. Gleadowe and made by Wakely & Wheeler. Presented to Corpus Christi,
Cambridge by Prof. A. L. Goodhart, former fellow.
Corpus Christi, Cambridge

clerk to the Goldsmiths' Company. He had just completed cataloguing the Company's antique plate and was in effect suddenly seized with a wish 'to remove the present stagnation from the gold and silverwork of this country'.[91]

The following year the Hall held open competitions for trophies and for domestic plate and the Company initiated a Plate Improvement Scheme, a role now diffused through the Craft Council run by the trade, whose annual prize competitions are partly funded by the Company.

The first public exhibition of modern silver to be held at the Hall was in 1938. But the Company had been buying current silver wares for its collection since 1925 and there had been earlier exhibitions of contemporary production elsewhere, for example annually at Dorland House, Regent Street from 1933, and the trade shows such as 'The British Industries' at Olympia. In 1937 a report on design in the *Jewellery, Silversmithing and Allied Trades* was published by the Council for Art and Industry, chartered by the energetic and persuasive Frank Pick. This recommended biennial exhibitions of current work at the Hall.

Fig. 105 **Mappin & Webb catalogue**

1937. Silver designed by Keith Murray. The term 'modern' was invoked just as 'in the new fashion' had
been for three centuries.

VAM

Fig. 106 **Coffee set**

1964 to 1966. Designed by Gerald Benney. H. coffee pot 24 cm. Commissioned by the first fellows and
some friends of Fitzwilliam College.

Fitzwilliam College, Cambridge

The first, in 1938, was visited by 37,000 people in six weeks. Most of the large London firms took part (Fig. 57).[92]

Despite all the commitment to current design at the Hall, this did not strike much spark in the trade generally. Both manufacturers and retailers were unable to accept that design could help sell their products. An anonymous Birmingham manufacturer 'catering for a clientele of the great middle class', with a limited turnover of five to fifteen thousand pounds, spoke for most of the trade. 'There is no cash to finance a designer, nor would he be of much use to us.' Why not? 'Because our clients have no serious need for good design. They want goods as near like the wealthy have at a price near to their own products.'[93] This point of view would have sounded depressingly familiar to Henry Cole and the design reformers of a century earlier. However, there was a certain self-consciousness about the poverty of design in the 1930s. The popular term 'fitness for purpose' was so widely used as to become an advertiser's cliché; Radcliffe, a firm making stampings for the silversmithing trades, advertised its products in the *Goldsmiths' Journal* by juxtaposing pictures of a medieval stone bridge and a plated tea service. The latter, although made in 1851, was 'still in good condition and only now replated'. The firm was claiming an association with the perceived purity of pre-industrial forms; 'No intricate shapes or superfluous ornament . . . It is this sense of "fitness for purpose" that distinguishes . . .'[94] But first the outbreak of war in 1939 and then the high rate of postwar tax (110 per cent on luxuries) stifled any potential response from the trade.

Since the 1950s the boom in art school attendance, coupled with a heightened awareness of design history, might have been expected to stimulate a renaissance in commercial production too. But the old divisions remain a stumbling block. For many people, their only knowledge of modern silver are the limited editions put out by cathedrals and stately homes to mark centenaries and royal occasions.

The Goldsmiths' Company, conscious of its roots in the trade and anxious to promote saleable and well-designed products, still encourages competitions and trade shows. The Craftsmen of the Year competition, organised by the trade's Craft Council, awards prizes annually for specific skills – enamelling, chasing, engraving and polishing. A separate competition for design has now been supplemented by a category for designers' own finished pieces. Opportunities for silversmiths' work in the past ten to fifteen years include the Topham Trophy competition run by the Walker Art Gallery, the Johnson Matthey awards for students and prize competitions run by Goddard's and, most recently, Dairy Crest, won in 1983 by Rod Kelly, an extraordinarily skilled young designer and chaser (Fig. 59).

Notes

1 Challis 1978, 36; Reddaway 1975, 128–31.

2 VAM 1980, 48–50.

3 Seymour MSS, HMC Longleat IV, f. 173. Bill of 17 June 1545.

4 Scouloudi 1937–41. In 1554 and 1558, statutes were passed blocking foreign craftsmen, an indication that they were here in large numbers. E.g. Hayward 1976, pl. 651.

5 Glanville 1971.

6 Hayward 1976; Oman 1961, pl. 145.

7 Hayward 1976, pl. 687.

8 VAM, Pembroke inventory.

9 Schroder 1983. Hayward 1976. Oman (Norwich) 1964.

10 Goldsmiths' 1979, no. 13.

11 Caryatid straps occur in English silver from

the 1550s. Some are coarsely modelled and crudely cast, others of exceptional quality and detail.

12   Hayward 1976, pl. 677–8. Another to this design is in Toledo.

13   *Goldsmiths' Review*, 1969–70, 16–18; Oman 1971.

14   Freshfield 1893. Others belong to S. Mary Abbots, Kensington and All Hallows, London Wall.

15   They still occur as late as 1646 (Fig. 115).

16   Tait 1982.

17   No one is sure how these finely detailed portrait plaques were done, whether by casting or engraving. Examples are in VAM and BM.

18   Lightbown 1968; Hayward 1976.

19   Burghley MSS; Inventory 1690.

20   One pair, from Thirkleby Church, Yorkshire, is split between VAM and Temple Newsam, Leeds. The other is in the Untermyer Collection. For auricular pieces, see Oman 1970; ter Molen 1984 Vol. I, 139–42.

21   Bond 1947, 243; Oman 1959.

22   Oman 1971.

23   The Staunton Harold set is split between VAM and Manchester; the other is in S. Paul's Cathedral treasury.

24   Oman 1970; Oman 1961.

25   Dauterman 1965. Safford 1983.

26   Boston MFA: salver 1691, porringer 1677; the chinoiseries chased about 1691 on both. The arms of Cromwell were added about 1720!

27   Gold chasers have been studied in detail; VAM 1984.

28   One snuffbox is VAM, another on loan to Leeds Castle. The canisters *Proceedings of the Society of Silver Collectors*, Vol. 11, 5–6, 1975, 96. Forbes *et al.* 1969, 51–4. Tests at Winterthur show that Chinese export silver (of the mid-eighteenth century) is marked differently in alloy from sterling.

29   Important silver of 1690 to 1720 is at the BM (Wilding Gift, Tait 1972), Ashmolean Museum (Farrer and Carter Collections, Grimwade 1947) and VAM. The Bank of England bought silver of about 1694 (the year it was founded): Oman 1967. For colonial silver, see Safford 1983.

30   Hayward 1970. Designs remained in use, often for years; Isaac Liger's 1728 toilet service uses Moelder motifs.

31   Paul Crespin had a steady run of orders from the Portuguese court in the 1720s, Jones 1940. Augustin Courtauld, with other Huguenots, supplied Russian orders in the 1730s. Hayward 1975;

Oman 1959; Museum of London 1985.

32   Hayward 1959; VAM 1984, 51.

33   For example, VAM 1982, 58.

34   VAM 1982 and 1984, *passim* and see p. 00.

35   Fiske Kimball 1943/1980, fig. 170, 199–201. VAM 1984, 43–4.

36   Brunetti: VAM 1984, 38. For auricular echoes, compare ter Molen 1984, pl. 35 & 36 with Willaume's coiled cream jugs.

37   VAM 1984, col. pl. IX. Hayward 1976, pl. 53, 70–2.

38   VAM 1984, 107–8. Jones 1911, pl. XXXVIII.

39   Carrington and Hughes 1926, pl. 61. VAM 1984, 111–12.

40   Rouquet, like the Abbe LeBlanc, was thoroughly disparaging about English design standards.

41   By Jacques de la Joue, Barr 1983; VAM 1984, col. pl. IV.

42   For example, Grimwade 1974; VAM 1982, 68 and 9 emphasises Linnell's debt to Stefano della Bella.

43   VAM 1982, 56–63 and refs cited.

44   Banister 1983.

45   And the Hermitage Kettle.

46   Jones 1911; Grimwade 1969; VAM 1984, 113–14.

47   Barr 1980, 94–6; Hayward 1970.

48   Hayward 1959a and 1970a.

49   Hayward 1973; VAM 1984, 122.

50   VAM 1984, 125; Heal 1935.

51   Young 1983; VAM 1984, 37–8.

52   Grimwade 1956; Oman 1970. A set of four by Kandler (1765) are in the Birmingham Museum, Alabama.

53   VAM 1913 and 1982; Grimwade 1961; Barr 1980; Laing A. G. 1979.

54   Bury 1966; Banister 1980 and 1983; Snodin 1978, 132.

55   Rowe 1965 undervalued other designers: Wyatt, Flaxman and the recently recognised J. J. Boileau; Snodin 1978.

56   Hayward 1959a and 1970a.

57   Discussed in VAM 1982.

58   VAM 1984. Ince and Mayhew illustrated 'a candlestick or girandole in gilt wood, gold or brass . . . might be equally the same executed in silver', *c.*1762, *Universal System of Household Furniture*.

59   Temple Newsam, Leeds, purchased by Manchester Art Gallery, 1984.

60   Hughes 1967.

61   Fergusson. Another Boulton set (1773) is in the Birmingham Museum, Alabama.

62 Hatfield 1981, 15.

63 Crisp-Jones 1981 and p. 108.

64 *Connoisseur Period Guides. The Regency Period,* 1112–13; Bury and Culme, *Art at Auction 1983–4* (1984).

65 VAM 1982, 678–9, 83; Snodin 1978.

66 Rowe 1965.

67 Udy 1978.

68 Penzer 1954; Banister 1980.

69 Penzer 1954; Jones 1979.

70 Webster 1984. For this and other revivals, see Collard 1985 and Thornton 1984.

71 Webster 1984.

72 Grimwade 1962, pl. 8. Spinks in 1983 had a later (1837) Crespin copy.

73 A tea/coffee service in the Teniers style (1816 and 1817) was sold by Christie's, New York, 5 October 1983.

74 Culme 1977, 79.

75 Culme 1977, 77–81.

76 At the 1848 Birmingham Exhibition, Elkington Mason & Co. showed both electrotypes and electroplate. See Ch. 6.

77 Hunt 1984, 347–8; Birmingham A. G., 1973, 'Elkington's'.

78 Royal Academy 1972. For more commercial products, see Waldron 1982.

79 Birmingham A. G. 1973, D18.

80 Culme 1977, 96, 101. For the 1862 display, 169.

81 Culme 1977, 96.

82 Bury, Snodin, Wedgwood 1979; Birmingham 1973.

83 Theophilus' treatise, published in 1847, was the point of reference for the *Journal of Art and Manufactures* discussing Hardman's 1848 exhibits.

84 National Museum of Wales 1981, 105–22.

85 Bury 1962; Birmingham A. G. 1973, 'Functionalism'.

86 Dresser 1873.

87 Anscombe and Geere 1978 gives a useful summary. See Ch. 6.

88 Harlow 1984.

89 Birmingham A. G., 1973, 'Arts and Crafts'.

90 Arts Council 1979; Goldsmiths' 1938.

91 His retrospective account was published in Goldsmiths' 1965.

92 Goldsmiths' 1938.

93 *Goldsmiths' Journal*, May 1937.

94 *Goldsmiths' Journal*, May 1937.

95 But there is very little interest in commissioning silver. Designers like Sarah Jones and Christopher Lawrance concentrate on small items, costing only a few hundred pounds or less, *Goldsmiths' Review*, 1983–4.

PART IV

SILVER AND SOCIETY

ANTIQUARIES,
COLLECTORS, FAKERS

O LD silver has survived for many reasons – family sentiment, the conservatism and
reverence for tradition of societies such as colleges, livery companies and corporations
or because, like so much plate in churches, it has remained in weekly use.

Only in the past two centuries has a market emerged which values old silver primarily for
its antiquity and historical interest, or for its contribution to a period interior. Already two
hundred years ago there was little enough ancient plate available, and silver of the late middle
ages up to the mid-seventeenth century was referred to more or less indiscriminately as
gothic. An observant German visitor to London in 1786, Sophie von la Roche, described her
visit to the antique silver showroom of the royal goldsmith – Thomas Jefferys in Cockspur
Street:

> These antique well preserved pieces, so Mr Jefferys said, often find a purchaser more readily
> than the modern. This is because the English are fond of constructing and decorating whole
> portions of their country houses, or at least one apartment, in Old Gothic style and so are
> glad to purchase any accessories dating from the same or a similar period.

Jefferys, as royal goldsmith, was peculiarly well placed to dispose of worn plate from the
royal collection. By 1808 his successors as royal goldsmiths, Rundell & Bridge, so clearly
recognised this demand that they offered to favoured customers (known to be collectors)
royal objects which had been sent to melt by the Lord Chamberlain. From this one source
several important collectors like William Beckford, the Earl Brownlow, Earl of Lonsdale and
Duke of Buccleuch obtained magnificent late Stuart silver with the royal arms.[1]

Old silver was often valued for its associations as much as its workmanship; pieces with the
arms of ancient English families or indeed of the English kings were prized by antiquaries.
The Parr pot (Fig. 107), a Venetian latticino glass with English mounts of 1546 has the arms of
Sir William Parr, uncle to Queen Katherine, enamelled on its lid. Misread as the arms of his
more famous niece these ensured this little alepot's loving preservation in the collections of
two famous antiquaries – William Barrett of Lee in Kent, Horace Walpole at Strawberry Hill
and later at Sudeley Castle. The rarity and interest of the Howard Grace cup was recognised
by 1720, when it was discussed by Humfrey Wanley as a possible acquisition for Robert
Harley, Earl of Oxford (Fig. 108).[2]

This recognition of the inherent interest of some old silver was already apparent in the
1640s. When Parliament proposed in 1644 that the contents of the Jewel House should be
sold, pawned or melted down, the House of Lords demurred, on the grounds of the

Fig. 107 **The Parr pot**
Venetian latticino glass, silvergilt mounts and lid. 1546. Mark a fleur-de-lis. H. 14 cm. Made for
William, Lord Parr of Horton, whose arms are enamelled on the lid; later in Horace Walpole's collection
at Strawberry Hill.
Museum of London

veneration in which this plate was held, 'The Fastion of it and the Badges upon it'; the
associations, coupled with the workmanship, made it too valuable merely to melt down.
When the Act for the sale of the late king's goods was passed in 1649, foreign dealers were
invited to bid for the contents of the Jewel House and for the picture collection, since their
potential appeal to the European market was generally recognised. One piece at least, a
crystal bowl, set in jewelled and enamelled mounts, has survived because it passed
immediately into the treasury of a German princely house. It was recognised within a
generation as being to a design by Hans Holbein and is now in the Schatzkammer, Munich
(Fig. 109).[3]

Fig. 108 **The Howard Grace cup**
Sketch made when this ivory cup in silvergilt mounts (1525) was exhibited at a Society of Antiquaries
ballot on 15 January 1741. By 1851 it was the best known piece of English historic plate.
Society of Antiquaries: Minute Book 4, 1741

Fig. 109 **Bowl from Henry VIII's Jewel House**
Rock crystal, mounts silvergilt, gem set and enamelled with mottoes. Its design is attributed to Hans
Holbein. Sold from the English royal collection in 1649–50.
Schatzkammer, Munich

Respect for old objects was shared by all levels of English society and common attitudes
can be traced through the recorded actions of corporate bodies such as colleges and livery
companies, although it is rather harder to reconstruct the motives of private people who have
left no note of their intentions.

Quite why Richard Weoley bought a souvenir of the Siege of Boulogne (Fig. 110) is not
clear. When he bequeathed this silver-mounted and repaired Venetian glass to the Founders'
Company, of which he was twice master (in 1631 and 1640) he left a careful account of its
history. 'My painted drinking glass . . . which by relation was brought from Bullen . . .
when Henry VIII had that place yielded – Pillage taken by a Yeoman (it had descended in the
yeoman's family) which glass I bought for a valuable consideration.' Pride in his Company
prompted the gift of this antique piece; Weoley, anxious to make it the focus of a new
tradition, left it on the understanding that it was only to be used on Election Day when the
retiring master was to toast the new master in 'a Cupp of Hippocrasse'.[4]

Masters' or founders' gifts were particularly valued and often respected because of their
age; at the Armourers' and Braziers' Company, a mazer, given by the first master Everard
Frere at the Company's incorporation in 1453, was carefully lined throughout with silver in
1579. The weight of the 'garnish' of silver on his original gift, thirteen ounces, was inscribed,

Fig. 110 **The Weoley cup**
Venetian gilt and enamelled glass *c*.1500, silvergilt foot 1547. Mark a baton (?). Given to his Company
by Richard Weoley in 1644; purchased from a family whose ancestor had brought the glass back as
booty from the seige of Boulogne, 1544.
Founders' Company

271

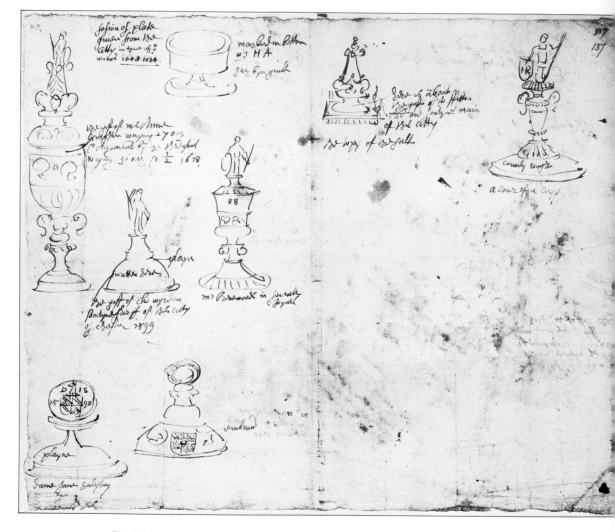

Fig. 111   **'Hasty Sketches of the Fashion of Many large Pieces of Plate given from the City, in tyme of the war'**

Part of the Chester town silver, sketched by Randle Holme II, Mayor of Chester, 1642. The collection was dominated by drinking vessels, some with steeple covers, with a few salts; the donors' arms were more important to record than the fashion, although several are 'curiously wrought'.

British Museum, Harl MS

as was the date of this restoration, presumably necessary because the wood of the bowl had cracked.[5] By that time the Company was well stocked with silver, but this simple wooden bowl had another significance.

Possessions which were recognisably both ancient, and closely associated with a particular society, acquired a special status. The Swan mazer at Corpus Christi College, Cambridge, a medieval joke-piece, was so highly regarded as a college treasure that it was copied in 1579.

The master and fellows presented this facsimile 'now made into the fashion of the said Swan Mazer at all points', to Sir Nicholas Bacon, the Lord Keeper, in gratitude for his generosity to their new chapel.[6]

When Oriel College, Oxford, purchased a secondhand beaker in 1493, the fellows may well have considered it desirable as a supposed relic of their founder, Edward II. Certainly by 1596 it was known as the Founder's cup; presumably the attraction was the combination of the initials E and S and crowns. In fact the piece was made in Paris about 1340 and the initials are those of its wealthy bourgeois owner, but the antiquarian appeal of the assumed association has ensured its preservation.[7]

When a corporate institution fell on hard times and was forced to dispose of historic treasures, prosperous members sometimes stepped in, prompted by sentiment rather than any wish to realise on the value. In 1640 when the Barbers' Company, embarrassed perhaps by its royal associations and imagery, sold a standing mazer given by Henry VIII, the surgeon Edward Arris purchased and re-presented it. Two years later at Oxford, Doctor Accepted Frewen (president of Magdalen College from 1626 to 1642) redeemed from the Oxford Mint for £11 11s 6d one piece of historic college plate, the Magdalen or Founder's bowl and by 1672 had returned it to the college. Although the cup he saved was actually made only forty years before, in 1602, it incorporated as its finial a figure of Mary Magdalen from a rather earlier piece, almost certainly a relic of the founder's time (he had died in 1486). Dr John Dale, a fellow of Magdalen who had concealed some other college treasures, including chapel plate, in 1648, felt it his duty later to commission a replacement of one of these pieces, a large crystal salt, which he had concealed. Unfortunately he had had to pawn the salt to pay his rent. Despite being prepared to give the goldsmith who had bought it 'any rate', Dale was unsuccessful in his attempt to provide a facsimile, because 'having no other pattern but what the Rude idias remaining in our memories suggest, he could make nothing of it'.[8]

A similar pious wish to recreate lost treasures may have stimulated the herald Randle Holme into sketching the Chester civic plate before it was handed over to the royal commissioners in 1643. He recorded the donors' names as well, presumably in the hope (unrealised) that the pieces might be refashioned in better times and their names be engraved on the new copies (Fig. 111).[9]

The Early Collectors

A small demand for old English silver was already apparent by the 1750s, although it was the associations, armorials or curiosity value, rather than the workmanship, which formed the bait and ensured the preservation of such pieces as the Howard Grace cup (VAM), Cardinal Bainbridge's snuffers (BM) or 'Queen Katherine Parr's jug' (the Parr pot, Museum of London, Fig. 107). These motives, particularly the appeal of the curious, were not peculiar to this period. A taste for fantasy pieces was characteristic of European collectors from the early sixteenth century, and the English were not immune, as the New Year's gift lists of the Tudor monarchs demonstrates. By 1600 cabinets of curiosities, like that of Sir Walter Cope, visited by Platter in the 1590s, contained porcelain, shells, nuts and gourds, often with appropriately rich mounts.[10]

There is little visual evidence for this taste for the fantastic, with one exception. An English oil painting of about 1665, now at Norwich Castle Museum, depicts the Paston treasure, family heirlooms of that Norwich family (Plate 2). It shows thirteen pieces of goldsmiths' work, two clearly English, two Dutch and the rest Dutch, Flemish or German. But only two are entirely of silver; one is a flagon embossed with shells of 1597 (now in the Metropolitan Museum) and the other is a simple flat-topped tankard. The rest are all mounted pieces – a strombus shell, mother-of-pearl and nautilus cups, and flasks of tortoiseshell and nautilus shell. Three of these items survive in Dutch museums, and one in the Castle Museum, Norwich, an indication of the continuous status attached to exotica, as compared with standard goldsmiths' wares. In the national collection; a quarter of the English silver before 1660 consists of mounted wares, a disproportionate rate of survival.[11]

Oriental porcelain too has retained its status as a decorative rarity and its popularity in England from the sixteenth century means that certain pieces are well provenanced, with a continuous line of descent to the present. A mounted celadon bowl belonging to New College, Oxford is said to have been a gift from Archbishop Warham before 1530 and a cup at the Percival David Foundation with mounts of 1569 is said to have been given to the Elizabethan gentleman Samuel Lennard.

A large group of mounted porcelain at Burghley House was apparently assembled in the late seventeenth century, although the mounts on the pieces from Burghley are English work of a century earlier (three sold in 1888 are in the Metropolitan Museum of Art). Porcelain was fashionable as interior decoration in court circles after the Restoration, and several mounted pieces such as a blue and white jar (VAM, Plate 4) fitted by Wolfgang Howzer with cast handles to make a curiously proportioned standing cup, were no doubt aristocratic commissions. These were sometimes intended for practical purposes; Barbara Castlemaine used 'a great basin of Chinese porcelain with silver handles' to demonstrate how to make syllabub to a visiting Frenchman, the Sieur Choran du Noyer, in 1671.[12]

At least from the 1750s silver played a significant part in the dressing of the antiquarian interior, which aimed sometimes at recreating a specifically, indeed artificially, gothic appearance, as at Strawberry Hill or Fonthill, and sometimes rather more at reviving a generalised impression of ancient splendour and hospitality, as at Hardwick or Cotehele. In the first case, mounted exotica were essential. William Beckford's eclectic taste procured for Fonthill a Chinese porcelain bottle of about 1300, fitted with enamelled mounts in Europe about 1380. This, the earliest piece of Chinese porcelain recorded in European mounts, had been in the collection of Louis XIV's son and of the French antiquarian Rogier de Gaignieres. The jug, stripped of its mounts, is in the National Museum, Dublin.

There has been a shift of interest; now the quality of the mounts, rather than the exotic material mounted, makes these pieces attractive to museums, particularly since workshops can sometimes be recognised where a group of similarly treated pieces has survived. To design and execute mounts for porcelain, tin-glazed ware, exotic woods or ostrich eggs was the speciality of one late Elizabethan goldsmith (so far unidentified) who had the mark of three trefoils within a trefoil. A crystal salt at the Goldsmiths' Company, a crisply mounted white stoneware jug (VAM) and a porcelain wine jug and bowl from Burghley all bear his mark. Another goldsmith, with a single trefoil mark, apparently carried on this speciality of

274

Fig. 112 **Ostrich egg cup**
Gilt 1623. Mark a trefoil. Engraved on the flag held by Minerva and on the lip is a record that this cup
was given to John Stopes by the parishioners of S. Mary Magdalen, Fish Street, London, in gratitude for
his sermons.
Formerly Swaythling Collection

mounting exotica into the 1620s. They may well have been father and son, or at least in the same workshop. The Jacobean goldsmith mounted, for example, an ostrich egg (Fig. 112) a lignum vitae cup, a mother-of-pearl bowl and the Dyneley casket (an alabaster box) all noteworthy for the quality of their punched and engraved ornament.

Mother-of-pearl plaques, cut from the shell of a marine snail (*Turbo marmoratus*) found in the Pacific, were widely used for bowls, boxes and cups from about 1600, presumably as a result of the opening up of direct trade by the East India Company. An interesting group of mounted mother-of-pearl, assembled by Lady Baillie and now on show at Leeds Castle, includes a York tankard by Thomas Mangey. Most family collections included at least a few mounted shells, hardstones or porcelain. William Beckford's appetite was voracious, in keeping with his emulation of Renaissance collectors.

By about 1800, two parallel strands of antiquarian activity are evident. Gentlemen studied English antiquities, sometimes including silver, their interest stimulated through books and discussions at the Society of Antiquaries so that Walter Scott could satirise the 'antiquary' in a novel in 1815. At the same time, the taste for the antiquarian interior, that style which Horace Walpole had termed 'good King James the first gothic', was spreading, disseminated partly through tours and guidebooks to Strawberry Hill and the reconstructed homes of Walpole's friends, houses such as Lacock Abbey (William Sharington) and the Vyne, near Basingstoke (John Shute).[13]

Old historic houses, like Cotehele on the Tamar which George III visited in August 1789 had become show places, consciously dressed to express the romantic idea of the 'Old English' way of life. Inheriting Browsholme Hall, in Lancashire, in 1797 Thomas Lister Parker remodelled the interior to create a Jacobean great hall and commissioned Jeffrey Wyatt in 1804–5 to create a gothic dining room. A contemporary watercolour shows his oak buffet dressed with what appears to be silver tankards and mounted stoneware jugs; two lignum vitae tankards, one with mounts of 1808, survive at the house, presumably part of this display.

The Prince Regent also had a gothic dining room at Carlton House, designed by Henry Holland. Depicted in Pyne's *Royal Residences* (1819), this was lavishly decked with both old silver and silver in an old style (Fig. 114). Brackets supported covered cups in the fireplace and sideboard laden with massive dishes and candelabra dominated the end of the room. The royal collection was stocked with heavily embossed baroque and chased rococo plate, and the prince clearly had a taste for late seventeenth-century silver – as his purchases from Rundell & Bridge show. He was of course particularly well placed to gratify his interest in picturesque old plate, an interest satisfied sometimes by composite pieces and sometimes by straightforward copies like the 'Jacobean' bowls made by Edward Farrell, copying genuine early seventeenth-century wooden bowls.[14]

The mixture of period detail in such interiors could become eclectic, not to say bizarre. By the 1830s, when Sir Samuel Rush Meyrick published Henry Shaw's *Specimens of Ancient Furniture* (in parts 1832–5; 1836) the demand for authentic material and consistency was generally recognised. As Meyrick said in his introduction 'However beautiful the elegant simplicity of Grecian forms, these are not of themselves enough to produce that effect that should be given to the interior of an English residence.'

In general the contemporary collectors' taste was for 'medieval' objects, preferably associated with a known donor, or mounted hardstones, glass and ceramics rather than wholly silver pieces. Meyrick illustrated ten examples of medieval English goldsmiths' works, mainly from Oxford colleges except the King's Lynn cup. Several were mounted, like Queen Philippa's horn at Queen's and a coconut cup from Oriel. But these were already seen as museum pieces.

By contrast, at least in great houses, certain types of old plate, particularly the large dishes, cups, basins and bottles associated with sideboards had remained constantly in demand and so survived in relatively large numbers. When the dining room layout crystallised in the second half of the eighteenth century, a sideboard dressed with plate emerged as the equivalent of the earlier buffet and, just as before, a mixture of periods and styles was quite usual. Designs for mid-Georgian dining rooms, such as that by Robert Adam for Kedleston,

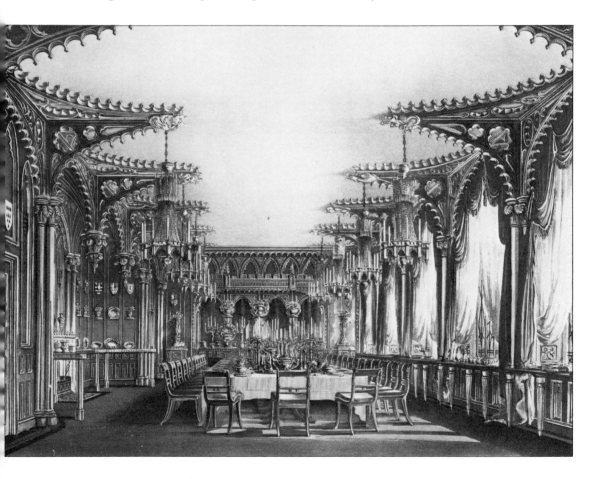

Fig. 113 **The gothic dining room, Carlton House, 1817**
Etching and aquatint by T. Sutherland from Pyne *The Royal Residences.* Note the 'gothic' display silver
on brackets around the fireplace; serving plates and so on are set out for use on the window-sills.
Museum of London

277

show a typical formal display, with pairs of fountains, cisterns, cutlery boxes and dishes of various dates ranged around a semicircular alcove.[15]

Sheraton's sideboards were fitted with brass rails to support silver dishes, so general was the custom. A guide book to Burghley House of 1815 describes the mixture of periods evident in the south dining room display; on 'two sideboards also are four large round dishes, being coronation plate, given to the family by King James II, Queen Anne and George I, several large cups, and a Ewer'. This Burghley custom of displaying plate went back at least to 1763, when the Rev. William Cole, touring country houses with Horace Walpole, commented on the 'Prodigious sideboard of plate, some with Kg James I's cipher on them. Gilt vases of great bigness. The most monstrous large cistern I ever saw big enough to bathe in' (Fig. 114). At Viscount Townshend's home in the 1760s there was a similarly mixed

Fig. 114   **The south dining room, Burghley, 1820**
Etching by Lady Sophia Cecil. A mixture of silver and gilt of many dates; the central fountain and cistern, and the massive late Stuart cistern, are still at the house, as are the Grand Almoner's dishes ranged at the back. The smaller objects, mostly seventeenth century standing cups and tankards, were chosen for their ornamental quality.
John Harris

278

display, with silver sideboard dishes bearing Queen Anne's arms alongside recent purchases from Paul Crespin.[16]

Institutions too retained the old custom; when Philip Hardwick designed a new Hall for the Goldsmiths' Company in 1835, he fitted a niche with shelves behind the high table, to show off their historic plate.

Lavishly worked plate, of whatever age, was always in demand and kept a reasonable secondhand value, but, a distinct market for antique plate can be detected both through the public auctions of major collections and private sales continuously from about 1800. Rundell & Bridge did not publicise their 1808 sale of old royal plate presumably, as John Hayward commented, because although they had allowed the palace only the melt price they were intending to ask much higher prices for its value as historic antique plate. William Beckford is only one of the collectors known to have seized this opportunity. He wrote to his agent Franchi on 16 September 1808 'the old pieces from the Royal silver are divine. I shall accordingly start felling [trees], being persuaded that these salvers and this plate etc will give me great pleasure'. Two of his purchases, a Restoration dish and a William and Mary salver, are a reminder that the royal collection, since the dispersal in 1650, had virtually no earlier silver.[17] The partial dispersal of his collection in 1822–3 was only one of a series of sales, most held by Christie's, which ensured a steady supply of antique plate between 1800 and 1850; much of the silver belonging to Queen Charlotte (sold anonymously in 1818), the Duke of York (1827), George IV and the Duke of Sussex (1843), plus the contents of Strawberry Hill (sold in 1842) and the Stowe sale of 1848 can be documented and their subsequent movements traced, whether to institutions or through private hands. George IV bought several antique pieces at the Duke of York's sale which are still in the royal collection. The Vintners' Company has a superb rosewater ewer with a dish made later to match, both purchased at the Duke of Sussex's sale.[18] A rosewater basin of 1616 in the Holburne Collection can be traced back to Beckford (Holburne paid £60 4s 9d for it at the Lansdown Tower sale in 1845). Frederick the Duke of York's arms are on a plaque over the boss, and Queen Charlotte's initials are engraved on it.

As far as smaller silver was concerned, institutions had no qualms about turning in old tankards, mugs or cups to pay for new plate and many of these found their way onto the antique market rather than to the refiner's furnace. The armorials of colleges or livery companies, with inscribed names and dates, or sometimes the arms of the donor; identify such pieces. A picture-back tablespoon, its bowl die-stamped with the arms of the Goldsmiths' Company, is now in a private collection, while two only from the set remain at the Hall.

By the 1820s the dealer in antique silver had definitely arrived on the London scene although it is significant that Kensington Lewis, apparently the first retailer to lay claim to this speciality on his trade card, was also known especially for his newly made historical plate, copying Tudor and Stuart models.

Sources of Silver

A significant proportion of the Stuart plate on the antique market in the past century was shed by institutions, much of it forced out in various campaigns of reform and closure in the nineteenth century.

Notable were the sales of corporation plate arising from the Municipal Reform Act of 1835. Boston in Lincolnshire in 1837 sold over a thousand ounces of its old plate at auction for about £539, a collection which had been accumulating since 1580. The prices ranged from 5s an ounce for spoons, to 23s an ounce for lot 73, a 'Very Antique Chalice' given in 1626. Its admiralty oar mace of 1725 (now back at Boston) was presented to the Earl Brownlow three years later and found a new home at Belton, to be lent from there to the 1862 Exhibition. Another piece of Boston town plate, a small silver mace of 1682, is part of the Harcourt Collection of maces at the Museum of London. The prices paid in 1837 show that antique plate was fetching by then markedly more than recent pieces; for comparison lot 79, a 'Handsome modern Tea Salver . . . with chased centre and massive embossed edge' given in 1821, made only 7s 2d an ounce.[19]

Silver peculiar to corporations, such as maces, also came onto the market during these nineteenth-century reforms and closures. A mace at the Goldsmiths' Company belonged formerly to the town of Portarlington in Ireland, from which it was sold about 1840, and at the Victoria and Albert Museum may be seen two handsome Stuart maces, of 1663 and 1694.

When the last two Inns of Chancery, Barnard's Inn and Staple Inn, were closed in the late nineteenth century, their possessions, including silver, were dispersed. A pair of wine cups of 1627, given to Barnard's Inn and inscribed with the donor's, Mr Anthony Risbie's name remind us of their past existence. At about this time, two early Stuart cups used at the Court Leet meetings of S. Andrew Holborn, came into the national collection, one 'The gift of John Crane to the quest (inquest) house . . . 1621' and the other given by William Londe in 1617 (VAM).

Livery companies and colleges inevitably sold plate from time to time, the former particularly in the dark days of the 1830s and 1840s. The Blacksmiths' cup, a handsome standing silver cup of 1655, was a special commission, ordered by Christopher Pym as a thanks offering to the Company when he was appointed clerk; a figure of Vulcan wielding a hammer at an anvil forms its stem. But Pym's gift, despite its close associations, was sold by the Company, came into the collection of Ralph Bernal, a wealthy sugar planter (who lent it to the 1850 Exhibition) and subsequently came back to the City again on loan, where it may now be seen at the Museum of London. Another commissioned group to have survived, Simon Owen's ewer and basin made for the Goldsmiths' in 1611, was sold as early as 1637 because building the Company's new Hall had proved burdensome.

In Oxford, the Taylors' Company was disbanded in 1838 and 300 ounces of its plate sold. One of these pieces, a tumbler cup of 1744 presented by William Ives, alderman, to his Company, was seen on the London market recently and Stuart cups from the Oxford and Salisbury Merchant Taylors' Companies are now in the keeping of the Merchant Taylors' Company of London.

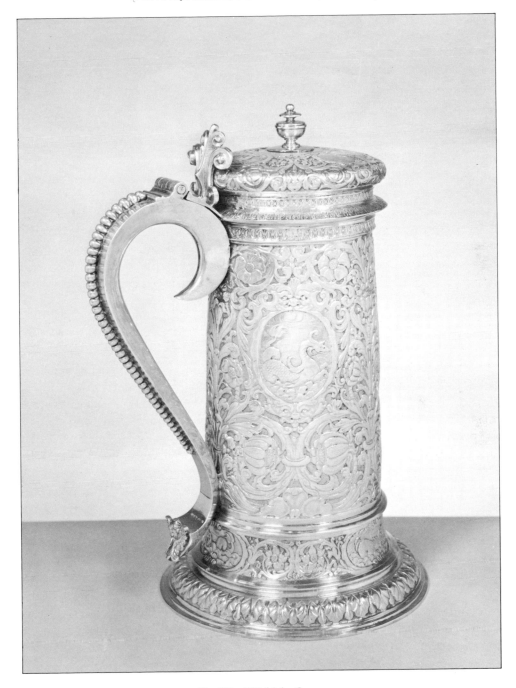

Fig. 115 **Thirkleby flagon**
1646. Mark a hound sejant. H. 26 cm. Chased with flowers, grotesque masks and plaques of marine
monsters; a rare survivor of highly fashioned mid-Stuart silver in the auricular style. One of a pair
formerly in use at Thirkleby church, Yorkshire, made for domestic use.
VAM

281

Fig. 116 **Communion cup**

Gilt 1545. Mark illegible. H.20.5 cm. A typical early Renaissance drinking cup, engraved with a band of
scrolling foliage. Copied for the church in 1649 to make a pair.

S. Margaret Pattens, City of London

Another major source of antique plate in the past century has been sales by churches, not so much of conventional communion cups, flagons and alms dishes (for which there is only a limited demand) but secular silver, given subsequently. Some Tudor cups have fortunately found safe havens in English institutions. The Deane cup (1551, given to All Saints Church, Deane in 1698) was sold by the church in 1971 and bought subsequently by the Hampshire Museums Service; a few years earlier Southampton Museum purchased from S. Michael's Church a tazza, or shallow wine bowl on a foot (1567), with a central scene embossed after a Flemish plaquette. Another standing bowl given in 1711 to the parish of S. Agnes, Cornwall, is now at the Cecil Higgins Art Gallery, Bedford.

A medieval covered bowl, the earliest example of English secular silver (Fig. 2) formerly at Studley Royal Church, Yorkshire, is now in the Victoria and Albert Museum, as is the Kimpton cup (late fifteenth century) and a flagon, one of a pair chased with auricular ornament in 1646, later given to Thirkleby Church (Fig. 115). At the Goldsmiths' Hall are a pair of livery pots of 1594, given to Westwell Church, Kent in 1630 and a standing bowl of 1532 from Arlington Church, plus a late medieval cup, one of the earliest hallmarked drinking vessels (1493) from Middleton Church, Yorkshire. But many other pieces, for example an Elizabethan tankard given to the Rector of Heddington, Oxfordshire in the 1830s, a Stuart tankard from Lambourn and a ewer and basin by Louis Mettayer, formerly at S. Martin-in-the-Fields, are now in private collections or museums overseas.[20]

The arguments for and against selling church plate have been rehearsed many times in the past seventy years, most recently in the consistory court hearing on the S. Mary-le-Bow plate in December 1983. One point sometimes urged is that the piece (particularly if it is a handsome 'domestic' and so saleable one) was not made for church use; but the short list above shows that this is faulty reasoning. Even if not made for church use; they were certainly seen as eminently suitable, at least until the Camden Society and the Tractarians persuaded church people otherwise.[21]

An exhibition held at Christie's in 1955 demonstrated both the quality and the quantity of secular plate of the sixteenth and seventeenth centuries held by English churches.[22] Almost all the pieces whose history is known were gifts; the reasons for this gradual accumulation of domestic silver are not difficult to understand. At the Reformation, the Protestant reformers stressed the eucharist as a common meal to be shared by all worshippers and consciously rejected the Roman Mass chalice, so that their new communion cup took its form from the simplest contemporary standing wine cup. Although the Elizabethan campaign to refashion chalices into communion cups appears to have recommended a standard design, it is clear that a domestic cup, or even a mazer, if one were offered as a gift, was quite acceptable.[23]

Churchwardens saw nothing improper in accepting other secular plate, particularly rosewater basins and flagons, also. A standing cup of handsome proportions and in a contemporary German shape (1545; Fig. 116) was presented to the Church of S. Margaret Pattens in the City sometime after the Reformation and then copied to provide an extra chalice in 1649. The Stuart goldsmith produced an exact facsimile, down to the Roman profile bust engraved below the rim.

A more famous Renaissance cup, now at Cirencester Church, bears English hallmarks of 1535. Traditionally it is said to have been given by Queen Elizabeth to her physician Sir

Richard Masters. He was granted the lands of Cirencester Abbey in 1565 and, it is thought, gave this cup as a thanks offering. Bearing the falcon badge of the Boleyn family, it is presumed to have been that unhappy queen's property. Another secular piece, given as an alms dish after the Reformation (1564) is a basin of 1524 displayed at S. Paul's treasury: only three early Tudor basins are preserved today, all because of their liturgical significance.[24]

In the two centuries after 1600 we find gifts to English churches of livery pots, sweetmeat dishes, salvers, steeple cups, beakers, cage cups, two-handled porringers and bleeding bowls, all given for baptism or for the communion. One parish, S. Mary, Monken Hadley in Hertfordshire, was fortunate in its lord of the manor. In 1619 Richard Emerson presented his church with an elegant curved rosewater ewer (1609, Fig. 74), a covered cup (1586) and a paten, all pounced with the donor's coat of arms; the first two are now on public view, in S. Paul's Cathedral and at the British Museum. The bucket-shaped Elizabethan communion cup was by no means universally adopted and a wide choice of profiles were acceptable in the seventeenth century. Tong in Staffordshire owns, and exhibits a superb crystal drum mounted in silvergilt, given in the 1620s, only a few years after its making.[25]

Steeple cups were clearly also acceptable as handsome altar plate. All Saints, Fulham owns three steeple cups. Two are London-made, and one, originally without a steeple, is German. This one had a steeple added to give it a uniform appearance, matching it up to enhance the display on the altar. There is no discernible pattern in the dates of giving; in 1664 the Hon. Elizabeth Byron gave a steeple cup of 1608 to her church in Nottinghamshire, while a century later (1747) Elizabeth Weedon gave one of 1629 to S. John's Church, Hampstead (VAM, Fig. 14). A pair of 1612 in Skye were apparently bought as chalices that year in London by the local laird, the McCleod of McCleod, at the prompting of King James. Their covers could not of course be used as bread patens for communion because of the steeple, however handsome they might look on the altar at festivals, and as a result not all have retained their covers.[26]

Because the parish was the basic unit for local government in Tudor and Stuart England and because the vestry was given administrative authority, some domestic silver now belonging to churches was intended for vestry meetings, such as the gourd cup belonging to S. Magnus in the City, which is said to be referred to in the *Merry Wives of Windsor*. Tobacco boxes were commonly passed round by the churchwardens at meetings on church business; a handsome silver one of 1766 belongs to S. Botolph, Aldersgate.[27] But some (domestic) pieces explained as gifts to the vestry for convivial use at meetings, were always intended for liturgical use and inscriptions on the plate make the donor's intention clear. For example, in 1684 James Newton gave a steeple cup of 1618 'for Ambleside Church to be used in the Chapel and for no other use'.[28] It seems that there was a period of improper activity during the Commonwealth and there is a rush of inscriptions like 'Mixe not holy things with profane' on plate given after the Restoration. One donor, Eleanor James, went so far as to invoke an anathema on those misusing her gifts to S. Beret Paul's Wharf in the City. They were 'Solely for the Sacrament'; her gifts included a Hamburg-made dish, elaborately embossed.[29]

Parishioners giving domestic plate naturally chose pieces which, although handsome, were no longer fashionable, particularly buffet plate such as steeple cups. Picturesque old plate was seen as particularly suited to a church setting. When in 1697 the churchwardens of S.

Fig. 117 **Hexagonal salt**

Gilt 1550. Mark W over a crescent. H. 14 cm. Treasure trove, found as the inscription says, in 1755 when digging in Stockport. A rare shape, described as 'sixsquare'.

Goldsmiths' Company

Mary Woolnoth in the City needed communion plate, they exchanged old and broken silver for two gilt flagons made a century before and handsomely engraved with a wholly secular subject, monsters among foliage to a design by Nicaise Roussel, no doubt purchased at little above the bulk bullion price because they were out-of-date both in form and ornament (Fig. 79).

Quite apart from the silver shed by churches, institutions and families, chance discoveries have added a little to our stock of early silver. Some was concealed in the ground and rediscovered, like a silvergilt porringer and a French toilet water bottle of about 1680 found in a hole in Parliament Hill in 1892. In 1893 boys out rabbiting near Leominster discovered a cache of four wine cups and three salts, made between 1578 and 1639, several pounced with a wolf's head crest, which were presumably removed from a nearby house and concealed during the Civil War disturbances (Fig. 118). Both were purchased for the national collection, like the Ramsey Abbey censer and incense boat discussed earlier. At Goldsmiths' Hall there is a hexagonal salt of 1550 (Fig. 117) found below a wall at Stockport and recently (1982) a very early spoon, found concealed in the thatch of a Devon farmhouse, was sold by Phillip's for a record price of £13,000.

Fig. 118 **The Stoke Prior treasure**
Wine cup, bell and trencher salts, various dates 1578–1639. Possibly a Civil War deposit (or loss) found
by boys rabbiting near Leominster in 1891.
VAM

As a means of preservation, chance loss is rarer than deliberate concealment, but mudlarks with metal detectors on the Thames foreshore recently retrieved from the silt two silver wine tasters, one of 1634 and the other with a Bordeaux mark, presumably dropped by vintners as they took boat.[30] A very rare item, a Stuart skillet or saucepan lid, now in the Rochester Museum in New York state, was excavated from a nearby Indian grave; a very battered mid-Georgian punch bowl (1764) turned up with native repairs in the Gold Coast after the Ashanti Wars; both had perhaps been trade goods. But the body of knowledge on early silver, which has been accumulating since the early nineteenth century, is not significantly altered by these and other discoveries, which shed light rather on the social history of silver than on its design or manufacture.

The Status of Antique Plate

Once historic plate had become recognisably ancient it was regarded as suitable for use in a formal, ceremonial or even, as we have seen, liturgical setting. Gifts to livery companies illustrate this attitude. The Elizabethan standing salt which John Powell, master, presented to the Vintners' Company in 1702 is still suited to the dining-in-state customary in the livery companies.

Equally, when Thomas Seymour presented the Catherine of Braganza crystal salt to his Company, the Goldsmiths', in 1693 he was no doubt extracting himself fairly cheaply by giving away something with a retail value lower than its original cost, but the Company accepted it with pleasure. They already had a good crystal standing salt of 1601, presented by Richard Rogers in 1632, which was even more out of keeping with contemporary domestic silver, but the two were in harmony as expressing ancient splendour and respect for tradition. The Company had sold plate in 1637 and overhauled their collection in 1664 (and again in 1740) replacing many old pieces but the Gibbon salt (1576; also crystal and given in 1632), the Rogers salt and the Bowes cup were held back on each occasion, and even survived the more drastic overhaul of their collection forced on the Goldsmiths' in 1667, after so much of their income from property had gone up in smoke.[31]

A century later rococo silver was in fashion; it retained its appeal for a hundred years, never becoming merely quaint or antiquarian. Handsome chased covered cups, such as one at the Vintners' by Kandler of 1729 and another at the Goldsmiths' by De Lamerie testify to the peculiarly high esteem enjoyed by this particular type of antique plate. As a matter of course, owners overhauled their plate cupboards regularly, sending silver to be boiled or to have bruises beaten out, as we see from the Wickes/Wakelin ledgers, or to be regilt, all cheaper alternatives to a complete refashioning. Institutions were even more concerned with appearances and ordered restorations of their historic treasures from time to time, often recording their dates on the pieces concerned. The King's Lynn cup, according to inscriptions under its foot, was repaired and 'New Enameled' in 1692, 1750, 1770 and 1782 (Plate 1).[32] The Leigh cup at the Mercers' Company was regilt in 1684, and the badges re-enamelled and a new finial attached earlier this century. The Goldsmiths' Company placed a large order for replacement plate in 1740; nearly a thousand ounces of it was gilt display plate for which William Linnell carved a new 'Beaufet' in their Common Hall; and at the same time their three historic salts, and three cups were regilt or recoloured to match up to the De Lamerie ewer and basin and the four new standing cups.[33]

Churchwardens sometimes did the same, particularly in prosperous town parishes; a Jacobean basin and an Elizabethan cup belonging to S. Peter le Poer were 'Repard and Beautified' in 1792 and again in 1831, as engraved inscriptions record.[34] A Stuart standing paten at Holy Trinity, Cambridge was heavily repaired (indeed, virtually reconstructed on a new core) in 1727, and a basin of 1721 at the Mansion House is engraved with the dates of no less than seven successive repairs and regildings between 1721 and 1886 – an indication both of the store set by it and the heavy wear it had received.

Gilding was the easiest and most commonly found alteration in condition, and was considered particularly appropriate for treasured old plate. The Founders' plate at Corpus Christi, Oxford, for instance, was clearly all regilt on one occasion in the mid-nineteenth century, a fairly costly exercise requiring a conscious decision (not so far documented) on the part of the president. One piece at least, Bishop Foxe's hourglass salt, was regilt with little knowledge of its original condition. When published by Meyrick & Shaw in 1836 (from an earlier watercolour) it retained blue and green glass or enamel sheets behind its openwork panels, but these had gone by the time it was regilt.[35]

The National Collection

From its inception in 1852 the Museum of Science and Art (Victoria and Albert Museum) collected English silver, both contemporary pieces and antique plate. Admittedly in the early years, before the technique of reading hallmarks had become general, attributions were sometimes confused and so pieces now recognised as English were acquired, and subsequently described, as German and Flemish, as was the Dyneley casket. But the art referee J. C. Robinson, initially buying for the museum, was as much trapped by what was currently regarded as desirable, that is intricately decorated pieces of the seventeenth century, as any private collector, and these dominated the early acquisitions. Following this policy, some good objects came in, like a cage cup of 1669 bought in 1864 for £34, and a superb standing cup of 1611 bought five years later for rather more, £260.[36] But mistakes were made; at least two fakes, both mounted pieces, were purchased in the 1860s.

These early purchases fulfilled Robinson's demand for ornamental plate; 'merely usable plate' could not in his opinion be regarded as decorative art and was, therefore, not desirable. As a result of this policy the national collection is still weak in dinner plate, entrée dishes and other standard Georgian tableware, although it is well provided with casters, cruets and creamers. The dealer William Chaffers was sometimes able to persuade Henry Cole, the energetic first secretary of the museum, to buy despite Robinson's opposition. In 1865, a good year for purchases, the museum acquired the Dyneley casket, an alabaster box which has long been recognised as coming from the workshop of a Jacobean goldsmith who specialised in mounting up exotic materials. Another purchase of the same year, a chinoiserie sugar box bought on Chaffers's recommendation, provoked Robinson to a furious minute; 'the best of these specimens even, under any circumstances would have been scarcely worthy of a place in the Museum, whilst all of them had been purchased at a very extravagant rate . . . Mr Chaffers' acquired knowledge is only enough to give him a dangerous amount of self-confidence' (Fig. 22).

The most expensive acquisition of those first forty years of the national collection of English silver again represented a fashionable collector's item. It was a large Elizabethan standing salt, offered by Lord Mostyn to the museum at a much higher price (2,000 guineas) than Cripps or the secretary felt reasonable. But when Lord Mostyn agreed to add three smaller salts and a caster associated with the drum salt, the purchase was agreed and these pieces have been for nearly a century (1886) an ornament to the early English silver collection. The provenance was regarded as impeccable and they were assumed to be old family possessions since the sixteenth century. But the family history, including massive confiscations in the Civil War, make this continuous descent unlikely; the present condition of the salts (and of the historic Mostyn plate sold subsequently) suggests the possibility of an antiquarian collector sometime during the eighteenth century.

Certainly several of the Mostyn pieces show signs of alteration; the salts in the national collection have been heavily regilt, so much so that the caster can no longer be unscrewed, a classic restorer's oversight when refurbishing antique plate for the collector. Heavy gilding had the advantage of concealing the traces of inserts and losses to the original, so could be regarded by the seller as a desirable addition. So few elaborate sixteenth-century pieces have been preserved and even fewer in unaltered condition that careful inspection is needed to decide which features are original and which additions. Often they are single examples; two early Jacobean wine cups in the national collection, one purchased in 1902 and the other in 1907, have damaged stems but their original profiles cannot be constituted as there are no exact parallels to follow.

With the aid of spectrographic analysis, it is possible to determine the constituents of any part of a silver vessel (as long as gilding and solder are not present), and this has been an increasingly useful aid in determining which pieces are in original condition and which have been modified. Those catalogues giving English silver draw on these analyses.

Exhibitions and Collectors

Although catalogues of church and college plate are largely a development of the 1880s and later, a string of public exhibitions from 1850 whetted the public appetite, and introduced historic plate to a wider audience than that coterie of antiquaries familiar with civic and local collections through the tours organised annually by the Archaeological Association in the 1840s, and through papers read to the Society of Antiquaries.

The purpose of the first, the Exhibition of Works of Ancient and Medieval Art held in the Great Room at the Society of Arts in 1850 was, as its organising committee declared, to complement the better known Exhibition of Works of Industry (the Great Exhibition) to be held the following year and 'would not only be extremely interesting to the Public but would also be useful to Manufacturers', since the exhibits were chosen 'with reference to their beauty of form or for the practical illustration they afford of processes of manufacture'. To ensure that craftsmen had a proper opportunity to benefit, a special low (threepence) entry fee for 'artisans' was introduced for the last fortnight of the exhibition. The assemblage of rich

Fig. 119 **Conversazione at Ironmongers' Hall 1861**
Etching. The splendour of the historic silver, massed both in a temporary buffet the width of the room,
and in the niche, demonstrates why the better known 1862 Exhibition at South Kensington drew so
heavily on the livery companies.
Museum of London

silver, jewels and hardstones was described as rivalling both Beckford's and Walpole's collections.[37]

While neither dates of making nor attributions to English goldsmiths were provided for the silver shown at this exhibition (Octavius Morgan's papers explaining the marks on early English silver was not read until 1852), it was the first opportunity for the general public to see an assemblage of historic plate. The royal family lent a nautilus cup; Prince Albert was president with a distinguished committee including two dukes, two earls and a marquis. A. W. Franks, then only 24, was honorary secretary. Livery companies and colleges lent plate and a few individual collectors, notably Ralph Bernal and Prince Soltykoff. But there was no old family plate from the great houses; the bulk of the identifiably English silver came from retail goldsmiths – Garrard's, Hunt & Roskell, Lambert & Rawlings – whose control of the antique market was already firmly established.

Lenders to this and to the Exhibitions of 1862 at South Kensington, 1868 (National

Exhibitions of Works of Art at Leeds) and 1869 (Manchester Art Treasures) such as Hollingsworth Magniac, Augustus Franks (later Keeper of Medieval Antiquities at the British Museum) and John Dunn-Gardner were not offering as exhibits plate inherited from their families' historic collections but showing prizes consciously assembled in the market place. Their taste in early plate, or rather the limited choice available to collectors, is clear from the 1862 Exhibition to which, for example, Sir Thomas Holburne lent a large part of his collection. This, at the Holburne of Menstrie Museum in Bath, is dominated by examples of embossing, chasing and generally ornamental plate of the late Elizabethan, Jacobean and late Stuart periods.[38]

English silver made up 282 of the 400 or so pieces of plate exhibited in 1862. Of the early (pre-1600) plate lent by private owners, twenty out of forty-seven were mounted objects – mazers, an ostrich egg, Chinese porcelain and a rock crystal candlestick – but the great majority were German stoneware jugs. Some of these, from Ralph Bernal's Collection (sold in 1855), are now in the national collection at the Victoria and Albert Museum. The collection of silver formed at about this time by Augustus Franks was equally dominated by mounted pieces. The British Museum, to which Franks left his collection, is rich in other superb Elizabethan silver but the bulk are mounted, including Iznikware and glass.[39] The 1862 Exhibition was immensely popular; nearly 900,000 people visited it in five months.

Another exhibition of 'rare works of art and antiquities' held the year before, the Ironmongers' Hall Conversazione, is rather less well known, although fully reported at the time. It ran for only four days and entrance was by invitation; so the attendance of 4,000 people was remarkable.

This was probably the first exhibition to include English silver at which hallmarks and date-letters were quoted. William Chaffers was on the committee (his *Hallmarks on English Silver* first appeared two years later, in 1863) and managed to extract loans of historic plate not only from twenty-four livery companies but also from private lenders, notably John Beresford Hope, John Dunn-Gardner, Henry Durlacher and J. P. Dexter. One dealer, George Lambert (of Lambert & Rawlings) lent heavily but Hunt & Roskell lent a German standing cup only. The plate was set out on two massive buffets dominating the Livery Hall, 'one blaze of beauty not only for archaeological eyes but for lovers of artistic excellence of every period' (Fig. 119). The most recent piece, in an admittedly miscellaneous display, was a newly made claret jug with silvergilt mounts 'designed after the manner of Cellini' and presented to the master of the Ironmongers' Company in 1860.[40]

The Howard Grace cup, also shown at Ironmongers' Hall in 1861, was well known to antiquarians. It had been discussed by the Society of Antiquaries in the previous century (in 1741 and 1768, and published in 1808 and 1851), and in the catalogue of the 1861 Conversazione (which was not published till 1864) its supposed association with Thomas à Becket was refuted. But despite Chaffers's help with choosing loans and with the catalogue, the date-letter was misread as 1445.

A centenary exhibition at Bath in 1982, which brought out the Holburne silver, demonstrated the preferences of one early Victorian collector. His taste was for gilding, and for adding his heraldry wherever possible, preferences he shared with two earlier collectors William Beckford and the Duke of Sussex, and were characteristic of contemporary

Fig. 120 **Bowl with later embossing**
1796. Mark illegible. A typical plain neo-classical bowl, presented to S. James Garlickhythe by the rector
Charles Goddard as a baptismal bowl twenty-five years later and redecorated with embossed rococo
scrolls and flowers over the original arms.
S. James Garlickhythe

attitudes. Equally typical was his cheerful acquisition of objects which to a modern eye are
spoilt by later chasing, like a porringer and cover by the hound sejant maker of 1660, or
altered to make them more attractive to later taste, like the porringer of 1671, which has been
extensively chased and had a foot added in the nineteenth century to turn it into a sugar
basin.[41]

A marginal piece is a two-handled cup of 1675, chased and embossed with flowers and
animals. To this has been added diaper chasing, matting, lambrequin ornament around the
rim and a cartouche with the initials and arms of the Duke of Sussex, from whose sale
Holburne purchased it with other, better, plate in 1843. This cup may not have been

ANTIQUARIES, COLLECTORS, FAKERS

enhanced with intent to deceive; a cover, fully hallmarked, was added to it in 1777 to make it functional in current terms.

But two at least of the Holburne pieces are clearly confections for the collector's market, designed, as Philippa Bishop comments in the 1982 Exhibition catalogue, 'by a 19th century craftsman who specialised in producing elaborate pieces of Tudor iconography adapted from earlier tankards'. One, an unmarked peg tankard, is replete with embossed Tudor badges and three massive acorn and oakleaf feet with 'Henricus Rex . . . 1527' (in reference to Henry VIII's assumption of the title Defender of the Faith in that year) engraved under the base. The other, a tankard hallmarked 1683, is heavily embossed with portraits of Queen Elizabeth and William Cecil and bears a Latin inscription about the queen. The incongruity of this ornament was not apparently recognised at that time, since both pieces were included as authentic Tudor plate in the 1862 and 1868 loan exhibitions. Another object, made to satisfy the appetite for historical relics is the so-called Saxon or 'Earl Godwin's cup' at Berkeley Castle. This was reconstructed about 1800 or so from a mace head bearing the London hallmark for 1610.

Fakes, Forgeries and Spurious Marks

The extravagance of the pieces just discussed is unusual; most silver identifiably altered or modified for the collector has been more discreetly and knowledgeably handled. The history of nineteenth-century fakes of antique plate has still to be written, but the comments of Williams Cripps in the 1878 and later editions of his *Old English Plate* indicate that a century ago a thriving if illegal cottage industry was at work to satisfy collectors' demands in the shortage of genuine old plate. Cripps explained that seventeenth-century silver, which had been much collected earlier in the century and, therefore, heavily faked, had fallen out of fashion and 'the market is now flooded with plain and fluted plate (of Queen Anne or the earlier Georges) which is made to all appearance, both at home and abroad, and brought hither by the waggon load'. Charles Eastlake (in 1867) also wryly described the commoner forms of faking and altering plate to be met with over a century ago.[42]

The problem of fabrication was recognised. In the foreword to the 1855 sale of Ralph Bernal's collection, an exceptional sale which ran from 5 March to 30 April, Planché admiringly commented that Bernal was 'Distinguished amongst English Antiquaries by . . . the extent of his knowledge, the difficulty of imposing upon him was increased by the necessity of the fabrication being fine enough in form, colour or workmanship to rival the masterpiece it simulated'; a mounted gourd, in the style of 1600 or so, has punched ornament in the 'Egyptian' taste of 1800 to 1810, and was probably not made to deceive but as a piece of fashionable decorative art around 1840 (VAM, purchased 1865). The profitable creation of 'antiques' was well under way by the 1840s.

The demands of the collector's market could only be satisfied by supplementing the tiny stock of genuine pieces in good condition with marriages, alterations and additions and outright fakes. The creativity of the dealers in Renaissance works of art is well known; the Castellani family can take credit for '16th century' jewels, and other examples of goldsmiths' work but identifying the craftsmen who worked with antique plate is more difficult. A

293

Fig. 121a, b, c **Caster with inserted marks**
*c.*1710. Originally struck on the base with maker's mark (SW) only, repeated. A disc, fully marked for,
was later soldered in, to make the caster more saleable as a dated antique.
Assay Office

recently published catalogue of the Schroder Collection separates out some historicist pieces formerly described as sixteenth or seventeenth century but now recognised as nineteenth century. In the 1860s J. C. Robinson, art referee for the South Kensington Museum (VAM) commented that Bath was notorious as a source of forgeries of silver.

The demand for antique silver, both here and in America, was constantly growing and inevitably the collectors' stress on hallmarked pieces stimulated a flood of forged marks. A pamphlet on the Lyon and Twinam forgeries issued by the Goldsmiths' Company in 1899 (to the trade only) listed the sets of forged date-letter, duty mark, maker's mark and sterling punches discovered on the London premises of these two men. Thirty-eight punches for date-letters for the years between 1719 and 1830 had been seized on an earlier search of Reuben Lyon's Holborn shop;[43] an early photograph shows his bottle glass windows crammed with old silver, a useful cover for these spurious pieces.

A recent article on these two cases, described at the time as 'the largest and most important seizure of forged antique silver plate in the history of the Goldsmiths' Company' follows in fascinating detail the complexities of the investigation and subsequent treatment of the two men. Two rooms in Twinam's house yielded almost 900 articles, all of sterling silver; about half were marked with forged punches and all imitated antique silver of between 1720 and 1830. Although all that was seized then was destroyed, pieces with these forged marks still turn up. Twinam's output over a number of years must have run to thousands of items. Apart from exporting to America, Lyons sold his spurious antique plate through trade outlets such as pawnbrokers.

A popular late Victorian collector's item was the porcelain goat and bee jug, a design produced by Nicholas Sprimont at his Chelsea factory from about 1750. Goat and bee jugs of silver are also found, with Sprimont's mark struck on the base and hallmarks for years as late as 1777, six years after he died and more than a quarter of a century after he abandoned silversmithing for porcelain. One is reproduced in Jackson's *History of English Plate* (figure 1351), and another is in the interesting collection of English silver at the Huntington Library, California. These silver goat and bee jugs were apparently cast from a porcelain original and the hallmarks on the base either cast or cut out and set in from a genuine piece of silver, to create an attractive and instant antique, with the advantage of a famous maker's name (Fig. 122).

Another Huntington piece, a mug marked by Thomas Mangey of York in 1678, has a strap handle struck with the Hull town mark. It is just possible that this anomaly is attributable to legitimate trade practice, since runs of components were sent for marking before assembly and members of the closeknit Mangey family were working as goldsmiths in both York and Hull, but it is more likely that the handle has been made up from an earlier spoon, legitimately marked in Hull.[44]

Repairers often used old plate; the flange of a covered dish in the Calverley toilet service (VAM 1683) is clearly a strip cut out of a cup with part of the coat of arms still visible. Less easily explained is a tankard chased with crisp chinoiseries (VAM) whose lid and body have respectively two workmen's marks and two hallmarks.[45]

An interesting faked piece produced about 1900 is a German tigerware jug with silver straps, neckmount and cover. The mounts are apparently constructed from an Elizabethan

Fig. 122 **Goat and bee jugs**
Gilt. With false marks in the base for London 1777, maker Nicholas Sprimont. These jugs were cast,
presumably from genuine examples in Chelsea porcelain.
Goldsmiths' Company

cup and paten cover, embossed for its new role with masks, strapwork and fruit. While the
hallmarks are genuine, the maker's mark (otherwise unrecorded) is probably a forgery. The
extraordinary demand among collectors for mounted wares at the turn of the century no
doubt accounts for this creation, which is by no means unique.[46]

Practices alter according to the demand of the market, as collectors of wine labels and
caddy spoons are all too well aware today. A toasting fork in the Victoria and Albert Museum
attracted attention because of its solid silver rod which seemed an apparently inconvenient
device. When examined, its grip turned out to be the handle from a cruet frame, fully marked
but reassembled in a new guise. Cutlery has its own pitfalls, described and illustrated in Ian
Pickford's recent book; the conversion of spoons into the rarer and more highly priced two-
or three-pronged fork is probably the easiest to recognise but apostle spoons are also a
dangerous area.[47]

The value added by an invented provenance is also not new; the antique market was
already familiar with this means of authenticating old silver in the 1870s, as Cripps describes.
The potent appeal to collectors of 'Real old family plate', sold 'in strictest confidence' and
with the armorials erased to avoid publicity and further embarrassment to the purported
original owners, was already recognised and manipulated to give colour to dubious pieces.[48]

There is of course a fine line between legitimate alteration and fraud. The appetite for relics, preferably associated with royal martyrs or heroes such as Mary Queen of Scots, Bonnie Prince Charlie, Charles I or Admiral Nelson has raged for almost two centuries. Characters from British history whose initials, armorials or badges appear on works of art enhance the interest and, therefore, the value of the silver, textile or jewellery in question. Often these elements were added relatively recently to reinforce an association. The National Maritime Museum has a collection of Nelson silver inscribed with his initials and armorials, as though given by Horatio Nelson to Emma, all made well after his death. An early beaker, recently exhibited at the Goldsmiths' Company, bears the pounced initials TW. These were firmly considered those of Thomas Wolsey, until research into its history demonstrated that a previous owner, in direct line, was Thomas Whately (1685–1765).

Two loans to the Ironmongers' Hall Conversazione, both from Lambert, show the commercial appeal such association were thought to have; this dealer lent cutlery 'engraved by Hogarth' and 'Josuha Reynolds' tea caddy case'.

Antique Silver since 1900

By 1900 the collectors' market was flourishing and able to support several specialist periodicals (*The Burlington Magazine* started in 1903, *Connoisseur* in 1901 and *Apollo* in 1925) all containing dealers' advertisements and accounts of recent auction sales. An early *Connoisseur* of 1901 had articles, for example, on the plate of the Innholders' Company, collecting old Sheffield plate and reading hallmarks. With the shortages and high prices of genuine old silver, Sheffield plate was just becoming collectable; 'it is only within the last decade (from about 1890) that Sheffield plate has attained to the dignity of finding itself among those objects which arouse the cupidity of the collector' (*Connoisseur* 1901). In 1924, Bradbury included examples of Sheffield plated candlesticks made three years earlier from dies of the 1760s, as a guide and a warning to collectors.

By the 1890s the drift of fashion towards the ideas of William Morris in interior decoration and the taste for uncluttered, simple forms had further stimulated demand for antique silver of the early eighteenth century, whose characteristic angular shapes and soft patina were seen as harmonious. 'We rummage Lambert's or Carrington's (two prominent dealers in antique plate) for real old Georgian silver punch-bowls to use as centrepieces', as Rosa Crandon Gill commented in the *Art-Journal* 1891; Queen Anne taste, commented on as fashionable in reviews of the 1878 Paris Exhibition, was for a fretted busy style which is not recognisable to a modern eye as of the early eighteenth century.

Two important exhibitions of silver, held in 1901 at the Burlington Fine Arts Club and in 1902 at S. James Court, drew for the first time on the great ducal houses (Knole, Belvoir and Welbeck), although Sir Samuel Montague (with other collectors) also lent lavishly. In the 1902 Exhibition attributions to makers were only given occasionally, with the exception of De Lamerie, whose name and mark had never been forgotten. By 1924 it was considered helpful by the Burlington Fine Arts Club to hold an exhibition of 'Counterfeits, Imitations and Copies' of works of art in which Dutch fakes and cast spoons featured.

At the 1862 Exhibition medieval had been generously interpreted as encompassing silver as late as 1750. By 1900 the subject was more subtly subdivided but at the Burlington Fine Arts Club Exhibition the emphasis was still on silver made before 1700, and particularly ornate Elizabethan pieces, a recognition of the prevailing taste which remained a factor in auction prices too until shortly before the Second World War. The appetite for mounted pieces continued to be fierce; a tin-glazed earthenware jug from West Malling Church, Kent (with mounts of 1581) was sold in 1903 for £1,522, a record at the time, although admittedly it was a great rarity in ceramics too and well publicised because of its provenance. Prices are hard to compare because of the extraordinary shifts in the value of money and of antiques in the course of this century but the prices for mounted stoneware jugs certainly dropped from their peak of around 1900, perhaps because of a general unease about the way in which old mounts could be (and had been) transferred from one piece to another, to create saleable antiques. Prices continued to be quoted as so much per ounce in the sale room reports well into the 1930s. E. A. Jones and other scholars like Moffat and Freshfield laid open all the historic collections of English institutions – Windsor Castle, the colleges of Oxford and Cambridge and London's churches. Jones followed in Cripps's steps to Russia and wrote up the superb plate purchased by, or given to, successive tsars and tsarinas since the sixteenth century.

A very popular exhibition of Elizabethan art was organised, again by the Burlington Fine Arts Club, in 1926 and an exhibition limited to English silver was held in aid of Queen Charlotte's Hospital in 1929. By this time silver from several historic family collections had been dispersed – Burghley in 1888, the Plomer-Ward heirlooms in 1914, the Ashburnham in 1914, the Foley Grey in 1921 (although some of this was repurchased for Dunham-Massey or sold quietly through the trade – Crichton in particular was buying for Baron Bruno Schroder, whose collection is one of the few containing important Tudor silver in private hands in England).

Some famous collections of English silver were formed and dispersed between 1850 and 1940. John Dunn-Gardner, who had lent to the 1862 Exhibition, introduced his collection (which extended from the sixteenth century to the rococo period) to the general public by lending it to the Victoria and Albert Museum from 1870. When it was sold in 1902, the museum, and the Goldsmiths' Company, made purchases of historic plate. The preference of Sir Samuel Montague (Lord Swaythling) was for mounted pieces and early silver generally, as the massive sale in 1924 demonstrated. This collection was also seen at the museum for many years; some of his pieces were acquired by the national collection, others by J. P. Morgan. Several are in the Metropolitan Museum.

Two good collections of plain late Stuart silver, one a gift in memory of A. J. Carter in 1927, the second put together by Captain C. D. Rotch before and after the First World War, came to the Victoria and Albert Museum; the latter, initially a loan, was bequeathed in 1962. During this period, up to 1938, wealthy American collectors were very active in Europe; J. P. Morgan's collection, when catalogued by E. A. Jones was well stocked with early pieces. These have been released into the market in a series of sales since the Second World War; in the most recent, held at Christie's in New York in 1982, an early Tudor beaker made a world record price for a piece of sixteenth-century silver, a quarter of a million dollars.

The market in antique plate is as much subject to waves of fashion as any other aspect of taste. While there has always been competition for Paul De Lamerie's silver, his rococo work was less highly valued than the Britannia standard wares until relatively recently. However, a high rococo coffee pot of 1738 (by De Lamerie, Plate 7) and an equally inventive ewer and basin by George Wickes set new heights in 1983, the first selling in New York for a quarter of a million dollars and the second in London for £176,000; both are now owned by the same collector.

Very little unrecorded English silver of real importance has turned up in London in the past half century. Some was sold from Russian collections in the 1930s and there is a steady trickle of sales from country houses, notably Belton and Althorp. Occasionally museums in the United States sell silver, in order to buy other items, but these do not normally return across the Atlantic.

There are occasional surprises. Sometimes churches own unexpected items, for example Fig. 115 and recently a very rare fifteenth-century spoon with a wodewose (wild man) terminal has turned up in America, still in the possession of the family whose ancestress emigrated, with the spoon, from Cornwall in 1848. In 1983 a Dorset landowner sold to the Victoria and Albert Museum a nautilus cup with mounts of 1557, which had apparently descended in his family for four centuries, and in 1984 an extraordinarily rare object, a silvergilt casting bottle (1553) was sold at Sotheby's, having gone unrecognised and so survived without later regilding; it had been sold as brass quite recently (Plate 1).

Four notable private collections have come to English museums in recent years. The British Museum has a collection of Huguenot silver, small but unrivalled in quality, bequeathed by Peter Wilding; the Manchester Museum and Art Gallery has a collection of late seventeenth- and eighteenth-century silver, largely teaware and candlesticks, formed by Mr and Mrs Assheton Bennett and at Nottingham Castle Museum may be seen the smaller but high quality, eighteenth-century collection of Richard Gibbs, a local jeweller and goldsmith. The Ashmolean Museum, in the Carter and Farrer Collections, has perhaps the largest concentration of high quality De Lamerie silver – from the early Treby toilet service to his shell baskets of the 1740s – and more De Lamerie was at Cheltenham, where the Dowty Collection was recently on loan.

Apart from the specialist clubs for collectors of wine labels, corkscrews, caddyspoons and other small silver, two societies devoted to the study of English silver flourish in England, stimulating their members through visits to collections, papers on recent research and study tours of museums and private collections here and overseas. One, the Silver Society, publishes annual proceedings while the Silver Study Group, more recently established, concentrates on talks and visits.

Although there have been few exhibitions recently of the scale of those extravaganzas between the wars and in the early 1950s, such as the Queen Charlotte's of 1929, Goldsmiths' Hall holds annually a short exhibition on a related theme, such as the history of hallmarking, or silver in the service of wine, and 1984 saw a major exhibition on the rococo in England (VAM). Another in 1985 focused on the Huguenots, to mark the Revocation of the Edict of Nantes (Museum of London). While at the Goldsmiths' Company *A Place for Gold* told the story of its successive Halls.

Add to these occasional delights the permanent displays in our cathedrals and civic treasuries and it can be seen that the student of English silver has now a greater chance than ever before of studying his subject. A critical approach to old acquisitions is gradually refining the displays in the national museums, so that either objects substantially altered from their original condition are removed into store or their full history, so far as it can be reconstructed, is explained to illuminate their present condition. The distinction between legitimate repair and alteration and the active interference of such nineteenth-century dealers as Frédéric Spitzer is now more generally recognised, and if this means that some old favourites are no longer visible in our national collections, or heavily qualified, then perhaps pieces of great quality but less well known may take the limelight.

Notes

1   Grimwade 1976: 'Thomas Jefferys'; Hayward 1959, 145; introduction to Christie's catalogue of Brownlow sale, 29 May 1963.

2   It was shown to the Antiquaries in 1741. Other plate shown included the Bainbridge snuffers (BM) in 1745 and 1774. One of the Rochester covered bowls was shown in 1829. Culme 1985 quotes others.

3   For the 1644 comment, see Collins 1955, 188; Hayward 1968, 120–4.

4   Goldsmiths' Company 1951, 16. Ch. 14.

5   Ellis 1892.

6   Fitzwilliam 1975, 16 and references quoted there. As the mazer is quite small, its interest was in its rarity and oddity, not its metal.

7   Lightbown 1978, 22–3, pl. XIX. This beaker (with another small cup) cost Oriel £40s 18d in 1493. It has the mark of a Paris maker, c.1440. See Varley, 'The Founder's Cup at Oriel', Connoisseur, CXVIII (June 1946), 36–7.

8   Hayward 1983, 160–5.

9   Randle Holmes's sketches are bound up with a collection of Chester papers; in BM Harl. MS. 2125.f. 316/317C.

10   Discussed in Collins 1955, 101–8. See Hayward 1976 for pieces and MacGregor 1983.

11   Hayward 1976, 311 for cabinets.

12   Glanville 1984.

13   But the antiquarian first Earl of Mount Edgcombe had undoubtedly purchased some antiquities to dress the great hall. At Burghley, the ninth Earl of Exeter had an exact copy of a 1609 steeple cup made in 1758: Webster 1984, 11 and 12; Collard 1985.

14   For example, Bury, Wedgwood, Snodin 1979, pl. 8. Composite pieces and copies, particularly of sideboard plate, were the speciality of Kensington Lewis: Culme 1975. See p. 118–21.

15   A French jar of c.1660 converted to a fountain,

and copied to make a pair, with two cisterns, the latter all made by Francis Leake in the 1690s. Adam had further alterations made to the jars, giving them neo-classical square plinths: Wilson 1983.

16   Rev. William Cole's tour, 1763; Wilmarth S. Lewis 1961, Vol. 10, 346. Goldsmiths' Company MSS, Townshend Plate Book.

17   Snodin and Baker 1980 illustrate other examples and copies of old plate ordered by Beckford.

18   The Vintners' set, given by John Tanner Kaye on 26 October 1843, consists of a basin by Harache (1705) and an ewer by Pitts (1811), both with the arms of Augustus Frederick, Duke of Sussex. Sideboard dishes in seventeenth-century style, made by Edward Farrell for the Duke of York and bought by the Duke of Wellington in 1827, may be seen in the dining room at Stratfield Saye: Bishop 1982, 2.

19   Hull too sold 1,500 ounces of civic plate in 1836, but started reacquiring within half a century. Three waiters came back in 1877, from a set of six 'for a glass' bought in 1738. The auction price in 1836 (£18 16s 3d) was within a few shillings of their original cost. Alec-Smith 1973, 49 and Appendix C.

20   The British Museum has the Rochester standing bowls and the Stapleford acorn cup. The Lambourn tankard is in the Metropolitan Museum of Art, New York and the MFA, Boston, has another acorn cup. The West Malling jug is in Scotland.

21   Goldsmiths' Review, 1969–70, 16–18; Alec-Smith 1973.

22   Christie's 1955. Some were sold subsequently. Two Exeter and two Colchester churches still own sixteenth-century mazer bowls.

23   As late as 1843 an Elizabethan tankard was presented to Holy Trinity, Arlington; this has now been sold.

24   Hayward 1976. Two are at Corpus Christi,

Oxford, given by Bishop Foxe, and a third belongs to S. Magnus in the City. An earlier basin (*c*.1400) is at Canterbury, Oman 1979, 49–52.

25 Freshfield 1894; Christie's 1955.

26 Freshfield 1894; Penzer, n.d. and 1959, *passim*.

27 Freshfield 1895; Oman 1957.

28 Freshfield 1894; Oman 1978, pl. 45 and 46. One is now in Vancouver, the other in S. Paul's treasury.

29 Phillips 1982, 22 January, lot 181, £13,000. A set of spoons was found in the wall of a ruined church in the 1960s; now in the Worcester Museum. In the 1862 Exhibition, item 5856 was a gold 'chocolate cup and cover found in the lake at Knowsley' lent by the Earl of Derby, presumably also stolen.

30 The 1634 taster is in the Museum of London.

31 Milbourn 1888; Carrington and Hughes 1926.

32 Penzer 1946; Lasko & Morgan frontispiece, 27–8.

33 Goldsmiths' Company committee minute book.

34 On loan to VAM; Freshfield 1894. Masters 1978 quotes other examples, 301–14.

35 Campbell, 1984.

36 Oman 1965. The date-letters on both were correctly read.

37 Society of Arts 1850.

38 International Exhibition 1862; Bishop 1982.

39 Read and Tonnochy 1928; Wilson 1984.

40 Ironmongers' 1869.

41 Bishop 1982.

42 Cripps 1881, 145–7. A good list of the commoner forms of ffaking marks (and objects) is in Goldsmiths' 1978, Forbes 1969, Grimwade 1982.

43 Goldsmiths' 1889; Johnson 1983, 25–36.

44 Wark 1978, 128, 22.

45 This was an early acquisition (1865) but the oddity of the crisp chasing around worn hallmarks should have been suggestive.

46 Forgery of marks still occurs. In May 1971 a Sheffield silversmith was found guilty of forging London and Sheffield marks of the late eighteenth/ early nineteenth century on to modern teapots, candlesticks and a tankard, in antique style. A Genoese firm, Paroli, put late Georgian marks on to modern Georgian silver. Grimwade 1982, illustrates some cups altered to make them more saleable.

47 Pickford 1983, 67–70.

48 Cripps 1878, 146. A covered cup of 1649 at Williamsburg (Davis 1976, pl. 44) has crudely scratched on the base: 'Purchased At Strawbery Hill'. It cannot be identified in the 1842 sale catalogue and the inscription was almost certainly added later to give it false colour.

FOURTEEN

THE SOCIOLOGY OF SILVER: GIFTS AND OBLIGATIONS

ATTITUDES to silver have remained constant for at least five centuries. Par excellence it was the gift for one's king, one's patron, one's brotherhood, the parish church, the local hero and one's heirs; and always a cup was the first choice. In 1478, when the Goldsmiths' Company elected to make two cups from the diets or sample scrapes taken by their assayer they were deliberately enhancing the dignity of their court dinners. In the lotteries popular between the 1560s and the early eighteenth century cups were always prominent among race prizes, and the milkmaids parading in their finery on Mayday crowned their headdresses with two-handled cups (Fig. 124).

In eighteenth-century England, silver was essential to both those rites of passage, baptism and burial. Quite apart from the normal gifts, a silver christening bowl was often used, and in funeral processions parish officers walked at the front with their silver-headed staves draped in black.

Certain occupations were distinguished by their silver badges, like those worn by the admiralty bargemen until the mid-nineteenth century, or the badge of the king's messengers. One recently on the London market was made in 1720–3 by Francis Garthorne; it weighs six ounces and the cast parcel-gilt lion and unicorn support the Garter badge, with a silver greyhound suspended below. Poverty and old age could be a route to wearing, if not owning, silver; the badges issued to almsmen from the sixteenth century were sewn onto their cloaks. These were often large and heavy, depicting the benefactor (as on badges from a Westminster almshouse; Museum of London; Victoria and Albert Museum) or incorporating some local reference (Fig. 123).

In London, silver was an essential element in the traditional Mayday festivities referred to above. On that day, as a French visitor records in 1698, milkmaids danced before the houses of their regular customers, their heads crowned with pyramids of silver, entwined with garlands and ribbons. The silver was hired, as was customary; the scene became so much a London setpiece that it is depicted in several paintings in the Museum of London. By 1800 if not long before, the pyramid had become so substantial that two chairmen were hired to carry it, as Pyne shows in his *Costume of Great Britain* (1808).

Honoured with a royal visit, towns were expected to present a cup. Three cups in the 1574 Jewel House inventory can be traced back to Elizabeth's progress through East Anglia in 1564; Huntingdon, Cambridge and Godmanchester had each made the customary gifts of a cup and purseful of coins. At least two of those cups taken to Russia by English envoys before the Civil War were the fruit of progresses by James I in 1617, to Warwick and another town; the Warwick town device is still faintly visible pounced on one. York and Lincoln each gave cups to Henry VIII on his 1540 visit, hoping to obliterate the memory of their share in the Pilgrimage of Grace.[1]

The launching of a ship, preaching sermons, winning a race, election to one's college or company, all were regarded as suitable occasion for a gift of plate and examples may be seen in most large museums (see Fig. 125). In 1795, Admiral Sir George Bowyer received a covered cup to mark a successful naval engagement between his ship the *Barfleur* and a French vessel; this now belongs to Abingdon Corporation.

Fig. 123 **Beadle's badge**
*c.*1693. Mark DA crowned. H.22 cm. Worn by the beadle (officer) of Cripplegate Ward; he also carried a
silver-headed stave of office.
Cripplegate Foundation

Fig. 124 **'Laitiere de May' 1698**
Engraving from *Memoires et Observations Faites par un Voyageur en Angletere*. On Mayday until about
1825 London milkmaids danced before their customers' houses, their headdresses crowned with silver.
Note the lidded tankards, fluted dishes and the two-handled cup crowning the pyramid.
Museum of London

Another gallant captain, who smuggled a French countess away from the terrors of
revolutionary France 'Concealed in his packet', and landed her at Brighton, was presented in
1792 with a typical race cup by the Prince of Wales. Pitts & Preedy, the makers, merely
substituted a plaque chased with a ship and another with a view of the Pavilion for the normal
racehorses.[2] Dinnerplate was equally popular and provided a convenient means of giving a
more generous present than a mere cup; it also offered greater scope for ornament (Fig. 125).

Civic heroism was rewarded too; Shrewsbury presented a local man, Thomas Hayes, with
a tankard and a standing cup at a cost of £15 – in recognition of his help when plague struck the
town in 1650. Charles II's generosity after the double disasters of plague and fire swept
through London in 1665–6 is well known through the group of engraved tankards which Sir
Edmund Bury Godfrey had made up from the silver vessel which had been the king's gift
(Fig. 135). But there were other recipients of Charles II's gratitude too: Samuel Pepys,
visiting Sir Robert Vyner's shop in May 1667, commented on the '2 or 3 great silver flagons
made with inscriptions as gifts of the King to such and such persons of quality as did stay in

Town . . . for the keeping of things in order'. These other Stuart royal gifts have apparently vanished. The City of London rewarded the persistent campaign by Brass Crosby, late lord mayor, John Wilkes and Richard Oliver, to get parliamentary reports published, with a massive cup embossed by John Romer with scenes from their campaign; this cup, of 1772, is at the Mansion House (Fig. 126).[3]

The highest mark of respect from a city to a national figure was the grant of its freedom and a standard gift evolved of a gold casket containing a suitably inscribed and sealed parchment roll; some of these freedom boxes are masterpieces of goldsmiths' work. The earliest reference to this custom (although this box has not survived) occurs in 1674, when Sir Robert Vyner, lord mayor, presented Charles II with the freedom 'in a large square box of massey gold, the seal of the said Freedom hanging at it enclosed in a box of gold set all over with large diamonds'. In 1681 the Skinners' Company presented silver freedom boxes 'fairly gilt and engraved with the Company's arms' to three courtiers. But apart from these boxes, plate, and particularly the silvergilt cup, remained the standard gift.

The custom of giving plate flourished particularly from the sixteenth century, with its

Fig. 125 **Tureen and ladle**
Gilt. 1798. Mark of John Schofield. Presented to Admiral Viscount Duncan by the County of Forfar to mark his victory at Camperdown in 1797 and 'in testimony of their satisfaction that so great a service was achieved by a Native of this County'.
Loan, National Maritime Museum

Fig. 126 **The Brass Crosby cup**
1772. Mark of John Romer, retailers Portal & Gearing, Ludgate Hill. 'A silver cup of the value of two
hundred Pounds', made by order of the Common Council of the City and chased with a vivid scene of
the Lord Mayor's Coach, escorted by a cheering crowd, bringing Alderman Brass Crosby home in
triumph.
Mansion House

great stress on secular societies, increasing prosperity and strongly masculine flavour to hospitality; drinking vessels were by far the commonest gifts. A lottery advertisement of 1567 depicts 113 drinking vessels (beakers, covered bowls and cups) to be offered as prizes, as against a handful of other plate – salts, ewers and spoons (Fig. 11).

A silver cup was regarded as a gracious and honourable form of compensating for refusing office. If a man of wealth wanted to avoid his term as unpaid ward or parish officer, he might give a beaker or wine cup as a fine, suitably inscribed; the officers of Vintry Ward clubbed together after the Fire to replace their lost 'biggin'. They purchased a lignum vitae loving cup with a silver lipband engraved with their names and the date, 1670. Cripplegate, a large ward

Fig. 127   **Cripplegate Ward beaker**
1608. Mark NR over a device. Engraved 'This was the Fyne of R. M. Vaus For beinge released from beinge scavinger 1608'. The design echoes that of another beaker, given in lieu of a fine to the Ward in 1604.
Cripplegate Foundation

straddling the City wall, has an interesting group of beakers and cups given to the 'Quest House' (local courthouse) between the mid-sixteenth century and about 1640, some of which may be seen in the treasury at S. Paul's Cathedral and a unique covered mug of 1646 has been preserved by Cornhill Ward (Figs. 127 and 23).[4]

Livery Companies

Just as in the later Middle Ages men and women had eagerly joined religious societies, fraternities offering mutual support in illness and in death, and expressed their sense of fellowship through gifts, so in the sixteenth and seventeenth centuries this corporate loyalty was expressed through membership of their secular successors, the livery companies, inns of court, or university colleges. Each of these bodies accumulated plate, sometimes through free gifts and sometimes in recognition of services rendered. Marcus, Earl of Tyrone, gave a gilt cup to the Fishmongers' Company in 1747 'for the granting to his Lordship a Lease of 3 lives of the Company's Irish Estate', as the engraved inscription records.

Gifts were by no means totally spontaneous, as sometimes inscriptions make clear; honourable obligations as between brotherhood and member could be discharged by a gift of plate. In 1743 Robert Willimott, a Cooper, was chosen Lord Mayor of London. He had promised the wardens that he would not transfer from the Coopers' Company to one of the twelve great companies, normal practice at the time. So the Company made him master and exempted him from the customary fines for the steps in the Company hierarchy which he had skipped over. 'To show his grateful Sense of these their Repeated Favours (he) Pray'd and Prevail'd with the Wardens' to accept two large waiters. These, made by Robert Abercrombie, are still in the Company's possession. When Sir Robert Vyner was Sheriff of London, the Goldsmiths' as was customary for liverymen, lent him plate for his official entertaining; the silver bell he gave in return in 1666, now incorporated into an inkstand made by Paul De Lamerie in 1740, may still be seen at their Hall.[5]

The livery companies acquired virtually all their plate as gifts or as fines, and an informal but generally recognised tariff seems to have applied. The fine of John Dethick for admission to the livery of the Mercers' Company was a scroll salt (1638). Sometimes one may suspect that the gift was a penalty exacted for a trade offence; the Gibbon salt (1576) was presented to the Goldsmiths' Company in 1632, at dinner after the customary S. Bartholomew's Day search of London's shops. To avoid the stigma of irresponsibility, those who were giving voluntarily stressed this and inscriptions such as 'Freely Given' often occur.

Entrance to the livery of a company was almost always marked by a gift of plate, and liverymen who had served as master often left a bequest too. The Leigh cup, at the Mercers' Company, was left for them 'to use it at the choseing of the Wardens . . . if they shall think it so good'. Gifts to livery companies inevitably varied in size and quality according to the taste and wealth of the donor, and the importance he attached to his term of office. The large and heavy standing cup, which Samuel Pepys presented to the Clothworkers' Company in 1678, after serving as master, was clearly a special commission; it has a caged or sheathed body, whose openwork foliage design incorporates the badges of the Company – griffins, rams' heads, and teazels – and another pastmaster considered his legacy equally carefully. John

Archer, who died in 1678, had been an active member of the Drapers' Company for over half a century. Although in his will he had left his Company £60 to buy 'a Dussen of silver Plates or four silver Candlesticks which they please', on his deathbed he changed his mind and specified a basin and ewer instead, as his widow and son testified. The basin and ewer, duly engraved with his arms, remain at Drapers' Hall.[6]

An interesting contemporary extension of this ancient custom flourishes at Goldsmiths' Hall. Here newly elected members of the court are given the opportunity to commission a personal wine cup, to stimulate their patronage of their Company's craft (Fig. 78). These cups, many of which were recently exhibited at the Hall (1983, Goldsmith and the Grape Exhibition) demonstrate the range of technical virtuosity achieved by English goldsmiths today – *plique à jour* enamel, gemsetting, casting and so on. The Company continues to commission cups as gifts, although their purpose is to create display pieces, as in the Dublin cup (Fig. 78).

Gifts made by companies were usually prompted by the need to acknowledge a favour or mark an achievement or honour conferred on a distinguished member. To celebrate the

Fig. 128   **The Stamford punch bowl**
Gilt 1685. Mark PR,? for Philip Rollos. D.40.5 cm. Presented with a ladle to the town of Stamford by
Charles Bertie, twice its MP, in 1685. It holds five gallons.
Corporation of Stamford

Fig. 129 **Presentation jug**
1832. Thomas Winbush. A handsome example of shell and wave chased ornament.
Loan, VAM

completion of the New River in 1613, Sir Hugh Middleton's project for bringing piped water to the City, the Goldsmiths' Company presented the energetic Sir Hugh with a steeple cup; he had recently served as prime warden so their pride in his achievement was understandable.

Gifts to and from Local Dignitaries

Gentlemen who served for a time as borough MP, or as recorder, were also drawn into the gift-exchange cycle. In the 1680s the convivial practice of presenting that fashionable item, a silver punch bowl or monteith, to the burgesses quickly caught on and both Stamford and Newark retain the handsome bowls they were given in 1685 and 1689 (remade 1693) by their respective MPs (Fig. 128). Boston also owns a punch bowl and ladle, given in 1740 and reacquired by the town after the 1837 sale. When Robert Clive was elected MP of Shrewsbury in 1760, he gave the mayor and corporation a handsome embossed tankard, made in Hamburg a hundred years earlier. This custom flourished into the nineteenth century; Dover has a bowl and shell ladle of 1814. In return the towns presented gifts too; Bristol spent about £150 on a splendid ewer and basin for its retiring recorder John Scrope in 1735, a set which is particularly interesting as one of the earliest in England to adopt rococo ornament, and four years earlier had presented him with that fashionable item, a silver epergne, also purchased from Wickes.[7]

The antiquary Elias Ashmole presented the town of Lichfield with his 'large chased silver bowl and cover, cost me £23 8s 6d' in January 1666. This handsome piece, a standing cup and cover in the auricular style, is engraved with the seal of the corporation and an inscription recording his generosity.[8]

In late Stuart England it was often the case that a gift of plate was reciprocated or even returned, with courtesy, to the original donor, as Pepys several times pleasurably noted. A characteristic illustration of the role of plate in the City of London's internal relationships is an exchange of gifts between the Drapers' Company and Sir Richard Brown. Elected sheriff in 1648, he was arrested before he could host the customary dinner for the assistants and livery of the Company. Two years later a purse of gold from the Company 'to manifest their cares' for him elicited a gift from him of 2½ dozen spoons. This evoked a return gift to his wife of the same value, £17 10s, in the form of a standing cup. So honour was satisfied on both sides and the corporate body made a substantial, if belated, contribution to the costs of his year as sheriff.[10]

When the finances of the companies were severely strained, as in the 1630s and 1640s, prosperous liverymen sometimes helped out with loans against the value of the corporate silver. At the Painter-Stainers' Company their benefactor George Willingham, past master, refused any 'consideration' (interest) for his generosity in 1643, and when his Company gave him twenty gold nobles in 1647 in gratitude, he returned them in the form of a cup 'to follow that bowle, which he formerly gave in remembrance of his wife'. Alderman Stephen Frewen, one of four men who lent the Skinners £2,000 in 1666 to pay their chimney tax, was, so family tradition claims, given a nautilus cup in gratitude (now VAM).[11]

Why Silver Has Not Survived

To explain the present scarcity of English silver made before the mid-sixteenth century, one must look not merely at the Civil War, so often simplistically quoted as the time 'when all old silver was melted down' and certainly the best documented melt, but more widely, and indeed back to the reign of Henry VIII.

To pay subsidies or forced loans in plate, instead of ready money which was often in short supply, was a device acceptable to both the subject and the Crown. Both the Jewel House goldsmiths and the Mint, ultimate recipient of the bulk of such contributions, were equipped to deal with bullion in whatever form it came. So in 1522 the Ironmongers' Company raised their contribution to the subsidy partly in cash – £27 13s 'all our money belonging to our Hall' – but largely by giving up their old plate, although a few pieces, including the mazer bowl inscribed 'Ave Maria' still at the Hall, were retained.[11] Robert Amadas, deputy master of the Mint, reported to Cardinal Wolsey that in Norwich he had gathered £700-worth of plate in subsidy payments. Again, between 1544 and 1548 the Vintners' Company sold virtually all its silver, in order to invest in property, retaining only thirteen ale cups.[12]

The conversion to coin could be instant; a crude and dramatic illustration is the money issued at Newark in 1646. Plates and dishes from the king's own dinner service were simply cut up with shears into diamond-shapes and punched with the figure six or nine, to designate their value in pence. Hallmarks and traces of the engraved arms of the royal household are still visible on these makeshift coins.[13]

This alternative to ready cash remained a constant feature. The Drapers' Company adopted the traditional time-honoured response when requested to contribute to William III's loan for military expenses in 1696. The court sold 3,400 ounces of its plate to raise £972-odd and only £27, the residue, was paid in cash. Benjamin Mildmay, Earl Fitzwalter, took 4,000 ounces of his stepson's 'wrought plate' as security for a loan in 1748. It was deposited with his bankers; however, he loaned some back to the young man, who had recently married and needed to set up house.[14]

Clearly sudden unanticipated demands for money, whether to meet taxation or for investment, remained an important factor in the disappearance of historic plate. The Goldsmiths' Company contributed to the forced loan of 1627, when £120,000 was demanded from the City, by selling £407-worth of plate. They sold more in 1637 and again in the early 1640s. Other urgent demands for cash arose too. After the Fire the cost of rebuilding was a great burden both to private citizens and to institutions in London. The Goldsmiths', faced with reconstructing their Hall, sold over 1,300 ounces of plate to Sir Robert Vyner in July 1667, followed by a further 1,000 ounces to another goldsmith in December. Earlier, on 19 October 1666, the Mercers' Company decided to sell all but six pieces of their plate, to raise capital to rebuild their destroyed property; this raised £702.[15]

A further incentive, if not temptation, to dispose of plate arose in the early 1700s from the Classis lotteries authorised by Parliament in 1709. On 26 May 1711 the Goldsmiths' authorised the sale of plate to a total of £482 17s 10d, and were allocated twenty lottery tickets. Most had been given between 1671 and 1692; the items sold comprised currently fashionable

Fig. 130 **Centre of alms dish**
Remade in 1708 for All Hallows the Great, using a mixture of 'Small plate belonging to ye Sd. Church'
and Lady Anne Glover's silver, given a hundred years earlier. Her arms, engraved in the centre, and the
chased marine plaques, indicate that her original gift was a Jacobean rosewater dish, lovingly reproduced
by the late Stuart goldsmith for a different purpose.
S. Michael Paternoster Royal, City of London

objects such as pipe-pans, monteiths, snuffers, forks and trencher salts. Another livery company, the Salters', sold all their plate in 1711 to invest in lottery tickets. Five years later they sold their holdings from the lottery and had the plate fashioned anew by Humphrey Payne, engraved with the arms and dates of gift of the original donors. For many years the existence of a monteith 'dated 1660' at the Salters' Company puzzled students of English silver, but on inspection it turned out to be part of the Humphrey Payne replacement order, but bore the original donor's name and date of gift.[16]

Because its weight and so value could be quickly assessed by any competent silversmith equipped with a scale, it was the obvious target for bailiffs in debt cases. In August 1739 the goods of Peter Hendon were distrained because he owed nine quarters' tithe payments to his church, S. Anne and S. Agnes, Aldersgate. The bailiff took two silver spoons, a silver watch and a dictionary to make up the £4 13s 4d owing. The Skinners' Company in 1604 asked their master to take away all their plate, to avoid distraint by the King's officers.[17]

The greatest threat to survival of old silver, as always, was the pride of owners and their relentless enthusiasm for refashioning. The phrase 'out of fashion, battered and unhandsome for service' with which Francis Meynell, goldsmith, described much of the City of London plate in 1662 neatly sums up why so little old silver has been preserved. Intended for regular, if not daily, heavy use, it was valued only while its appearance enhanced the standing of its owner and users. Only one piece of the London civic plate pre-dates the Fire, that is the Christopher cup of 1662, not because the rest was destroyed then but because the aldermen had no hesitation in refashioning it.

Much of the eighteenth-century plate now at the Mansion House had its origin in gifts made to the City of London two centuries earlier. The increasing port of the Tudor mayor, expressed in his assumption of the prefix 'lord', can be demonstrated in the swelling tide of gifts of plate from the 1520s onwards. Perhaps the culmination of this process is Sir John Alen's bequest in 1545 of the Collar of SS, a royal gift to members of the king's council, to be worn henceforward by the Lord Mayor of London and his successors.[18]

The policy of refashioning can be demonstrated particularly well in the London corporation plate; three great pilgrim bottles or flagons made by Benjamin Pyne in 1721 were descended, through at least one refashioning, from a pair of 'great gilt pots, a parcel of the fine of Mr John Brown', given in 1527 to excuse him from further civic office. These do not have Brown's arms but usually the City, like other institutions attracting gifts of plate, ensured that the donor's memory be honoured by reproducing his arms or a commemorative inscription on to the replacement plate. The widow of Sir Ambrose Nicholas, lord mayor 1575–6, left two dozen parcel-gilt trenchers, a symptom of the prosperity of London's leading men and of the enhanced status achieved by the mayor's office in the sixteenth century. These trenchers, bearing the arms of Lady Nicholas and of the City, had heavy wear and were exchanged in 1633, 1654, 1662 (when they were enlarged) and now exist only as part of a set of ninety-two dinner plates made by Paul De Lamerie in 1737. The Christopher cup of 1662, unique pre-Fire survivor among the civic plate, is in fact a remake of Christopher's original gift of a bowl in 1580.[19]

Sometimes there is a gap of several years between the apparent (inscribed) date of gift and the hallmark date. This may be simply because the executors were slow to pay up or because the bequest was temporarily used as ready cash, but often the original gift was converted later into a more appropriate or more useful form and the name and date of the gift transferred. Thus the mace of the Court Leet of S. Andrew, Holborn is engraved with a total of twelve names, benefactors from 1612 to 1696, whose bowls, cups and other gifts were melted down and with cash gifts enabled the mace to be fashioned in the latter year (VAM).

A remorseless transmogrification of its plate, while carefully preserving the memory of the donors, is characteristic of virtually all English institutions, at least until the late nineteenth century (see Fig. 130). Sir Humphrey May, Chancellor of the Duchy of Lancaster to James I, gave a gilt cup fashioned from his Duchy seal, to Lancaster in 1630. When the town purchased 'a new silver presenter' from Isaac Cookson of Newcastle in 1740, they cheerfully sacrificed May's cup, while transcribing the Latin inscription from his original gift onto the replacement, a salver which was more to the current taste.

Those bequeathing money for a purchase of plate recognised this practical attitude and often specified merely 'something of Use' or, as William Camden did in 1622, left a bequest 'to buy them a piece of plate in memorial of me'. A two-handled cup at Great Yarmouth of 1737 is inscribed 'Mr. George Morse's gift of a Silver Salver & Tankard was exchanged for this cup in the year 1737'; but Morse's gift of 250 ounces of plate, had been made 90 years before in 1648.

Even between friends, this was acceptable behaviour. When Horace Mann wrote from Florence in 1744, explaining that he had sold a handsome coffee pot given him by Horace Walpole, he justified his action to his friend, by saying it was done 'with a view of making some useful plate, nay to begin a service'. Although there is a hint of irony in his assurance that 'In every plate and dish I buy I will write, Ex dono HW, for without that beginning I should never have begun', this is a salutary warning against assuming that the name of a donor implies any but the most remote connection of courtesy with the object in which it appears.[20] The Norwich goldsmith Peter Peterson left at his death in 1603 a long list of bequests. The plate, to be ordered and distributed by his executors, was to be inscribed 'the gift of Peter Peterson', although made after his death.

Although silver was not apparently a normal marriage gift until the nineteenth century (with the exception of the toilet service which the husband was expected to present to his new wife), there is one inscribed piece, an epergne or centrepiece by De Lamerie, which appears to have been a wedding present (VAM). Inscribed 'The gift of Ye Rt Hon[able] Sophia Baroness Lempster to Sir Roger and Lady Newdigate AD 1743', it was a grandmother's gift to the Newdegate family of Arbury Hall, but even in this case the inscription and the engraved armorials, were added at the recipient's expense and it is quite likely that the gift actually took the form of old plate, refashioned into a currently fashionable shape.

The Market for Secondhand Silver

In the past the greatest threat to the survival of old silver was not the depredations of the king or his tax-gatherers but the relentless social pressure to demonstrate one's status through one's plate. This assumption was spelled out by Elizabeth Smyth who shrewdly advised her son Thomas (1609–42) of Ashton Court, Somerset who had recently inherited and was furnishing his home, to buy 'Strong substantial plate' since money spent on this 'will do you more service and credit than in your purse'.

Pride in family was expressed rather through handsomely engraved newly fashioned plate than through an elaborate but impractical display of old buffet plate. A series of goldsmiths' bills for the Ingram family of Temple Newsam, Leeds demonstrate the process in action. In November 1631 when Sir Arthur needed new dishes, trencher plates, basins and ewers, he simply sent down to his goldsmith 'two old dishes' followed by other plate to a total value of £242, plus £100 in cash. The goldsmith then supplied him with new plate, including that innovation, a tobacco box. His new basins, ewers and 'flagon pots' were engraved with the Ingram arms, crest and mantling whereas more utilitarian kitchen service plate bore only his arms 'in a Lorrell'; the former cost 5s apiece for engraving but the latter only 2s. [21]

A ewer and basin commissioned by the Goldsmiths' Company in 1611, lavishly embossed with their motifs – cups and buckles, leopards' heads and unicorns and set with an enamelled boss of their arms – was sold with other plate in 1637; then the new owner erased the arms, removed the enamelled boss and had his own pounced on the centre in its place. [22]

Since senior church men doubled up as great officers of state, bishops and abbots were expected to maintain the way of life and spending on plate characteristic of the nobility. Without daughters and sons to provide for, they could do so most lavishly, although it could rebound on them, as Wolsey found in 1530. A generation earlier in 1476, George Neville, Archbishop of York also sacrificed all his wealth, partly because of his political activities but partly also because the king envied him his enormously lavish lifestyle. The trap took a classic form. The king invited himself to come and hunt at the Abbot's Manor of the More in Hertfordshire; 'he was right glad and went home to make perveyance therefore; and set out in London and diverse other places all his plate and other stuff that he had his after Barnetfield and Tewkesburyfield and also borrowed more stuff of other man and perveyed for the King for two or three days for meat and drink and lodging and arrayed as richly and pleasantly as he could'. But the king arrested him, confiscating all his treasure and 'his said Archbishop's mitre in the which were full many rich stones and precious, and made thereof a crown for himself. And all his other jewels, plate and stuff the King gave it to his eldest son and heir Prince Edward'. [23]

It is hardly surprising, given this attitude to overmighty subjects and their possessions, that virtually no medieval plate which can be associated with a noble family has survived. Armorials of the original owner could be removed, as Henry VIII did with Wolsey's in 1532, although it was little more trouble and expense to have plainer plate refashioned and its earlier history erased. But secondhand silver has always had a resale value, particularly if its workmanship was handsome and elaborate, as the 1649–50 sales of the king's goods demonstrated.

At the Restoration there was a sudden demand for large and lavishly worked silver; English towns felt compelled to make presentations to the king, and their agents scoured the London goldsmiths' shops for appropriate gifts. Since conditions in the previous decade had not been conducive to a lively trade in plate 'of curious workmanship', several would-be purchasers preferred to buy foreign pieces made several years earlier. The silvergilt castle studded with gems (actually a salt) which the city of Exeter presented to Charles II had been made by Johan

Fig. 131 **The Exeter Salt of State**
Gilt and set with gemstones. Made in Hamburg *c.*1630 by Johann Hass. Purchased for over £700 and
presented to Charles II by the City of Exeter in 1660; perhaps bought initially in Germany by
Cromwell's agents as a gift for the Tsar. Plymouth gave a fountain and perfume burner, also by a
Hamburg goldsmith, 'of very curious workmanshipe'.
Jewel House, HM Tower of London

Hass of Hamburg about 1630 (Fig. 131). Plymouth gave the king a table fountain made about 1650 by another Hamburg goldsmith, Peter Oer. Oman suggested that these two pieces might have been part of an order assembled in Hamburg by English agents as gifts for the tsar, who had refused to receive an embassy from the regicide Oliver Cromwell in 1658.[24]

Foreign plate, particularly Dutch and German, was generally available here in the seventeenth century, as the large number of Nuremburg cups belonging to English churches demonstrates. A splendid Dutch centrepiece of three dolphins, supporting shells, at the Fishmongers' Company, was made by Johan Lutma of Antwerp and presented to the Company by John Rushout, prime warden in 1654. Presumably its fishy references led him to choose it as peculiarly appropriate. A massive standing cup made by Martin Dumling of Nuremburg is displayed with other civic treasures in King's Lynn; it was purchased in 1634 in fulfilment of the will of Thomas Soame, three times mayor of the town. His legacy of £20 could not have purchased anything so large or impressive as this cup, had it not been both foreign-made and secondhand. The campaign of the London Company against dealing in Nuremburg plate, unless taken for assay and hallmarking, meant that many cups ended up with churches and institutions, given away because they could not be profitably resold.[25]

Sometimes the arms of successive owners enable us to trace the history of a piece. An embossed and chased rosewater dish of about 1595, now in the Kremlin, illustrates the circumstances whereby plate moved as gifts. Originally part of the Jewel House stock, it went to Denmark, perhaps as a gift to Christian IV who visited his brother-in-law James I in 1606 and 1614, or else as the perquisite of a departing Danish ambassador (they customarily received gifts of 1,500 ounces of plate). Marked with CIV, it was then taken to Russia when Christian's bastard son married the daughter of Tsar Mikhail Romanov in 1644.[26]

A flow of orders to various goldsmiths is the characteristic pattern before the twentieth century, presumably because no one retailer carried ready stock of all the current forms. While a group of plate can be linked to a specific event, such as a marriage, by an agreement of dates and the appearance of a wife's armorials with those of her husband, it is clear that silver was regularly overhauled, with old plate sent in to cover much of the cost of the new. This meant that customers had a wide choice of secondhand plate and several incentives to buy it. It was already in stock, there was no charge for working it, the duty (post-1721) was payable only on 'newly wrought' plate and objects not of the latest style were charged at less than current items. The 'dressing set' or toilet service which Sir Walter Calverley bought for his new bride in 1707 was already over 20 years old. Weighing over 300 ounces it cost £119, only a few pence above the melt price (VAM).[27]

Both private treaty sales and, from the early eighteenth century, auction sales of household goods were popular methods of obtaining good quality secondhand plate more cheaply than through the retail trade and high rank was no barrier to following this practice. When Henry Howard, Earl of Northampton, died in 1614, all his gilt buffet plate and mounted porcelain and crystal was bought by two goldsmiths for resale, but his serviceable white silver such as a basin and ewer 'scollop fashion' – perhaps like the mermaid sets (VAM and Toledo Fig. 89) – and his pie plates, salad dishes, lamp and so on were all sold to the lord treasurer. The figures are large, almost £1,000 for gilt and £705 for the white silver. Where such large sums were involved, very few members even of the aristocracy were in a position to pay cash outright except when their rent rolls fell due, and it is clear from the Ingram account that his goldsmiths were acting also as a source for long-term credit.[28] The leading goldsmiths apparently acted as agents at sales; in 1727 David Willaume bought at the Duke of Shrewsbury's sale a case of gilt cutlery for John Hervey. In 1697 John Hervey, first Earl of Bristol, bought over 1,100 ounces of wrought plate from the executors of Baptist May (d. 1698) at 5s4d the ounce whereas David Willaume the following year charged him 7s0d an ounce for new silver sconces. But it should be remembered that the Huguenot goldsmiths

Fig. 132 **The Jerningham cistern**
Engraving and etching *c*.1740. This massive cistern (Hermitage, Leningrad) was commissioned in 1730 to show 'that the sculptors and artificers of Great Britain are not inferior to those of other Nations'! George Vertue designed it, Rysbrack modelled the figure-handles (much copied by silversmiths both at the time and in the 1760s) and Kandler made it. No one bought it, it was offered as a prize in the 1737 Westminster Bridge Lottery and by 1740 it belonged to Empress Anna of Russia.
VAM

could always charge above the going rate, that is more than the office allowed, because of their particular skills.[29]

The advertisements which Stafford Briscoe, goldsmith, published in the *General Evening Post* in 1751 make clear that much of his stock of 'useful and ornamental Second Hand Plate' from bottle cranes to coffee pots was available 'for a Trifle more than the Weight of the Silver'. Most goldsmiths indicated on their trade cards their willingness to take old plate in part-exchange. Better items, particularly those with elaborate fashion, were retained for resale. Briscoe had several chased bread baskets and 'chased plain and monument Candlesticks' in stock. His largest items, which from their size and price must have represented a considerable outlay, were a cistern and fountain 'of modern and elegant Workmanship' weighing 525 ounces. Since these massive vessels were in use only in the wealthiest homes and since Briscoe's shop was not adjacent to fashionable Piccadilly or the Haymarket but on the corner of Friday Street and Cheapside in the heart of the City, this seems a curious investment. It had presumably been 'turned over' against the part-replacement of a dinner service which would be comparable in weight. It is probable that Briscoe's was entirely a retail business, with what newly made stock he carried supplied by other workers.[30]

From an annotated catalogue of a sale of Lady Frederick's property held at her house in Savile Row on 29 June 1767, we can see both the demand for old silver and the prices paid. Prices ran from 5s 4½d the ounce for the least desirable of the plate (a set of casters) to 9s the ounce for '6 wrought teaspoons and a pair of tongs and strainer', listed with jewels and curiosities and presumably elaborately finished.[31] Since the tea ceremony was an occasion on which the hostess herself served her guests it was desirable that the accoutrements should be as lavish as possible. A bill sent by David Willaume to Temple Newsam in 1726 indicates the cost of such a set; on 11 October he supplied six teaspoons, tongs and a strainer weighing five ounces. The price of fashion was £1 3s, gilding a further 18s and engraving another 8s. The total cost, at £3 19s, plus 3s for the case, was just under 16s an ounce, considerably more than any item of tableware.[32]

Another item from Lady Frederick's sale, a pair of superb rococo sauce boats 'with eagle handles', curiously wrought and decorated with masks and festoons, weighing almost fifty ounces and presumably close in style to those by Kandler in the Ashmolean Museum (and elsewhere), fetched only 6s an ounce, but by this date these boats would have been looking distinctly old fashioned.

Silver as Heirlooms

Wills are selective, normally mentioning only those items most highly valued by their owners, which might well not be all or even exclusively plate. When John Baret, treasurer to the Abbot of Bury, made his immensely long and specific will in 1463, he offered one legatee a choice between his 'best gay cup of earth, covered' or another ceramic pot but barely troubled to mention his plate. Most was to be sold to execute his charitable bequests although the abbot was left his 'best standing cup'.[33]

Only where there was little to divide was the plate specified. John Coote (d. 1502) wanted his eldest son to have 'mine silver salt with the cover' while his daughter Alice was to have the other salt (without a cover) and also his second-best and fourth-best cups without covers. Normally before the Reformation silver as the major capital asset was sold off to pay for religious intentions; when Richard, Bishop of Chichester died in 1253 he made six specific bequests of drinking vessels, all but one were gifts to him, but the 'silver food dishes and goblets not assigned' were all to be sold.[34]

Items in wills which were curiosities, or pieces specially valued, often elicit more detail. When John Stourton of Preston Plucknet near Yeovil left 'a silver cup covered which belonged to St Thomas the Martyr' he clearly considered it a great treasure; hardly less valued was his daughter's gift of 'a covered cup gilt in the likeness of a costard (apple) with leaves'.[35]

Heirloom silver is normally confined to cups and spoons, the most intimate of a man's silver and so most highly valued. Cups associated with state office were likely to be specifically valued in wills since they expressed a family honour. The office of hereditary cupbearer at the coronation banquet, a service associated with the manor of Wymondley, passed in the fifteenth century by marriage from the Argentines to the Alington family. In 1485 Sir William Alington left his son Giles the two gilt standing cups his perquisite from and used at the Coronations of Edward IV and Richard III. A generation later, in 1522, Sir Giles left his son two cups for service rendered at the Coronation of Henry VIII. These cups, like almost all bequests, have vanished, no longer valued once their gilding wore away and their design ceased to be acceptable.[36]

Family affection and loyalty to ancestors undoubtedly were often the motives for preserving early silver. Pieces of no great monetary or artistic value, if associated with a founder of the family's fortunes, often became heirlooms, particularly in the fluid social conditions of the sixteenth and seventeenth centuries, when the professions of the law, medicine and government office were providing opportunities for rapid advancement for men with little inherited wealth. In 1639 the Bury gentleman, Francis Pinner, was presumably acting in this spirit of family piety when he left to his great-grandson Francis Goodrich 'My stone pot (which was my father's) footed and tipped and covered with silver with letters for my father's name engraved upon the cover'. In Pinner's long and detailed will, this silver mounted pot is the only household item specified, although its low value and old-fashioned appearance made it inappropriate both to his standing and time.[37]

A New England family owned a similar saltglazed pot with engraved silvergilt mounts which became a heirloom in the Winthrop family, descending through seven generations. Given to Adam Winthrop, father of the first governor of Massachusetts, by his sister Lady Mildmay 'at the Feast of S. Michael Ano 1607', this little pot was by then already 50 years old and had presumably some greater symbolic importance to the family than its simplicity warranted.[38]

A similar motive, a wish to secure personal immortality, is to be seen in Sir Nicholas Bacon's gift of three gilt cups to his three sons 'To remain an heirloom'. Of no great elaboration, these seal cups were nevertheless both a perquisite and a memory of his term as Lord Keeper of the Great Seal to Queen Elizabeth and so were engraved not only with the family arms but also with a representation of the great seal of Queen Mary, from the metal of which they had been made (the seal weighed 120 ounces, the three cups 121 together). The

Fig. 133 **The Lowther porringer and salver**
Gilt 1660. Mark DR between two mullets. H. 20 cm. Given by 'Richard Lowther and Anne his Relicte'
to John Lowther. The influence of Van Vianen's auricular ornament is clear; note the dissolving masks
between the profile busts of Romans.
Loan, VAM

family crest of a boar is the only other ornament, modelled in relief on the cover; to Bacon aesthetic considerations were secondary to the evidence of family achievement and continuity (Fig. 73).[39]

At least from the Restoration, for seventy years or so, a cup or porringer accompanied by a salver, normally gilt and engraved with armorials, was regarded as an appropriate presentation gift. A substantial number are known, bearing the marks of goldsmiths supplying the Jewel House and hallmarks in the 1660s; several are clearly royal gifts, from the inscription 'Ex dono Regis'. A porringer, now lacking its stand, presented by the king in 1673 to Archbishop Sterne is an example of the type; more elaborately chased is the set presented by Lady Savill as a bequest from her husband to Sir James Lowther in 1660 (both VAM, Fig. 133). On this the ornament consists of profile heads of Roman emperors in laurel roundels within auricular embossing.[40]

To identify such family treasures, we are normally dependent on commemorative inscriptions, or sometimes groups of initials. A Stuart lobed bowl (1677), in the Huntington Collection at San Marino, California, is engraved with the arms of Towneley and on the underside the birth and death dates of four members of that family, successive owners of the bowl from 1685 to 1748. In 1937 the Croft cups, a pair of massive two-handled cups of 1685 appeared on the London market. Inscriptions on the cups record that in 1719 Sir Herbert Croft gave one to each of his daughters. However, the cups had been, as other earlier inscriptions show, legacies a generation before from Sir Herbert's mother-in-law and grandmother-in-law.[41]

Even gifts of low value could be dignified with an inscription; a single-eared porringer (bleeding bowl) of 1684 has on it 'Ex dono Annae Aris Virg: Caritas: sorori Eliz: Eston 1686' and the steels (stems) of spoons lent themselves to commemorative engraving (Fig. 136).[42]

That ambitious public servant Samuel Pepys refers several times to receiving 'noble presents', such as 'a fair state dish of silver and a cup with my armes ready cut upon them', worth about £18 (February 1663) or (given ostensibly to Mrs Pepys) 'a small silver state cup and cover value about £3 or £4', but this Pepys exchanged at Alderman Backwell's for a tankard.

These sets have often become separated, but the City of Bath retains a salver and standing cup, delivered to Beau Nash to mark the visit of Frederick Prince of Wales in 1738. Recently the Museum of London purchased another set, a cup and salver of 1715, which bears the arms of the East India Company.[43]

A strong sense of property operated where silver was concerned. Margaret Gill quotes from the 1793 will of a Newcastle goldsmith, Robert Scott, who had a bad conscience about misappropriating his mother-in-law's silver and, worse, engraving it with his own initials 'without her knowledge I took the liberty of marking them with the initials of my own and my wife's names . . . a Teacannister, on the one side Tempest Arms on the other the letters RES'. This plus a teapot and stand, a milkpail and ladle, six tablespoons and four salts and shovels 'were brought with her when she came to live with me' and were now to be returned.

Customary Gifts and Expectations: the Monarch as Gift Giver

Inevitably gifts from royalty have been particularly valued, both at the time and later. In his *An Illustrated History of English Plate* Jackson illustrated a mounted stoneware jug, the Frances jug (plate 1009) which is said to have belonged to Mrs Frances Jefferson, servant to Elizabeth I. Bequeathed with the condition that it should pass always to the females of the family with that Christian name, it followed that line of descent until 1801. Although sold away from the family, the association remains. A snuffbox with Chinese figures and trees is engraved on the back with a record that it was given to Nell Gwyn by Charles II and then passed to her son's butler (VAM).

A covered bowl of 1671 and a standing cup of 1660, still at Charlecote House, Oxfordshire, were presented to Bishop Lucy of S. David's by Charles II. These are displayed in the Elizabethan great hall with a Tudor wine cup 'found in the house'; here we meet the merging of family sentiment with antiquarianism. The hall is a recreation of about 1830 and Charlecote is a monument to that energetic pursuit of the romantic 'old English' interior, which was already being revived and recreated from the 1740s, just as it was finally dying.

As the puritanical but realistic William Ames commented in 1633, 'a display of plate was for public servants' essential 'for the comportment and lustre of state'. To accumulate or, as a minimum, to have the use of table silver was an essential element in gentility; even prisoners of state, if they were noblemen, were issued with a set of essential plate for their personal use in the Tower, often drawn from their own forfeited possessions. Until his execution the Duke of Buckingham, whose fall in 1521 so greatly enriched the royal Jewel House, had basins to wash in, ewers and cups to serve his wine, and bowls, presumably for his breakfast ale. Envoys too, even those of relatively low status, expected to eat from silver. In September 1542 Sir Anthony Browne, then conferring with the Scots at York, protested 'seeing that the Lord Erskine is here everyday served on silver, I think it should not be for the King's honour, I being Master of his horse and Captain of his Pensioners, but (that) I should be served with the same'.[44]

This emphasis on dignity of port, which was regarded as a necessary attribute for a representative of the monarch's honour, led to the custom of making generous provision of plate for all royal servants travelling abroad. Ambassadors in the late seventeenth century expected a handsome provision of 4,000 ounces of silver and many attempted, successfully, to claim their plate as a recompense for expenses incurred on the king's business. This initial justification turned into the practice of claiming it as a perquisite, an onerous burden on the Jewel House which was finally abandoned early in the nineteenth century.

Much of the antique silver found engraved with royal arms can be traced back to these Jewel House issues, which went also to successive Speakers of the House of Commons and certain other officers of state; Sir John Cust, for example, ordered two services at Jewel House expense in 1761 and 1768. Benjamin Mildmay as Treasurer of the Household ordered himself a service in 1739.

In great households, the senior servants too expected to eat with silver; the steward's table at Dunham Massey, George Booth's principal residence, was equipped with 280 ounces of plate, largely in the form of spoons and forks but including two soup (serving) spoons, three casters and eight salt cellars. Leaving aside these more or less involuntary issues, there were other customary gifts from the crown which were almost as rigid and, if less bulky individually, amounted to quite large sums over a year.

NEW YEAR'S GIFTS

The ancient custom of presenting to the monarch gifts at the New Year is well documented from the early sixteenth century and there are several gift rolls recording not only what was received but what the monarch gave in return (Fig. 134). It was formalised at court, so that the rank and standing of the donor dictated the weight of the return gift he was due from the Jewel House. In the sixteenth century the royal goldsmiths can be seen building up a stock of suitable gifts – largely salts and cups in various sizes, and spoons – by midsummer, when they normally received an advance of several hundred pounds. The system was revived after the Restoration and Pepys in January 1661 had the task of selecting a piece of plate for his employer, Lord Sandwich. The tankard he chose at the Jewel House weighed slightly more

Fig. 134 **'A New Year's Gift to the King of Scotland'**
Watercolour of a silver, brass and gilt lantern, a New Year's gift from John Harington to James VI; 1602.
An accompanying poem plays on the symbolism of the light shed by a newly arrived monarch. In MS of
Harington's *Epigrams*, 1605.
Folger Shakespeare Library, Washington

Fig. 135 **Plague and Fire tankard**
1675. Mark IN over a star. One of several ordered by Sir Edmund Bury Godfrey as gifts in 1675–6. The
inscriptions, scenes and Garter badge refer to Charles II's gift in recognition of Sir Edmund's bravery
and hard work as a London magistrate in 1665–6.
Loan, VAM

than Sandwich's allowance of thirty ounces, so Pepys paid the difference – 12*s* for one and a half ounces.[45]

Although apparently the custom of distributing plate at New Year died in the 1680s, within the royal household spoons remained customary gifts to certain officials well into the nineteenth century. Some years ago three came onto the market; large tablespoons ordered for presentation to the King's Master Cook, and Yeoman of the Confectionery, they are of standard old English pattern, two by Mary Chawner (1834) and one by William Eley, William Fearn and William Chawner (1810). In 1811 one spoon cost £6 6*s* 1*d* including engraving the royal crest, crown and garter, which represents a substantial gift in kind, when set beside the recipient George Rawlinson's annual salary of just over £200.[46]

Traditionally, at the Coronation the new king presented his hereditary butler with a cup, and the Oxford civic collection still retains the magnificent silvergilt cup, embossed with royal badges among flowers, which Charles II presented to Sir Sampson White, twice lord mayor of that city. The cup, by Francis Leake, bears the 1665 hallmark. The Goldsmiths' Company owns another Coronation souvenir; Tobias Cleve, representing the town of Sandwich, was chosen as one of the canopy supporters at Charles II's Coronation. Receiving the silver of the canopy pole as his perquisite, he had it made into a tankard appropriately inscribed.[47]

Seal cups and, from the late seventeenth century, seal salvers, were the customary means of recording for one's family the honour of a royal appointment, such as Chancellor of the Duchy of Lancaster, or Keeper of the Privy Seal; each post carried with it the normal perquisite of the discarded silver matrices. These weighed up to 120 ounces, sufficient for one heavy covered cup or standing salver or, as in the case of the Bacon heirlooms, three smaller cups. Two seal salvers of the 1720s may be seen at the Victoria and Albert Museum; another, earlier, one is at the Burrell Collection and there are examples of seal cups at the British Museum. A seal salver (1738) belonging to Kingston-upon-Thames is associated with Queen Caroline.

These contribute relatively little to the history of silver design, but are often handsomely engraved with carefully integrated heraldry, in which the two faces of the discarded seal are integrated with references to the armorials of the recipient. In the case of the famous salver made by De Lamerie in 1728 for Sir Robert Walpole, his crest, arms and cypher all appear in the engraved border (Fig. 82).[48]

The Concept of Courtesy

In considering silver made before the mid-seventeenth century, it is essential to reconstruct its function in order to understand its appearance. At court and in great princes' households an elaborate ritual was observed both in laying tables and in serving food. This was dictated by a dual hierarchy of birth and office and governed not only eating and drinking but also the utensils supplied. The constant distinction made by inventory clerks between covered and uncovered vessels was of course to ensure a complete record, but also serves to remind us of the inexorable etiquette attached to their use; in all aspects of court life but pre-eminently at meal times, gold and silver reinforced the message of status.

The peak of this ritual at the English court is described in the so-called Black Book of the Household of Edward IV, a set of regulations drafted between 1471 and 1473 when a reform of the royal household was in train. Based both on English court practice and on the highly refined ceremonial of the Burgundian court (Edward's sister had married the Duke of Burgundy), it specified which ranks of the nobility and household officers were to be served their food in covered dishes, or drink from covered cups. A duke 'when he dineth or suppeth in his own chamber out of the high presence (was) then to be covered in all services', but even in the privacy of his chamber a marquess could not have covers on his food dishes. However, the steward of the household, who represented the 'great estate' of the king, was always served covered, unless he was eating in the royal chamber and in the king's presence. The cofferer, again a royal household official, was to be issued with a standing salt and spoon for his personal use while the sergeant of the pantry had only a salt.[49]

No silver serving vessels now survive earlier than the late seventeenth century, by which time the medieval rules on ceremonial dining had crumbled away and others had been substituted; even from this relatively recent period, very few covers survive, although saucepans and dishes were normally supplied with them. But where cups and salts are concerned the great majority had covers and those listed as without covers were either originally part of a set, of which one at least would have been covered, or intended for low-grade officers in large households. Sets of two, three and six drinking vessels and small salts frequently occur, but always at least one cover is included. This etiquette was followed further down the social scale too; late medieval wills often specify that the eldest son is to have the covered salt, along with the best covered cup, while other lesser pieces went to the younger children.

Unfortunately there are very few surviving covered cups or salts to underline this point: from the end of the fifteenth century, there is a small group, one being the salt presented by Warden Hill to his Oxford college in 1494. Sometimes the cover was mislaid, or sent for melting; in some cases it was attached to the foot of the cup later, to make it more stable. A steeple cup of 1599, given later to S. Mary Abbots, Kensington as a chalice (VAM) has had an outer foot ring added which has clearly been cut from its own cover; having left private hands it was used with a paten.

This attitude to the formal use of tableware and drinking vessels survives fossilised today, in that race and other presentation cups almost always have covers. They have no longer any function other than to confer status on their owners and so merit the ancient courtesy of a cover.

THE SPOON AS SYMBOLIC GIFT

Inevitably spoons, as the least expensive means of possessing or giving silver, were the focus of a range of attitudes. Often a spoon was a token of admission, for example to the livery of a company or as at Exeter and Ludlow, where on being elected one of the twenty-four burgesses, a man had to present a gilt spoon worth at least 10s and weighing two ounces or more, double gilded 'and of the form and fashion of the spoons now' before he was sworn. At Ludlow in 1639 the town owned forty-seven spoons and eleven were outstanding, still due to be delivered. 'Spoonsilver' was a commuted payment of 20s, representing the price of a silver spoon, paid by free men as admission to the Plumbers' Company in the 1660s; but an additional fine of 20s was also paid.[50]

Another attribute was as a memorial gift; Sir Robert Wingfield, at his death in 1538, left a gilt spoon to each of his colleagues on the king's council 'as a remembrance'. This came to be supplanted by the custom of presenting memorial rings, already established in the late fifteenth century; Sir Edmund Shaa left in 1488 money for rings with 'wells of pity' engraved on them, an early example of a practice which continued into the nineteenth century.[51]

The livery companies were in general no more sentimental about their collections of spoons than about their other plate. The Founders' Company sold all their spoons in 1633, with the single exception of one given by Humphrey Bourne on his admission ten years

Fig. 136 **Plague and Frost Fair spoons**
a) Gilt 1665. The seal top spoon is engraved with a total of deaths from plague in 1665.
b) 1683. The trefid end spoon is a souvenir of the Great Frost of 1683, when booths were set up on the frozen Thames.
Museum of London

329

before, which has the hopeful inscription 'If you love me keep me ever, that's my desire and your endeavour'. The Plumbers' Company, no doubt desperate for cash after the Fire, sold sixty spoons on 29 September 1666, to raise £66 7s 6d.[52]

The splendid series of spoons from 1561–1693 at the Innholders' Company demonstrates that a sense of continuity and loyalty towards past members sometimes protected even such small items. The spoon finials, each with a cast figure of S. Julian (patron saint of the Innholders') were made to a pattern supplied by the Company, and it was specified by the court of the Company that they should be made up into sets and so enhance their dinners. Few of the liverymen would be entitled by rank to adopt a personal armorial device, which might otherwise be their choice. A large parcel-gilt spoon of 1630 at the Wax-Chandlers' Company, suitably engraved with a beehive on the knop, is another gift which was sold but regained. The stem is engraved '1667 Twise presented to ye Company for their use and no otherwise to be disposed of'.[53]

When John Bankes, citizen and mercer, was preparing for his mastership of the Mercers' Company in 1630, he ordered from Robert Jygges a set of spoons with the Company's maidenhead crest as finial, presumably to distribute during his year of office. He died a week after the election, in September 1630, and one set of his maidenhead spoons, carefully marked with his initials, was bequeathed (with other silver) to Christ's Hospital (Horsham) where it remains today. One from his 1630 order has been acquired recently by the Mercers' Company. All his gifts and bequests, to his Company, Christ's Hospital and two City churches, bear his arms, although one flagon was not purchased until a decade after his death.[54]

Where a set of spoons was associated with a particularly noteworthy past benefactor, the spoons might survive more or less intact or as, in the case of the set left by Sir Richard Whittington in 1442 have been made up subsequently. Seven new spoons copied from the old ones were added in 1565, presumably because of losses. The risk of loss or sale was considerable; the Arundel spoons at Trinity Hospital were almost lost in 1666 when the 'poor men' of the hospital pawned them after the Fire for £3 16s.[55]

Until the end of the seventeenth century, a single spoon was an acceptable gift, and could also, once inscribed, be regarded as a souvenir. A trifid-end spoon at the Museum of London was 'bought at the faire kept upon the Middle of Y^e Thames at Ye Temple in the great Frost' in 1683–4, a souvenir of that phenomenon of the Thames freezing over which vanished with the building of a wider-arched bridge and the coming of milder winters (Fig. 136b). A silver-mounted tin mug 'bought by Mr Gabril Tanner at Ice Fare' is another souvenir from the same winter, sold at a booth on the river. A grimmer London memorial in the same museum is a sealtop spoon which has, engraved on its stem, a note of the mortality rate in plague year, 1665, when 68,000 out of 97,000 deaths were attributable to the epidemic (Fig. 136a).

Souvenir spoons have been commercially available for well over a century, with royal occasions, military victories and institutional centenaries all popular excuses for commemoration issues. Recently some firms have created a somewhat artificial new collector's item by issuing sets of spoons on a theme and a century ago there was a thriving market in reproduction apostle spoons.

CHRISTENING GIFTS

From the eighteenth century the single spoon fell out of favour, except as a christening gift, since a man's spoon was no longer his personal eating tool. Each child of the Tudor lawyer, Edmund Bowyer, received one from his godparents in the 1560s; and the Norwich goldsmith Peter Peterson left one to each of his godchildren in 1603. But other plate was equally acceptable, particularly porringers; a York porringer of 1680 is engraved (in Latin) 'The Gift of JH who stood as godfather 2 Aug 1682'.[56] Samuel Pepys, setting off to a family christening in 1661 with a porringer and a set of spoons, returned home with his gifts undelivered, annoyed because he had not been asked to name the child (although eventually he compromised by giving just the spoons). Another time, in 1668, his wife gave a basin costing over £10 to their parson's newborn child.[57]

Edward Howes, writing in 1631, regarded the custom of a christening gift of silver as a Tudor innovation; 'it was not the use and custom (as now it is) for godfathers and godmothers generally to give plate at the baptism of children (as spoons, cups and such like) but only to give christening suits with little bands and cuffs wrought either with silk or blue thread'. No consistent pattern of christening gifts is discernible before the nineteenth century, when the normal gift became a mug or cutlery set. A rather more bizarre and much more substantial christening present is a Britannia standard tureen with cast lion and unicorn handles which the newborn Lady Emilia Lennox received in 1733. This tureen or pot à l'oille was already old and presumably, from its use of the royal supporters, part of a Jewel House order (Plate 6).[58]

By the mid-nineteenth century, christening plate had become both standardised and, responding to the pressure of renascent Anglicanism, laden with appropriate Christian imagery. One of the most attractive of the Summerly commissions is a mug designed by Richard Redgrave on which standing angels clasp hands. In a standing cup by Hunt & Roskell (VAM 1852) three kneeling angels support the bowl above a coiled serpent, a design in the French gothic spirit. The young Queen Victoria, whose godchildren were very many, ordered a standard cup from Mortimer & Hunt (VAM 1841); this incorporates a lion and a lamb, putti representing the virtues of prayer, gentleness and pity and a serpent symbolising eternity. Quite apart from the queen's cypher and a dedicatory inscription, it is recognisably a display piece and far less useful than the Redgrave mug. Later designs for mugs, notably by Elkington's, drew on Kate Greenaway's illustrations of children, which were engraved or etched onto standard simple forms.

Monarchs were always vulnerable to such requests. Henry VIII seems to have made a standard gift of a salt weighing sixteen to twenty ounces to the children of royal officers. In the careful accounts of Sir John Petre of Ingatestone Hall, we see that he too purchased salts, in December 1567, for two godchildren. Both were gilt, one 'with a pepper box in the top' cost 39s 9d and the other 52s. These were standard items with no indication of engraving to record the gift. This was the recipient's business. Several christening gifts of George II are recorded; one, a cup by Paul Crespin presented to the king's godson Tollemache in 1744, is the standard two-handled presentation cup of the time, merely differentiated by the engraved royal arms and cypher (see Pl. 6).[59]

nus JOHANNES SHAW
Baronettus necnon L.L. D.
(de quo supra Pag. LXX.)
Diotam argenteam cum oper-
-culo *anaglyptico* opere ela-
-boratam donavit.
1751

ONORABILIS JUVENIS D.ˢ
FREDRICUS NORTH
Filius natu maximus
HONORATISSIMI D.ⁿⁱ D.ⁿⁱ
FRANCISCI Baronis
NORTH et de GUILFORD
Hujus Collegii Primi Ordinis Commensalis dedit
Viginti Avreos ———— £ 2J.
1749

DVARDUS WINNINGTON
Arm.(de quo supra Pag. LXXI.)
duos Cantharos ex argento
affabrè factos dedit.
1754

Fig. 137 **Page from college gift book**
Mid–eighteenth century. A very rare example in England of a pictorial record of gifts kept between the
late seventeenth and late eighteenth centuries. Many of the pieces are still in the college's hands.
Trinity College, Oxford

Security

A constant factor unique to silver is that it has been the only form of decorative art, in daily use throughout the house, which also has an immediate resale value. It is innately precious, a quality which has always demanded special treatment from owners, the craft and the king. Precautions against clipping and more spectacular acts of theft have ranged from the unobtrusive but careful marking of scratch-weights on the undersides of objects, to the indentures customarily signed by those household officers with responsibility for plate. Thanks to this inherent and constant value, we have relatively full documentation of early plate, even though there may be very few actual examples.

When Cardinal Wolsey's plate was to be handed over to the king in 1529 it was all set out on tables in two rooms off the gallery in his archiepiscopal palace at Westminster (Whitehall); 'under the tables in both the chambers were set baskets with old plate, which was not esteemed but for broken and old, not worthy to be occupied, and books containing the value and weight of every parcel ready to be seen'. When on semi-public display, as for example at a banquet for French ambassadors held in 1546, the King's laden buffets were guarded by men-at-arms throughout the meal.[60]

There were always leakages of plate, particularly from the scullery, the household department where silver was most in use. Between 1558 and 1596 the royal household lost 15,600 ounces of plate from the scullery alone, 'stollen and embeaseled by untrewe persons as well at gret Feastes and marriges, Banquets and Progresses'. The Jewel House paid an annual reward to the beadles at Goldsmiths' Hall until the Civil War, in recognition of their looking out for stolen royal plate offered for sale in the shops of Cheapside.[61] The Goldsmiths' Company was the obvious route by which to persuade tradesmen not to deal in stolen plate or jewels or to pass on the word about particular thefts.

The enormous sums locked up in plate, and the relative ease with which it could be embezzled by dishonest servants, meant that specified household officers were made responsible for the plate in their individual charge. As George Cavendish, Wolsey's usher, explained, 'every officer was charged by indenture with all such parcels as belonged to their office'. The Skinners had their plate weighed, valued, the weights marked on each piece and a new inventory drawn up on four occasions in the seventeenth century, a typical institutional pattern of care.

An inventory of Edward Seymour's plate made in 1546 lists offices normally holding and answerable for plate; trenchers, salts and spoons were kept in the pantry, drinking vessels (bowls, glass flagons and jugs) in the cellar, serving pots and cruets in the buttery, basins and candlesticks in the ewery and tableware (plates, dishes and 'saucers') in the scullery. Chamber (bedroom) plate in Mistress Barbara de la Roche's charge included a looking-glass and a casting flagon for perfumed water, bowls and small covered cruses 'made jug-fashion all gilt with arms' and a stoneware jug ribbed and covered with silvergilt.[62]

The Hardwick Hall plate inventory of 1601 appears at first an inchoate jumble, a miscellaneous mixture of silver, but once the entries are grouped according to their function, it becomes clear that the clerks preparing the inventory moved round the house from office to office, dealing separately with dining, drinking, washing and cooking plate, although not troubling to separate the categories on their list. Most household and probate inventories continued to adopt this approach; the 1750 list prepared for George Booth, Earl of Warrington, lists plate in the still room, pantry, chapel and tea room.[63]

In the first half of the nineteenth century a crop of grand new country houses were built. They all had one feature in common; plate storage was centralised in a strong room and the butler was responsible for it, often sleeping in a room adjacent and so controlling access, as the plans of early Victorian country houses published by Franklin demonstrate. The weight of each piece was carefully recorded and sometimes engraved on to the base, and these precise details enable one sometimes to identify specific items or to trace alterations.[64]

Despite all these precautions, thefts from private houses did occur, as a glance at the published calendars of Middlesex Quarter Sessions records or the advertisements in the London Gazette for the late seventeenth century shows. One incident at Ham House, Surrey in 1763 concerned not tableware but silver trimmings for furnishings, characteristic of that lavishly equipped house and still to be seen there.

The wife of a local gardener, Francis Lambert, dishonestly came by the cast silver foot from 'an hearth for burning wood or coals'. When attempting to sell it, she chose the royal goldsmith, Thomas Heming, in Old Bond Street. Her story to him was that a sea officer had given it to her as payment for his lodging. An alternative version, offered when she wanted the silver weighed before taking it to sell, was that her husband's servants had found it in a load of dung, purchased in London! She clearly had an accomplice among the Ham House staff; two cast lion feet detached from hearth boxes are now displayed at the house.[65]

Heming's part in reporting her visit and the attempt to sell the silver is characteristic of the responsible honest goldsmith; all London retailers were required by the Company to enquire the source of any plate offered for sale and keep a list of the information. The Goldsmiths' Company employed 'Warning Carriers' to alert the trade to recent thefts. A Company Walkbook of 1744 names three officers who were, between them, to visit 162 goldsmiths plus pawnbrokers, jewellers, toymen and watchmakers.

An Elizabethan basin belonging to Bristol Corporation of 1595 is a well-documented example of a recovered theft. Stolen in the 1831 town riots, it was cut up by the thief into 167 pieces. But when these were offered to a Bristol silversmith, the thief was captured and the basin, reconstructed on to a new silver backplate, is back among the corporation plate. The commonest theft was of a spoon or fork, easily concealed in a servant's apron or pocket. Advertisements in the Newcastle papers analysed by Margaret Gill show that goldsmiths were expected to check up even if the piece offered was worth relatively little.[66]

Churchwardens often engraved their names and that of the parish, along with the weight, underneath chalices, flagons and alms dishes. S. James Garlickhythe, in the City of London, owns one of the earliest post-Reformation communion cups (1549) onto which, a century later, a large scallop shell was engraved as a mark of ownership. But while there were dishonest goldsmiths prepared to shut their eyes and ask no questions for the sake of obtaining silver for melt at a bargain price, a ready market for stolen silver flourished.

The problem with plate, as with cash before paper money appeared, was its weight. In July when the Dutch fleet was menacing Harwich, Samuel Pepys set about ensuring the safety of his valuables. Some he sent to be buried in his country garden at Broughton but he complained of the difficulty of wearing £300-worth of gold 'around my body with some trouble'. Burial was a time-honoured way of securing silver against marauders; in 1745 churchwardens terrified of the approaching Scottish army of Bonnie Prince Charlie, buried the Newcastle church plate for safety, and the Drapers' Company saved theirs from the Great Fire by burying it in the garden of their Hall.

Churches were also vulnerable to thieves since they had open doors, coupled with a concentration of precious vessels. The benefactor of Layer Marney Church, Essex in 1523 gave not only two complete services of altar plate (one for the parish altar and one for his chantry chapel) but also explicit instructions for their security. The normal custom, of different keys to be held by several responsible people, was adopted here and several churches still retain their iron-bound Nuremburg chests with two or three locks, intended to guard against an individual dishonest churchwarden.[67]

Occasionally church plate reappeared without explanation. S. Mary, Ealing owns a handsome group of various dates, including a chalice by George Garthorne (seventeenth century), a later copy of it and several alms dishes and patens, all with the typical revived rococo floral embossing of the 1820s. The entire group was 'left at the Vicarage on Christmas Day by a stranger', perhaps someone with a guilty conscience? Two flagons at Christchurch Newgate Street were recovered from Islington Horsepond, slightly dented but otherwise unharmed, two centuries ago; again, it seems that an uneasy conscience led to a 'hunt as to its whereabouts' which was successful because someone suggested where to look.

One spectacular raid of church plate took place at S. Paul's Cathedral in 1810. With the minimum of damage and no signs of forced entry, thieves removed 2,000 ounces of silver from the strong room above the dean's vestry, penetrating eight locked doors and leaving behind a skeleton key. Even the silver binding on Bishop Sancroft's great bible was ripped off. The theft was discovered only when preparing for the following Sunday's services. None of the plate was ever recovered. Grantham Parish Church, which lost its plate a few years later, issued handbills with full details of engraved inscriptions and weights, but none was returned; S. Mary, Boston was equally unfortunate in 1775, in spite of offering a £50 reward for information.[68]

Criminals today are well aware of the difficulty of disposing of antique plate, unless it is of a type familiar enough to be hard to trace. In 1968, when a plate cupboard in Canterbury Cathedral was broken into, the silver stolen included a medieval ablution basin of about 1400, but this was discarded on a dump at Streatham Common and later recovered by the police, whereas the large Caroline flagon and other, later, silver has not reappeared. Presumably the basin's timeworn and superficially dull appearance saved it.[69]

Security of church plate has become more problematic in the past century, as people depart from rural parishes and town churches are empty even during the week, leaving their treasures vulnerable even where a secure store exists. To reduce this risk, and to bring at least some plate back into the public eye, the Victoria and Albert Museum in 1915 opened a gallery of English church plate, which has now about 300 exhibits. More recently the Goldsmiths' Company initiated in 1958 a series of diocesan treasuries, of which there are now eighteen installed in English cathedrals. Each contains a selection of plate lent by the churches of that diocese, each piece chosen because it is old, a local variation in shape, given by someone noteworthy, or simply because it is a beautiful piece of craftsmanship. Other historic church silver has been deposited in local museums; with the exception of those originally made for domestic use, most pieces have a relatively limited interest outside their locality, since the communion vessels were normally produced to standard designs and have no great intrinsic importance as decorative art. Often the engraving, dedicatory or more rarely pictorial, is their most interesting feature. But the sheer bulk of plate inherited by some town churches where several parishes have been amalgamated into one, which is a situation peculiar to the ancient cities of Norwich, Exeter, Bristol and London, means that some plate inevitably lurks 'in the bank vaults, where no one can see it'.

Notes

1   Collins 1955, 111; Oman 1961, pl. 18.

2   Goldsmiths' 1951, pl. LXXVII; Preston 1958; Goldsmiths' 1978.

3   Grimwade 1951; Lushington 1975.

4   Goldsmiths' 1951, nos. 33, 38, 49, 56, 66, 74.

5   Goldsmiths' 1951, no. 238; Carrington and Hughes 1926, 163.

6   Oman 1970; Greenwood 1930, 37–9. Another past-master, John Sanderson, left minute instructions as to the shape of the ewer to be bought with his bequest of £50: 'of the old fashion, with a nose and not a round spoute nor an anticke end'.

7   Jewitt and Hope 1895, CXVIII and *passim*. Altogether twenty towns still own punch bowls or monteiths. Barr 1983, and p. 69 and p. 80–1.

8   Jewitt and Hope 1895.

9   Greenwood 1930, 56–8. His spoons were converted into candlesticks in 1738.

10   Painter-Stainers' 1972.

11   Nicholl 1866.

12   Crawford 1977, 91. Five purchasers, all senior members of the Company, spent £156; more was sold in 1548. Milbourn quotes earlier inventories.

13   Oman 1934.

14   Greenwood 1930, 4.

15   Prideaux 1896, Vol. II, 161.

16   Prideaux 1896, Vol. II, 185–6. The Ironmongers kept till the 1640s a Jacobean lottery prize: Nicholl 1866.

17   McMurray 1925, 130.

18   Masters 1978, 308–9.

19   Masters 1978, 311.

20   W. S. Lewis, *Letters of Horace Walpole* (1954) Vol. 18.

21   Leeds RO; Ingram MSS.

22   *Goldsmiths' Review* 1969/70, 16–18.

23   Halliwell 1839, 'Warkworth's Chronicle'.

24   Oman 1973, 54–8.

25   Jewitt and Hope 1895, King's Lynn. Two Nuremburg cups among the Kremlin ambassadorial gifts, bear the mark of the London goldsmith RB (for Richard Brooke); Oman 1961, pl. 21, 24. p. 172.

26   Oman 1961, pl. 33.

27   Yorkshire Diaries *Surtees Society* (1886) 115.

28   Howard Inventory 1614; Leeds RO; Ingram goldsmiths' bills 1650s.

29   Quoted in Hayward 1959.

30   Wills 1983. Culme 1985.

31   Kingston-on-Thames RO: Frederick MSS.

32   Leeds RO: Ingram MSS.

33   *Bury Wills*. Quoted in Myers 1850.

34   *Bury Wills*.

35   *Somerset Wills*.

36   C. E. Parsons, 'Horseheath Hall and its Owners', *Cambridge Antiquarian Society* (1948) 41.

37   *Bury Wills*. Stone pots, silver mounted, were the universal drinking vessel for yeomen upwards: Allan 1984, Ch. 3.

38   It had been mounted about 1550–70. Boston MFA, pl. XVI, 389–90.

39   Banister 1981. Stone 1966, 1973.

40   Oman 1970.

41   Wark 1978, pl. 219; Jackson 1911, pl. 445, 721.

42   In VAM.

43   Banister 1968, 13; Barr 1980, 158.

44   Collins 72–3. Ambassador archdeacon Hawkins, in Bologna in 1532 stressed this point, 'Judge you how they are content to be served in tin or pewter, who are accustomed to dine at home off silver'.

45 Banister 1968.

46 With Brand Inglis 1979.

47 Jewitt and Hope 1895. The tankard is hall-marked 1661; Carrington and Hughes 1926, pl. 37. At Hastings a punch bowl was made from the silver staves from George II's Coronation.

48 Banister 1981, 278–9, 334–5. A later formula· was to set the seal matrix into a rose bowl.

49 Myers 1959, *passim*. Northumberland Household Book. Eames 1971.

50 Royal Albert Memorial Museum, n.d.; Plumbers' 1965.

51 Reddaway and Walker 1975, 176.

52 Ironmongers' 1866; Plumbers' 1965.

53 Butler 1901; Ironmongers'.

54 Information from Jean Imray, former archivist to the Mercers' Company. In 1603 the Norwich goldsmith, Peter Peterson, left twenty spoons 'with knoppes of the sonne' (his device) among his family.

55 Imray 1978; 1981.

56 Lee 1972, pl. 22.

57 Banister 1968.

58 Sotheby's May 1984 and p. 236.

59 Salts were used in the medieval baptismal ritual. Trevor 1955.

60 Cavendish 1959; Oman 1979 a and b.

61 Collins 1955, 153 and 156, note 4. In 1597 when the queen's silver and pearl standish was stolen at Theobalds, the theft was cried through the London streets and an informer betrayed the culprit.

62 Seymour MSS.

63 Hardwick inventory 1601. Plate inventory of George Booth 1750, photocopy in Department of Metalwork (VAM).

64 Franklin.

65 Tollemache MSS.

66 Jewitt and Hope 1895, 'Bristol'. Goldsmiths' 1952. For example, Gill 1980, 266, 277, 284.

67 Oman 1979.

68 Oman 1957; Pishey Thompson 1856.

69 Oman 1979.

BIBLIOGRAPHY

Primary Sources

MSS

Amadas Inventory 1532, Inventory of Robert Amadas 1532, Public Record Office PROB 2/486

Ashbee MSS, Unpublished memoirs, typescript vols., VAM Library

Bowyer MSS, Estate book of John Bowyer, *c*.1550–70, Minet Library, Camberwell, MSVI/230

Darnley Inventory 1831, Goods of the Rt Hon. Earl Darnley at Cobham Hall, Kent, taken 10 June 1831, VAM, National Art Library

Elkington Pattern Books MSS, *c*.1840–1920, Archive Dept., VAM

Fox MSS, History of Rundell, Bridge & Rundell by George Fox, 1843, Baker Library, Harvard, MSS 597, 1843, F792 (photostat copy, VAM, London)

Goldsmiths' Company MSS

— Wardens' accounts and minute books, 1334 to the present (one volume only, 1578–92, is missing)

— Apprenticeship registers, vol. 1 [the book called the Dormant] 1578 – the present

— Assayers' books 1740 – the present, assay office records

— Survey and view of property 1651

— 'Gouldesmythes Storehouse' by H.G. (Hannibal Gamon) 1604, Citizen and Goldsmith of London (copies in the Folger Shakespeare Library, Washington; the Goldsmiths' Company; the British Library)

— Townshend plate book *c*.1760.

Hirst MSS, *c*.1832, Robert Michael Hirst, 'A Short Account of the Founders of the Silver and Plated Establishments in Sheffield', Sheffield City Libraries, acc. no. 33243 special collections (Bradbury Records 299)

Holland Inventory 1447, Plate and jewels of John Holland, late Duke of Exeter, taken 8 September 1447, Westminster Abbey Muniments 6643

Ingram MSS, Temple Newsam archives deposited at Leeds district archives

Newdegate MSS, Arbury Hall, Warwickshire, deposited at Warwick Record Office

Pembroke Inventory 1561–7, 'Gold & Sylver Plate, Jewelles, Apparell & Wardrobe Stuffe . . . of William Herbert, Earl of Pembroke, VAM, MS L.30–1982

Randle Holme MSS, Collection of Chester papers, BM, Harl. MS 2125

Sudbury Inventory 1683, Probate inventory of plate etc. of John Sudbury, Dean of Durham, 5 June 1683

Tollemache MSS, Inventories, bills and other papers relating to the plate of Elizabeth Dysart, later Countess Lauderdale, *c*.1650–1700

— Bills, notebooks and other papers of Lyonel, fourth Earl Tollemache 1727–44

Wickes/Wakelin MSS, Gentlemen's ledgers (nineteen vols), 1740–1818; Workmen's Ledgers and Day Books (8 vols) 1766–1816, Dept. of Metalwork, VAM

PRINTED

Royal Inventories 1326–1817

Inventory 1326, W. Rees, *Caerphilly Castle and its Place in the Annals of Glamorgan* (Caerphilly, 1974) pp. 114–28

Inventory 1521, 'King Henry VIII's Jewel Book' [1521] (transcript from MSS, formerly at Welbeck), *Associated Architectural Societies Reports and Papers*, vol. 18 (1883) pp. 155–229

Inventory 1542, 'Contents of Westminster Palace, 1542, Listed by Sir Anthony Denny', *Archaeological Journal*, XVIII (1864) p. 134 [PRO Wardrobe and Ho'hold A/C E351/42]

Inventory 1574, A. J. Collins, *The 1574 Inventory of the Jewels and Plate of Queen Elizabeth* (1955)

Inventory 1649, *Inventories and Valuations of the King's Goods 1649–1651*, O. Millar (ed.), Walpole Society, vol. 43 (1972)

Inventory 1703, 'The Goods and Chattels belonging to King James the Second', *Archaeologia*, 18 (1817)

Private and Institutional Inventories 1384–1804

Bond, M. F., *Inventories of S. George's Chapel Windsor 1384–1667* (1947)

Boynton, L., 'The Hardwick Hall Inventory of 1601', *Furniture History*, 7 (1971)

Brears, P., 'Yorkshire Probate Inventories 1542–1689', *Yorkshire Arch. Society Record Series*, 134 (1972)

Bury, *Bury Wills and Inventories*, Camden Society (1850)

Carpenters' Company Inventory 1627, 'Plate and Jewels', Appendix 4, in B. W. E. Alford and T. C. Barker, *A History of the Carpenters' Company* (1968)

Cathedral Inventories 1536
   Salisbury Cathedral, *Ecclesiastical Art Review* (April 1878) pp. 84–5
   Winchester Cathedral, *Ecclesiastical Art Review* (May 1878) pp. 114–15

Fastolf Inventory 1459, 'Inventory of Sir John Fastolf', *Archaeologia*, 21 (1827)

Gloucester Inventory 1392, Thomas of Woodstock, Duke of Gloucester, *Archaeological Journal*, liv (1897)

Gloucestershire Inventories 1539–1804, J. S. Moore, *The Goods and Chattels of our Forefathers – Frampton Cotterell (Glos) Inventories 1539–1804* (1976)

Halliwell, J. O., *Ancient Inventories* (1854)

Howard Inventory 1614, 'Inventory of Henry Howard KG, late Earl of Northampton, 1614', *Archaeologia*, XLII, part 2 (1869) pp. 347–74

Inventories 1642–3 (Oxford and Cambridge colleges), Gutch, *Collectanea Curiosa*, vol. 1, p. 227; *HMC Fourth Report*, Appendix 467; *HMC Second Report*, Appendix 127

Inventory 1761, S. Leighton, 'An Inventory Taken at Park Hall, Shropshire in 1761', *Transactions of the Shropshire Archaeological and Natural History Society*, n.s. 7 (1895) pp. 97–119

Legg and Hope, J. W. Legg and W. H. St John Hope, *Inventories of Christchurch Canterbury* (1902)

Oxford Inventory 1513, John De Vere, Earl of Oxford, *Archaeologia*, LXV (1914)

Oxford Inventories, *Household and Farm Inventories of Oxfordshire 1550–1590*, Oxford Record Society XLIV (Oxford 1965)

Queens' College Inventory 1642, 'The Plate of Queens' College Cambridge, melted in 1642', *Cambridge Antiquarian Society*, 1882, vol. 1, paper 31, p. 19

Seymour Inventories 1539, 1546, *Bath Longleat MSS, vol. IV, Seymour Papers 1532–1686*, HMC (1968)

Steer, F. W., *Farm and Cottage Inventories of Mid-Essex 1635–1749*, Essex R.O. VIII (rev. ed. 1969)

Suffolk Inventories 1539, *Suffolk Probate Inventories 1583–1631*, Suffolk Record Society, 22 (1981)

Weavers' Company Inventory 1677, 'Inventory of Plate, Linen etc. in Weavers' Hall 1677', Appendix I in A. Plummer, *The London Weavers' Company 1600–1970* (1972)

Family and Institutional Records

Brasbridge, J., *The Fruits of Experience* (1824) [memoirs of a silversmith]

Early English Text Society — *Babees Book*, Vol. 32 (1868)

—*A 15th c. Courtesy Book*, Vol. 148 (1914)

Edwards, A. C., *The Account Books of Benjamin Mildmay, Earl Fitzwalter* (1977)

Emmison, F. G., *Elizabethan Life: Wills of Essex Gentry and Merchants Preserved in the PCC* (Essex Record Office, 1978)

1980, *Elizabethan Life: Wills of Essex Gentry and Yeomen Preserved in Essex Record Office* (Essex Record Office, 1980)

1983, *Elizabethan Wills of South West Essex* (Waddesdon, 1983)

Freshfield, E., *Minutes of the Vestry Meeting of S. Christopher le Stocks* (1886)

Howard, *Household Accounts of John Lord Howard and Thomas Earl of Surrey 1481–1490* (Roxburghe Club, 1844)

Langford, A., *Sale Catalogue [of property in Saville Row and contents] of Lady Frederick, dec. 29 June 1767* (1767)

Levine, G., 'Some Norwich Goldsmiths' Wills', *Norfolk Archaeology*, XXXV, IV (1973)

Lewis, W. S., *The Correspondence of Horace Walpole*, 48 vols. (1961; New Haven, 1937–83)

London Record Society, *London Consistory Court Wills 1492–1547*, 3 (1967)

McMurray, W., *The Records of Two City Churches* (1925) [S. John Zachary and S. Anne and S. Agnes]

Middlesex County Records 1886, *Indictments, Coroners Inquests Postmortem and Recognizances from 3 Edward VI to 1603*, vol. 1 (1886; reprint 1972)

Myers, A. R., *English Historical Documents*, Vol. 3 (1969)

Myers, A. R., *The Household of Edward IV* (The Black Book) (Manchester, 1959)

Nichol, H., *Testamenta Vetusta* (1826)

Nichols, J., *Illustrations of Manners and Expenses of Ancient Times* (1797)

Paston, *Paston Letters and Papers*, Norman Davis (ed.), part I (1971) part 2 (1976)

Pepys, S., *The Diary of Samuel Pepys* 1660–1669, R. Latham (ed.), 10 vols. (1970–83)

Percy, *Household Papers of Henry Percy 9th Earl of Northumberland 1564–1632*, Camden Society Third Series, Vol. 93 (1962)

Prideaux, W. S., *Memorials of the Goldsmiths' Company*, 2 vols. (1896–7)

Sheffield, *The Sheffield Assay Office Register* (1911)

Somerset, *Somerset Medieval Wills*, XLI (Somerset Record Society, 1901)

Temple, Sir R. C. (ed.) *Travels of Peter Mundy 1608–1667,* Hakluyt Society series 2, vols 45 & 46 (1919)

Wood-Legh, *A Small Household of the XVth Century, Being the Account Book of Munden's Chantry, Bridport* (1956)

Catalogues of Exhibitions and Collections

Alec-Smith, R. A. *Catalogue Raisonne of the Corporation Plate of Kingston upon Hull* (Kingston upon Hull, 1973)

Arts Council 1979, *The Thirties: British Art and Design before the War*, Ex. Cat. (1979)
— 1984, *English Romanesque Art 1066–1200*, Ex. Cat. (1984)

Ashmolean Museum, *British Plate in the Ashmolean Museum* (Oxford, n.d.)

Baker, M., Schroder, T. and Clowes, E. L., *Beckford and Hamilton Silver from Brodick Castle*, Ex. Cat. (1980)

Benton, G. M., Galpin, F. W. and Pressey, W. J., *Church Plate of Essex* (Colchester, 1926)

Birmingham City Museum, *Omar Ramsden 1873–1939, Centenary Exhibition of Silver*, Ex. Cat. (Birmingham, 1973)
— *Birmingham Gold and Silver 1773–1973*, Ex. Cat. (1973)

Birmingham (Alabama) Museum of Art, *Silver from the Birmingham Museum* (1982)

Bishop, P., *Holburne of Menstrie Museum, A Guide to the Collections*, centenary exhibition (Bath, 1982)

Boston, Museum of Fine Arts, *New England Begins*, 3 vols., Ex. Cat. (Boston, Mass., 1982)

Bowes Museum, *Old Sheffield Plate 1750–1850*, Ex. Cat. (Castle Barnard, 1966)

British Museum, *British Heraldry to c.1800,* Ex. Cat. (1978)

Buhler K., *Church Silver of Colonial Virginia*, Ex. Cat. (Virginia Museum, Richmond, 1970)
— 'The Silver', *Campbell Museum Collection* (Camden, New Jersey, 1972)

Burrell, *Silver in the Burrell Collection* (Glasgow Art Gallery booklet, n.d.)

Busch-Reisinger Museum, *Eucharistic Vessels of the Middle Ages*, Ex. Cat. (Busch-Reisinger Museum, Harvard, USA, 1975)

Carrington, J. B. and Hughes, G. R., *Plate of the Worshipful Company of Goldsmiths* (Oxford, 1926)

Carver, B. S. and Casey, E. M., *Silver by Paul De Lamerie at the Sterling and Francine Clark Art Institute* (Williamstown, Mass., 1978)

Christie's, '*The Swaythling Collection of Silversmiths' Work*, catalogue of sale (6 May 1924)

— *Silver Treasures from English Churches*, exhibition catalogue (1955)

— Sale (29 May 1963)

— Sale (24–5 May 1816)

Colman, *The Colman Collection of Silver Mustard Pots*, edited by J. Culme (Norwich, 1979)

Cooper, J. C., 'The Gibbs Collection of English Silver' (Nottingham Castle Museum), *Connoisseur*, 202 (October 1979) p. 135

Cripps, W., *College and Corporation Plate* (1881)

Davis, J. D., *English Silver at Williamsburg* (Colonial Williamsburg, 1976)

Ellis, H. D., *Ancient Silver Plate Belonging to the Worshipful Company of Armourers and Braziers* (1892)

Fitzwilliam Museum, *Cambridge Plate*, Ex. Cat. (Cambridge, 1975)

Ferguson, W., *Old Church Plate in the Diocese of Carlisle* (1888)

Folger Coffee Company, *Folger Coffee Company Collection of Antique English Silver Coffee Pots*, Ex. Cat. (Nelson Gallery, Kansas City, Missouri, 1959)

Freshfield, E., *The Communion Plate of the Churches in the City of London* (1894)

— *The Communion Plate of the Churches in the County of London* (1895)

Gardner, J. S., *Old Silverwork, Chiefly English . . . Exhibited in 1902 at S. James's Court London* (1903)

Goldsmiths' Company 1938–1983. Exhibitions held at Goldsmiths' Hall, London.

— *Exhibition of Modern Silverwork* (1938)

— *Historic Plate of the City of London* (1951)

— *Contemporary Silverware* (1951)

— *Corporation Plate of England and Wales* (1952)

— *Treasures of Oxford* (1953)

— *Treasures of Cambridge* (1959)

— *Plate at Goldsmiths' Hall, London* (1960)

— *The Sterling Craft: Five Centuries of Treasures from the Worshipful Company of Goldsmiths, London*, touring exhibition (1966)

— *Copy or Creation – Victorian Treasures from English Churches* (1967)

— *Touching Gold and Silver: 500 Years of Hallmarks* (1978)

— *The Schroder Collection: Virtuoso Goldsmiths' Work from the Age of Humanism* (1979)

— *Leslie Durbin . . .* (1982)

— *Matthew Boulton and the Toymakers: Silver from the Birmingham Assay Office* (1982)

— *The Goldsmith and the Grape* (1983)

— *A Place for Gold* (1985)

Great Exhibition 1851, *Official Descriptive and Illustrated Catalogue of the Great Exhibition of the Works of Industry of all Nations* (1851)

Greenwood, M. A., *The Ancient Plate of the Drapers' Company* (1930)

Grosvenor Museum, *Chester Silver*, Ex. Cat. (1984)

Hackenbroch, Y., *English and Other Silver in the Irwin Untermyer Collection* (New York, 1969)

342

Hawkins, J. B., *Masterpieces of English and European Silver and Gold* (Sydney, 1979)
— 1984, *The Al-Tajir Collection*, privately printed (London, 1984)

Hope, W. St John and Fallow, T.M., 'English Medieval Chalices and Patens', *Arch. Jour.* XLIII (1887), pp. 137–61, 364–402

Ironmongers', *Catalogue of the Antiquities and Works of Art, Exhibited at Ironmongers' Hall, London in the Month of May 1861*, 2 vols (1869)

Jewitt, L. and Hope, W. St J. *The Corporation Plate and Insignia of Office of the Cities and Towns of England and Wales*, W. H. St John Hope (ed.) (1895)

Jones, E. A., *Old Royal Plate in the Tower of London* (Oxford, 1908)
— *Collection of Old Plate of J. P. Morgan*, privately printed (1908)
— *The Old Plate of the Cambridge Colleges* (1910)
— *The Gold and Silver of Windsor Castle* (1911)
— *Catalogue of Plate Belonging to the Duke of Portland at Welbeck Abbey* (1935)

Jones, W. E., *Monumental Silver: the Gilbert Collection*, Ex. Cat. (Los Angeles, 1979)

Kingston upon Hull, *Silver Made by Hull Goldsmiths*, Ex. Cat. (1951)

Laing Art Gallery, *Thomas Bewick*, Ex. Cat. (Newcastle, Laing Art Gallery, 1979)

Lang, G., *The Wrestling Boys: An Exhibition of Chinese and Japanese Ceramics . . . at Burghley House* (Stamford, 1983)

Lasko, P. and Morgan, N. J., *Medieval Art in East Anglia 1300–1520*, Ex. Cat. (Norwich, 1973)

Lee, G. E., *British Silver Monteith Bowls* (Byfleet, 1978)

Manchester City Art Gallery, *The Assheton Bennett Collection* (Manchester, 1965)

Metropolitan Museum of Art, *Highlights of the Untermyer Collection of English and Continental Decorative Arts* (New York, 1977)

Miles, E. B., *English Silver: The Elizabeth B. Miles Collection* (Wadsworth Athenaeum, Conn., 1976)

Milbourn, T., *The Vintners' Company Muniments and Plate* (1888)

Moffat, H. C., *Old Oxford Plate* (1906)

Molen, J. R. ter, *Van Vianen* (Utrecht, 1984)

Moss, M. A., *The Lilian and Morice Moss Collection of Paul Storr Silver* (Miami, Florida, 1972)

Mulliner, H. H., *The Decorative Arts in England*, catalogue of private collection (1924)

Museum of London, *London Silver 1680 to 1780*, Ex. Cat. (1982)
— *The Quiet Conquest. The Huguenots 1685 to 1985*, Ex. Cat. (1985)

National Museum of Wales, *The Strange Genius of William Burges*, Ex. Cat. (Cardiff, 1981)

Norfolk Museums, *Norwich Silver in the Collection of Norwich Castle Museum* (Norwich, 1981)

Oman, C., 'English Plate at the Hermitage Leningrad and State Historical Museum, Moscow', *Connoisseur*, CXLV (August 1959) pp. 14–16
— *The English Silver in the Kremlin 1557–1663* (1961)
— 'The Plate of Winchester College', *Connoisseur*, CXLIX (January 1962) pp. 24–33
— 'The Civic Plate and Insignia of the City of Norwich', *Connoisseur*, 155 and 156 (April and May, 1964)
— *Catalogue of Plate Belonging to the Bank of England* (1967)

Painter-Stainers', *Treasures of the Painters' Company* (1972)

Penzer, N. M., 'The Hervey Silver at Ickworth', parts 1 and 2, *Apollo*, LXV (February/April, 1957)

— 'Tudor Font-shaped Cups', parts I–III, *Apollo* (December 1957, February and March 1958)

— 'The Steeple Cup', parts I–IV, *Apollo*, 71, 72 (1959–60)

— 'The Plate of Christ's Hospital', 3 parts, *Apollo* (July/August/September 1960)

— 'An Index of Steeple Cups', *Proceedings of the Society of Silver Collectors* (n.d.)

Preston, A. E., *The Abingdon Corporation Plate* (Oxford, 1958)

Read, H. and Tonnochy, A., *Catalogue of Silver Plate: the Franks Bequest* (British Museum, 1928)

Robinson, J. C., *Catalogue of the Special Exhibition of Works of Art on Loan to the South Kensington Museum June 1862* (1863)

Royal Academy, *The Arts and Crafts Society Fiftieth Anniversary Exhibition* (1938)

— *Victorian and Edwardian Art – The Handley-Read Collection* (1972)

Royal Albert Memorial Museum, *Exeter and West Country Silver* (1978)

— *Early West Country Spoons from the Corfield Collection* (n.d.)

Royal Collection, *Inventory of Plate by Garrard's,* privately printed (1911)

Royal Ontario Museum, *English Silver*, Ex. Cat. (Toronto, 1958)

Safford, F. G., 'Colonial Silver in the American Wing', *Metropolitan Museum of Art Bulletin*, XLI, 1 (1983)

Schroder, T., *The Dowty Collection of Silver by Paul De Lamerie*, Ex. Cat. (Cheltenham, Cheltenham Art Gallery, 1983)

Sheffield Polytechnic, *The Silversmith: An Exhibition to Celebrate the Bicentenary of the Sheffield Assay Office*, Ex. Cat. (Sheffield, 1973)

Sheffield City Museum, *Sheffield Silver 1773–1973*, Ex. Cat. (Sheffield, 1973)

Society of Arts, *Catalogue of Works of Ancient and Medieval Art Exhibited at the House of the Society of Arts* (1850)

Spinks, *Sixty Years of English Silver 1878–1938*, Ex. Cat. (1984)

Victoria and Albert Museum, *Old English Pattern Books of the Metal Trades*, catalogue (1913)

Victoria and Albert Museum 1953–1984, Catalogues of exhibitions

— *Exhibition of Victorian and Edwardian Decorative Arts* (1953)

— *Royal Plate from Buckingham Palace and Windsor Castle* (1954)

— *Victorian Church Art* (1971)

— *The Hennells: Silversmiths and Jewellers 1735–1973* (1973)

— *Liberty's 1875–1975* (1975)

— *Masterpieces of Cutlery and the Art of Eating* (1979)

— *Pattern and Design* (1982)

— *Art and Design in Hogarth's England* (1984)

Ward, B. M. and Ward, G. W. R., *Silver in American Life*, Ex. Cat. (New York, 1979)

Wark, R. R., *British Silver in the Huntington Collection* (San Marino, California, Huntington Library, 1978)

Watts, W., *Works of Art in Silver and Other Metals (the Lee of Fareham Collection)* (1936)

Watts, W. and Mitchell, H. P., *Catalogue of English Silversmiths' Work: Civil and Domestic in the Victoria and Albert Museum* (1920)

Watts, W., *Catalogue of Chalices and Other Communion Vessels in the Victoria and Albert Museum* (1922)

Webster, J., *Silver at Burghley House, Stamford*, Ex. Cat. (Stamford, 1984)

Wilson, D. M., *Catalogue of Antiquities of the Later Anglo-Saxon Period Vol. I Anglo-Saxon Ornamental Metalwork 700–1100* (1964)

General

Anon., *Memoirs of the Late Philip Rundell Esq.* (1827)

Addleshaw, G. W. O. and Etchells, F., *The Architectural Setting of Anglican Worship* (1948)

Alec-Smith, R. A., 'Silver Bearing the Hull Assay Mark', *Apollo*, LIV (1951) pp. 75–8

Alford, B. W. E. and Barker, T. C., *A History of the Carpenters' Company* (1968)

Allan, J. P., *Medieval and Post-Medieval Finds from Exeter 1971–1980* (Exeter 1984)

Anscombe, L. and Gere, C., *Arts and Crafts in Britain and America* (1978)

Ashbee, C. R., *Modern English Silverwork* (1908)

Badcock, W., *A New Touchstone for Gold and Silver Wares* (1679; reprint New York, 1971)

Baker, M., 'Patrick Robertson's Tea Urn and the Late Eighteenth Century Edinburgh Silver Trade', *Connoisseur* (August 1973), pp. 289–94

Banister, 'A Basketmaker's Accounts with Some 18th Century Silversmiths', *Proceedings of the Society of Silver Collectors*, I, 9 (1967) pp. 21–4

— 'Silver for the Careful Cook', *Country Life Annual* (1967) pp. 90–5

— 'Pepys and the Goldsmiths', *Proceedings of the Society of Silver Collectors*, I, 10 (1968)

— 'Silver Nutmeg Graters', *Proceedings of the Society of Silver Collectors*, II, 2 (1971) pp. 45–7

— 'Identity Parade: Some People and Pieces from the Emes and Barnard Ledgers', *Proceedings of the Society of Silver Collectors*, II, 9/10 (1980) pp. 165–70

— 'Seal Cups and Salvers', *Country Life*, 1169 (1981) pp. 278–91, 334–5

— 'Highlights from the Assheton Bennett Silver Collection', *Antique Dealer and Collector's Guide* (June 1983) pp. 82–4

— 'Master of Elegant Silver: Peter Archambo', *Country Life* (9 June 1983) pp. 1594–5

— 'A Postscript to the Barnard Ledgers', *Proceedings of the Society of Silver Collectors*, III, 1/2 (1983) pp. 28–40

Barr, E., *George Wickes 1698–1761 Royal Goldsmith* (1980–83)

— 'The Bristol Ewer and Basin', *Art at Auction the Year at Sotheby's 1982–83* (1983) pp. 284–91

Barrett, G. N., *Norwich Silver and its Marks 1565–1702* (Norwich, 1981)

Beard, G., *The Work of Robert Adam* (Edinburgh, 1978)

Beecroft, J., 'On Collecting Wine Labels', *Proceedings of the Society of Silver Collectors*, II, 2 (1971) pp. 34–6

Berain, *100 Planches Principales de l'Oeuvre Complet de Jean Berain* (Paris, 1930)

Blair, C., 'The Rochester Plate' (Rochester Cathedral), *Connoisseur*, 200 (April 1979)

— 'A Drawing of an English Medieval Royal Gold Cup', *Burlington Magazine*, 121 (June 1979)

Bradbury, F., *History of Old Sheffield Plate* (1912; reprinted 1968)

Burshe, G., *Tafelzeir des Barock* (Munich, 1974)

Bury, S., 'The Prince Consort and the Royal Plate Collection', *Burlington Magazine*, CIV (August 1962)

— 'The Silver Designs of Dr Christopher Dresser', *Apollo* (December 1962)

— 'The Liberty Metalwork Venture', *Architectural Review* (February 1963) pp. 108–11

— 'The Lengthening Shadow of Rundell's', 3 parts, *Connoisseur* (February, March, April 1966) pp. 78–85, 152–8, 217–23

— 'Felix Summerly's Art-Manufacture', *Apollo* (January 1967)

— 'An Arts and Crafts Experiment: The Silverwork of C. R. Ashbee', *Victoria and Albert Museum Bulletin*, III (1967) pp. 18–23

— 'Assay Silver at Birmingham', *Country Life*, CXLIII (1968) p. 1615

— *Victorian Electroplate* (Country Life Collectors' Guides, 1971)

— 'Pugin and the Tractarians', *Connoisseur* (January 1972)

— 'Trophies from the Great Exhibition of 1851', *VAM Album*, 2 (1983) pp. 208–22

Bury, S. and Fitzgerald, D., 'A Design for a Candlestick by Georg Michael Moser', *Victoria and Albert Museum Yearbook* (1969) pp. 27–9

Bury, S., Wedgwood, A. and Snodin, M., 'The Antiquarian Plate of George IV: A Gloss on E. A. Jones', *Burlington Magazine*, CXXI (June 1979) pp. 343–51

Bury, S. and Snodin, M., 'The Shield of Achilles', *Art at Auction Sotheby's 1983/4* (1984)

Butler, A., 'The Old English Silver of the Innholders' Company, London', *Connoisseur*, I (1901) pp. 236–44

Campbell, R., *The London Tradesman* (1747; reprint Newton Abbot, 1969)

Campbell, M., 'The Gold Chalice and Paten', *The Pelican*, Corpus Christi annual report 1981/2 (Oxford, 1982)

— *Medieval Enamels* (1983)

— 'Bishop Foxe's Salt', *The Pelican* 1983/4 (Oxford, 1984)

Cavendish, G., *The Life and Death of Cardinal Wolsey* (Early English Text Society, 1959) p. 243

Cellini, *The Treatises of Benvenuto Cellini on Goldsmiths' Work and Sculpture*, C. R. Ashbee (ed.) (1898; New York, 1963)

Challis, C. E., *The Tudor Coinage* (Manchester, 1978)

Charleston, R. J., *English Glass* (1984)

Clayton, M., 'Silver at Polesden Lacey', *Apollo* (May 1963) pp. 380–2

— *The Collector's Dictionary of the Gold and Silver of Great Britain and North America* (1971; revised edition 1984)

Clowes, L., 'The Rothermere Silver at the Inner Temple', *Connoisseur* (February 1957) pp. 29–32

Collard, F., *Regency Furniture* (Woodbridge, 1985)

Connaissance des Arts, *Les Grands Orfèvres de Louis XIII à Charles X* (Paris, 1965)

Connoisseur Complete Period Guides, ed. R. Edwards and L. G. G. Ramsey (1968)

Cooper, J. K. D., 'A Reassessment of Some English Late Gothic and Early Renaissance Plate', parts I and II, *Burlington Magazine*, CXIX (June and July 1977) pp. 408–12, 475–6

— 'An Assessment of Tudor Plate Design 1530–1560', *Burlington Magazine*, CXXI (June 1979) pp. 360–4

Corbett, M. and Norton, M., *Engraving in England (Charles I)* (Cambridge, 1964)

Crawford, A., *History of the Vintners' Company* (1977)

Cripps, W., *Old English Plate* (1878)

Crisp-Jones, R., *The Silversmiths of Birmingham and their Marks 1750–1980* (1981)

Crosby Forbes, H. A., Kernan, J. D. and Wilkins, R. S., *Chinese Export Silver 1785–1885* (Milton, Mass., 1975)

Culme, J., 'Kensington Lewis', *Connoisseur*, CXC (1975)

— *Nineteenth Century Silver* (1977)

— 'Beauty and the Beast: The Growth of Mechanization in the Trade', *Proceedings of the Society of Silver Collectors*, II, 9/10 (1980) pp. 158–65

— *Attitudes to Old Plate 1750–1900* (Sotheby, 1985)

Dauterman, C. C., 'Dream-pictures of Cathay-Chinoiseries on Restoration Silver', *Bulletin of the Metropolitan Museum of Art* (New York, Summer 1964)

— 'English Silver in an American Company Museum' [Folger Coffee Company], parts 1 and 2, *Connoisseur*, CLIX (1965) pp. 208–11, 274–9

Davis, J. D., 'Domestic Silver of the Colonial United States', *Spanish, French and English Tradition in the Colonial Silver of North America* (Winterthur, 1968)

Delieb, E. and Roberts, M. *The Great Silver Manufactory* (1971)

Dickinson, H. W., *Matthew Boulton* (Cambridge, 1937)

Dresser, C., *Principles of Decorative Design* (1873; reissued 1976)

Dresser, C., 'The Art Manufactures of Japan from Personal Observation', *Journal of the Society of Arts* (February 1878)

Dodwell, C. R., *Anglo-Saxon Art: A New Perspective* (Manchester, 1982)

Eames, E., 'Domestic Furnishings in England in the Fourteenth and Fifteenth Centuries', *Furniture History*, vol. 7 (1971)

Edwards, A. C., 'Sir John Petre and Some Elizabethan London Tradesmen', *London Topographical Record*, 23 (1962) pp. 71–89

Elphinstone, N., 'The Church Plate of All Saints Newcastle upon Tyne', *Burlington Magazine*, CIX (1967) pp. 645–6, pl. 49–53

Evans, J., *Pattern: A Study of Ornament in Western Europe 1180–1900*, 2 vols. (1931)

Evans, J., 'Huguenot Goldsmiths of London', *Proceedings of the Huguenot Society*, vol. XIV, no. 4 (1933)

Evans, J., *Huguenot Goldsmiths in England and Ireland* (1933; reprinted from *Proceedings of the Huguenot Society* , XIV, 1933)

Fales, M. G., *Early American Silver* (New York, 1973)

— *Joseph Richardson and Family, Philadelphia Silversmiths* (Middletown, Connecticut, 1974)

Fallon, J. P., 'The Goulds and Cafes Candlestick Makers', *Proceedings of the Society of Silver Collectors*, II, 9/10 (1980) pp. 146–51

Fedden R., *Treasures of the National Trust* (1976)

Fergusson, F., 'Wyatt Silver', *Burlington Magazine*, 116 (December 1974) pp. 751–6

Forbes, J. S., 'Fakes and Forgeries of British Antique Silver Ware', *Criminologist* (February 1969) pp. 71–85

Gilchrist, J., *Anglican Church Plate* (1967)

Gill, M. A. V., *Marks of the Newcastle Goldsmiths 1702–1884* (Newcastle, 1974)
— 'The Latter Days of the York Assay Office', *Yorkshire Archaeological Journal*, vol. 49 (1977)
— *A Directory of Newcastle Goldsmiths* (Newcastle, 1980)

Girouard, M., 'English Art and the Rococo', 3 parts, *Country Life* (13 and 27 January, 3 February 1966) pp. 58–61, 188–90, 224–7

Glanville, P., 'The Parr Pot', *Archaeological Journal*, CXXVII (1971)
— 'The Plate Purchases of a Tudor Lawyer', *Collectanea Londiniensia: Studies Presented to Ralph Merrifield* (London and Middlesex Archaeological Society, 1978) pp. 281–300
— 'Chinese Porcelain and English Goldsmiths, *c*.1560–*c*.1660', *Victoria and Albert Museum Album*, 3 (1984)
— 'Bishop Foxe's Ablution Basins', *The Pelican*, Corpus Christi annual report 1983/4 (Oxford, 1984)
— 'Tudor Drinking Vessels', *Burlington Magazine* Special Supplement Sept. 1985, 19–22
— 'Robert Amadas, Tudor royal goldsmith', *Proceedings of the Silver Society* 1985

Glynn, G., 'Heraldry in English Silver', *Proceedings of the Society of Silver Collectors*, vol. III, 1/2 (1983) pp. 6–10

Goldsmiths' Company, *Spurious Antique Plate*, list of pieces with their marks, seized in the Lyon-Twinam forgery case (1899)

Goldsmiths' Company, Hughes, G. R., *The Worshipful Company of Goldsmiths as Patrons of their Craft 1919–53* (1965)

Goodall, J., 'Cambridge Plate: Six Centuries of Heraldic Silver,' *Connoisseur* (August 1977)

Goodison, N., 'The Victoria and Albert Museum's Collection of Metalwork Pattern Books', *Furniture History*, vol. 11 (1975) pp. 1–30.

Grimwade, A., 'The Farrer Collection of English Silver', 3 parts, *Country Life* (11 April, 20 June, 25 July 1947)
— 'Changing Taste in the Collecting of Silver', *Apollo Annual* (1949)
— 'Shrewsbury and Boston Plate', *Apollo*, LIV (1951) pp. 103–6
— 'Royal Toilet Services in Scandinavia', *Connoisseur*, 137 (1956) pp. 175–8
— 'The Garrard Ledgers', *Proceedings of the Society of Silver Collectors*, I (1961)
— 'Silver at Althorp: part 1 The Marlborough Plate; part 2 Candlesticks and Candelabra; part 3 Huguenot Period; part 4 Rococo and Regency; part 5 Continental', *Connoisseur* (October 1962; March, June, December 1963; March 1964)
— 'Family Silver of Three Centuries', *Apollo*, 82 (1965) pp. 498–506
— 'Crespin or Sprimont? An Unsolved Problem of Rococo Silver', *Apollo*, 90 (1969)
— 'Some Treasures of Anglo-Jewish Silver', *Proceedings of the Society of Silver Collectors*, II, 1 (1970) pp. 11–17
— *Rococo Silver 1727–1765* (1974)

— 'The Rise and Fall of Rococo', *Proceedings of the Society of Silver Collectors*, II, 5/6 (1975) pp. 91–5

— *London Goldsmiths 1697–1837 their Marks and Lives* (1976; revised edition 1982)

— 'The Altar Plate of the Chapel Royal', *Connoisseur*, 195 (June 1977)

— 'The Study of English Silver Fakes', *Apollo*, 116 (September 1982) pp. 181–4

Grimwade, A. and Banister, J., 'Thomas Jenkins Unveiled', *Connoisseur,* 195 (July 1977)

Gubbins, M. C. B., 'Pseudo Hall-marks on Silver', *Connoisseur* (August 1974) pp. 256–61

— 'The Assay Office and Silversmiths of York 1776–1858', *Proceedings of the Silver Society* , III, 3 (1982) pp. 74–8

— *York Assay Office and Silversmiths 1776–1858* (York, 1983)

Halliwell, J. O., *A Chronicle of the First Thirteen Years of the Reign of King Edward the Fourth by John Warkworth* (Camden Society, 1839)

Harlow, K., 'Gilbert Marks Forgotten Silversmith', *Antique Collector,* 7 (1984) pp. 42–7

Hare, S., 'William Denham and the Gylte Cupp', *Goldsmiths' Review* (1983/4) pp. 27–9

Harrison, F., *Annals of an Old Manor House* (Sutton Place, 1893)

Hatcher, J., and Barker, T. C., *A History of British Pewter* (1974)

Hatfield, L. C., 'A Set of English Silver Condiment Vases from Kedleston Hall', *Bulletin of the Museum of Fine Arts, Boston*, 79 (1981) pp. 4–19

Hawley, H., 'Meissonier's Silver for the Duke of Kingston', *Bulletin of the Cleveland Museum of Art* (December 1978)

Hayward, H., 'Some English Rococo Designs for Silversmiths', *Proceedings of the Society of Silver Collectors*, II, 3/4 (1973) pp. 70–5

Hayward, J. F., 'Royal Plate at Fonthill', *Burlington Magazine,* CI (April 1959)

— 'A Surtoute Designed by William Kent', *Connoisseur* (March 1959)

— *Huguenot Silver in England 1688–1727* (1959)

— 'A Rock Crystal Bowl from the Treasury of Henry VIII', *Burlington Magazine* (April 1968) pp. 120–4

— 'The Restoration of the Tudor Clock-Salt', *Goldsmiths' Company Review* (1969/70)

— 'Silver Made from the Designs of William Kent', *Connoisseur* (June 1970)

— 'A William and Mary Pattern-Book for Silversmiths', *Proceedings of the Society of Silver Collectors*, II, 1 (1970) pp. 18–22

— 'Rundell, Bridge & Rundell, Aurifices Regis', *Antiques*, 2 parts (June/July 1971)

— *The Courtauld Silver* (1975)

— *Virtuoso Goldsmiths and the Triumph of Mannerism 1540–1620* (1976)

— 'The Tudor Plate of Magdalen College, Oxford', *Burlington Magazine*, CXXV (May 1983) pp. 260–5

Heal, A., *The London Goldsmiths 1200–1800* (1935)

Heckscher, M., 'Lock and Copeland', *Furniture History*, 15 (1979)

Hennell, P., 'The Hennell Family of Silversmiths', *Proceedings of the Society of Silver Collectors*, I, 11 (1968)

— 'The Hennells: A Continuity of Craftsmanship', *Connoisseur* (February 1973)

Hernmarck, C., *The Art of the European Silversmith 1430–1830* (1977)

Hind, A. M., *Engraving in England (James I)* (Cambridge, 1955)

Holland, M., *Old Country Silver* (1971)

Holme, R., *The Academy of Armory* (Roxburghe Club, 1905)

Holmes, C. G., 'British Silverware Today', *The Studio*, CIV (1932) p. 216

Honour, H., 'Silver Reflections of Cathay', *Antiques*, 81 (March 1962) pp. 306–9
— *Goldsmiths and Silversmiths* (1971)

Hope, T., *Household Furnishings and Interior Decoration from Designs by Thomas Hope* (1807)

Hope, W. St. John, 'On the English Medieval Drinking Bowls Called Mazers', *Archaeologia*, 50 (1887) pp. 129–93

Houart, V., *Antique Silver Toys* (New York, 1981)

How, G. E. P., 'The Cult of the Teaspoon', *Notes on Antique Silver*, no. 4 (1944–5)

How, Mrs G. E. P., 'The Goldsmiths of Bristol', *Connoisseur* (August 1974) pp. 252–5

How, G. E. P. and How, J. P., *English and Scottish Silver Spoons*, privately printed, 1 (1952) 2 (1953) 3 (1957)

Hughes, G. B., 'Silver Standishes and Inkstands', *Country Life Annual* (1951)
— 'English Silver Epergnes', *Country Life* (19 May 1955) pp. 1317–24
— 'Silver Wine Labels', *Country Life Annual* (1955) pp. 78–82
— 'Georgian Milk and Cream Jugs', *Apollo*, 63 (1956) pp. 199–206
— *Small Antique Silverware* (1957)
— 'The Georgian Vogue of the Tea Urn', *Country Life*, CXXXII (25 October 1962) pp. 1026–7
— 'The Art of Close Plating', *Country Life* (19 December 1969)

Hughes, G., *Modern Silver throughout the World 1880–1967* (1967)

Hughes, P., 'An Adam Punch Bowl', *Burlington Magazine*, CIX (November 1967) 646, pl. 53–5

Hughes, T., 'Tomorrow's Treasure: The work of Edwardian Silversmiths', *Country Life* (24 October 1974)

Hunt, L. B., 'The Mystery of the Galvanic Goblet', *Burlington Magazine* (June 1984) pp. 347–8

Impey, O., *Chinoiserie* (1977)

Imray, J., *The Charity of Richard Whittington* (1968)
— 'The Early Days of Trinity Hospital', *Transactions of the Greenwich and Lewisham Antiquarian Society*, 9, 3 (1981)

Ince, W. and Mayhew, J., *Universal System of Household Furniture* (c.1762)

Inder, P. M., 'Silver in the Exeter Museum', *Connoisseur*, 183 (July 1973) pp. 184–5

Ingram, W., *Francis Langley: The Brazen Age* (biography of late Elizabethan goldsmith/ businessman) (Harvard, 1979)

Irons, N. J., *Silver and Carving of the Old China Trade* (1983)

Jackson, C. J., *An Illustrated History of English Plate*, 2 vols (1911)
— *English Goldsmiths and their Marks* (1921)
— *English Goldsmiths and their Marks*, I. Pickford (ed.) (revised edition Antique Collectors' Club, 1986)

Jervis, S., *The Penguin Dictionary of Design and Designers* (1984)

Johnson, P., 'The Lyon and Twinam Forgeries', *Proceedings of the Silver Society*, III, 1/2 (1983) pp. 25–36

Jones, O., *Grammar of Ornament* (1857)

Jones, E. A., 'Some Builders of Ships for the Royal Navy and their Gifts of Plate', *Burlington Magazine*, 37 (September 1920)

— 'Paul Crespin', *Proceedings of the Huguenot Society*, XVI, 3 (1940)

Kaellgren, P., 'The Teapicker Design on English Rococo Silver Tea Caddies', *Antiques* (February 1982)

Kent, T. A., 'Edward Sweet, West Country Silversmith', *Proceedings of the Society of Silver Collectors*, II, 5/6 (1975) pp. 100–3

— 'The Goldsmiths of Falmouth', *Proceedings of the Society of Silver Collectors*, II, 9/10 (1980) pp. 155–8

— *London Silver Spoonmakers 1500–1697* (1981)

— 'The Great Days of Exeter Silver 1700–1750', *Proceedings of the Silver Society*, III, 3 (1982) pp. 53–63

— 'Salisbury Goldsmiths and London Wardens 1631–1637', *The Hatcher Review*, 2, 15 (Salisbury, 1983)

Kimball, F., *The Creation of the Rococo* (Philadelphia 1943; reprint New York, 1980)

Levine, G., 'Norwich Goldsmiths' Marks', *Norfolk Archaeology*, XXXIV, part III (1968)

Lightbown, R., 'Christian Van Vianen at the Court of Charles I', *Apollo*, 87 (1968) pp. 426–39

— *Secular Goldsmiths' Work in Medieval France* (1978)

Link, E. M., *The Book of Silver* (1973)

Lushington, R., 'The Tankards of Sir Edmund Berrie Godfrey', *Connoisseur*, 190 (December 1975) 258–64

MacGregor, A. (ed.), *Tradescant's Rarities: Essays on the Foundation of the Ashmolean Museum 1683* (Oxford, 1983)

McFadden, D. R., 'American and British Silver in Minneapolis Institute of Art, *Apollo* (March 1983)

McNab Dennis, J., 'London Silver in a Colonial Household', *Bulletin of the Metropolitan Museum of Art*, 26 (December 1967)

Marks, R., *Burrell: Portrait of a Collector 1851–1958* (Glasgow, 1983)

Maryon, H., *Metalwork and Enamelling*, third edition (1954)

Masters, B. R., 'The History of the Civic Plate 1567–1731', *Collectanea Londiniensia: Studies Presented to Ralph Merrifield* (London and Middlesex Archaeological Society, 1978) pp. 301–15

Meyrick, S. F. and Shaw, H., *Specimens of Ancient Furniture* (1836)

Moger, V., 'A Conversazione at the Ironmongers' Hall', *Collectanea Londiniensia: Studies Presented to Ralph Merrifield* (London and Middlesex Archaeological Society, 1978) pp. 453–63

Morgan, O., 'Table of the Annual Assay Office Letters', *Archaeological Journal*, vol. X (1853)

Nicholl, J., *Some Account of the Worshipful Company of Ironmongers* (1866)

Noel Hume, I., *James Geddy & Sons, Colonial Craftsmen* (Colonial Williamsburg, 1970)

Oman, C., 'Goldsmiths of S. Albans', *Transactions of S. Albans and Hertfordshire Archaeological Society* (1932) pp. 215–36
— *English Domestic Silver* (1934 and later editions)
— 'Coining of the Royal Plate at Newark in 1646', *Numismatic Chronicle*, fifth series, vol. XIV (1934)
— 'The Bermondsey Dish', *Burlington Magazine,* XCIV (January 1952) pp. 23–6
— 'False Medieval Plate', *Apollo* (March 1952) pp. 74–5
— *The Wellington Plate: The Portuguese Service* (1954)
— *English Church Plate 597–1837* (1957)
— (Royal Sale 1808), *Burlington Magazine* (December 1958)
— *The Gloucester Candlestick* (1958)
— *English Silversmiths' Work, Civil and Domestic* (1965)
— 'The Civic Plate and Insignia of the City of Portsmouth', *Connoisseur* (December 1965)
— 'A Hundred Years of English Silver', parts 1 and 2, *Victoria and Albert Museum Bulletin* (April 1965, 1966)
— 'The Civic Plate of the City of York', *Connoisseur* (October/November 1967)
— *Caroline Silver 1625–1688* (1970)
— 'Chippendale-Gothic', *Antiques* (January 1970) pp. 94–6
— 'Eton College Plate', parts 1 and 2, *Connoisseur* (June/July 1971)
— 'The Civic Gifts to Charles II: Failure of a Mission', *Proceedings of the Society of Silver Collectors*, II, 3/4 (1973)
— *English Engraved Silver* (1978)
— 'The Plate and Jewels and their History', Appendix 4 in *A History of the Carpenters' Company* (1978)
— 'Plate from a Lost Oxford College', *Archaeologia Cantiana*, XCV (1979) pp. 49–52
— 'Security in English Churches AD 1000–1548', *Archaeological Journal,* 136 (1979) pp. 90–8
— 'The College Plate' in J. Buxton and P. H. Williams (eds), *New College Oxford 1379–1979* (Oxford, 1979)
Oman, C and Rosas, J., 'Portuguese Influence upon English Silver', *Apollo*, 51 (June 1950)
Ormond, R., 'Silver Shape in Chelsea Porcelain', *Country Life* (1 February 1968) pp. 224–6
Penzer, N. M., 'The King's Lynn Cup', parts 1 and 2, *Connoisseur*, CXVII–CXVIII (March/July 1946) pp. 12–16, 64, 79–84
— 'The Howard Grace Cup and the Early Date-Letter Cycles', *Connoisseur* (June 1946) pp. 87–92
— *Book of the Wine Label* (1947)
— 'Scroll Salts', *Apollo Annual* (1949) pp. 48–52
— *Paul Storr* (1954; reprinted 1971)
— 'The Mazarine', *Apollo* (1955) pp. 104–5
— 'The Jerningham-Kandler Wine-Cooler', *Apollo*, 64 (September and October 1956) pp. 80–2, 111–15
— 'The Early Silver Teapot and its Origin', *Apollo*, 64 (December 1956) pp. 209–10
— 'The Great Wine Coolers', parts 1 and 2, *Apollo*, 66 (August/September 1957) pp. 3–7, 39–46

Percival, S. T. B., 'Thomas Merry, Citizen and Goldsmith', *Connoisseur,* 176 (1970)

Phillips, P. A. S., *Paul De Lamerie 1688–1751* (1935, reprinted 1968)

Pickford, I., *Silver Flatware, English, Irish and Scottish 1660–1980* (Woodbridge, 1983)

Platt, C., *Mediaeval England* (1978)

Plumbers' Company, *Short History of the Worshipful Company of Plumbers* (1965)

Plummer, A., *The London Weavers' Company* (1972)

Poliakoff, M., *Silver Toys and Miniatures* (1986)

Pugin, A. W. N., *Designs for Gold and Silversmiths* (1836)
— *The True Principles of Pointed and Christian Architecture* (1841)

Quickenden, K., 'Boulton & Fothergill Silver: Business Plans and Miscalculations', *Art History*, III, 3 (September 1980)

Quimby, I. M. G., (ed.) *Arts of the Anglo-American Community in the 17th Century* (Charlottesville, Virginia, 1975) incorporating Mrs G. E. P. How, '17th Century English Silver and Its American Derivatives'

Reddaway, T. F., 'The London Goldsmiths circa 1500', *Transactions of the Royal Historical Society*, fifth series, 12 (1962)
— 'Elizabethan London – Goldsmiths' Row in Cheapside 1558–1645', *Guildhall Miscellany*, 2 (1963)

Reddaway, T. F. and Walker, L. E. M., *The Early History of the Goldsmiths' Company 1327–1509* (1975)

Ridgway, M. H., *Chester Goldsmiths from Early Times to 1726* (Altrincham, 1968)
— *Chester Silver 1727–1837* (Chichester, 1984)

Rijksmuseum, *The Ceramic Load of the Witte Leeuw 1613* (Amsterdam, 1983)

Rogers, H. M., *The Making of a Connoisseur* (1951)

Roth, R., 'Tea Drinking in Eighteenth Century America: Its Etiquette and Equipage', *U.S. National Museum Bulletin 225, Contributions from the Museum of History and Technology* (Washington DC, 1961) pp. 62–91

Rowe, R., *Adam Silver 1765–1795* (1965)

Scouloudi, I., 'Alien Immigration into and Alien Communities in London 1558–1640', *Proceedings of the Huguenot Society*, vol. XVI (1937–41)

Schroder, 'Sixteenth Century English Silver. Some Problems of Attribution', *Proceedings of the Silver Society*, III, 1/2 (1983) pp. 40–7
— 'English Gold', *Grosvenor House Antique Fair Souvenir Guide 1984*, pp. 8–15

Schrijver, 'Europe's Earliest Silver Teakettle', *Connoisseur*, 166 (1967) pp. 81–4

Seaby, W. A. and Hetherington, R. J., 'The Matthew Boulton Pattern Books', *Apollo* February and March 1950) pp. 48–50, 78–80

Seaby, W. A., 'A Letter Book of Boulton & Fothergill 1773', *Apollo*, LIV, 2 parts (1951) pp. 83–6, 113–16

Sheffield, *The Sheffield Assay Office Register 1773–1907* (Sheffield, 1911)

Sitwell, H. D. W., 'The Jewel House and the Royal Goldsmiths', *Archaeological Journal*, CXVII (1962)

Smith, E. J. G., 'The Fox Family of Victorian Silversmiths', *Antique Dealer and Collectors' Guide* (August and September 1974)

Snodin, M., *English-Silver Spoons* (1974; revised edition 1983)
— 'Silver Vases and Their Purpose', *Connoisseur*, 194 (January 1977) pp. 37–42
— 'J. J. Boileau', *Connoisseur* (June 1978) pp. 128–33
Snodin, M. and Baker, M., 'William Beckford's Silver', parts I and II, *Burlington Magazine,* 122 (November and December 1980)
Stalker, J. and Parker, G., *Treatise on Japanning and Varnishing* (1688; Dover Reprint 1960)
Stancliffe, J., *Silver Bottle Tickets* (1986)
Stone, L., 'Social Mobility in England 1500–1700', *Past and Present*, 33 (1966) pp. 29–36
— *Family and Fortune* (1973)
Stone, P., 'Some Famous Drinking Horns in Britain' parts 1 & 2, *Apollo* (April & May 1961)
Tait, H., 'The Stonyhurst Salt', *Apollo*, 179 (April 1964) pp. 270–8
— 'The Peter Wilding Bequest', *Connoisseur*, 180 and 181 (August and September 1972)
— 'The Use of Silver Filigree and Granulation on Jacobean Silver', *Proceedings of the Silver Society*, III, 3 (1982) pp. 66–9
Tatham, C. H., *Etchings of Ancient Ornamental Architecture* (1799)
— *Designs for Ornamental Plate* (1806)
Taylor, G., *Silver* (Harmondsworth, 1956)
— 'Some London Platemakers' Marks 1558 to 1624', *Proceedings of the Silver Society* III, 4, 1984, pp. 97–100.
Theophilus, *On Divers Arts,* Hawthorne and Smith (eds), (Chicago, 1963)
Thompson, P., *History and Antiquities of Boston* (Boston, 1856)
Thornton, P. K., *Seventeenth Century Interior Decoration in England, France and Holland* (1978)
— *Authentic Decor 1620–1920* (1984)
Toyeska, I., 'The Royal Clock Salt', *Apollo* (October 1969) pp. 292–7
Udy, D., 'The Influence of Charles Heathcote Tatham', *Proceedings of the Society of Silver Collectors*, II, 5/6 (1975) pp. 104–6
— 'Piranesi's "Vasi", the English Silversmith and His Patrons', *Burlington Magazine,* CXX (December 1978) pp. 820–38
Vardy, J., *Some Designs of Mr Inigo Jones and Mr William Kent* (1744)
Waldron, P., *The Price Guide to Antique Silver* (Woodbridge, 1982)
Ward-Jackson, P., *Some Main Stream and Tributaries in European Ornament from 1500 to 1750* (1969; originally printed in *Victoria and Albert Museum Bulletin*, vol. 3, 1967)
Wardle, P., *Victorian Silver and Silver Plate* (1963; New York, 1970)
Watts, W., 'Belonging to C. D. Rotch', *Connoisseur*, 48 (1917) pp. 79–83
Wells-Cole, A., 'Two Rococo Masterpieces', *Leeds Art Calendar* (Leeds Art Gallery and Museum, 1974)
Wenham, E., *Domestic Silver of Great Britain and Ireland* (Oxford, 1931)
Westwood, A. H., 'An Assayer's Notes', *Proceedings of the Society of Silver Collectors,* I, 11 (1968)
Wilkinson, W. R. T., *Indian Colonial Silver* (1973)
— 'China Trade Silver from Canton', *Connoisseur* (January 1975) pp. 46–53
Williamsburg, *The Silversmith in Eighteenth Century Williamsburg* (Williamsburg, 1966)
Wills, G., 'Stafford Briscoe, a London Silversmith', *Burlington Magazine* (1983) pp. 50–3

Wilmot, R. T. D., 'The Dorrien Cup', *Proceedings of the Society of Silver Collectors*, I, 8 (1966) pp. 22–6

Wilson, D. M., *The Forgotten Collector A. W. Franks* (1984)

Wilson, G., 'The Kedleston Fountain. Its Development from a Seventeenth Century Vase', *J. Paul Getty Museum Journal*, vol. II (1983)

Wilson, H., *Silverwork and Jewellery* (1902, revised edition 1978)

Wilson, T., 'Bishop Foxe's Crozier', *The Pelican*, Corpus Christi annual report 1980/1 (Oxford, 1981)

Wyatt, M. D., *The Industrial Arts of the Nineteenth Century* (1851–3)
— *Metalwork and its Artistic Design* (1852)

Wyler, S., *The Book of Sheffield Plate* (New York, 1949)

Younghusband, Sir George, *The Jewel House* (1921)

Young, H., 'Thomas Heming and the Tatton Cup', *Burlington Magazine* (May 1983)

Zahle, E., 'Queen Caroline Mathilde's Toilet Set', *Virksomhed 1954–1959* (Copenhagen, 1960)

INDEX

Figure numbers are shown in *italics*